# The Wind Will Not Subside

$3^{98}$
HP
ST
4.3

$2^{48}$
HP
ST
4.3

*Joe Patrick Bean*

D1009496

# The Pantheon Asia Library

## New Approaches to the New Asia

No part of the world has changed so much in recent years as Asia, or awakened such intense American interest. But much of our scholarship, like much of our public understanding, is based on a previous era. The Asia Library has been launched to provide the needed information on the new Asia, and in so doing to develop both the new methods and the new sympathies needed to understand it. Our purpose is not only to publish new work but to experiment with a wide variety of approaches which will reflect these new realities and their perception by those in Asia and the West.

Our books aim at different levels and audiences, from the popular to the more scholarly, from high schools to the universities, from pictorial to documentary presentations. All books will be available in paperback.

Suggestions for additions to the Asia Library are welcome.

### *Other Asia Library Titles*

*The Japan Reader,* edited by Jon Livingston, Joe Moore, and Felicia Oldfather
>    Volume 1 *Imperial Japan: 1800–1945*
>    Volume 2 *Postwar Japan: 1945 to the Present*

*A Chinese View of China,* by John Gittings

*Remaking Asia: Essays on the American Uses of Power,* edited by Mark Selden

*Without Parallel: The American-Korean Relationship Since 1945,* edited by Frank Baldwin

*Chairman Mao Talks to the People: Talks and Letters, 1956–1971,* edited by Stuart Schram

*A Political History of Japanese Capitalism,* by Jon Halliday

*Origins of the Modern Japanese State: Selected Writings of E. H. Norman,* edited by John Dower

*China's Uninterrupted Revolution: From 1840 to the Present,* edited by Victor Nee and James Peck

# The Wind Will Not Subside

Years in Revolutionary China—1964-1969

by

David Milton and Nancy Dall Milton

PANTHEON BOOKS
A Division of Random House
New York

Copyright © 1976 by David Milton and Nancy Dall Milton

All rights reserved under International and Pan-American Copyright Conventions. Published in the United States by Pantheon Books, a division of Random House, Inc., New York, and simultaneously in Canada by Random House of Canada Limited, Toronto.

Grateful acknowledgment is made to Oxford University Press for permission to reprint 25 lines from the poem "Changsha" (p. 355) and 9 lines from the poem "Return to Shaoshan" (pp. 356–7) by Mao Tse-Tung, translated by Michael Bullock and Jerome Ch'en. Reprinted from *Mao and the Chinese Revolution* by Jerome Ch'en. Copyright © 1965 by Oxford University Press.

Library of Congress Cataloging in Publication Data

Milton, David, 1923–
  The Wind Will Not Subside.

  (The Pantheon Asia Library)
  Includes bibliographical references and index.
  1. China—Politics and government—1949–
I. Milton, Nancy, 1929–     joint author. II. Title.
DS777.55.M536   1976   320.9'51'05       75–10370
ISBN 0–394–48555–6
ISBN 0–394–70936–5 pbk.

Manufactured in the United States of America

9  8  7  6  5  4  3  2

To our families—parents, sons, brother, and sisters—
to those who went along and to those who remained
behind.

*"The tree may prefer calm, but the wind will not subside."*

A favorite old Chinese saying of Chairman Mao

# Contents

# List Of Illustrations

(between pages 190 and 191)

# Foreword

In this book based on what we learned and saw in China from 1964 to 1969, our first thanks go to our Chinese friends—teaching colleagues, students, and cadres—at the Peking First Foreign Languages Institute, who taught us so much about China and its Cultural Revolution. Had it not been for them, we could easily have lived in Peking through those momentous five years and learned little. However, our analyses are our own, and our friends should not feel responsible for any conclusions with which they do not agree.

We have been helped in the writing of this book by the knowledgeable and perceptive advice and criticism of good friends—of three in particular. Our editor in San Francisco was Tom Engelhardt, who, in a labor of love, brought his editorial expertise to a stern review of the entire manuscript, strengthening and simplifying it. The ongoing seminar we have had with Franz Schurmann, growing out of our work together on *People's China,* has illuminated our insights into China, and his reading of the manuscript produced helpful suggestions. Jack Service was the meticulous scholar who standardized into Wade-Giles our diverse styles of Chinese romanization and whose eagle eye caught more than a few other problems in the process. We are indebted to all of them.

We would also like to mention our gratitude for an exchange of ideas to Hong Yung Lee, who we feel has done some of the finest scholarship we have seen on the Red Guard movement.

Because so much of this book is based upon our own experience in China, we have attempted to keep documentation to a minimum. The Chinese are understandably sensitive about the use of unofficial documents because of problems of accuracy and interpretation. However, all of the leaflets, *ta-tzu-pao,* editorials, and speeches used in this book are ones with which we were familiar in China. Undoubtedly some of them are, and were then, inaccurate, but they were the materials that influenced millions of people who read them, in whatever form, and acted upon them. We have found that the English translations available in libraries and centers of Chinese studies in this country correspond in general to materials with which we were acquainted in Peking.

We are grateful to the Louis M. Rabinowitz Foundation, whose grant made it possible for us to spend several uninterrupted months working full-time on the manuscript.

# Introduction

Standing aloof and secure in their separate world states, ancient Rome and China coexisted for several centuries; they traded through intermediaries but never intersected. In the totality of their respective political and philosophical systems, neither, it seemed, had need of the other. And so there developed from the two great civilization states, an East and a West whose differing thought systems would diverge over the centuries to mutual exclusion. For more than 1,000 years, the two developed independently, until China's enforced collision with a Western world propelled forward not only by its aggressive search for markets, but by its technological dynamism, produced shock waves throughout the entire Chinese social organism. The history of that violent encounter has shaped not only the dynamics of modern Chinese development, but has altered the course of the West as well. Because of the forcible nature of the long delayed interaction between the two world systems, it is perhaps ironic but not illogical that the Chinese of the twentieth century should seek the answer to the crisis of their ancient civilization in the rebel branch of Western thought, Marxism–Leninism. In a sense, when the West at last confronted China, it was confronting itself.

For the Chinese themselves, the assimilation of an ideology of Western stock has not been painless. There is indeed a close analogy to the long and complex process by which they transformed Indian Buddhism into a form congenial to their own culture. The Great Proletarian Cultural Revolution was a great historic convulsion of Chinese society coming at the end of a half-century of struggle, led and articulated most specifically by Mao Tse-tung, to extract from Soviet Marxism–Leninism those elements most appropriate for China and to reshape them into a Chinese whole.

Marxism had given to China a tenet quite alien to traditional Chinese views of harmony. It was the concept of class struggle, which provided the key to the overturning of the old oppressive class order and the creation of a new social unity. However, along with the classical Marxist concept of class, the Chinese found that they had also imported a new system of class division based on twentieth-century Russian social and political development. The new system turned out to be startlingly congenial with the overthrown Confucian bureaucratic state. The vanguard party, the centralization of state power, and the Soviet reliance upon an intellectual and technological elite for achieving the industrialization they believed to be the prerequisite for socialism, all fit entirely too neatly into the long Chinese experience with a society of ordered inequality. The ancient scholar literati and the new technocratic elite have much in common.

Mao Tse-tung, the philosopher and theoretician of the Chinese Revolution, while standing as the firmest advocate of class struggle, understood this concept in its classical Marxian context of equality. Mao's conception of the struggle for equality includes not only the battle against the bureaucracy, deeply institutionalized into the traditional Chinese system of hierarchy, but also those Marxist commitments to lessening the differences between mental and manual labor, city and countryside, and leaders and led. In this battle, Mao has indeed taken on some of the most tenacious elements of China's cultural and political inheritance. China has never had a democratic system. Thus Mao's attack on the new elitism and bureaucracy accompanying Soviet-style Marxism has also been an attack on the very roots of the old Chinese social structure.

However, Mao wished to combine the concepts of equality that he took from the Western world with one of the positive aspects of Chinese historical experience—collectivity. The concept of equality, so precious a part of modern Western political thought, has long been linked, at least in the philosophical abstraction, to individual freedom. It is not illogical that current Western visitors to China should find it difficult to comprehend how the Chinese can believe so passionately in the one while rejecting the other. Nevertheless, there was a consistency to Mao's formula defining the targets of the Cultural Revolution which would provide a symbolic framework for what he saw as China's philosophy of the future. Those who would be regarded as enemies of the people were "Those in the Party in power [bureaucracy] taking the capitalist road [individualism]." The opposition to both elitism and individualism would be encapsulated in the slogan "Serve the People," the central principle of China's new ethical system of socialism.

Mao also had little use for the determinism of Western Marxism, for it was that determinism, according to the Russian argument, which gave legitimacy to the reassertive elitism spawned by the productive forces of society. It has always been the Chinese view that good people, ethical citizens, are created not so much by the external forces of society as by conscious thought and moral education.

Their commitment to a leadership embodying the ethical values of the society indicates why the Chinese saw the Cultural Revolution itself, a rebellion of the people against some of its leaders, as being entirely within the bounds of political legitimacy. The people were told by the man who had come to be considered the personalization of the revolution that they had the mandate to overthrow evil leadership. Such revolutions have the blessing of morality, based not upon law, as we heirs of Rome understand morality, but upon a central social principle. It is for this reason that questions of equality were fought out in China in a popular mandate.

The Chinese Cultural Revolution of the 1960's was a colossal social movement devoted to questions of power and values. Those Westerners who have written about this historic event have taken basically two approaches. Writers sympathetic to the Chinese Revolution have emphasized the struggle over values; those less sympathetic or hostile have concentrated their attention on the struggle for power. We who consider ourselves friends of the Chinese Revolution believe that only by a description and analysis of both aspects, the struggle for a new world view and the real struggle for political power by live political actors, can one arrive at any depth of understanding of what the Cultural Revolution was all about. We had gone to China to teach English, to learn about the country, not to write about it. We had already spent two years in a peaceful and well-organized China before the outbreak of the impassioned struggle, when we found ourselves in the rare position of foreign participant-observers at the making of Chinese history. Our role as participants derived from the fact that our Chinese colleagues and students had become accustomed to our being sometime sharers of their lives and activities, and because they, like we, sensed from the very beginning of the Cultural Revolution that the remaking of a thought system in the international intimacy of the twentieth century could not be a matter of Chinese history alone.

As we look back on those remarkable few years, we realize the extent to which we read editorials, interpreted big-character posters, felt the passions of factional loyalties in a mood and political framework shared with our Chinese friends. Yet, at the same time, as twentieth-century American heirs to the Roman world center, we could not but see the Chinese experience through our own Western spectacles as well. Increasingly, we were struck by the range of historically and culturally different meanings that we brought to common terms and expressions, used with assurance by both Chinese and Westerners. We learned the lesson taught anew to generations of pilgrims and scholars in other lands —that the translation of the experience of another people defies the confines of language. For it is not just the problem of the accurate equivalent of the word, but the equivalent concept which often simply does not exist. One feels the "existential shock" which Paul Mus says the Western mind experiences upon contact with Chinese civilization. For us, it was necessary to experience, to study, and to attempt to understand the Chinese political struggles within their own context before it was possible to interpret them. We became increasingly aware of the difficulty of understanding Chinese interpretations without an insight into their roots.

Perhaps no people is quite satisfied with the way in which outsiders interpret their "own" system. Certainly the Russians are displeased with the way in which the Chinese interpret Leninism, and it would be doubtful that the Chinese would not find dissatisfaction in any foreign explanation of their Cultural Revolution. In a sense, of course, both are right. No outsider, no matter how close his involvement, ever feels the politics of a country in the same way that its own people does, nor can the conclusions of transient political participants be quite the same as those of the people who must live with the consequences. Any transference of one thought system into the terminology of another culture inevitably alters it. However, that is the history of the movement of human ideas since the beginning of civilization. Even science now agrees that all knowledge is made imperfect by the presence of the experimenter. Like almost everyone else in China, we saw the Cultural Revolution from the perspective of the one place in which we happened to be, but, like the rest of the inhabitants of Peking, we had the good fortune to be at the political center of the nation. Almost everything of consequence which we learned about China can be traced to those extraordinary years when a whole society opened up and exposed light and dark aspects alike to the inspection and criticism of its people.

# The Wind Will Not Subside

*Chapter I*

# The East Wind
# Prevails

IN THAT BRIEF INTERLUDE between the oppressiveness of the monsoon summer and the onset of North China's long gripping winter, Peking enjoys an atmosphere of singular exhilaration. It is but a few weeks' respite from the unrelenting cycle of natural forces which, from the time of man's beginnings, have determined the necessities and possibilities of Chinese civilization. From late May to early September, the fierce heat which covers the continent is tempered by the damp masses of air coming from the sea. By mid-October, the cold of the Siberian winter is already sweeping across the unprotected North China Plain, bringing the dry and dusty winter monsoon from that great barren land, the Gobi Desert. Because of the might and the duration of the two major seasons, it is not surprising that the poignancy of spring has figured so prominently in Chinese painting and poetry. But for the inhabitants of Peking, whose spring is the briefest of moments, their month of autumn is the time of holiday, of renewal, and celebration.

The skies, cloudless and blue, are tinted with the faint yellow North China dust, as if reflecting the tiled roofs of the old Imperial Palace. The air has an almost tangible clarity, and in these crystalline days, the people of Peking make their annual pilgrimages to see the red leaves of the Western Hills and the beloved chrysanthemums of the city's centuried parks. The gray city is suddenly splashed with red. Banners and flags fly everywhere. The Imperial Palace, long the symbolic center of China, is covered with scaffolding and painted yet again with the color the world has come to call Chinese red. The faceless gray walls that hide from public view the old courtyard homes of central Peking display newly painted red doors. Red, which for China has always symbolized that which is life-giving—marriage, birth, victory—now incorporates all past associations into the symbolism of revolution. For it is the celebration of the revolution around which the autumn holiday atmosphere now centers. It was with that great traditional regard for harmonizing the affairs of men with the authority of nature that the leaders of the Chinese Revolution chose October 1 as the day on which Mao Tse-tung would appear on the rostrum of the red palace of emperors now vanished to state: "The Chinese people have stood up."

We arrived in Peking just a few days before National Day, October 1, 1964, the fifteenth anniversary of the People's Republic of China. The decade-and-a-half anniversary would have been an important one to the Chinese under any circumstances, but the events of the preceding year found particular focus in the holiday ceremonies.

China in the fall of 1964 was a nation under the gun. The American Seventh Fleet lay in wait off the coast as the United States actively engaged in the aerial and naval bombardment of China's neighbor and socialist ally, North Vietnam. To the southwest, India was once again building up her shattered forces with the help of the United States and the Soviet Union. From the summer of 1963 until a few months before our arrival, the Chinese were engaged in an increasingly fierce polemical struggle with the Soviet Union, the closing stage of a relationship turned bitter with disappointment and distrust. Observing also the re-emergence of a powerful and hostile Japan, and fending off the armed emigrés from Taiwan, the Chinese people, like the French in 1793, understood that they were surrounded by the threat of armed counterrevolution.

A few weeks before we arrived, Ch'en Yi, China's Foreign Minister, had told an audience of foreign experts working in Peking that the Chinese were prepared for an attack by the United States from the south, the Russians from the north, and the Japanese from the east. "Let them all come," he said. "If necessary, we will give up some of our cities, retreat to the hills, and fight for a hundred years." His wry remark that his hair was turning white as he impatiently awaited these developments was taken by his countrymen not so much as an expression of their foreign minister's toughness as of their own cool defiance under pressure.

The extent to which China felt herself, and was, in fact, besieged was as yet only dimly realized by Americans in those early days of the Vietnam War. It was no more than a time of portents, of early and ominous suggestions of what would follow. For America, the remainder of the decade would be a period of great domestic turbulence, a turbulence resulting directly from the intensification of the war in Asia. For China, there would be a prolonged period of internal struggle of an intensity that astonished the world. The seeds of that struggle were already deeply rooted in the structure of Chinese society, in China's relationship with the outside world, and in past struggles to establish her national identity and international position, but none of this was apparent in October 1964.

We found instead a mood marvelously in harmony with Peking's bright and tranquil weather. In 1964, this seasonal mood was heightened by the symbolization of China's early successes in breaking out of her encirclement. The several thousand foreigners who swept through the hotels and streets of the city in those few days preceding National Day represented China's intensive efforts to consolidate new friendships and alliances able to turn the encirclement against the encirclers. For the first time since 1919, a socialist country was challenging the Soviet Union's "right" to eternal guardianship over world revolution. China was welcoming to her revolutionary celebrations a heterogeneous group of nations and individuals, allied in no formal way, sharing, however, the elusive but compelling interest in standing up to one of the two superpowers. There came together in Peking the fraternal parties of Vietnam, Korea, Japan, and Indonesia, drawn together in their varying degrees of anti-revisionism by the American superpower's Southeast Asian war; Romania and Albania, the small resistors to the Eastern European policies of the other superpower, and the tiny pro-Chinese splinter parties which had appeared in Ceylon, Belgium, Australia, and New Zealand. These were the fragile links in China's 1963–64 alternate socialist camp.

In addition, the Chinese had established a modest constellation of relationships outside the socialist sphere. Prince Sihanouk, still successful in his long struggle to maintain Cambodia's tenuous neutrality, turned comfortably and confidently toward his giant neighbor. Later, his Peking welcome would be as consistent in defeat as it was in success; but in 1964, his presence was a triumphant component of China's policy of uniting all those threatened by US imperialism. So, too, was the presence of the brilliantly robed representatives from the hopeful nations of Africa. Chou En-lai's trip to fourteen African nations earlier in the year had carried with it the hope for a second Bandung Conference, and increasing Sino–African solidarity seemed a not unreasonable expectation.

In the area termed by the Chinese the intermediate zone —those countries allied with neither of the two major powers but subject to their pressure, particularly that of the US— China's most dramatic diplomatic achievement of the year had been the opening of relations with France. Accompanied in France by a vogue in *chinoiserie,* the new diplomacy opened trading possibilities for both nations, a Paris–Shanghai route for Air France, and a large and permanent embassy in Paris, China's first major diplomatic outpost in Western Europe. The long and brilliant tradition of Chinese studies in France; the delight with which the eighteenth-century French elite had imbibed the elixir of Chinese civilization; both nations' assumption of their respective superiority in language, culture, and food gave this diplomatic breakthrough a pleasant historical consistency. By October, France had settled into diplomatic status in Peking.

The 2,600 National Day guests, whom the Chinese counted so precisely, were not impressive by the standards of other capitals. For the Chinese, however, their significance went beyond their numbers. Each one was regarded in a highly symbolic way as representative of his people and country. The Chinese press listed with great solemnity not only the princes and ministers honoring China's revolutionary holiday with their presence, but also individuals such as the American black leader Robert Williams and his wife. Today, Robert Williams' early advocacy of armed self-defense for Blacks seems a distant chapter in contemporary America's instant history; but for the Chinese then, Robert Williams was, in fact as well as symbol, a leader of yet another rebellious people.

Thus, National Day 1964 was the triumphant celebration not only of a decade and a half of the People's Republic, but of the growing success of an audacious foreign policy. With the new policy came a plethora of needs that had not existed during the period when China had leaned on the expertise of the Soviet Union. In order to develop the tenuous new links of diplomacy and friendship, the Chinese would quickly need to train a corps of young professionals with proficiency first of all in a variety of languages, and perhaps more important than the languages themselves, the ability to analyze and interpret the politics, the journalism, the diplomacy, in fact, the culture of the world from which they had been so long separated. China's isolation after 1949 had not been of her choosing, but it had been a reality. Although we went to China in a technical capacity to teach language, in a symbolic sense we were crossing the barriers which had shut the experience of the Chinese Revolution off from so much of the world. Many of those who came as we did brought with them languages and relationships unknown to modern China. The teaching of Urdu, of Swahili, Bengali, Persian, and Arabic represented a remarkable breakthrough in China's contact with unfamiliar societies, but so indeed did the teaching of Spanish and Portuguese. By and large, the teachers and editorial workers found themselves, as we did, regarded as representative of their people. Many were learners more than teachers, coming to China to witness and study the accomplishments of the revolution, hoping to learn a few lessons which could be applied at home. Whether or not China intended seriously to organize a new center, the reiteration in speeches and editorials of her position as "the base of world revolution" could have only one meaning to those who realized that such a center was historically not possible anywhere else.

Peking's American community contained representatives of each period when America had faced two choices in its relationship with the Chinese Revolution. Just as a few early friends of the Chinese Revolution, such as Anna Louise Strong and George Hatem (Ma Hai-teh), had come to live in China, so several victims of the McCarthy holocaust, men like Frank Coe and Sol Adler, once among the US Treasury Department's brilliant young staff members, had done the same. So it was when we arrived during the Vietnam War. We found ourselves heirs to a thirty-year-old tradition established by our fellow countrymen and women. Yet the People's Republic of China on its fifteenth anniversary was, of course, quite different from the legendary government in the caves of Yenan. The Chinese found it quite natural that we should arrive as a family with three children. A great many of the new foreign community of 1964 did the same, and just as the Chinese were expecting us to teach their young people our languages, so they had already established a school to teach our children Chinese.

In January 1964, Mao Tse-tung had issued two of his rare statements concerning the revolutionary struggles of the world's peoples. Both touched with great immediacy upon US imperialism. In the first, Mao spoke in support of tiny Panama and its people's just struggle for national sovereignty and control over the Canal Zone. The second challenged another aspect of American world domination, its stationing in Japan of F-105D nuclear armed aircraft and submarines, its maintenance of troops and military bases in Japan, its Security Treaty with Japan, and its control of Okinawa. The Panamanian struggle was a classic battle of a third world

country, long weakened by colonialism and imperialism.
Japan was one of the growing economic powers of the world
threatened by America's military force in Asia. Not coin-
cidentally, the struggles in the two countries to which Mao
threw China's support were two of the disparate components
of the world united front against US imperialism which the
leader of earlier and brilliantly successful united fronts was
now formulating. The closing summations of both statements
were close to identical:

> "The people of the countries in the socialist camp
> should unite, the people of the countries in Asia, Africa,
> and Latin America should unite, the people of the con-
> tinents of the world should unite, all peace-loving coun-
> tries and all countries that are subject to US aggression,
> control, interference, and bullying should unite and
> should form the broadest united front to oppose the US
> imperialist policies of aggression and war and to safe-
> guard world peace."[1]

It was the seductive logic of a new popular alliance led by a
new and pristine revolutionary center which brought that
diverse group of guests, of kings and revolutionaries, together in Peking that October.

So China, ancient center of civilization, now radiating the
irresistible attraction of the new, was once again discovered
by the world. The shock of recognition, transmitted through
time from Marco Polo to the Nixon press corps, was experienced by "outside country" people from every continent.
They, like travelers before them, found a remarkable people
living in a society extraordinary for its order and harmony
and now characterized by an egalitarianism generated by the
closeness of their revolution. This revolution, like all great
human events, had created its own distinctive rituals and
ceremonies. Among the 2,600 guests attending the pre-
National Day banquet in the Great Hall of the People, we
were to encounter for the first time the culture of post-'49
China.

Built in 1959 to celebrate the tenth anniversary of the
People's Republic, the Great Hall of the People in T'ien An

Men Square is a monument of symbolism, both numerical and political. It was built in ten months. Its main auditorium holds 10,000 people. As is well known, Chou En-lai's visits with honored guests have often taken place in rooms dedicated to each of China's provinces, and the formidable corridors through which they are reached contain marbles from every part of the country. But the popular character of the hall is not determined merely by such ceremonial reminders of the regional individuality of China. Rather, it is contained in the building itself. Many times during our stay in Peking we were to hear stories of the participation of the city's citizenry in the construction of the Great Hall, and on several occasions, as our bus passed the square, fellow passengers pointed to some part of the building and said, "You see—that's the part our group built." Like much that is Chinese, the Hall of the People is rhetoric become reality—a hall created by the people.

It is difficult to know what synthesis of the old and new created the diplomatic rituals of the new China, but rituals they are, with a protocol that is modern yet timeless and a style singularly definable as post-revolutionary Chinese. In spite of the gulf in policy which separated the National Day banquet of 1964 from the one honoring Richard Nixon in 1972, there was little to distinguish them in form—the combined pomp and jollity of a military band; the flawless food served with dignified informality by white jacketed young men and women; the self-conscious enthusiasm with which hundreds of guests imitated the Chinese custom of circulating from table to table to exchange toasts.

There is, no doubt, something about the unexpected scale of things Chinese which proves exhilarating to those encountering them for the first time, and so it was with a banquet for 2,600. It was an exhilaration tempered, however, by order, personified in a way which did not seem strikingly relevant until a few years later. The main speaker at the banquet was the Chairman of the People's Republic of China, Liu Shao-ch'i, white-haired, austere, uncharismatic. In accordance with the custom which was soon to become familiar to us, he read his speech while we at our tables followed the text word by word. His voice was startlingly high-pitched, his Hunan accent almost unintelligible to speakers of Mandarin. The procedure was emotionless, impersonal, but the speech was not. After welcoming the guests in all their proper classifications and briefly reviewing the accomplishments of the previous fifteen years, Liu's speech consisted primarily of specific affirmations of support for struggling people in all parts of the world. He began with the people of Vietnam and ended with support for ". . . the working class and broad masses in Western Europe, North America, and Oceania in their struggle against monopoly capital and for democratic rights, the improvement of their living conditions, and social progress!" In the spirit of Chairman Mao's recommendation to "turn a bad thing into a good thing" Liu inverted the encirclement of China into the bold contention that ". . . US imperialism is increasingly encircled by the people of the whole world."[2]

The National Day parade of the following day was yet another embodiment of the reversal of assumptions. Great numbers of people, perhaps a million, participated, while a small number, perhaps a few thousands, watched. It was as if the China of 700 million were displaying representative parts of her society to the watchers, who, for their part, personified the rest of the world. The parade marchers practiced for weeks before the event. Every schoolyard and neighborhood lane echoed with loudly amplified music, the shuffling of cloth-shod feet, and the abrupt directions for which the curt consonants of Peking dialect seem so well suited. The area surrounding T'ien An Men Square was marked off like a giant chessboard, and each of the hundreds of marching groups gathered at its assigned starting place in the chilly October dawn. The guests began arriving early, since veterans of many National Day parades told us that it was possible to set one's watch by the beginning and end of the parade, so precise was the organization of this mammoth event. To arrive at the back entrances of the Imperial Palace in the crisp morning, walk through the timeless courtyards, down the ancient carved marble steps and across worn paving stones now embellished with gray pots of autumn asters and chrysanthemums, was to feel for a few moments the weight of China's centuries. We parade watchers, a strange new breed of foreign envoys in the Forbidden City, were present to bear witness to the re-emergence of that center of influence which had disappeared into chaos only to rise again.

The parade that day was in the style familiar to those who had seen several National Days, but to the first-time observer it was a marvel of enormous numbers and perfect order—millions of paper flowers, their oranges, reds and pinks so unexpectedly harmonious, hundreds of doves and balloons released into the clear skies, and marchers by the hundreds of thousands, their long rows impeccably straight, their animation and seriousness contagious to the viewers in business suits, saris, military uniforms, African robes, and the "native costumes" of the world. As athletes, workers, schoolchildren, peasants, militiamen, and national minorities swept past the reviewing stand, their numbers, their organization, their purposefulness stamped upon the celebration the authority of a people cognizant of their destiny. P'eng Chen, Peking's mayor, spoke as had Liu Shao-ch'i the previous evening of domestic accomplishments and the positive trend of the revolutionary struggle in the world. He spoke of the need for modesty in the face of accomplishments, of the necessity for strengthening one's weaknesses, and of the obligation of a large party to practice the principles of equality with "all parties, whatever their size," of reaching unanimity through consultation, and not imposing one's views on others.[3] It was a speech characterized not only by optimism and a sense of success, but with the caution of a young world power seeking to lead but not control. It represented a high point in China's policy of creating a base for a third world force.

The optimism of National Day did not diminish throughout the month of October. On October 14, Khrushchev was removed as Chairman of the Soviet Council of Ministers. His fall came at the end of a particularly strong series of attacks by the Chinese, who saw his political demise as at least a partial verification of their prolonged criticisms of his policy. Two days later, with the pointed poetic logic so congenial to Chinese political culture, China exploded her first nuclear device, developed in spite of Moscow's termination of all nuclear, military, and economic aid. China's remarkable scientific and industrial achievement was entirely her own, an achievement reached years earlier than even the most optimistic outside estimate. Militarily weak China, having already dared to break out of the domination of the Soviet bloc, had now taken the first step into the small and jealous circle of nuclear powers.

On the night that the explosion was announced to the Chinese people, we were awakened at midnight by the clashing of drums and cymbals outside our windows. (No matter what time important events occur in China, they are nearly always announced and celebrated in the middle of the night. It is, no doubt, a custom arising out of both China's ancient history, when the court of the Emperor convened at sunup, and of her revolutionary history, during which, for reasons of exigency, meetings and announcements often had to come at night.) There was an air of gaiety quite bizarre to recent arrivals from America, where announcements of nuclear explosions had long been greeted with solemnity and despair. People piled into trucks and buses, unfurled red flags and sang songs as they converged on T'ien An Men Square from all parts of the city. Special editions of the *People's Daily* printed the Chinese Government statement, and a press communiqué was read everywhere over Peking's ubiquitous loudspeakers. But the gaiety of the people was not bizarre, nor was it macabre, for they accepted China's first nuclear explosion in the spirit of the government statement. It said: "To defend oneself is the inalienable right of every sovereign state . . . China cannot remain idle and do nothing in the face of the ever increasing nuclear threat posed by the United States. China is forced to conduct nuclear tests and develop nuclear weapons." In the few weeks that followed, we were interested to observe in the general exchange of congratulations a conspicuous absence of hawkish sentiments. The people of China took very literally the further statement that "The Chinese Government hereby solemnly declares that China will never at any time and under any circumstances be the first to use nuclear weapons."[4]

Mao himself had spoken about nuclear weapons to Dr. W. E. B. Du Bois, the eminent black American scholar, when he visited China in 1958. During the course of their long conversation, Du Bois observed that the American atomic arsenal posed a fearful threat to the people of the world. Mao responded that it was a good thing that people in America had become pacifistic and were afraid of the bomb. Since the threat of nuclear war came from the West, it was useful in Mao's view for Western peoples to fear the bomb, but since the Chinese themselves were the target and potential victim of the bomb, it was not useful for the Chinese to be afraid of nuclear weapons. If it would do any good for him to be frightened, Mao said, he might become the most frightened man in the world, but he didn't think his adopting that attitude would serve any useful purpose.[5]

In the five years that we spent in China, there were to be other nuclear explosions and other celebrations which became successively lower in key and in the intensity of public interest. But the attitude generated by the first one never changed. Through the remarkable shifts of policy and world relationships which we were to see, the bomb remained for the Chinese as it had been from the beginning—a necessary evil in the face of aggressive enemies.

So we first saw China at a kind of pinnacle of national confidence and optimism. There was a freshness in the application of the new policy which extended also to ourselves. We were anxious to start work either before or soon after National Day. But to the Chinese, our eagerness to throw ourselves into whatever work awaited us, although demonstrating an admirable attitude, was clearly a bit shortsighted. How was it possible, they wondered, to travel so far, to a country so different, and not take some time to observe the new country, to feel it? They thought we should first become acquainted with each other in order to determine the most suitable situation in which we should work. The Chinese sense of pace was impossible to resist. It is not, as is sometimes suggested, simply a slower pace, but one with very different rhythms from our own. Some things take great, to us even dangerous, amounts of time in China. Experiments, whether as gigantic as the Cultural Revolution or as limited as teaching methods, are stretched far beyond a point that seems either efficient or psychologically feasible. But there are other things which must be done with breathtaking speed and intensity. China is moving very rapidly into industrial time. One feels it immediately in Shanghai, the most industrially advanced of China's cities and the most "Western." In most of China, however, the century-weighted patterns of agricultural time are still pervasive—the long periods of the somnolence of the earth, and the rush to plant and harvest. Peking, an ancient as well as modern capital, is still deeply rooted in this agricultural society. In no part of the city is one far from the green commune fields which grow the city's fresh vegetables or from the sound of the donkey-pulled carts on which pipe-smoking peasants ride winter and summer to deliver produce to the seventh largest city in the world.

We slid gently into Chinese time. We spent our first two months visiting China's monuments, old and new, the parks and lakes, so formal in conception and so informally enjoyed by the hard-working, simply-dressed population; the factories, the new and modern ones, the small neighborhood ones, all functioning with a casual pride; and the communes, the backbone of all the rest. They were the kinds of sights now familiar to Americans through the accounts of hundreds of recent visitors, virtually all of whom report similar impressions of energy, confidence, and purposefulness. But this was a world only dimly glimpsed in the America of 1964, even to those who attempted to study it. We wrote glowing letters to friends at home, who no doubt thought us bedazzled, but that is a China experience repeated a thousand times since Marco Polo.

It is probably not possible for visitors from the outside

ever to absorb the totality of China—the area is too vast and varied, the regions of the country too differentiated, the history too extensive, the culture too intricate. As in all civilizations, there are strata of experience and consciousness; the penetration of one inevitably reveals yet another, and China has accumulated thousands of years of such layers of experience. Yet there are in contemporary China certain essential qualities of life and spirit which are powerfully communicated, and which, whatever the complexities and subtleties that created them, must be seen as those which most sharply characterize what modern China is. It was those qualities of a powerful unity, optimism, and collective purpose which we felt in our first few months.

The first months of our first winter in Peking flew by rapidly, consumed not only by the dramatic events of the world but also by the domestic requirements of winter clothes and bicycles for the whole family, and a new teaching and studying life. We had scarcely become settled in our teaching jobs at the Peking First Foreign Languages Institute, "our" school for the remainder of our stay in China, and our children in school to study Chinese, when it was time for the several weeks of winter vacation which coincide with the traditional Chinese New Year around the first of February. It is a time for visiting, for seeing old friends or one's distant family, and it seemed an appropriate time for us to do the same. We joined the throngs at the Peking Railroad Station departing for the far reaches of the country. Everyone seemed to be carrying a plastic handbag or string bag filled with Peking delicacies, cold buns of steamed bread to eat on the train, and the bright enamel cup owned by every traveler. We went, our family of five, quite alone, on the comfortable, old-fashioned train that would take us to visit an American friend living with her daughter and Chinese grandchildren in Kaifeng, Honan Province, center of China's earliest civilization.

From the earliest memory of man, the Yellow River has carried huge accretions of fine silt from the lands in the far west and deposited them in the Central Plain, creating an alluvial soil of great fertility. It was this phenomenon of nature which stimulated China's early development of an agricultural civilization in much the same way that the accretions of the Nile gave rise to Egypt. What is now Honan Province was the area of Chinese man's first home, and the fertility of its soil was the foundation of the prosperous dynasties which rose, fell, and rose again in or around Kaifeng. But the great deposits of the Yellow River, source of the Central Plain's fertility, were also the source of its disasters, for with the years and the centuries, the mud has unceasingly raised the bed of the great river until it has come to rise high above the level of the plain. This terrifying phenomenon is the reason for the gigantic floods which have again and again swept over the plain, claiming lives in the millions and ruining land and crops uncountable. The Yellow River became "China's Sorrow," and the history of the Yellow River Plain has been determined by men's ability or inability to deal with this marvel and terror of nature.

One does not forget the first view of "The Lord of the Rivers." The climb to the top of the bank is steep, and breathing is difficult in the sharp dry cold. There is no sight of the river until one clambers onto the summit of the incline, and then the view is endless, like an ocean, not a river, wide without end, and indeed yellow, yellow-brown like a serpent of mud. This is the central fact in the lives of the tough and wiry peasants of Honan, and there is little in their daily farming existence which is not somehow influenced by the reality of the great river.

The land through which we passed on the train was barren and harsh, like all of the north central plains area, virtually treeless except for the neat rows of post-1949 afforestation seen throughout the country. An enormous concentration of hydraulic projects is gradually forcing the great giant back into its original course, but there are anomalous remains of the past. In 1938, Chiang Kai-shek, in a reckless attempt to stop the Japanese advance on the town of Chengchow, cut the dykes of the Yellow River and diverted it south. The Japanese were stopped at a cost of eleven cities and 4,000 villages submerged, and 2 million peasants homeless. This is a chapter of history long past, but a bitter residue remains. The soil of the area suffers from either excessive salinity or excessive alkalinity, and the struggle to deal with the problem continues still. There is not, in China, the possibility which Americans accepted from the very beginning of their agricultural development, of simply leaving behind that land which was unsuitable for crops. The population is too large for that and the arable land too little, so there is no answer but to "move mountains," to create terraces out of rocky ravines or tidelands out of the sea, and to use the soil in the intensive way traditional to Chinese agriculture. In Honan, which the Chinese frankly speak of as a poor province, one is brought to an abrupt realization of the drama of the Chinese peasant to survive which is at the root and the heart of the Chinese Revolution. It is a drama now much mitigated by the ending of the landlord system which, even in fertile areas of the country, squeezed the peasants into famine and destitution; but it is a drama which is not yet finished. The history of the political movements since 1949, the establishment of the communes, and even China's profound disagreements with the Soviet Union must be seen in relationship to this question.

We had arrived in China at the end of the period the Chinese call the hard years (1959–62). In July 1960, the Chinese had been informed that all economic aid and the 10,000 Russian technicians in China were being withdrawn. By August, the Russian technicians had departed with blueprints under arm, and major construction projects throughout China ground to a halt. China, confronted with the worst droughts and floods in a century, and attempting to recover from the dislocations caused by faulty planning in the Great Leap Forward, faced a serious economic crisis. The Chinese did suffer from malnutrition in those years, but there was no famine. Seven hundred million Chinese, in an unprecedented effort of collective will, shared out each grain of rice, and bent their backs to repair the damage. City people and intellectuals took to their beds for a few hours each day in order to conserve body energy, while those doing physical work were allotted more food. People showed us snapshots of themselves, looking very thin indeed, and asked with amusement if we did not think there was a great difference from the present "fat" selves. There was. By 1963, the grain crop was sufficient; in 1964, it was good; by 1965, it was excellent.

In February 1965, the psychology of the Honan peasants was not that of people who had just come through a famine, but of ones who had emerged victorious from a battle. We were to hear in Kaifeng first what we later heard throughout the country—that without the communes "we would not have survived." Contrary to the near-unanimous view of Western experts that the communes had been the cause of the food shortages, it was the firm view of the peasants that without this new form of extensive farming they could never have dealt with the exigencies of the natural disasters.

The creation of large-scale agricultural communes incorporating more than 500 million peasants stands as one of the greatest innovations of the Chinese Revolution. Yet they did not spring from a vacuum, but from the uninterrupted revolution on the land unleashed by China's peasant war. After the victory of the revolution in 1949, the peasants, lacking draft animals and farm implements, had moved rapidly to set up mutual aid teams which pooled resources while retaining private ownership of land, animals, and tools. These teams, encouraged by Party leaders and aided by state loans, soon evolved into farming cooperatives in which each contributor was repaid for his contribution out of joint funds. By the winter of 1956, much of the countryside had been organized into cooperatives, most of which, by the spring of 1958, had paid off their debts incurred in the purchase of land animals and farm implements. At this point, the movement to establish communes began. This remarkable stage-by-stage revolution in the world's largest peasant country, although a tumultuous and stormy process, appears, when contrasted with the agony of the Russian peasant under Stalin's policy of collectivization, as a relatively smooth transition to the creation of a stable, socialized agriculture system. By merging 740,000 agricultural cooperatives into some 74,000 communes, a new social institution emerged which combined farming, industry, commerce, education, and defense. The communes continue to run their own schools and banks. They perform governmental functions, much like an American county seat, and handle military affairs through the establishment of local militia units.

Thus, very early in our stay in China, we encountered the nation's stern imperative to create a good and viable existence for her 500 million peasants—and in her own way. It was an awareness that would remain with us in the coming period of great complexities. We traveled the following summer to the lush countryside of south central China and visited communes, fragrant with tea and flowers, where the peasants lived in two-story lath and stucco homes of an Elizabethan elegance. But it is on the harsh northern plains, where the peasants, no longer lashed by landlords, are still lashed by nature, that one begins to understand why, to Mao, the question of the Chinese peasant has always been central to China's revolution.

As we adapted ourselves to the currents of life generated by a people making up one-fourth of humanity, we found that the Chinese lived and thought on two planes. One was the lively workaday existence of ordinary people concerned with practical economic, political, and personal problems. The other involved an almost cosmic consciousness of China's place in the global scheme of things—an awareness of the historic past, the present as the product of that past, and the emerging future. We were often struck by the time-frame thinking of our friends, who, when we discussed the student, worker, or minority movements in our country, wished to know in what stage we thought that movement was. Stages were important to them, because they felt what was appropriate at the beginning of any historical or political process might not be appropriate in a subsequent stage. And so we, too, gradually began to think in the Chinese way of a beginning, a middle, and an end to each historical process, slowly absorbing the knowledge of China's past political and historical development in order to understand the present.

## Chapter II

# Two Roads—Two Lines

ON THE HOLIDAYS of the Chinese Communist Revolution six giant portraits look out on Peking's T'ien An Men Square. The portraits are always the same, and each appears in the same place. Centered on the red wall directly under the yellow-tiled roof of the Gate of Heavenly Peace is the portrait of Mao Tse-tung. To the left of the great square, in the shadow of the vast Museum of the Revolution, are pictures of Karl Marx and Friedrich Engels. On the right, in front of the Hall of the People, are portraits of Lenin and Stalin, and directly across the multi-acred plaza opposite T'ien An Men, situated at the base of the Monument to the Revolution, rests the portrait of Sun Yat-sen. Mao and Sun thus face each other under the broad expanse of the northern Peking sky, while Marx and Engels, Lenin and Stalin, stand guard on the flanks of the revolution. The precise symbolism of these prophets of revolution reflects the synthesis of Chinese and European idea systems attempted by the Chinese people in the twentieth century.

Not long after our arrival, we were taken across the immense square to look at the Monument to the People's Revolutionary Martyrs. Inscribed on its towering granite face were the names of patriots who, from the middle of the nineteenth century up to China's liberation in 1949, had fought for Chinese national independence. What struck us was this official recognition that the Chinese Revolution encompassed a century-long process of struggle and that the Chinese Communist Party had appeared only in the last act. It was soon apparent to us that the Chinese people of today see themselves as actors in a 100-year drama of revolution. To them, the four volumes of Chairman Mao's works represent a history of their own lives and that of their parents and grandparents. The dynamic quality of life in China that we were to share for a time stems from the belief of its people that they are both living and making history.

It would become clearer to us as time passed that the Chinese people were engaged in one of those climactic periods of their long history which involved the struggle to transform an appropriated foreign doctrine into a new cultural synthesis uniquely Chinese. Just as, in the distant past, China had reshaped Buddhism imported from India into a system fit for Chinese use, the Chinese have found in Marxism an affinity with Chinese collective life patterns and dialectical philosophic traditions. China's remolding of Marxism has been a stormy and revolutionary process. Yet the remarkable harmony achieved by Chinese civilization throughout the centuries has often arisen out of chaotic struggles not so different from this. Unity, as Mao asserts, can emerge only from struggle.

As we were to learn, a bitter conflict between Chinese leaders over which road to follow had existed within the Communist Party from the beginning of the revolution. Even seventeen years after the victory of the Chinese Revolution, the dispute remained unresolved. We had come to China at the decisive stage of that massive effort to appropriate, translate, and then break loose from the Russian revolutionary experience. Like many non-Chinese observers in the fall of 1964, we believed that the Chinese Communist leadership constituted a monolithic, veteran group, united in policy and direction. Despite periodic arguments at the top and the occasional replacement of individual national leaders, the Chinese Communist Party was noted for possessing the most stable group of leaders of any political organization in the world. Within two years, not only would that "stable" leadership divide into hostile camps, but the nation would move to the brink of civil war. Believing that the debate with the

Russians was just about over, we found that among the Chinese themselves it had just begun. Along with millions of ordinary Chinese, we were drawn into a political struggle over the meaning of a half century of Chinese history. The Chinese political war of the mid-Sixties was, in fact, a conflict over the two models of revolutionary development produced by the fundamentally different experiences of the Russian and Chinese revolutions. Which model should China choose? Which would be more relevant to its future development? It was a political struggle rooted not only in theory, but in the historical experiences of the two great revolutions of the twentieth century. Labeled by the Chinese as "the struggle between the two lines," it was a contest among leaders influenced by the model of revolution developed by Mao Tse-tung in his guerrilla capital of Yenan and those determined to follow the classic Moscow formula for modernization.

Throughout the whole protracted course of the Chinese Revolution, the effort to synthesize the experience of the Russian Revolution produced strains and tensions within the ranks of the Chinese Communist Party. Mao's writings clearly reflect the search of generations of Chinese thinkers for a formula to revive a collapsing civilization. Mao once described how he had himself engaged in that search:

> "From the time of China's defeat in the Opium War of 1840, Chinese progressives went through untold hardships in their quest for truth from Western countries [. . .] every effort was made to learn from the West. In my youth, I, too, engaged in such studies. They represented the culture of Western bourgeois democracy, including social theories and natural sciences of that period, and they were called the 'new learning' in contrast to Chinese feudal culture, which was called the 'old learning.'

> "Imperialist aggression shattered the fond dreams of the Chinese about learning from the West. It was very odd—why were the teachers always committing aggression against their pupil? The Chinese learned a good deal from the West, but they could not make it work and were never able to realize their ideals."[6]

According to Mao, the Chinese finally discovered a universally applicable truth from the Russian October Revolution of 1917—"The salvoes of the October Revolution brought us Marxism–Leninism."

If the salvoes of the October Revolution brought the Chinese Marxism–Leninism, then the history and traditions of peasant revolt that had existed for centuries provided the social forces and indigenous form for China's revolutionary transformation. Hunan had been the center of Chinese revolutionary thought for over half a century prior to the 1911 Revolution. Moreover, Hunan, unlike Peking, was influenced directly by the concepts of peasant revolt, specifically the Taiping rebellion of the 1860's. It was in Hunan that Mao developed intellectually and where he spent more than eight years of his youth as a student and teacher at the Hunan Normal School in Changsha. It required a peasant intellectual to lead China's peasant revolution.

The scholars of Hunan, isolated from the main currents of Chinese history and thought during the eighteenth and early nineteenth centuries, developed their own pragmatic and interpretative approach to the Confucian classics. These writings, stressing economic and political aspects of Confucianism, challenged the scholasticism predominant in the rest of the country. It was Wang Fu-chih (1619–92), the anti-Manchu philosopher of Hengyang, who first developed an evolutionary approach to Chinese political institutions asserting that each historical period produced its own unique form of political organization. He therefore argued that it was futile to attempt to revive ancient institutions. This notion was, of course, an attack on a fundamental tenet of Confucian philosophy. For Wang, political and social systems, as well as human nature, and social customs were all subject to change:

> "What is not yet complete can be completed; what is already completed can be reformed. There is not a single part of human nature already shaped that can not be modified."[7]

The ideas of Wang Fu-chih were not well known outside his own province during his lifetime, but by the second half of the nineteenth century they influenced a whole generation of scholars and officials in Hunan, and during Mao's youth these ideas were widespread in the progressive school system with which Mao became associated.

Wang Fu-chih had stated, "Action can reap the result of knowledge, whereas knowledge might not lead to action." His theory of knowledge, while embracing a theory of observation and deduction, placed the weight on action. In 1937, Mao Tse-tung wrote in his famous essay "On Practice":

> "If you want knowledge, you must take part in the practice of changing reality. If you want to know the taste of a pear, you must change the pear by eating it yourself [. . .] If you want to know the theory and methods of revolution, you must take part in revolution."[8]

Did this come from Wang Fu-chih or Marx and Engels, from the Chinese dialectical system or the dialectics of Hegel? Undoubtedly Mao was influenced by both Western and Chinese schools of thought and found them compatible. What he could not digest from the West he discarded, and as he and other Chinese Communists gained experience, they discarded more and more of the theory which did not fit their own environment.

In the late summer of 1965, André Malraux, then French Minister of Culture, asked Mao when he had formulated the idea that the peasants were the main force of the Chinese Revolution. Mao replied:

> "My conviction did not take shape; I always felt it. But there is a rational answer all the same. After Chiang Kai-shek's coup in Shanghai, we scattered. As you know, I decided to go back to my village. Long ago, I had experienced the great famine of Changsha, when the severed heads of rebels were stuck on poles, but I had forgotten it. Two miles outside my village there were trees stripped of their bark up to a height of twelve feet; starving people had eaten it. We could make better fighters

out of men who were forced to eat bark than out of the stokers of Shanghai, or even the coolies. But Borodin understood nothing about peasants."[9]

Nor, he added, did Stalin. However, a number of young Chinese Communists took a different road than Mao's. In the early days of the revolution, they made the pilgrimage to Moscow, studied at the Lenin School, and returned to China to apply the urban-oriented Russian formula of revolution. They brought with them a blueprint for revolution and a charter of leadership issued in Moscow. Mao was referring to these early Chinese Communist leaders and others who would follow them when he told Malraux that "there is no such thing as abstract Marxism, but only concrete Marxism, adapted to the concrete realities of China, to the trees as naked as the people because the people are busy eating them."

Mao undersood, as had all great revolutionary leaders before him, that revolutions are created by monumental social forces which sweep aside everything standing in their way:

> "Everything arose out of a specific situation: We organized peasant revolt, we did not instigate it. Revolution is a drama of passion; we did not win the people over by appealing to reason, but by developing hope, trust, and fraternity. In the face of famine, the will to equality takes on a religious force. Then in the struggle for rice, land, and the rights brought by agrarian reform, the peasants had the conviction that they were fighting for their lives and their children."

What Mao was describing was the reality of a massive social movement which characterizes revolution from below. "You must realize," he told Malraux, "that before us, among the masses, no one addressed themselves to women or the young. Nor of course to the peasants. For the first time in their lives, every one of them felt involved."

By the time of our arrival in China, Mao and a few others had fully understood, and were beginning to elaborate upon, the differences between the Russian and Chinese models of revolution. The Chairman reminded his French guest: "When Westerners talk about revolutionary sentiments, they nearly always attribute to us a propaganda akin to Russian propaganda. Well, if there is propaganda, it is more like that of your revolution [French Revolution 1789–93]. If propaganda means training militiamen and guerrillas, we did a lot of propaganda." In the late 1920's, the battered remnants of China's revolutionary leadership retreated to the countryside after the disastrous defeat of the revolutionary uprisings in Shanghai and Canton. There they sank roots in soil which had traditionally sprouted the social instrument for transferring political power in China—peasant rebellion. The ancient Chinese theory of revolution, as developed by Mencius, was meant solely for removing tyrants. The "Mandate of Heaven" stood as a religious sanction and after-the-fact legitimation of a new ruler. Such new emperors, often of peasant origin, frequently rode to power on the back of massive armed peasant revolt. It has been argued that every Chinese dynasty has arisen from a period of war involving peasant rebellion, a time of troubles when "the great fight each other for power and the poor turn against all government."[10] There is enough truth in this simplified concept of Chinese history to suggest how Mao and the Chinese Communists were able to transform peasant rebellion, a traditional Chinese political form, through Western Marxist–Leninist theories of class struggle and revolutionary seizure of state power.

The first great revolutionary manifesto of the Chinese Revolution, written by the young Mao in 1927, contained the seeds of the unique Chinese view of modern revolution:

> "The present upsurge of the peasant movement is a colossal event. In a very short time, in China's central, southern, and northern provinces, several hundred million peasants will rise like a mighty storm, like a hurricane, a force so swift and violent that no power, however great, will be able to hold it back. They will smash all the trammels that bind them and rush forward along the road to liberation. They will sweep all the imperial-

ists, warlords and corrupt officials, local tyrants and evil gentry, into their graves. Every revolutionary party and every revolutionary comrade will be put to the test, to be accepted or rejected as they decide [. . .] Every Chinese is free to choose, but events will force you to choose quickly."[11]

Mao put the revolution before the Party; the Party was to be tested by the revolution. Thirty years later, Mao would use the same concept to test the Party once more in the fires of revolution from below, and we as foreign teachers would find ourselves with the rest of the Chinese urban population submerged in a mass politics involving millions of activists. This was hardly the concept of the role of the vanguard party developed by the Russians.

Concepts of revolution from below were further elaborated and developed by the Chinese communists when they sank roots once again in the peasantry after their epic Long March to secure Northwest China base areas. For more than a decade, Mao and other Chinese leaders learned the rudiments of popular rule in the vast Liberated Areas the Chinese Communist armies carved out for themselves. The new political system worked out by Mao and his followers from the caves of their capital town in the dry plateau region of Shensi Province included: an anti-bureaucractic style of simplified administration, reliance on local-level organization, the dispatch of intellectuals to the countryside, co-operative forms of production, mandatory cadre labor at the point of production, and the systematic spread of popular education.[12] All these were to become the hallmarks of the new Maoist revolutionary theory and practice, very different indeed from the Russian bureaucratic system of top-down rule. The new popular forms of Chinese communist government grew naturally in the decentralized environment of protracted revolutionary guerrilla war.

After decades of successful organization and popular rule in the Liberated Areas of the Chinese countryside, the Chinese peasant revolutionary armies conquered the major coastal cities by storm in 1949. There, they confronted entirely new problems for which their past experience provided little guidance. Mao and his followers had learned how to make revolution, but they knew little about building a modern economy. Naturally, the Chinese Communists, including Mao, turned to the Russians for guidance in constructing a modern socialist economy and administration. The art of revolution has always been a cumulative endeavor, and Mao, like Lenin before him, looked to history for models in constructing a new social order. Although the Russians had done little to support the final surge to power of the Chinese Communists, Russian backing was needed to counter the American military threat and economic boycott of the new revolutionary regime. In these circumstances, Mao made the decision that it was necessary for Chinese survival in a hostile world to "lean to one side."

There were a number of factors which accounted for the tenacious hold of the Russian version of Marxism–Leninism on the Chinese Communist Party. For one thing, the Russian concept of the vanguard party was directly exported and transplanted in Chinese revolutionary soil by representatives of the Communist International in the 1920's. Some Chinese leaders, particularly those educated in Moscow, saw the new Chinese Communist Party as nothing more than a replica of the Russian Bolshevik Party. While Mao accepted the theory of the Leninist vanguard party, over the years he was to interpret that theory differently from some of his colleagues. A second factor was the creation of a Chinese Communist underground apparatus in the White Areas of the country under the domination of Chiang Kai-shek's Kuomintang government and the Japanese during the decades of revolutionary civil war. Under conditions of illegality and terror, parallels with the Russian historical experience occurred. Ideological and organizational patterns characteristic of the Russian Bolshevik Party were reproduced in a Chinese environment. It was no accident that, by the 1960's, Liu Shao-ch'i, the leader of the underground party in the White Areas, should have become the major representative of the "revisionist" line in opposition to Mao and the indigenous Chinese political and organizational line created in Yenan. The Party in the White Areas was secret, highly disciplined, centralized, and by necessity rigidly hierarchical in structure, while the Party in Yenan enjoyed an open existence leading popularly elected governments enthusiastically supported by the masses of poor peasants. Policy and command in the underground Party in the White area flowed from the top down. Loyalty to the Party, rather than to the revolutionary classes, governed the outlook of the majority of the Party members. In Yenan, the situation was almost the reverse.

Finally, and perhaps most decisively, there was the direct influence of thousands of Russian advisors who came to China during the 1950's. Looking back on those days, Mao admitted that he lacked experience and knowledge in constructing a modern economy. He himself led the argument that China must seek Russian aid and learn how Russia had transformed herself from a backward country into a powerful industrial socialist state. As a result, the Russians laid the foundations of China's machine tool industry, trained corps of technicians, and established the framework for China's secondary and higher educational systems.

The more than 10,000 Russian advisors who came to China during this period succeeded in winning over an important section of the Chinese leadership to Soviet concepts of economic development, Party organization, and educational goals. The Russian economic formula was to build heavy industry first, deferring agricultural development until agricultural machinery would become available for the countryside. Surplus capital for investment in industrial enclaves would be extracted from the peasantry as it had been in Russia. This Soviet model of development called for the creation of a technological elite through specialized and intensive education of the few. The Russian concept of Party building was to consolidate and firmly establish the vanguard party as a surrogate for the urban working class. A highly professionalized army divorced from politics was to be created after the Soviet Red Army and the rank and file guerrilla tradition phased out.

Within two years of our arrival in Peking we were to witness the massive denunciation of all these concepts of modernization as "revisionist." If such policies were continued, the Maoists argued in the mid-Sixties, China would "change color" and head down a road that could lead only to the restoration of capitalism. They charged that a new oppressive class system similar to that of the Soviet Union would be established. The "two-line struggle" which erupted in the Cultural Revolution and almost led to civil war, counterposed the Yenan tradition to what was essentially the Russian model of modernization. In opposition to the program of giving priority to heavy industry, the Maoists promulgated an economic policy centered on agricultural development as the foundation of the national economy. The surplus for industrial development would come from an expansion of agricultural output rather than from existing peasant reserves. The Maoists refused to build the country by exploiting the 500 million peasants who had made the revolution in the first place. As for Party building, rather than consolidating an elite, Mao wished to expose the vanguard party to periodic rectification by the masses. In education, the Maoists hoped to dismantle the elite school system and substitute a program of widespread popular schooling based on the Yenan tradition. In the army, politics was to come first, technical efficiency second. By 1964, this criticism of the Russians was more than apparent to all China's foreign guests, but the fact that the nation was on the verge of an internal political revolution was not. We were, of course, curious to know what the feeling of the average Chinese was toward their former "comrades in arms"—the Russians.

A Chinese friend told us his version of the evolution of the Russian advisory program in China. The first group of Russians who came in the early 1950's, he said, had been true comrades and friends, enthusiastic about China's revolution and sharing the ideological commitments of the Chinese. He told of one advisor, working in drought-stricken Honan, who, on seeing the first rain in months, jumped out of his car in suit and tie and, standing in the deluge, shouted, "This is good for the Revolution." The second group which replaced the first was more aloof, our friend told us. They were good technicians, competent, professional, and serious about their work, but also determined to establish Soviet-style regulations in a uniform manner in every possible project and factory. They lived apart in elite quarters designed to provide them with luxuries unknown to their Chinese counterparts and showed little enthusiasm for China's development aside from their own technological input. The third group came in the late Fifties. The only thing they were interested in was data and statistical information on every factory in the country. "We considered that espionage," our friend exclaimed, "and we refused to give them what they wanted."

This, then, constituted the broad outline of the tensions produced by the Chinese effort to synthesize world revolutionary experience and to construct from the ground up revolutionary institutions capable of sustaining a new modern nation. Since 1958, the Sino–Soviet conflict developed from a Party dispute to that between the two largest socialist states in the world. China was now confronted by the two superpowers, both declaring hostility to China's revolutionary system, both devoted to undermining that system and, if possible, to overthrowing it. The triangular pattern of world power relationships had already begun to affect world history.

Changes in the Soviet Union, not China, precipitated the growing crisis within the world system of communist states and parties. It had all begun when Khrushchev, at the XXth Congress of the Soviet Communist Party, without any prior consultation with other parties, arbitrarily jettisoned the basic line of the international movement and substituted one of his own. His total denunciation of Stalin, in effect, put into question thirty years of revolutionary experience, and his revision of Lenin's position on "peaceful coexistence" laid the foundation for what was to become the new Russian world view which envisioned Soviet–United States cooperation for the settlement of world problems.

Observers of world communism are fond of citing the Chinese as the modern Protestants breaking with the Holy doctrine established in Moscow. If analogies are in order, it might be more accurate to view Khrushchev's secret speech at the XXth Congress in another light. Was it not as if the Pope rather than Luther had nailed the ninety-five theses to the door of the church at Wittenberg? Revision of fundamental doctrine by the center of world communism created the greatest crisis in the world communist movement since the founding of the Third International. Within a few months, a leading saint of world communism had been proclaimed a devil, revolution had been discarded for the doctrine of "peaceful transition," and peaceful coexistence, by implication, became the substitute for revolution as the agency of global change. In the future, the leaders of the United States and the Soviet Union would attempt to decide the affairs of the rest of the world by themselves. At this historical juncture, the Chinese Communist Party, standing firmly on the rock of the Chinese Revolution, emerged as the foremost defender of a European-originated belief system now in danger of disintegration.

Chinese Communists, and especially Mao, had few historical reasons for revering Stalin—and even a few for detesting him. The Chinese, however, were less interested in defending Stalin as leader than they were in constructing a defense of the Russian Revolution, out of which their own revolution had sprung. Acutely aware of the importance of symbols, the Chinese understood that the Russians were smashing more than the image of Stalin. They were not just dispensing with an icon, but dismantling the Church itself.

In April 1956, the Chinese published the famous essay "On the Historical Experience of the Dictatorship of the Proletariat," to be followed nine months later by a second document, "More on the Historical Experience of the Dictatorship of the Proletariat." These two essays established the Chinese as the most consistent and able defenders of Marxist political theory in the world. It was during this period that Mao told the Russian Ambassador to China, "Stalin deserves to be criticized, but we do not agree with the method of criticism, and there are some other things we do not agree with."[13] The Chinese themselves had rejected the Stalinist work style, the Stalin formula of rule by command, and many other Stalinist precepts of Party organization, but they were not about to trample on forty years of world revolutionary history.

By 1957, the Chinese Communist leadership under Mao had gained a great deal of experience both in agricultural and industrial development and was confidently beginning to assert itself as a group of mature and experienced Marxists within the international communist movement. This was the period when Khrushchev's new line had unloosed a revolt in Eastern Europe and the United States stepped up the pace of the international arms race. On October 15, 1957, the Russians, desperately needing China's support, signed an agreement to help China develop her own nuclear weapons systems. In the following month, representatives of the socialist bloc nations and communist leaders throughout the world adopted in Moscow the Declaration of World Communist Parties. This declaration appeared to reverse some of the Soviet XXth Congress theses and reinstated much of the old international line. Soviet euphoria over Sputnik, the new tough line of the United States, and opposition within the Soviet elite to the doctrinal revisions of the XXth Congress, all may have encouraged Khrushchev to make concessions on ideological issues. In any case, the Chinese were able to force through their own thesis that "US imperialism is the center of world reaction" and amend the Khrushchev "peaceful transition" theory by inserting the caveat: "Leninism teaches, and experience confirms, that the ruling classes never relinquish power voluntarily." This was the moment of history when Mao proclaimed to the Chinese students in Moscow that "the East Wind prevails over the West Wind!"

However, the spirit of Sino–Soviet unity proved to be short-lived. By the spring of 1958, Mao had renewed the revolution at home by launching the Great Leap Forward and the agricultural commune movement. The Yenan model of revolution was reasserting itself. The year 1958 was a turning point in the Chinese Revolution, as we were to learn in many discussions with our Chinese friends. Whether or not one enthusiastically supported the Great Leap and the communes became a test of loyalty to Mao's revolutionary line. Within two years of our arrival, all Chinese had to account for their record during the tumultuous years of the Great Leap.

During those days when the new revolution was sweeping over the Chinese countryside, the counterrevolution gathered strength in the Taiwan Straits. By July 1958, Chiang Kai-shek, with American support, had transferred approximately one-third of his army, some 200,000 troops, to Quemoy Island, within a stone's throw of the Chinese mainland. Engaged in a decisive stage of revolutionary mass mobilization and threatened with outside attack, the Chinese looked for unequivocal support from the Soviet Union. In July, Khrushchev arrived in Peking. In discussions with Mao, he made it clear that as a quid pro quo for Russian support against the United States, the Russians would demand that Soviet naval and air bases be established at the principal Chinese port cities. Mao later said that he had responded by telling Khrushchev that if the Russians forced through this demand, the Chinese would go up in the hills to fight the new occupiers of Chinese territory.[14] It was during this discussion that Khrushchev remarked that guerrillas and militiamen in an era of nuclear weaponry were nothing but a heap of flesh and that the Chinese People's Communes were "nonsense."

Russian failure to back China in the Taiwan Straits crisis and Russian antagonism to the Maoist concept of uninterrupted revolution strengthened Mao's conviction that the Russians were no longer interested in revolution. Mao and other Chinese leaders feared that the Russians were once again turning toward collusion with the United States for superpower control of the world. On November 17, 1958, Khrushchev told Hubert Humphrey in a public interview that the Chinese communes were "old-fashioned and reactionary." For the first time, the Russians had publicly interfered in Chinese affairs. They had aligned themselves with the

United States in condemning the continuing revolutionary process in China. We were, of course, more or less familiar with the main elements of the dispute between the Chinese and Russians over international strategy and revolutionary theory. What we did not know, but would soon learn, was that internal and external pressure during the period of the Great Leap had created serious divisions among the Chinese national leaders which proved in the long run insoluble. In the month following Khrushchev's public criticism of the Chinese communes, the Central Committee of the Chinese Communist Party met at Wuchang to criticize the dislocations and errors arising from the Great Leap Forward. It was at this meeting that Mao resigned as Chairman of the People's Republic so that he could devote "more time to Marxist–Leninist theoretical work." He relinquished the leading position in the nation to Liu Shao-ch'i, but remained as Chairman of the Communist Party. Whether or not he was compelled to resign, we were told during the Cultural Revolution that Mao said, "I was most dissatisfied with that decision, but there was nothing I could do about it."

It was in the spring of 1959 that the Chinese Revolution entered a conclusive, decade-long struggle to break loose from the influence of the Russian Revolution and its international organization. The first five years of this process involved breaking with the Soviet Party and State. The second five years, corresponding with our own years in China, involved the attempt to break with the internal influence of the Soviet political, economic, and social model of modernization.

For over forty years, major internal power struggles within the Chinese Communist Party have in one way or another been linked to leaders connected with Moscow. The overthrow of Li Li-san in the Thirties, Wang Ming in the Forties, Kao Kang and P'eng Teh-huai in the Fifties, and Liu Shao-ch'i in the Sixties have all involved the Russian connection. At the 1959 Lushan Conference, the struggle between the Defense Minister, Marshal P'eng Teh-huai, and Mao Tse-tung reflected the persistent pressure of the Soviet

Union as a key factor in China's internal politics. That conference witnessed the most bitter political and personal attack on Mao Tse-tung in the history of the Chinese Communist Party. We, together with millions of Chinese, would soon be reading the hitherto restricted speeches of the Lushan meeting. Marshal P'eng Teh-huai, an acerbic peasant soldier, veteran of the Long March, and commander of the Chinese Volunteers in the Korean War, led the political faction opposed to the Great Leap and Mao's concept of agricultural organization. P'eng led his attack on Mao by criticizing the formula for "putting politics in command." Moreover, he ridiculed the Great Leap Strategy as a program of petit bourgeois fanaticism which violated all known economic and scientific laws. P'eng stood instead for a strategy of planned economic development dependent upon Russian aid. As Defense Minister, P'eng's notion of a modern professionalized army was predicated upon Soviet weapons aid and would have meant a return to a heavy industry economic strategy. Mao Tse-tung, in contrast, hoped to guarantee China's independence by concentrating on the development of atomic weapons, either with or without Russian aid, and by building a mass, rather than a Western-style, professional army. The Maoist army, backed by local militia, would be geared to a strategy of "defense in depth." Mao had outlined his concept of the road to follow as early as 1956:

> "Do you want atomic bombs? If you do, you must decrease the proportion of military expenditure and increase economic construction. Or do you only pretend to want them? In that case, you will not decrease the proportion of military expenditure, but decrease economic construction. Which is the better plan? Will everybody please study this question. It is a question of strategic policy."[15]

It was clear that the question of Chinese national independence was an unshakeable principle for Mao.

On July 23, Mao launched his counterattack against P'eng Teh-huai and his supporters; it was the beginning of a protracted political war. While admitting shortcomings and errors in the Great Leap and commune movements, Mao stood firmly by his conviction that it is social forces that make history and not technique alone. In his reply to Marshal P'eng, Mao showed in characteristic fashion that he was willing to take the risk of disorder and chaos in return for revolutionary transformation:

> "The People's Communes will never collapse. At the present, not a single one has collapsed. I am prepared to have one-half of them collapse. Even if seventy per cent of them collapse, we will have the remaining thirty per cent."[16]

The People's Communes subsequently withstood every test and may well be recorded as the greatest social innovation of the Chinese Revolution.

Mao characterized the political struggle at Lushan as a class struggle and his opponents as right opportunists who were attempting to split the Party. After a complex and bitter fight, including a threat by Mao to return to the hills to organize a new revolutionary army of peasants to fight the leadership which had opposed his revolutionary line, Mao won a decisive victory. P'eng Teh-huai was removed as Defense Minister and replaced by Mao's close ally Lin Piao. But history would show that a substantial portion of the Chinese leadership shared the views of the deposed Marshal P'eng.

The struggle against Marshal P'eng over internal policies and with the Russians over their strategy of collusion with the United States now merged and in a sense became inseparable. However, not wishing to make the conflict with the Russian Communist Party a dispute between nations, the Chinese hoped to argue out differences in terms of the philosophy which both countries claimed to share. Khrushchev, on the other hand, responded to the new Chinese theoretical broadsides with insulting attacks on Chinese Communist leaders. At the famous Bucharest Meeting of Representatives from Fraternal Communist Parties, he lashed out at the Chinese delegates, calling them "madmen" who wanted to unleash a new world war. He labeled the Chinese as pure nationalists in the Sino–Indian boundary dispute and characterized the Chinese Communist leaders as "left-adventurist, pseudo-revolutionaries, and sectarian." By the 1960's, the Russians escalated the conflict from the realm of ideology to one between national states by withdrawing the 10,000 Russian technicians from China, which in turn created a crisis in the already strained Chinese economy.[17]

Chinese society and politics of the 1960's were marked by the intensification of the conflict engendered by Mao's attempt to extricate the Chinese Revolution from the Russian embrace. Criticism, both veiled and open, continued against Mao's domestic policy of uninterrupted revolution. Despite the dismissal of P'eng Teh-huai for his opposition to Mao's line of "self-reliance" and politics in command, and the more veiled charge that P'eng was in "collusion" with Russian leaders, the deposed Marshal retained much of his influence. We, who knew something of the P'eng Teh-huai case from the foreign press before we had come to China, had no idea that the issue was still smoldering under the surface, nor that the Chinese leaders were badly split, some wishing to "reverse the verdict" on P'eng Teh-huai. Later, it was disclosed publicly that at the Party's Enlarged Work Conference held in January 1962 the debate over the justice or injustice of P'eng's removal from office was reopened. P'eng himself circulated an 80,000-character document defending his criticism of the commune movement and the strategy of the Great Leap.

When the Tenth Plenum of the Eighth Central Committee of the Chinese Communist Party opened in late July 1962, Mao Tse-tung put forth a new slogan which, during the Cultural Revolution, became a battle cry of the masses— "Never Forget Class Struggle." On the first day of that meeting, Mao declared that it was necessary "to rename right opportunism as revisionism in China."[18] In ancient China, the Confucian "rectification of names" required that each member of society be properly classified and publicly noted in his correct status. This new rectification of names by Mao was undoubtedly carefully noted by many symbol-conscious Chinese. By this move, Mao had linked the conflict with the Soviet revisionists to China's domestic politics and class struggle. It was a development which would profoundly influence Chinese revolutionary politics for the foreseeable future. It was a logical outcome that, within five years, the Chief of State, Liu Shao-ch'i, would be renamed "China's Khrushchev." By initiating the class struggle against domestic enemies identified as representatives of Soviet style revisionism, Mao laid the foundation for establishing the Soviet Union on the level of the United States as a principal enemy, and eventually as *the* principal enemy.

Inexorably, the Sino–Soviet conflict moved toward a final break between the two parties and two giant states. While the Chinese army delivered a humiliating defeat to the Indian troops carrying out Nehru's forward policy in Tibet, the Soviet–American duel in the Caribbean ended in a deal between the two superpowers. China accused the Soviet Union of adventurism for introducing nuclear missiles in Cuba and of capitulationism for taking them out. The final settlement between Kennedy and Khrushchev was viewed by the Chinese as a new Munich. Two months after the Cuban missiles crisis, Khrushchev announced that the Soviet government was abandoning its long-standing opposition to a nuclear test-ban agreement. China had made it clear to the Russians that she recognized the right of the Soviet government to refuse to give technical aid in manufacturing nuclear weapons, but that any attempt by the Russians to deprive China of her right to produce a nuclear defense of her own would be considered a violation of China's sovereignty. Despite frequent Chinese official protests, the Russians intensified their efforts to reach an agreement with the United States on a treaty for the nonproliferation of nuclear weapons.

From October 1962 to April 1963, the Chinese carried on a public debate in the international communist movement against revisionism. Specifically, they attacked Russian surrogates Togliatti and Thorez, the heads of the Italian and

French Communist Parties. The final break between the two great socialist powers came in June 1963. At the very moment when the United States and the Soviet Union signed the test-ban treaty, a Chinese delegation was waiting in Moscow for one final futile effort to settle Sino–Soviet differences. It was the last humiliation the Chinese were prepared to accept. A doctrinal debate between communists now turned into a conflict between two of the largest nation states in the world.

From the summer of 1963 until July 1964, the Chinese Communist Party engaged in the greatest polemical struggle within the international revolutionary movement since Lenin's historic debate with the Mensheviks and the Second International. No longer were the Chinese communists attempting to force the Russian leaders to return to their traditional and "correct" leadership of the world revolutionary movement. A Chinese campaign was launched to establish China as the new center and base for world revolution.

Lenin, a true European, at home in Germany, France, and Italy as well as Russia, had visualized a process by which the socialist revolution in one country would soon be supported by an international wave of revolution at least in the advanced countries. Later he conceived of the revolt in the colonial world of the East supporting and stimulating revolt in the West. In either case, he incorporated an internationalist world outlook. Mao Tse-tung, on the other hand, was the product of a vast peasant revolution in a great civilization which for millennia had stood as a world of its own. Mao, a proponent of revolutionary self-reliance, had a record of disregarding advice from the Communist International on how to conduct revolution in China. He has always shown a certain ambivalence on the question of whether it would be either feasible or practical for China to become the center of world revolution or to attempt to found a new Communist International. It was our impression that it was Liu Shao-ch'i and other Chinese leaders, not Mao, who hoped to take over the old Moscow international apparatus. Whatever the case may be, the Chinese movement in 1963–64 to become the world center of international communism was short-lived. Mao concentrated his attention on the one-fourth of the world's population who were Chinese, convinced that Russian revisionism, both externally and internally, was the principal contradiction in Chinese life.

China's polemical onslaught against Soviet revisionism resulted in the famous Nine Comments in reply to the July 14, 1963 Open Letter which the Central Committee of the Soviet Communist Party sent to its millions of Party members. For months, millions of Chinese diligently studied the Nine Comments. The Chinese documents, issued one after another in the course of one year, skillfully laid out the theoretical foundations for the Chinese critique of the Soviet line on Stalin, wars of national liberation, the questions of war and peace, and Soviet–US collaboration. They accused the Soviet Party of causing the split in the international communist movement. It was assumed by the foreigners working in China during the first half of the 1960's, and perhaps by Western scholars, that the Nine Comments represented the theoretical conclusions of a united Chinese leadership including Chairman Mao. But this may have been a questionable assumption. A leadership that split so completely one year after the final Chinese Comment was issued on July 14, 1964 could hardly have been in full agreement on all the theoretical issues packed into 500 pages of tightly argued discourse. By the end of the decade, all the Comments, except the Ninth, would be forgotten. The Ninth Comment, "On Khrushchev's Phony Communism," reflected the views of Chairman Mao, who wrote many of its key passages.

The Ninth Comment represented Mao's study of the outcome of the Russian Revolution and his attempt to avoid the negative consequences of the Soviet system.[19] It was an impassioned summing up of what had gone wrong in the Soviet Union, arguing that the world appearance of Khrushchev's revisionism was "the most important negative experience, enabling Marxist–Leninists in all countries to draw appropriate lessons for preventing the degeneration of the proletarian party and the socialist state." Looking at the complex interrelationships of the Chinese Revolution within a world system of interacting revolutionary and nonrevolutionary sovereign states, Mao saw the internal class struggle in China as decisive. He was not as worried that China would be conquered from without as he was that it would be conquered from within.

The Ninth Comment was a theoretical blueprint to ensure the success of socialism and to prevent the restoration of capitalism. It described socialist society as a process of uninterrupted revolution and proclaimed the necessity of carrying the socialist revolution through to the end "on the political, economic, ideological, and cultural fronts." The goal of this continuous revolution and class struggle was to be the final abolition of all exploiting classes. The differences between workers and peasants, between town and country, and between mental and manual labor would disappear. Continuous revolution would lead to a communist society characterized by the principle enunciated by Marx: "From each according to his ability, to each according to his needs." Measurement of socialist progress or capitalist degeneration could be determined by whether the gap between the incomes, and presumably the status, of "a small minority and those of the workers, peasants, and ordinary intellectuals" was becoming wider or narrower.

Khrushchev and his followers were accused of usurping the leadership of the Soviet Party and State as the political representatives of a new privileged stratum which the Chinese labeled "the new Soviet bourgeoisie." This new stratum, the Chinese argued, was propelled by self-interest, and dominated rather than served the masses. It had, in effect, created a bourgeois socialism, and a new polarization of classes was rapidly emerging. In essence, the Maoists were calling for the primacy of politics over economics, while the Russians staked everything on productive forces. In the West, Khrushchev's new program was referred to as "goulash communism." The Chinese agreed.

In order to prevent what had happened in Russia from

happening in China, the Ninth Comment listed fifteen propositions based on the theories and policies of Mao Tse-tung that were designed to prevent the degeneration of China's revolution. These included the recognition of contradictions in socialist society, the necessity of carrying out a revolution on the political and ideological fronts, and the call for launching huge mass movements to realize socialist goals. Reaffirmation of the commune system as a suitable form of organization for the transition to communism, cadre participation in labor, and low salaries for government officials were all considered essential to prevent the emergence of a new privileged class. Finally, it was deemed essential to bring up the youth to carry on the cause of the revolution. These young successors would have to be "tempered in the great storms of revolution."

The most remarkable and startling paragraph in this Chinese manifesto of continuous revolution was a statement written by Mao in 1963, but never before quoted publicly:

> ". . . If our cadres were thus dragged into the enemy camp or the enemy were able to sneak into our ranks, and if many of our workers, peasants and intellectuals, were left defenseless against both the soft and the hard tactics of the enemy, then it would not take long, perhaps only several years or a decade, or several decades at the most, before a counterrevolutionary restoration on a national scale inevitably occurred, the Marxist-Leninist Party would undoubtedly become a revisionist party or a fascist party, and the whole of China would change its color."[20]

Never before had a leading communist suggested that a communist party maintaining a monopoly of political power might turn into a fascist party. For the first time, a leading communist statesman and theoretician asserted that political power, even under socialism, might be utilized as an instrument for one class to exploit another. Mao saw that class was more than an economic category; it was a political category determined by unequal distributions of power as well as control over property. An exploiting class under socialism was one which used political power for private gain.

There was a certain logic to the fact that it should be a Chinese peasant intellectual and revolutionary who would lay the foundations for transforming Marxist theory in the second half of the twentieth century. Throughout Chinese history, there has always been a close correlation between the distribution of power and the distribution of status. The primary source of wealth, prestige, and privilege had been the bureaucracy, a political institution. In the Maoist view, political consciousness contributes decisively to the class stand of the individual and social groups as a whole, and since the question of consciousness is indeterminate, so then is the future, which can be only what men make of it. The source of contemporary China's new bureaucracies was its universities, and it was there that the future consciousness was being determined.

## Chapter III

# The Successors

THE PEKING First Foreign Languages Institute, like many of the western suburb's institutions of higher learning built under Soviet influence in the 1950's, is an island of academia within the peaceful, manicured fields of vegetables belonging to its neighbor, The Evergreen People's Commune. Reached by a narrow road lined with locust trees and traveled mainly by trucks and the carts and bicycles of the commune members, it surprises one with its air of rural tranquility. It is divided by the road into two campuses. At the time of our stay, students and younger teachers generally lived on the east campus, and older professors, Party cadres, and administrators on the west campus. That is probably still the case.

Except for a few small buildings owned by the commune and used for such activities as making bricks, the only neighboring center of activity is the co-op store just a few steps from the iron entrance gates which face each other from either side of the road. The community, including faculty members of the Institute, take the leisurely walk there to buy eggs—by weight, not number—to have their own bottles filled with soy sauce, and in summer to buy the magnificent local tomatoes, eggplants, and string beans sold for a few pennies from the mountainous piles dumped casually on canvases on the ground. In the dry goods section of the co-op, there are always a few students carefully selecting notebooks, bars of soap, or brightly striped nylon socks. In the spring and summer, willow trees, brilliant hibiscus, and flowering judas soften the look of the utilitarian concrete buildings; but during the long winter, only the lively coming and going of students, engaged in unending conversation, gives color to the surroundings.

The Institute, with its pastoral setting and Soviet architecture, was to prove an illuminating base from which to observe the monumental "struggle between the two lines" of the Cultural Revolution. Organizations like the Institute were at the epicenter of the ideological conflict then raging within the context of academic debates. As an institute functioning directly under the Chinese Foreign Ministry, with the responsibility to produce not only foreign language teachers, but embassy personnel for other countries, and interpreters and translators to work for China's foreign policy at home, its fundamental task was by definition a cosmopolitan one.

Inevitably, the temptation had been great to follow certain policies of the 1950's, especially to recruit students from urban bourgeois families, in particular from Shanghai, where the facility for language learning was accelerated by earlier training in mission schools, by parents who spoke other languages, by a generally high level of education, and by that combination of factors which in all countries gives to the sons and daughters of the educated their significant academic headstart. This had been a natural tendency immediately after 1949, and a substantial core of the bright and sophisticated young teachers who had made up the Institute's first student body did come from precisely such backgrounds.

There had also been a long period when the Institute had been seen by some of its intellectual leaders, themselves products of the best of Western university education, as a kind of "Oxford of the East." The curriculum of the English Department, for example, had proceeded in classical fashion, from Beowulf through Shaw. This, plus emphasis on the mastery of a formidable amount of esoteric grammar, was not in substantial contradiction with the expectations of Soviet educational methods, which had prevailed in Chinese educational circles during the middle and late 1950's. It was perhaps a surprise to both the Western-trained "bourgeois intellectuals" and the Moscow-trained Party cadres to find themselves in basic agreement.

However, there was in this school, as in many other Chinese institutions, another tradition of education, one close to the recent revolutionary past and to the peasant guerrilla origins of the revolution. For some universities, created in accordance with their own grand design by the Russian experts, these revolutionary origins were rather remote and formalistic, but for the Peking First Foreign Languages Institute, they were not. The Institute had been established in one of the communist Liberated Areas before the victory of 1949, and although many administrators and Party cadres had been assigned to it in its later and more prestigious period, there were others who held shared memories of carrying rations of millet and their few precious textbooks on their backs as they moved their school in accordance with the requirements of the war. Their first institute had been on the K'ang Ta model, a model which had arisen out of the experience of the Yenan period, in which soldiers had been farmers and intellectuals had been soldiers; in which an entire community provided for its own food, housing, and clothing by its own efforts; officers taught soldiers and soldiers had taught officers; and what was learned was put into practice for a further refinement of theory. The K'ang Ta model arose out of the necessities of war, of a blockade of supplies, and the need for every revolutionary to become proficient at a multitude of tasks.

For Mao, K'ang Ta was to become the educational model for the China of the future, to ensure that China would embody a classically Marxist conception of the elimination of the differences between mental and manual labor, between city and countryside, between worker and peasant. It was a philosophic concept of the harmony of people—with each other and with their natural environment—that was, like many of Mao's concepts, highly compatible with much that was old in Chinese thought. But it was a concept that would encounter unrelenting opposition from those who saw the

Soviet experience as a viable model for China's industrialization.

There was another side of the K'ang Ta model which broke with Chinese traditions. It was Mao's pioneering effort to cast off the old Confucian teacher worship, the whole ancient system of rote memorization, and the dreary rituals of traditional education which had for so long prevented China from entering the twentieth century. One of Mao's most important contributions has been the popularization of inductive methods of learning. We visited a factory not long after our arrival in China and saw on a wall, in a room used for night classes, ten simple methods worked out by Mao in the old guerrilla areas. The principles listed were:

1. Use the inductive method, not the "stuffing the duck" method.
2. Proceed from near to far (known to unknown).
3. Proceed from shallow to deep (simple to complex).
4. Use language that is simple and easily understood; explain new terms.
5. Be exact, not vague.
6. Make things interesting.
7. Use gestures.
8. Repeat the concepts you have given.
9. Have teaching notes or outline.
10. For cadre students, the method of talking things over is good.

Painted boldly on the same schoolroom wall was Mao's simple sixteen-character slogan for solving problems: "Discard the dross and select the essential; eliminate the false and retain the true; proceed from one thing to another; and from the outside to the inside." This rudimentary but scientific methodology, when set against the traditional Chinese learning methods, stands for a revolution in the approach to knowledge. It explains how the Chinese Communists were able to bring hundreds of millions of illiterate peasants into the modern world.

The Peking First Foreign Languages Institute had had a

long and complex history of differing educational policies, but by the winter of 1965, at least some of its personnel were consistently engaged in an attempt to divest the institution of the predominantly Western or Soviet orientation of the 1950's. Many of the questions raised a few years later in all educational institutions were raised rather earlier in the Languages Institute. Perhaps the reason was that its parent organization, the Chinese Ministry of Foreign Affairs, still remained quite closely under Mao's direct surveillance, even during the period of the early Sixties, when he had lost control of the Party organization in other areas. At the same time, that Foreign Ministry, struggling to carry out a daring diplomacy in the third world and the "intermediate zone," had found the excessively traditional training of the Institute's graduates inadequate to these needs. We were to hear before long about a criticism which had come from the Foreign Ministry in 1962. "What kind of teaching are you doing there?" the Institute, in essence, was asked. "We keep getting graduates who write in the style of Thomas Hardy and don't understand a word of the *Wall Street Journal*."

We were thus made aware very early in our stay at the Institute that there was a difference in policy which was reflected in the everyday work of our teaching, but not that it arose from anything as serious as the "two-line struggle" in the Party. There is a tendency in Chinese politics to discuss current struggles obliquely within the context of struggles already concluded, whether they be historical analogies of a 1,000-year distance or the well-known inner Party struggles of the immediately preceding period. We had the impression from all that was stated officially in the school that the struggles over student admission, teaching materials, faculty-student relationships, had been successfully and correctly won and that all that remained was their proper implementation.

As neophytes in the obscurities of Chinese political culture, we were undoubtedly more ingenuous than most. However, as the bitter factional struggles of the Cultural Revolution were soon to prove, our Chinese colleagues and students also interpreted the results of these years from a great variety of personal and political perspectives. A large percentage of the incoming students that year and the next were from peasant backgrounds, bringing with them problems remarkably similar to those of disadvantaged students in the United States. Their presence would not only give impetus to the theoretical criticisms of the old literature-cum-grammar approach of language learning, but point up many practical problems as well. Both methodology and materials were affected, not merely by the political debate regarding the merits of the several models, but by the needs of the students themselves. Not yet daring or wishing to give up entirely its accustomed program, the English Department was running its revamped five-year course concurrently with a new three-year course, based on the listening-speaking method long accepted in many countries, but seen in China, with its timeless respect for the written word, as daringly new. It was an approach compatible with Mao's notion of knowledge arising from practice and then conceptualized into theory. The older professors were surprised and the younger ones triumphant when, at the end of a year of running two parallel groups of first-year students through the two programs, the three-year students surpassed the traditionally trained ones, not only in speaking and comprehension, but in reading and writing as well. The claim that it was a victory for Mao Tse-tung's Thought was not, in fact, inaccurate.

The question of materials was more difficult. Having done away with syntactical analysis and the Romantic poets, what then should replace them? The Foreign Ministry's remark about the *Wall Street Journal* had not been ignored. Upper level and graduate students worked busily away at mimeographed sheets of reprinted articles from *Newsweek,* and *US News and World Report*. By the time they graduated, they were expected to intelligently analyze editorials from the *New York Times* and the London *Times*. Teachers searched for contemporary Western literature that was politically relevant, well written, and culturally comprehensible, but often found themselves thrown back on the socialist standbys earlier recommended by their Russian advisors. They liked Jack London, for example, for his fierce class view; but most agreed that it was not of great value for students to ingest a conceptualization of American society no longer in existence. They debated the merits of teaching the students translated stories of contemporary Chinese heroes nationally familiar through films, comic strips, and newspaper editorials. Some, however, argued that since these students were going to work in a complex world of which many knew very little, they should be learning about that world while they learned the language. It was in an attempt to deal with a few of these requirements that one of us used sections from Conor Cruise O'Brien's *To Katanga and Back* that winter of the Congo crisis.

There was also the unending debate over the use of Chinese materials translated into English. These were anathema to linguists and language teachers of all schools but, to the Chinese, irreproachably logical. How, they asked, would these future servants of the government know how to state their country's positions in another language if they did not study how their government stated its position in another language. They saw *Peking Review* not only as the source of correct political policy statements, but as a model for phrasing such statements in foreign languages. The unshakeableness of their views was not simply a result of ideology, but of a tradition refined through centuries that there is a correct way, whether ethical, political, or literary, and that the good student devotes himself to the mastery of the model, not to his individual interpretation of the subject. A writing class of eleven bright graduate students courteously indicated that they felt it rather capricious of their American teacher to suggest that each of them write on the assigned current events subject according to his or her individual view of the question. If the teacher would write a perfect model, they would learn from that.

However, the immemorial Chinese habit of bending the self to the mean of official virtue does not imply, as is often assumed, the abnegation of the Chinese personality. We found our students to be highly differentiated individuals. In fact, in China, there seems to be a cultivation of personality highlighted by the popularity of pointed and descriptive nicknames. One of the young teachers was always referred to by his friends as "the bird." The common use of the affectionate "*lao*" and "*hsiao*" before proper names means more than just "old" and "small"; it denotes personality. Some people are just "*lao*" and others "*hsiao*," and everyone understands why. The Chinese are acute psychologists, but their sophisticated assessment of different personality traits is not, as in the West, to understand the individual for himself, but rather to mesh the individual, with all his expected idiosyncrasies, harmoniously into the larger group. Thus, conscious and precise understanding of the individual is necessary to determine how he or she will relate in a group setting, how the group will have to adjust to each differing personality, and what necessary adaptations might have to be made in order to guarantee group survival. In this way, the group culture incorporates and tolerates a wide range of personality types, and through an atmosphere of intensive debate and lively discussion, seeks consensus through persuasion rather than command.

It is also the diversity of an enormous country which gives to its people such variety of character, for the impetus of the revolution and socialist construction has caused a mixture of regional populations historically unknown in this land of many dialects and local cultures. Everywhere we went during our years in China we met Chinese from distant provinces who had found the adjustment to different food, different dialects, different climates, nearly as unsettling as it is to visitors from thousands of miles away. This is one of the elements of China's present unity—that a people for so long united through written language and political structure, but so separated geographically have come to feel at home throughout the gigantic spaces of China. There are now few urban people who have not, for however short a time, known the rigorous life of the countryside; and the opposite process, while not so dramatic, proceeds as one of the inevitable concomitants of modernization. So it was with our students at the Institute, who brought with them to Peking their characteristic regional culture and their dialectal differences, which produced in an English class as many variations in pronunciation as in any multilingual group. From the tall, strong-boned Northerners to the small, round-faced Southerners, the varying physical types of China are, except for coloring, as different from each other as those of the various peoples of Europe.

There was a simplicity to their lives at school which exists in the industrialized West only as a rather idealized memory of the past. Their central concern was their studies, which they approached with seriousness, heightened by the enthusiasm of those to whom it is still a great privilege, an unimagined luxury, to be chosen from among millions to go to college and be cared for while there. They were indeed the new elite which the Cultural Revolution called into question, but they were a modest elite, conscious of their privilege. One of our peasant students, an intelligent young man much admired by his classmates, spoke for all of them when he stood up in class one day and said in his careful second-year English, "Our parents still believe in the old Chinese idea that those who do mental labor rule, while those who do manual labor are ruled. Now that we are here in Peking, we must remember to struggle against those ideas that we heard at home."

They wore the traditional clothes of China, either the old frog-fastened, high-collared, black padded jackets or the new blue or khaki jackets, buttoned and military collared. Their trousers were cotton or corduroy, usually faded and often patched. But this, in addition to indicating the frugality of their lives, was also the badge of a student, as it has become in other countries as well. On one of their periodic trips to the countryside, a group of them was asked by the peasants why they felt impelled to wear the worst-looking clothes they could find when they came to work in the rural areas. There was more than a slight implication that they were suspected of the same kind of inverse snobbishness of which American students are also accused. Except for those young women who wore their hair in long or short braids, they all cut each other's hair and wore the brushlike results with equanimity, for matters of personal vanity are of small importance in China. They took care of their tiny dormitory rooms, each with two double-decker bunks, somehow housing four students. Each did his or her own laundry, consisting of clothes and small towels, and dishwashing—a bowl, chopsticks, an enamel cup and a spoon, all of which could be washed at the outdoor tap after leaving the dining hall. It was a lifestyle of rustic simplicity.

In the evenings or on weekend afternoons, the sounds of traditional musical instruments—the three-stringed *erhu* and the Chinese flute—could be heard as one passed the student dormitories, for musical accomplishment was very common and one of the students' main sources of entertainment. Accompanying the performance, as is traditionally the case in Chinese theater, there was appreciative chatter and laughter rather than appreciative silence. Singing was popular. Unlike our own culture, there was never anyone who stated with embarrassment that he could not sing, and the cultivation of a polished, professional style was much admired. Informal pingpong games went on in the dormitory hallways and outdoors on homemade tables with a makeshift brick "net," and in late afternoons the playing fields resounded with the shouts of basketball and volleyball players. When we first arrived, there were outdoor movies on the playing fields on Wednesday and Saturday nights. Everyone brought his own stool, and one would meet the community, the old professors and their wives, the children of the younger teachers, stools in hand. But, as with Chinese students everywhere, these, too, always managed to have an extra seat for the teacher who was welcomed as a long-absent friend into the circle of his or her class.

In the coldest weeks of the long winter, the students flooded a level field to make a skating rink, and there was much amusement in teaching classmates from the semitropical South to skate and in admiring the accomplishments of the experts from the northern provinces. In the summer of 1965, the students built an enormous swimming pool out of local rock, and each year thereafter, as soon as the weather became warm enough, the pool was filled not only with swimmers, but with at least as many non-swimmers, particularly young women. Raised with old prohibitions against "dangerous" sports and the exposing of one's body, they had never learned to swim, but were now determined to. Chairman Mao's exhortation "to brave the winds and waves" was taken very seriously, even though its implementation often involved hours of standing waist-deep in the water while helpful classmates demonstrated the simplicity of floating on one's back. The real swimmers avoided the crowd and swam in the muddy but uncongested waters of the nearby irrigation canals. These were also, to some extent, a student product, for all had taken a turn with wheelbarrows and handbaskets in the construction of their local section of a complex network of canals extending from Tientsin and following the direction of the ancient Grand Canal.

Along with these familiar pleasures, the students of the Peking First Foreign Languages Institute, like students all over China, threw themselves into passionate debates and discussions, whose apparent abstruseness merely demonstrated the difficulties of understanding the popular application of an unfamiliar politics. Wednesday and Saturday afternoons are, by long revolutionary tradition in China, political study time. Classes and offices close down, and attendance at the study sessions is obligatory. The articles and editorials read, discussed, and dissected during these afternoons are as much a part of the everyday life of the Chinese as his work is on the other days of the week. For students and teachers, since the context of the discussion in those days had much to do with education and the training of youth, it was a central part of their existence both in and out of the classroom.

The great debate on education had deep roots in the differing political conceptions of what China's road to socialism should be. It was a debate which can be traced back to the early years of liberation, a debate which intensified from 1958, the period of the Great Leap Forward and the Lushan Conference, and reappeared in a battle of gigantic proportions during the Great Proletarian Cultural Revolution.

In 1949, following the communist victory, the question had high priority on the national agenda, and the First National Education Work Conference was held in December of that year. Its statement was a prophetic indication of the policy struggle which would begin immediately and continue for decades. "The education of New China should use the new educational experiences of the old Liberated Areas as the basis, should absorb the useful experiences of the old education, and should make use of the experiences of the Soviet Union." There could be no question of which model was fundamental and which one secondary. Based on Mao's directive, K'ang Ta type schools were established in the large Liberated Areas and in some of the provinces and municipalities.[21]

But the opposing historical and political forces were formidable. The overwhelming majority of the intellectuals thrown into the gigantic task of creating a modern educational system for a nation 85 per cent illiterate and lacking a substantial body of professionally trained personnel in virtually every field had themselves been trained under the "old education." They were to find that there was a far closer meeting of the minds with communist cadres trained in Moscow than with the graduates of K'ang Ta. As early as 1953, the Ministry of Education was putting forward teaching plans and outlines for middle schools which adopted *in toto* those of the Soviet Union. The Soviet reliance upon a small and highly trained elite of specialists as the means toward rapid industrialization was in little contradiction with the traditional Chinese concept of an intellectual elite. By the mid-Fifties, courses from primary school through medical school were being lengthened and intensified. The worker and peasant rapid-course middle schools had been suspended.

China had begun to adopt such Soviet conventions as their "Regulations for Academic Degrees, Academic Titles, and Honorary Titles."

It was, therefore, not remarkable that Chairman Mao, when he spoke to the directors of educational departments and bureaus of seven municipalities in March 1957, should say: "Does the Ministry of Education belong to China or to the Soviet Union? If it is the Soviet Union's Ministry of Education, then we must abolish our Ministry of Education." A month earlier, he had released his important "On the Problem of Correctly Handling the Contradictions Among the People," in which he reiterated in broad but unmistakeable terms his concept of the aim of education in China: "Our educational policy should be that those who are educated be able to develop morally, intellectually, and physically and become workers with culture and socialist consciousness." Clearly he felt that moral development was being lost through the termination of political study, that a gradual alienation of the young intellectuals from the worker-peasant population was taking place, and that physical development was being lost both through a decreased emphasis on sports and labor and through the increased study load. Over the years, he commented again and again that the students of China were ruining their eyesight and their health through unreasonable hours of study.

Mao has repeatedly followed a similar strategy in his inner Party struggles. He from time to time issues a warning, often consisting—as above—of deceptively casual and ironic remarks to the inner circle, at the same time putting forward to the Chinese people a brief but comprehensive statement of his political position. The same pattern was to be followed in the prelude to the Cultural Revolution. And so his 1957 statements were a mild forewarning of the stormy events of the following year. As the Great Leap Forward and the communalization of the rural areas swept turbulently over the nation, Mao moved simultaneously to break China's military and political dependence on the Soviet Union through the dismissal of P'eng Teh-huai at the

Lushan Conference. His political positions of those years, seen as proof of the old revolutionary's madness by both the West and the Soviet Union, were entirely consistent with his highly original concepts of mass politics. We were to hear many times during our years in China of the concept of the "pendulum swing"—that the pendulum in order to move from one side to the center, must first swing to the opposite side. It was an explanation which often seemed maddeningly simplistic when applied to the social complexities being explained, but it has assumed an axiomatic centrality in the popular philosophy of contemporary China.

Mao's left swing of 1958 also gave a mighty push to the pendulum of education, by then firmly stabilized on the side of quiescent traditionalism. He opened his attack in January 1958 with his "Sixty Articles on Working Methods," which contained explicit directives on educational work, of which this is a sample:

> "The relation between being red and expert and between politics and business is the unity of two opposite things. We must criticize the tendency of political apathy. On the one hand, we have to oppose the empty-headed politicians; on the other hand, we must oppose pragmatists who have lost their compass.
>
> "In all middle-level technical schools and polytechnic schools, where it is possible, factories or farms should be launched experimentally to engage in production in order to be self-sufficient and semi-self-sufficient. The students should implement half-work and half-study.
>
> "In laboratories and workshops of all higher engineering institutes where production can be undertaken, besides insuring the needs of teaching and scientific research, production should be implemented as much as possible. Additionally, it may also be possible for students and teachers to enter into labor contracts with the local factories.
>
> "In all agricultural schools, besides undertaking production in their own farms, it may also be possible for them to sign contracts with local agricultural cooperatives for labor participation. Also, teachers may live in

these cooperatives so that theory and practice can be coordinated. Cooperatives should send some qualified persons to enroll in agricultural schools.

"All rural middle and primary schools should sign contracts with local agricultural cooperatives to participate in productive labor for agriculture and subsidiary industry. Rural students should also utilize their vacations and holidays or extracurricular time to return to their respective villages to participate in production.

"In the case of colleges and urban middle schools, wherever possible, several schools may establish a factory or workshop jointly; they may also sign labor contracts with factories, construction sites, or service enterprises."[22]

It was the K'ang Ta model updated to the necessities of China's socialist construction in 1958. Along with the rest of the country, the students not only did their share of backyard steelmaking, but followed the Chairman's instructions to link themselves with industry or agriculture. The Peking First Foreign Languages Institute also had its own Great Leap traditions. In 1964–65, the teachers and a few graduate students still reminisced about the days when they had grown their own food and run a small factory.

The campaign which followed the "Hundred Flowers" movement of 1957 hit hard at the bourgeois intellectuals in the field of education, but since their educational philosophy had not been in fundamental contradiction with that of the Soviet wing of the Party, that philosophy reemerged from under the Chairman's attack with remarkable resiliency. As problems at least partially attributable to the Great Leap Forward began seriously to affect the economy, the defenders of the educational policies of the Fifties attempted to negate the results of the educational revolution of 1958 along with the other developments of that period that had affected national life. By early 1959, Lu Ting-yi, long a leader in educational circles, was stating that the educational revolution had been "chaotic, sloppy, and slanted" and that education "is bound to collapse if things continue in this way." By September 1962, the Central Work Conference of the Chinese Communist Party had adopted the "Sixty Articles on Higher Education," a programmatic document for all of China's schools that was an almost total reversal of Mao's "Sixty Articles." By September of the following year, the final draft of "Temporary Work Regulations for Regular Middle and Primary Schools" had been adopted.

Mao did not withdraw from an active strategic role in this educational battle of the early Sixties, but, as he had often recommended in his military writings, retreated from direct confrontation in order to organize indigenous forces to strike back guerrilla-fashion. In this battle, his forces were to be the People's Liberation Army, the peasant army which had won China's peasant revolution and which, in spite of all Soviet influences, was once again being trained and educated on Maoist principles. By the summer of 1960, Lin Piao, a general of brilliant and impeccable military record, was directing a movement within the Army to study Mao's thought. In October of that same year, Lin issued a directive for correct political study in the Army, using as the basic principles the "Four Firsts," which give first place: 1) to man in handling the relationship between man and weapons; 2) to political work in handling the relationship between political and other work; 3) to ideological work in relation to routine tasks in political work; and 4) in ideological work to living ideas in handling the relationship between ideas in books and living ideas.

The "Four Firsts," in the tradition of the propaganda work of the PLA and Mao himself, concentrated rather complex philosophical views into tightly conceptualized slogans simple to internalize. It was, in essence, the kind of "living Marxism" as opposed to dead theory which Mao had long believed must be practiced if that Marxism were not to become the petrified dogma of a rigid and hierarchical church. Lin Piao taught the Army that it was not necessary to study great amounts of abstract theory, but rather that it was preferable to take to one's political studies the "living" problems of everyday life and resolve them one by one. To go from practice to theory would not only give one the capacity to deal with practice but to master theory as well. It was an argument well understood as a counterattack by those advocating the traditional Chinese mastery of an immense coda of theory.

Thus, in the early 1960's, side by side with the revised educational manifestoes of the firmly anti-Maoist Ministry of Education, there were concurrent calls to the people to learn from the PLA and to follow Comrade Lin Piao's method of political study. There is little doubt that most of those in the field of education, students and teachers, were, to one degree or another, influenced by both currents. The decision of the Peking First Foreign Language Institute's English Department to run two parallel courses—one of five years in which the heaviest reliance was placed upon "theory" and traditional methods of learning, and one of three years with the stress on "practice"—is an indication of how the debate was sometimes resolved on an operational level.

In March 1963, the campaign to learn methods of political study from the PLA moved into the area of the popular culture. The convention of the popular hero has a very long history in China, for it was part of the Confucian method of moral education. Usually the heroes were not saints, but people who had made social contributions; but in time they became deified in the popular religion as well, and the local temples and shrines of China had long maintained a place for them. Chairman Mao's "Three Old Articles," also extensively studied in China during the early Sixties, all eulogize good men who died in the service of their fellow men—the army charcoal burner, the Canadian doctor Norman Bethune, and the old man who removed the mountain. So, in March 1963, when Mao issued a directive for the whole country to learn from the example of Comrade Lei Feng, a young PLA soldier, those cognizant of the countervailing tendencies in the battle over education must have understood that the Chairman was intensifying his campaign.

Chinese youth, during the Fifties, had been instructed by

means of emulative models whose life histories had become internalized into the thinking of everyone who went to school during that period. Because of China's long decades of national and revolutionary war, it was natural that they were all war heroes and heroines. The ones whose names we were to hear most often were Tung Ts'un-jui, a hero of the liberation war; Huang Chi-kuang, killed during the Korean War; and Liu Hu-lan, a fifteen-year-old girl cadre and civil war martyr, whom the KMT executed by cutting her body in half. In spite of the ever-present threat of war, the generation who learned to venerate these martyrs were themselves raised in an era of peace, and their glorious and romantic heroes were becoming increasingly distant in terms of the real possibilities of modeling one's life after them.

Lei Feng embodied a new concept of the model hero. He was a soldier, but a soldier in a peacetime army. The importance of his military role was less that of traditional heroism than the exemplification of that army's ideological training. Lei Feng was a hero in the struggle over education—education in the broadest sense, just as "culture" was used in its broadest sense in "The Great Proletarian Cultural Revolution." The question of education to Mao had never been simply a problem of how best to learn information, but rather, how to create the "new man," whom he saw as fundamental to the creation of a new society. This concept was concentrated in the first point of "The Four Firsts" as "The Human Factor Comes First." Having rejected the experience of the Soviet Union in building socialism, and particularly its underlying conviction that utopia would be built upon a base of heavy industry, the Chairman was to speak with increasing explicitness of the need for each person to struggle toward that devotion to the public good which alone would permit a future classless society to evolve.

Lei Feng was in many ways a very ordinary young man sharing much in his life and background with the millions of postliberation young Chinese. His early childhood had been passed in poverty, hunger, and sickness, but his memory of those years consisted as much of the reminders of his parents as of his own recollections. He had entered school with the joy of those deprived of learning for generations, and spent his youth in the arduous, but no longer exploited, labor of the vast Chinese countryside. Like many poor peasants who see Mao as a savior, he expressed his gratitude to the forces which had rescued him from peasant destitution with a direct and religious simplicity. These forces— Chairman Mao and the Chinese Communist Party—had, in fact, saved his life, as they had saved the lives of millions like him, and his politics were a reflection of that reality.

Like many young people in China, Lei Feng kept a diary which was a record of his ideological progress, not unlike the diaries of Christians of centuries past. As a vehicle for moral education, the diary as a literary form had great advantages over the narrative style in which the stories of earlier heroes were told. It was immediate and lively. Lei Feng's conceptualization of Mao's Thought was neither sophisticated nor intellectual. There was almost no direct reference to passages in Mao's works and no analysis of his writings. Rather, Lei Feng had internalized into his own life several of Mao's general concepts, and his diary dealt with his day-to-day attempts to make those concepts work. Although Lei Feng was often spoken of as a man who never forgot class struggle because of his hatred of the landlord class remaining from childhood, his life in the PLA gave him little opportunity to exercise this principle. The political concept of Mao's which had most relevance to the ordinariness of Lei Feng's life and, symbolically, to the ordinariness of most people's lives, was "Serve the People." A great number of the entries in Lei Feng's diary are descriptions of his daily good deeds, of helping his army comrades with their washing and mending, performing extra tasks to help the cooks, or repairing his truck in freezing weather though his fingers bled. However, his praises of Chairman Mao and his repeated comments that it was his love for Chairman Mao which inspired his life make it clear that Lei Feng was a conscious "student" whose example could be followed by anyone. Lei Feng's death did not come through an act of heroism as had the deaths of earlier heroes, but through an accident of rather prosaic absurdity, the pedestrian fate of an Everyman. He was killed by a falling telephone pole. But this, too, was the essence of this new hero of the early Sixties—that both his life and his death should be quite ordinary, except for his exemplary love for his fellow man; and to the degree that he put this selflessness into conscious practice, he was the man of the future utopia.

One of the main sources of Chairman Mao's Thought for people such as Lei Feng was the collection of three of Mao's essays known familiarly as the "Three Good Old Articles." The first of them, "Serve the People," was a simple funeral oration which Mao delivered in 1944 at the funeral of Chang Szu-teh, a soldier in the Guards Regiment of the Central Committee of the Chinese Communist Party. He was perhaps the genesis of the Lei Feng hero, a simple soldier who had lived for his comrades and died in an accident. In the second essay, "In Memory of Norman Bethune," delivered once again in honor of a selfless man's death, in December 1939, Mao elaborated on the theme of the Canadian doctor's devoted service to the people. He spoke, too, of the concepts of internationalism that have always been present in Marxist thought. It was in this essay that Mao ended with the leitmotif that was to characterize the models of the early Sixties and give a moral example to millions of citizens whose lives consisted mostly of their daily work.

> "We must all learn the spirit of absolute selflessness from him [Bethune]. With this spirit everyone can be useful to the people. A man's ability may be great or small, but if he has this spirit, he is already noble-minded and pure, a man of moral integrity and above vulgar interests, a man who is of value to the people."[23]

"The Foolish Old Man Who Removed the Mountains," based on a character from an early Chinese folk tale, emphasizes self-reliance, diligence, and perseverance in the face of seemingly insurmountable difficulties. The old man takes on the task of removing with his hoe the two great mountains in front of his house. His relevance to traditional Chinese ethics is ironically demonstrated by the fact that the story is also utilized in Taiwan's primary school education. In Chairman Mao's version, he urges the Chinese people to remove the two mountains of imperialism and feudalism from their backs in the same way. They should work with the confidence that, with the help of future generations if necessary, the mountains cannot but get smaller. The spirit of the old man who removed the mountains is invoked throughout China by peasants who move mountains with their hoes and fill in bays with handbaskets of rocks in order to create a few acres more of productive land.

The "old man," mythical product of a country with limited arable land, was alien indeed to the American assumption of unending resources. This was brought home to us in a visit with the teacher of our youngest son, then eleven. She was intensely earnest about her responsibility of teaching Chinese to what must have been a rather intimidating class of obstreperous youngsters from all over the world. She looked almost as young as they, with her serious face and long braids down her back. As would always be the case, she began her periodic report to the parents with the positive accomplishments first. But after that, yes, there was a problem, and clearly it disturbed her very much, for it was so distant from her experience that she had no means of understanding it, much less resolving it. It seemed that this bright child could not, would not, understand the story of the old man who removed the mountains, which was one of the basic reading texts of the Chinese primary school classroom, this one included. Always he argued with her that the old man's idea was ridiculous, that no one in his right mind would try to remove the mountains from in front of his house with a hoe, but would of course move to another place, to better land beyond the mountains. She was not disturbed by his arguing, but that she could not make him understand. And so they confronted each other, a fifth-generation Californian, whose ancestors had long ago moved beyond the mountains, and the daughter of generations of land-husband-ing farmers, each bewildered by the other's obtuseness. We assured her that we would do our best to help her pupil understand the story, but it was a cultural chasm of too great proportions to be resolved at age eleven. The arguments ended, mostly from a sense of the uselessness of it all, but neither mind was changed.

As we came to know our own students, we also tried to understand what made them as they were and asked them the question asked of students everywhere: "What do you like to read?" Again and again, until finally we understood that the answer would always be the same, we were told, "I like to read Chairman Mao's 'Three Good Old Articles.' " The articles are very short, three or four pages apiece and, because of the lucidity of the language, easily memorized. Many of the students who had read the articles hundreds of times had also carefully committed them to memory. "But how is it possible to reread something you already know so well?" we wondered, and they told us with unremitting enthusiasm that they really did not yet understand the articles well. It was clear that we were not talking about reading, but about studying in the sense in which the Bible is studied—not simply in order that its contents be understood, but that they be learned and that this learning finally be extended to a habitual practice of the principles. The popular and simple style of the Chairman's "Three Good Old Articles" is far from the formalism of the Confucian Analects, but their moral intent and the method by which they are studied by individuals who apply their learning to a social whole contain much that is traditional in China.

Lei Feng was followed within a year by another PLA hero, Wang Chieh, also an ordinary soldier, but more sophisticated in applying the Chairman's political principles to his everyday life. Rather than simply recounting his good deeds as Lei Feng had done, Wang Chieh analyzes his own behavior. His treatment of Mao's Thought is less emotional and simplistic, and his diary contains many of his own paraphrases of the Chairman's instructions. He is far more conscious of his own remolding than Lei Feng had been, and, not inappropriately, his death is a conscious act of self-sacrifice. He goes out of his way to seek dangers, and no doubt his action of throwing himself over a defective mine to save his comrades from injury was such a conscious act of heroism.

In 1965, yet another PLA hero—Ouyang Hai—was popularized in a novel which had enormous popular success. Ouyang Hai had also met his death in a spectacular act of self-sacrifice, pushing a horse loaded with ammunition out of the path of an oncoming train. These young men and others who would follow them were the Chairman's reply to the traditionalist educators, who were firmly consolidating their positions in the Ministry of Education. He saw these young models as personifying the ethic of the socialist man, and there is no doubt that they enjoyed widespread popularity.

Few ordinary Chinese had the opportunity or inclination to emulate the sacrifices of Wang Chieh or Ouyang Hai, but the good cadre Chiao Yü-lu provided an example which all could follow, the middle-aged and prosaic as well as the young and heroic. Assigned to Party work in the bleak Honan plains area which we had visited, he struggled with the severe difficulties of that arid province at the same time that he was losing his own unmentioned battle with cancer. He ignored doctors' recommendations for rest and medical care and died in his forties, a martyr to the battle against China's agricultural backwardness. It was models such as Chiao Yü-lu who were imitated by a few perfectly reasonable and sober people we knew who refused to seek medical help for illness and, even more strange, refused to take medicine that was prescribed. It seemed most illogical in a society which took pride in its new, inexpensive, and popularly available medical service, for people who did not suffer from the burden of old superstitions to consciously refuse to utilize this great accomplishment of China's liberation. But there were many who could find little opportunity in their commonplace lives to court the dangers of self-sacrifice except by a denial of the flesh. The problem of transcendence has immutable laws, it would seem, whether with a God or without.

The year 1962 reaffirmed Mao's position. His thematic statement "Never forget class struggle" was widely quoted, but the Plenum, like the Lushan Conference, was the source of a further hardening of opposing positions rather than a unification of the Party. The battle of the 1960's up to the Cultural Revolution was, in traditional Chinese fashion, a battle fought with opposing words and opposing models and in the guise of literary and philosophical debate. The PLA propagated the "word" of Mao Tse-tung; the opposing "word" in a political sense was embodied in Liu Shao-ch'i's work *How To Be a Good Communist,* published in a newly edited edition on August 1, 1962.

Later attacks on Liu's "poisonous book" would criticize it for its reliance on the maxims of Confucius and Mencius rather than those of Mao; for its attacks on the cult of the personality; its concept of absolute obedience to the Party and lack of reliance on the masses. Fundamentally, the two methods of political study differed in their basic tenet of how man is remolded. Liu's book, originally and more pertinently titled *On the Cultivation of a Communist Party Member,* was fundamentally conceived of as a manual for Party members and outlined a method of "cultivation" that was to be accomplished largely internally by the individual communist through political study and within the closed hierarchy of his Party membership. Mao's concept of study, always called "ideological remolding" was political study for the masses, not just the 17 million Party members, and it embodied the concept exemplified by the PLA and Lei Feng to practice what one had learned through the study of Mao's works in the "winds and waves" of class struggle and the struggle for production.

It is difficult to know to what extent the average Chinese who read the much-heralded reprinting of *How To Be a Good Communist* in the *Red Flag* and the *People's Daily* and, six months later, the many important *People's Daily* articles on Chairman Mao's good student Lei Feng, understood that he was reading the two sides of an increasingly fierce debate within the Party. The enormous practical difficulties in separating the "two lines" in the Cultural Revolution would indicate that there were serious problems in extending a policy debate carried on in innuendoes into an open mass evaluation of the contending issues. Even the novel about Ouyang Hai, one of Chairman Mao's good soldiers, had to be "corrected" in the Cultural Revolution, for its author had seen no incongruity in his character's study of Liu's book.

The students and teachers whom we knew apparently saw no contradiction between the word of Mao Tse-tung and the word of Liu Shao-ch'i. Everyone read Mao's "Three Good Old Articles," and both Party members and others read Liu's *How To Be a Good Communist*. Clearly Mao's line had a bit of an edge in the Peking First Foreign Languages Institute, at least among the students, for no one ever volunteered the information that Liu's book was among his favorite reading. On the other hand, there was never any indication that anyone disliked it or saw any discrepancy in the two approaches. However, there can be little doubt that many higher-level Party cadres and non-Party intellectuals who had been closely involved in the debate since 1958 understood a great deal about the implications of the popular campaigns. The Cultural Revolution would reveal that different organizations throughout the country had been influenced to different degrees by one line or the other. It would also reveal that, since the overwhelming majority of local Party leaders had paid at least lip service to both sides of the debate, their clear separation into one camp or the other proved to be virtually impossible.

The debate of the early Sixties was carried on in more than verbal dialogue. Nowhere was the polarization between Mao's concept of the mass revolutionary process and the traditional Party view of disciplined bureaucratic procedure more evident than in the Socialist Education Movement. This, however, for us at least, was clear only in retrospect. It was not until the Cultural Revolution that we, along with the rest of the non-Party masses in China, were to study and understand the differences in approach. The purpose of the Socialist Education Movement was to rectify the four "uncleans" in rural administration (lack of political discipline, ideological deviations, organizational deviations, and the mismanagement of economic affairs) and thus became popularly known as the "Szu Ch'ing" (four cleanups) Movement.

In May 1963, Mao issued what were to become known as the "First Ten Points," the directive for Party work in this rural movement. He stressed that it was of primary importance to wage class struggle in the villages against "landlords and rich peasants who [. . .] are employing all kinds of schemes in an attempt to corrupt our cadres in order to usurp the leadership and power" and he stated that in order to fulfill this task, reliance must be placed on the organizations of poor and lower-middle peasants.[24] It was a statement once again of his view that the political process is both generated and regenerated from below, and it was a view not well-received by a Party leadership oriented toward a top-down method of political management.

In September, there followed the "Later Ten Points," to be attributed in the Cultural Revolution, if not to Liu Shao-ch'i personally, at least to Liu's thought. Reliance in the movement should be placed, the revised "Ten Points" stated, not on the poor and lower-middle peasants, but on the Party leadership, for, among the peasant masses, there are those "who are backward ideologically and are unable to draw a clear line between classes."[25] However, in 1964, the new Poor and Lower-Middle Peasant Associations, which Mao saw as a counterweight to the Party in the countryside, continued to grow, and in January 1965, a new document, the "Twenty-Three Articles," appeared, in which Mao's position was stated even more explicitly than it had been in the original "Ten Points." The document spoke of the Socialist Education Movement as a movement meant to confront the "contradiction between socialism and capitalism in China's countryside." In order to accomplish this, it called once again on the peasant masses to supervise the Party cadres by their criticism and, for the first time, there appeared the formulation that was to be the central political focus of the Cultural Revolution—to direct the "spearhead" of criticism against "those people in authority within the Party who take the capitalist road."[26]

In the spring and summer of 1965, faculty members from the Institute went to the countryside to help lead the "Szu Ch'ing" Movement in a village located on the barren plains of Shansi Province, west of Peking. In retrospect, when one reviews the long struggle between Mao's concept of a mass-based criticism of the Party and the Party's own concept of movements of class struggle led by itself, it would seem that they went in the familiarly accepted role of a Party work-team. In the political movements of 1958 and 1963–65, the use of work-teams was taken as a matter of course, not only within the Party but by the people as well. The organization of the old Liberated Areas and of the guerrilla armies that emerged from them had been done by Party and Army work-teams. The people remembered them as a dedicated force that helped lead them to final victory. The early land reform movement had been directed by similar work-teams.

By the late Fifties and early Sixties, Mao feared a Party in power, now firmly entrenched and increasingly bureaucratic and elitist; but probably very few of the Party members who participated in the leadership of these earlier rural movements went as the "tyrannical overlords" which the popular simplifications of the Cultural Revolution were to require. Young teachers we came to know well told us of their adventures in the countryside during the organization of the communes, and their picaresque accounts said more of their naïveté in attempting to deal with the enormity of unfamiliar tasks than of any wish to dominate the peasants. They laughed at themselves for their ignorance of the realities of rural life. They described their group of urban intellectuals, trying hard to "integrate with the peasants in their daily lives," and told how, after a few days of muscular agony from squatting in the vegetable plots, they were discovered by the peasants in a variety of unorthodox working positions, sitting or lying on the ground. Without comment, the peasants politely brought small stools to the fields for the guests and "leaders" to sit on while they worked.

In 1958, these young teachers and older professors had, in a sense, taken their English Department along with them to the countryside. It seemed quite reasonable that they should live together and spend their evenings singing the English songs they had learned. As they did, the peasants clustered outside to peer through the doors and windows at these madmen, looking Chinese but gibbering in a strange tongue. The message gradually became clear. It was not enough to have studied politics, to have been a Party member in one's own unit. Those working in the countryside would have to learn to bend to the countryside's realities. In coping with the unfamiliar demands of rural domesticity, one young woman set the house on fire when it was her turn to cook on the strange stove, and a distinguished professor achieved delighted notoriety when he somehow included soap in the pot of cabbage soup he was cooking. But they learned something of the severe demands of rural Chinese life, did help with the establishment of the new communes, and forged bonds of friendship with the peasants, to whose homes they often bicycled on Sunday visits in later years.

The students and teachers who went to Shansi during the Socialist Education Movement were far more knowledgeable than their predecessors. When they returned, looking lean and brown, they told us of conditions of daily life so inexorable that literally every drop of water had to be cherished, for the parched plains to which they had been assigned suffered an acute and endemic lack of water. Only a few wells existed near the village, and these were very deep and with only a limited supply. Life centered around the availability of water, and since the crops had to have water in order to feed the people, the people's need for water had to come second. There was no question of indulging in the luxury of washing one's clothes or even oneself. These Peking people, accustomed at home to a life of simplicity, but with a steadily increasing variety of food, running water in their apartment buildings, and adjacent bathhouses, lived for three or four months eating the rough cornbread of the northern peasant diet and going without baths. But they were filled with enthusiasm and a sense of accomplishment. They had helped the peasants, not only with some of the organizational problems of their everyday lives, but also in the prescribed class struggle against former rich and middle peasants attempting to undermine the collective productivity of the village. They had not, however, uncovered any "people within the Party taking the capitalist road." To most of them, as to us, this formulation remained in the realm of editorial rhetoric. That concern of the Chairman's was to be deferred to the future.

Even though a number of the members of the Shansi work-teams had had earlier experience working in the countryside, there was probably in 1965 a rather special sense of breaking new frontiers when one was sent to such a difficult and deprived area as this one. The stress on national models for agriculture and industry—Mao's models once again—was on precisely such problem areas offering little in the natural environment but challenges. Like the rest of China, these students and teachers were caught up in the most "living" of the Maoist examples, Tachai.

The struggles of the Tachai Brigade, under the leadership of its tough, intelligent peasant leader, Ch'en Yung-kuei, came to symbolize for all China, and does to this day, living proof of the philosophic efficacy of the old man who removed the mountain. Cursed with a heritage of bleak and rocky land, the Tachai peasants had carried on a Sisyphean struggle to create nothing more than a modest amount of arable land. They had carried rocks by hand and moved mountains with tablespoons, only to see their epic efforts swept away by storms. They started over again, and the terraced landscape of Tachai stands now as a monument to the capacity of man to bend mountains and rivers to his will. Tachai was symbolic of the possibilities which the 700 million people of China could realize if they would but bend their backs and their collective will to the task.

Taching offered a similar inspirational lesson in the field in industry. In the bitter sub-zero weather of the northern oilfields, Wang Chin-hsi, an oil worker, performed feats of heroism representative of those of all the workers who fought so hard to achieve China's industrialization. Taching arose from an empty plain to become a community which not only produced oil for China's hungry factories, but grew its own food and built its own houses. It was the self-reliant frontier of America's lost past, but a frontier organized around the concept of collectivity rather than individualism. To learn from Tachai and Taching became the guiding expression for all of China, for those who struggled with the problems of newspaper deadlines and lesson plans as well as for the workers and peasants at the base of the superstructure. For the intellectuals whose political duties took them into areas as bleak as the Shansi plains, Taching and Tachai provided the models for self-sacrifice.

The Socialist Education Movement, the movement to learn from the PLA and to model oneself after its exemplars in the study of Mao's Thought were all at the center of the great struggle between the representatives of the "two roads" in China. But there were other debates which the students followed avidly in the *People's Daily* and which they brought with them into the classroom every day. Mao had referred in his "Sixty Articles" on education in 1958 to the concept of "red and expert." Students, by definition among the experts, threw themselves into intense discussions about how they could also maintain their "redness." It was, in fact, a particularly difficult feat for our students to achieve in light of the nature of their specialization. It did not take much political sophistication to understand that if engineering students combined their study with factory work, they improved their chances of maintaining links with the working class, or if agronomy students applied their knowledge on a farm, they would remain closer to the problems of the peasantry. But for students of foreign language, the contradiction was apparent. If they took their new "technique" to the countryside, they were likely to find themselves in the position of the teachers singing their English songs, further estranged from the peasants than their advanced education had already made them. One could go to the countryside and work; that was the practical side of "redness." And one could involve oneself in political study, in political movements; that was the theoretical side of "redness." But how to achieve a synthesis between these activities and the central activity of their lives, the study of language?

Because of the importance of the Army as exemplar, the students took many of their arguments from a framework of military experience. Which was more important, the argument went, to know how to shoot a gun or to have a political realization of the reasons for fighting? The answer was clear. If one knew what he was fighting for, anyone could learn weaponry techniques; but without "politics," his ability to shoot would prove to be of little value. It was a reaffirmation of the first of the "Four Firsts," that in the relationship between man and weapons, man takes first place. It was the synthesized experience of the Chinese Revolution, of Mao's development of the principles of people's war, in which an initially inferior force can defeat a superior force. Contemporary proof was as close as the news in the *People's Daily*. America with its advanced weapons could not defeat the struggling people's forces of Vietnam.

So the students attempted to extend the lessons of the PLA to the problems of their future work as diplomatic translators and interpreters. Language was their gun, but before this gun could function effectively, there must be a political understanding of what it was for. In 1964–65, that was the implementation of the policy which had keynoted National Day. The framework of their politics, they said, was the world revolution, and their language ability the means by which they would spread the experience of the Chinese Revolution and Mao Tse-tung's Thought to the oppressed nations of Asia, Africa, and Latin America, to the countries of the intermediate zone, and to all those fighting imperialism and revisionism. Although the students grappled with the abstruseness of this particular dialectical unity with enormous sincerity and energy, the difficulty of the task perhaps indicates the process by which Mao came to believe that it was impossible for China's younger generation to make revolution in their heads. However, their attempts to do so were indeed persistent.

In September 1964, there appeared in the literary journal *Wen-yi pao* a plea by the well-known literary theorist Shao Ch'üan-lin for writing about "people in the middle," those who did not fall clearly on one side or the other in the class struggle and were not decisively good or bad. He was quoted as having said the following: "The simplified portrayal of people, consisting merely of descriptions of their heroism and their courage in thought and action, does not fully reflect the complexity of the struggle." It was a viewpoint with long and honorable roots in the humanism of both Chinese and Western literature. However, "bourgeois humanism" was antithetical to the vision of struggle which Mao was attempting to maintain in a society he felt was far from having eliminated not only classes, but class interests.

The fiction-reading population in China is of moderate size, but the film-going public is enormous, so it was logically in the area of film criticism that the popular campaign against "the middle character" took place. Our students were very excited about the showing one Saturday evening of one of the most heavily criticized "middle character" films and urged us to be sure to come. We did, joining the crowd of students and teachers on the athletic field of the east campus. Usually, films were shown on the west campus, but the larger area had been decided upon because of the expected size of the audience, and the estimate had been correct. Chattering merrily as befits attendance at a Saturday night movie, good or bad, everyone was bundled up in padded jackets and wool scarves against the chill of the Peking evening. Children ran from group to group to see their friends, while their elders organized the family stools in close rows, and at last, it was time for *Threshold of Spring*.

Based on a novel by Jou-shih, one of the prominent young left writers of the 1920's, who was killed by the Kuomintang in 1931, it was a lush Technicolor production, romantic in a way which seemed rather poignantly old-fashioned, thematically accentuated with bursts of Chopin piano music and the willow trees of the beautiful southern China landscape. It is the story of a young intellectual, himself on "the threshold of spring," who is the prototypical middle character. In the long tradition of unsuccessful mandarins, he has become a teacher in an obscure village school. He falls in love with a widow, sympathizes with the revolution to the extent of receiving the latest radical literary journals from Shanghai, and, in general, suffers from the ambiguities and uncertainties which history has forced upon his life. As the film ends, in the critical period of the late 1920's, when Chinese intellectuals were faced with radical political choices, he cannot make a choice and therein lies his tragedy. However, the Hamlet dilemma was not appreciated in the class-conscious critical atmosphere of such ideological campaigns. The protagonist of the film represented to the audience of university students a rather simple fact. In the political atmosphere of the late 1920's, right-minded intellectuals should firmly have chosen the revolution as all their nation's leaders had done. It was a neat retrospective assumption, so neat that no one ever really "debated" *Threshold of Spring*.

And so, with movies to criticize, the Army and its heroes to emulate, literary debates, a Socialist Education Movement, and the "Three Good Old Articles" to study, students in Peking for the three or four years before the Cultural Revolution, lived in what seemed to them, and to us, too, at the time, an atmosphere of unending politics. They understood that all of this activity had a central meaning and that fundamentally that meaning was related to the Chairman's warnings not to forget class struggle. But what was class struggle? In the countryside, it must be former landlords and rich peasants who were still trying to reinstate the old land system. In a personal sense, for students especially, it had to do with thinking of oneself before the larger society, as had the central character of *Threshold of Spring*, or of secretly harboring hopes for a bourgeois career now that one was among the educated few.

But the precise significance of all of these movements of

the early 1960's, each in its own way a reflection of Mao's inner-Party struggle for his line, would not become entirely clear until the summer of 1966. When the events of that year finally burst upon the stage of China, our students, destined by history and personal fate to become the immortalized Red Guards of future history books, acted out their parts upon that stage with a sudden recognition of all that had preceded their moment in the drama. The recognition of different Red Guards was different; such is the nature of politics. But for them, unlike the rest of the world, the Cultural Revolution was not chaos arising out of order, nor the frightening spectacle of a nation gone mad, but finally the enactment of the class struggle they had talked about almost every day of their peaceful university lives.

*Chapter IV*

# Chairman Mao Talks To
# Some Foreign Friends

DURING OUR FIRST WINTER, an important visitor intruded briefly upon the calm, self-contained life of the Foreign Languages Institute. Edgar Snow, known to virtually every one of the Institute's nearly 1,000 students of English for his *Red Star Over China,* arrived one January morning with a phalanx of Chinese cameramen to shoot some footage for his latest film on China. It was indeed an unrehearsed documentary. The quiet English faculty library, its neat shelves displaying recent British and American newspapers and periodicals as well as an interestingly eclectic collection of critical and linguistic works, was inhabited by teachers busily reading, preparing lessons, or correcting papers. Some of us were suddenly and briskly arranged around one of the library tables to discuss the problems of English teaching for the film makers. Most of us—Chinese, British, and American—had worked together and we enthusiastically launched into a discussion of some of our pet pronunciation problems. Snow seemed intrigued that people who spoke a dozen kinds of English—Canadian, British, New Zealand, Australian, American, and varieties of Chinese English—were attempting to teach a single language to speakers of a dozen kinds of Chinese. However, Edgar Snow's morning in our library must have been one of the less successful accomplishments of that China trip, for we seem to have ended up on the cutting room floor.

A few evenings later, we had dinner with Edgar Snow,

Anna Louise Strong, and Rewi Alley, the New Zealand poet and writer. Snow never mentioned that he was seeking another of his celebrated interviews with Chairman Mao, but we were well aware of the symbolic role the veteran American newsman had played for three decades. Somehow he had reappeared in China whenever Sino–American relations were at decisive turning points. He would not return to China until 1970, after the Cultural Revolution, when the picture of him standing next to Chairman Mao atop T'ien An Men would signal to the Chinese people that the long struggle with the United States was reaching an historic juncture. His death in Switzerland in the winter of 1972, with Chinese doctors at his side, seemed strangely allegorical as Americans and Chinese prepared for the Nixon visit. It was the end of a long era which had begun in 1936 with Snow's first visit to the communist Liberated Areas and the publication of his classic *Red Star Over China.*

Not long after our dinner, Snow had his long interview with Mao, who, if not speaking for the government, had a few unique and interesting ideas of his own on United States aggression in Vietnam and other topics. Apparently, the Chairman talked to Snow in January 1965 not only to convey a message to the United States government, but also to express some of his ideas to other Chinese leaders.

After remarking to his American visitor that perhaps there was some personality cult in China, the Chairman added that Khrushchev had probably fallen because he had no cult of personality at all. On the question of Vietnam, Mao's position was clear and unambiguous. China's armies "would not go beyond her borders to fight. That was clear enough. Only if the United States attacked China would the Chinese fight. Wasn't that clear? The Chinese were busy with their internal affairs. Fighting beyond one's borders was criminal. Why should the Chinese do that? The Vietnamese could cope with their situation." In response to a question by Snow concerning the Chinese attitude toward the complete withdrawal of American forces from Vietnam, Mao listed a number of alternatives, among which was the sug-

gestion that an international conference might be held in
Geneva and further that "United States troops might stay
around Saigon, as in the case of South Korea."[27] This position undoubtedly went further in its attempt to conciliate
the American government than other Chinese leaders were
prepared to go.

The Chairman's interview with Snow was never published
in China but a few months later, when the *New Republic*
arrived in the English department library, our Chinese colleagues silently arrived one by one to read it. Despite our
close relationship with our fellow teachers, none chose to
make even one comment on the interview. It was obvious
that Mao had said a few things that did not fit the current
line. Perhaps they were startled by Mao's assertion to Snow
that one possibility for the future might include the negation
of the revolution by the youth. China's youth might, he said,
"make peace with imperialism, bring the remnants of the
Chiang Kai-shek clique back to the mainland, and take a
stand beside the small percentage of counterrevolutionaries
in the country." The Chairman's remarks that he was "going
to see God soon" and that, in 1,000 years, even Marx, Engels, and Lenin "would appear rather ridiculous" were indeed strange.

One thing was clear. Mao believed that China's internal
class struggle should have priority over any active counter
to the American threat in Southeast Asia. The former, if
left unattended would, in Mao's view, result in the reversal
of China's revolution, while the latter would probably take
care of itself: "Fighting would go on perhaps for one to two
years. After that, the United States troops would find it
boring and might go home or somewhere else." The problem
in 1965 was that the State Department was not interested
in what Snow had to report.

Only a few weeks after the Mao-Snow interview, the
United States, contemptuous of Chinese restraint, launched
large-scale air attacks on North Vietnam. Taking advantage
of the Sino–Soviet split, the US bombed North Vietnam at
the very time Soviet Premier Kosygin was visiting Hanoi.

The Chinese reaction to this new aerial aggression by the United States was immediate and angry. One hour after the North Vietnamese government had broadcast its statement condemning the US raids, the entire student body of our university was armed and assembled in their militia units on the school playing field. Soon they were on their way in perfect formation, rifles slung and bandoliers of ammunition crisscrossing young chests, to join hundreds of thousands of Peking citizens engaged in a massive demonstration to support Vietnam and condemn US imperialism. For three days, February 8, 9, and 10, the citizens of the capital took to the streets and marched in endless columns beneath red silk flags and behind swaying portraits of Ho Chi Minh and Mao Tsetung. The total number of participants in this Chinese version of the Gallup Poll was 3 million. On January 10, the foreign experts and "fraternal guests" were ushered to waiting automobiles. We proceeded in caravan through miles of organized marchers to T'ien An Men Square, where we entered the reviewing stands to witness the most impressive of all demonstrations we had seen in China. A vast sea of blue-clad armed citizenry arrayed under thousands of crimson banners confronted us. It is rare, if ever, that one sees a million human beings in one sweep of the eye. Here were the people, that abstraction that forever escapes translation except in China, where it always calls up a concrete visual image. Foreigners in China are often struck by the youthfulness and handsomeness of the Chinese people en masse. On this day of the people in arms there was no hint of hysteria, only a determined, tough kind of militant exuberance that took one's breath away. If Lyndon Johnson had been present, he might have understood why counterrevolution was bound to fail in Asia.

P'eng Chen made the main speech. Stating that the entire Chinese people would take concrete action to support their Vietnamese brothers and sisters, P'eng warned the United States that the Chinese Government "would not stand idly by with regard to US imperialist outrageous bombing and strafing of the towns and villages of the Democratic

Republic of Vietnam." In the months ahead, the Chinese statements in response to continued escalation of the war by the US would become tougher and more explicit. After P'eng's speech, when nearly a million Chinese had emptied the square with the same precision with which they had filled it, a British lady, who had somehow been hired by the Chinese to teach English, remarked, "I had no idea they were so well organized this far East." Apparently, the Pentagon was equally ignorant.

In the second week of February, Russian Premier Kosygin stopped off in Peking for a talk with Mao on his way home from Vietnam. The Russians were pushing for joint Sino–Soviet action on the Vietnam question leading to negotiations with the United States. Mao saw the joint action proposal as a new Russian device to control China and would have none of it. As Mao was to tell us at the end of the year when, as part of a small group of Americans, we spent a number of hours with him, the meeting with Kosygin was not very friendly; the chasm between the two parties, the two states, and the two peoples was becoming virtually unbridgeable.

A month later, Russian soldiers and mounted police broke up an anti-US demonstration of foreign students in front of the American Embassy in Moscow. More than 130 students were injured, and the Soviet government in a protest note accused the Chinese of instigating the incident and assaulting Soviet police. China's Foreign Ministry in an angry note of reply accused the Soviets of brutally injuring Chinese and students of other nationalities on the one hand while abjectly apologizing to the American Ambassador on the other.[28] Sino–Soviet relations appeared to have passed the point of no return. Many of our own students joined the crowds at the airport to welcome home the "martyrs" from Moscow.

The first of many demonstrations by the Chinese against the Soviet Embassy in Peking began a process which, for years, was to turn the huge building into a besieged fortress. A third massive volume of *Statements by Khrushchev*, which the Chairman wished the people to read as negative education, poured off the presses. Our students confessed to us that they considered this required reading an onerous and boring duty which they were attempting to avoid.

During the winter and spring of 1965, we were gradually incorporated into the workings of our organization, as Chinese throughout the nation are incorporated into, and identified with, their own places of work. Organizations, whether commune teams or brigades, schools, factories, retail stores, or administrative units, had replaced the traditional village, family, and clans, as primary units of identity. In America, one is asked, "What do you do?"; in China one is asked, "What organization do you belong to?" Most of these institutions have walls around them. The Chinese feel naked without walls and gates, which clearly demarcate the boundaries of each particular organization. Some of the foreign experts, who lived in the vast Friendship Hotel built for the Russians, felt that they had been deliberately fenced off by the Chinese, but the Chinese never understood this complaint. They themselves lived and worked behind walls which for thousands of years had protected them from the uncertainty of life outside their own communal shelter. Yet what went on behind the walls was no longer feudal or traditional; the walls encompassed large organizations engaged in modern endeavors. Our own physical incorporation into our organization was now complete. We had moved into an apartment at the Institute and now worked, ate, and slept in the largest organization in China devoted to the teaching of foreign languages.

By the spring of 1965, the external threat to China posed by the United States concretely affected the activities of all organizations throughout the country. In March, the Johnson Administration had expanded its aerial assault in South Vietnam into the sustained bombardment of the North. By April, the United States had embarked upon a process which would, within four months, bring US troop strength in South Vietnam to 125,000. It was becoming apparent that China was now actively preparing to counter possible American aggression on her borders. It looked like Korea all over again.

In May, *Hung-ch'i* (*Red Flag*), the theoretical organ of the Chinese Communist Party, published a major article by Lo Jui-ch'ing, Chief of Staff of the Chinese People's Liberation Army. Titled "Commemorate the Victory Over German Fascism! Carry the Struggle Against US Imperialism Through to the End!," the double slogan hailed the Soviet victory over the old fascism and called for the defeat of the new. This article had little in common with Mao's contention that the US would probably get bored in Vietnam and go either home or somewhere else. General Lo declared that US imperialism was playing a more ferocious role than Hitler and had become the main source of aggression and war on earth and the sworn enemy of the people of the world. He warned of a new Far Eastern Munich and reminded his readers of Hitler's undeclared blitzkrieg against the Soviet Union two years after the conclusion of the Soviet–German treaty of nonaggression. Lo advocated the theory of active defense which, although opposing the firing of the first shot in war, prepares for the enemy assault by utilizing space and concentrating superior forces to destroy enemy forces through decisive engagements. This was the formula the Chinese had utilized in the Korean War, when MacArthur's Christmas offensive drove toward the Chinese frontier. Lo added to Mao's strategic concept(s) a few notions of his own: "The strategy of active defense does not stop with driving the aggressor out of the country, but requires strategic pursuit to destroy the enemy at his starting point, to destroy him in his nest. [ . . . ] We seriously warn the US imperialists that they must not expect us to refrain from counterattacking once they have attacked us."

The Chinese Army Chief of Staff warned that the American theory of escalation was "leading its war of aggression in South Vietnam in the direction of a local war of the Korean type. It has already spread the flames of war to North Vietnam and is preparing to spread them further to China." Ridiculing US nuclear strength, Lo Jui-ch'ing reminded the

United States that its monopoly of the atomic bomb "was broken many years ago. Now other countries have the bomb." By implication, Lo was invoking the Soviet as well as the Chinese nuclear deterrent.

The article made it clear that not only would the Chinese support the Vietnamese people in their struggle against the US politically, morally, and materially, but that China was prepared "to send our men to fight together with the people of Vietnam when they need us." The article concluded by expressing confidence in the great Soviet people and the great Soviet army, stating, "We are deeply confident that we will be united on the basis of Marxism–Leninism and proletarian internationalism" and would "fight shoulder to shoulder against US imperialism."[29] Western scholars and government analysts have debated the meaning of Lo Jui-ch'ing's statement; the Chinese people with whom we came into contact understood it as the official warning of imminent, full-scale war with the United States. Each organization had its own contingency plans for evacuating the urban centers and setting up again deep in the countryside.

In the late spring, we were invited with other foreigners to an army camp near Tientsin to witness one of the famous military tournaments and jousts sponsored by Chief of Staff Lo Jui-ch'ing. The performance was nothing less than sensational. We sat like spectators at the Olympics and watched small squads of soldiers scale four-story buildings by drawing on that centuries' old acrobatic tradition of which the Chinese are so fond. Equipped with the traditional rugged tennis shoes that all soldiers in China wear, a team of four soldiers manipulating a fifty-foot bamboo pole, one in front, three behind, charged the building and with the aid of the pole the leading soldier, automatic rifle slung on his back, literally walked up the side of the building onto the roof. We were, of course, all astounded at the agility of the performance, and one European exclaimed, "My God, is that the way they're going to take Wall Street?"

But this was only the beginning. The next team scaled the same building without a pole by utilizing window ledges.

One soldier pulled the next up, then the first clambered up the back of the second to the next ledge, and so on to the roof. For six hours we watched bayonet jousts and night fighting techniques, the PLA officer explaining to us that soldiers of the advanced imperialist powers did not like to fight close or at night, and these techniques were designed to offset an enemy's technological superiority. We watched trucks being driven over ditches on narrow pieces of steel rail, sharpshooting exercises with AK47 automatic rifles fired while on the run, and other special events. The exhibition was obviously designed to impress foreigners with the expertise and fighting ability of the Chinese Army. In a short time, the "tournaments and jousts" sponsored by Lo Jui-ch'ing would be criticized as the wrong emphasis for an army which should above all devote its energies to increasing its political awareness. Our students would debate for many months the issue of which was more important for a soldier, to be an expert marksman or to possess an advanced revolutionary consciousness. The debate finally came down in favor of the latter, the argument being that almost anyone can learn to shoot, but that revolutionary consciousness was harder to obtain and more important in the long run.

China's domestic politics in those crucial months were inextricably tied to foreign policy. A move in one area inevitably affected the other. While it was not so clear at the time, in retrospect it becomes clearer that intervention by the Army in Vietnam would certainly have deferred, and more likely, ruled out, Mao's design to carry the domestic revolution "through to the end." Both sides of the crucial dispute over the possible response to the growing United States military threat must have been well aware of the domestic as of the strategic effects involved in alternate courses of action. Mao appears to have been convinced that a policy of "joint action" with the Soviet Union to meet the Vietnam crisis meant the establishment of Soviet air and naval bases on Chinese soil, once again raising the specter of Soviet control over China's internal affairs. Perhaps most important, Mao's political instrument for continuous revolution was the Army under Lin Piao. Chinese military intervention in Southeast Asia would with one stroke remove that army from its role as the shock force for a new cultural and political revolution. Without the Army, such a revolution would become impossible.

Mao's response to his opponents' line on the Vietnam question came quickly, and in the area where he had the most influence. On June 1, the system of ranks, insignia, and titles of office was abolished in the Chinese People's Liberation Army. Every soldier in the three services, whether private, admiral, or general, was now to wear only a single red star on identical caps, and uniform red collar flaps with nothing to designate rank. The State Council announced that this decision had been made so that "the revolutionary spirit and the glorious tradition" of the PLA should be fully expressed. The *Liberation Army Daily* stated: "Ten years of practice has proved that the rank system is not in conformity with our Army's glorious tradition, with close relations between officers and men, between the higher and lower levels, and between the Army and the People."[30] The ranking system that was overthrown was the Soviet system; the tradition referred to was Yenan. Mao had begun his counterattack by giving priority to politics over expertise. The new proclamation on Army ranks marked the beginning of his campaign for the revolutionary transformation of the whole society. It was easier to abolish insignia than social reality, however. When we asked a Chinese friend how one would now be able to distinguish the officers from the men, he laughed and said, "Oh, that's no problem. The officers are the fat ones."

Mao had launched his fight to control foreign policy. Within six months, he would begin his domestic revolution. The campaign to "learn from the Army" spread rapidly, and the *Liberation Army Daily* emerged as the most influential political voice in the nation. During the summer of 1965, Mao and his Defense Minister, Lin Piao, were engaged in the process of preparing public opinion for a showdown struggle. During that summer, we embarked on a tour of those southern Chinese cities immortalized by the Chinese saying "There is heaven above and Hangchow and Soochow below." Thirty foreign teachers of all nationalities made the tour, each of us accompanied by a Chinese teacher-interpreter-friend, the whole orchestrated by an efficient team of "responsible comrades." The tour of the "beauty spots" of the South indeed proved to be the Western traveler's imagined conception of a journey to Cathay, a Cathay which had retained its ancient temples and gardens, while adding a prosperous countryside maintained by a contented peasantry.

Having become accustomed to the austere northern plains, we were exhilarated by our transposition into the China of the landscape painting. In Wusih, our comfortable hotel was within walking distance of the huge Lake Tai, where brown-sailed boats swept across the choppy waters. One afternoon, a storm which had been threatening for hours broke as we were exploring one of the small pine-covered islands that dot the lake. Somehow, in this country of well-organized expeditions, there were neither umbrellas or raincoats. With the hilarity with which the lesser caprices of fate are so often greeted by the Chinese, we crowded together into a tiny temple which stood at the top of the island's hill. A few old paintings hung undisturbed on the walls and as we waited for the rain to subside, our companions told us about them. The lady in one dark corner was Yang Kuei-fei, the illustrious concubine of the T'ang emperor Hsuan-tsung, immortalized in poetry by Li Po and Tu Fu. She was strangled to death by a mutinous army as their price to the emperor for loyalty. The eyes of the beautiful lady, we were told, would follow us no matter where in the temple room we went. It was true, and we ran about the dark temple testing the marvelous skill of the long dead painter. But we were also told more recent stories about the communist guerrillas and boatmen who had fought on this historic lake during the revolutionary wars. The intermingled threads of China's imperial past and her socialist present, which came together on that afternoon, were to be the realities of our tour of the South.

The canal city of Soochow is an historical showcase with its elegant gardens, pagodas, pavilions, and temples built through the Sung, Yuan, Ming, and Ch'ing dynasties. The cultivation of the ancient arts continues in workshops where young men produce hand-carved sandalwood fans and in an embroidery institute where young women learn the painstaking skills which will finally permit them to embroider their exquisite cats, as perfect on one side as the other. However, Soochow's charm is not that of a museum piece but of a live town which has gracefully incorporated its romantic history into its contemporary progress. The prosperous neighboring commune which we visited was fragrant with the scent of the flowers which were grown as part of the regular crop, the flowers mixed with tea to produce such blends as the famous jasmine.

In Hangchow, a model commune grows one of the great teas of China, Dragon Well tea, and the textile mill produces bolts of brilliant silk brocade on its antiquated looms. We were welcomed to the historic Buddhist temple by a smiling monk who was, in addition to his other responsibilities, a member of the National People's Congress; we walked through parks which grew varieties of rare bamboo and pastures of pink and white lotuses, cultivated for their succulent roots; and rested in pagodas scattered about at reasonable distances from each other. In Hangchow, the West Lake, immortalized in poetry, painting, opera, and story, is the center of the landscape, and like all visitors of both ancient and modern times, we were rowed on the lake to view the scenery, to walk about the park-like islands, and to perform the ritual feeding of the huge orange goldfish.

This trip included our first visit to Shanghai, where we would return once a year during our five years in China. After the beauties of the lake and garden cities, Shanghai's architectural ugliness was startling. The now shabby Victorian buildings of Shanghai's colonial past seemed peculiarly symbolic of the predatory nature of that past. But we loved Shanghai from the moment we arrived in the old and chaotic train station. Like the people of all the largest cities in the world, Shanghai's people are fast-moving, fast-talking, and have a style immediately recognizable any-where in China, just as New York City style is recognizable anywhere in the United States. The streets are filled with bicycles, and there is a crackling vitality among the crowds doing their downtown window-shopping and nibbling on Shanghai delicacies sold at hundreds of small shops. A few years later, we came to Shanghai accompanied by a young teacher of peasant background raised on the harsh North China Plain. It was his first visit to the great city of the eastern seacoast, and he rather poignantly characterized what seemed to him most different in the Shanghai shoppers from their more stern Peking brethren: "They're always eating," he said quite disapprovingly.

On summer evenings, the population of 10 million pour out of their crowded quarters, and the sidewalks are alive with families eating dinner, gossiping, or playing chess, while their fans wave back and forth interminably. The children play and then fall asleep on bamboo beds carried outside, while their grandparents nod in bamboo reclining chairs. In Shanghai, one visits factories from the huge modern Shanghai Number One Machine Tools Plant to the neighborhood housewives' cooperative making plastic toys. Shanghai provides the sharpest urban perspective on China's past and future. This former metropolis of criminality, where the buying and selling of human beings was once a common-place of life, and every morning garbage trucks picked up the corpses from the streets, is now a city virtually without crime. We asked our Shanghai guide, a cultivated lady who spoke impeccable English, what she felt to be the greatest change in Shanghai since liberation. "For me personally," she said, "it is the fact that I can go anywhere in the city, at any time of the day or night, without ever having the slightest worry about being safe."

Memories of the past remain. The gray buildings lining the waterfront are a brooding reminder of Shanghai's past. For the education of the young, a few memorials are care-fully preserved, such as one small section of squatters' shacks left standing in the midst of newly constructed housing units.

But the industry which Shanghai displays so proudly, is, as every member of Shanghai's vital working class knows, the key to the future. One feels in the city on the Whangpoo the confidence and pride of those who are knowingly creating that future.

In August, while we were in the South, another of those extraordinary, symbolic conversations between Mao and a foreign guest took place in Peking. Entirely different in tone and content from the one with Edgar Snow eight months earlier, Mao's colloquy with André Malraux, the French Minister of Culture, included neither musings about seeing God nor passivity in the face of youthful negation of the revolution. Rather, Mao ranged over the whole history of the revolution and revealed that once again he had decided to intervene in the Chinese political process. Once again, the Chairman was using a foreigner to air his dispute with opponents within the Chinese leadership, and once again the interview would not be published in the Chinese press.

Flanking Mao were Liu Shao-ch'i, the Chairman of the Republic, and twenty leading Chinese political figures who sat in silence. Malraux noted that their presence gave the impression of a tribunal as Mao launched into a passionate discourse on the need to renew what he believed to be a faltering revolution. Lucien Paye, the French Ambassador, told Mao about his travels throughout China and how he had found the youth deeply devoted to Mao and the future he envisioned for them. Mao replied, "Revolution and children have to be trained if they are to be properly brought up. Youth must be put to the test." He had told Snow earlier in the year that hearing and reading about revolution and the old society was not the same as living it. Undoubtedly, he meant that the legends of the Chinese Revolution might not be enough to sustain revolutionary commitment in succeeding generations. And yet we, as foreign teachers in China, shared with the French Ambassador the impression that the young people of China were thoroughly devoted to the revolution. It was obvious that Mao did not agree with the

French Ambassador, foreign teachers, nor the majority of his own colleagues on the Central Committee of the Chinese Communist Party.

Declaring that Soviet revisionism was an "apostasy" moving toward the restoration of capitalism, Mao outlined to Malraux what he considered were the dangers for a victorious revolution:

> "Humanity left to its own does not necessarily reestablish capitalism [. . .] but it does reestablish inequality. The forces tending toward the creation of new classes are powerful. We have just suppressed military titles and badges of rank."

He went on to state what was to become the ideological foundation for the revolutionary upheaval he was planning:

> "Equality is not important in itself; it is important because it is natural to those who have not lost contact with the masses. The only way of knowing whether a young cadre is really revolutionary is to see whether he really makes friends with the workers and peasants."

Mao then told Malraux that the old thought, customs, and culture of China must be replaced by the new thought, customs, and culture of proletarian China.

> "What is expressed in that commonplace term 're-visionism' is the death of the revolution. What we have just done in the Army must be done everywhere. I have told you the revolution is also a feeling. If we decide to make of it what the Russians are now doing—a feeling of the past—everything will fall apart. Our revolution cannot be simply the stabilization of a victory."

Stating that the Communist Party constituted only 1 per cent of the Chinese people, the Chairman asserted that the Party could only "express the Chinese people in a real way if they remain faithful to the work upon which the whole of China has embarked as if on another Long March." As Malraux got into his car, Mao told him, "Whatever your Ambassador may think, this youth is showing dangerous tendencies. It is time to show that there are others." Out of earshot of the other Chinese leaders, Mao's final private statement to a foreign dignitary was nothing less than extraordinary. He told Malraux, "I am alone with the masses. Waiting."[31] Thus it was, in August 1965, that Mao Tse-tung gave a non-communist foreigner his blueprint for the great political movement he was about to launch.

We, and probably the overwhelming majority of Chinese on the lower levels, were unaware of the deep cleavages among China's top leaders. When we resumed teaching in the fall, the dominant role of the Army and its national newspaper in the nation's political life was apparent. We attended many discussions devoted to detailed analysis of key editorials in the *Liberation Army Daily*. This was part of the national campaign to learn from the Army how to put politics in command and apply Mao Tse-tung's Thought in a practical way. By the middle of September, hundreds of millions of Chinese throughout the country began the intensive study of a new document. It was "Long Live the Victory of People's War" by Lin Piao, a careful summary of Mao's theory of people's war, the Maoist answer to the theoretical position put forward by Chief of Staff Lo Jui-ch'ing and his supporters. General Lo had chosen a symbolic day, May 5, the anniversary of the Soviet defeat of German fascism, to set forth his views on the strategy of war. Lin Piao, in traditional Chinese fashion, chose a symbolic day to publish the Maoist reply—the twentieth anniversary of Chinese victory in the War of Resistance Against Japan. Each side had chosen its symbols carefully; it was clear that the polemic concerned the ever-present debate between the Soviet road and the Yenan road.

On September 3, the same day of the publication of "Long Live the Victory of People's War," Chief of Staff Lo Jui-ch'ing gave a major speech at a political rally in the Great Hall of the People. Delivered in the presence of Liu Shao-ch'i, Chou En-lai, Teng Hsiao-p'ing, and other leaders of the Party and the Government, it was a repeat of Lo's pronouncement in the spring. Within two months, Lin Piao had consolidated his control of the Army, and Lo Jui-ch'ing was removed as Chief of Staff. Mao had won this bitter struggle over the control of foreign policy; now he was ready to launch his domestic revolution.

Lin Piao's essay was a virtual textbook on people's war. In effect, it outlined a strategy to avoid confrontation with the United States on the one hand, while excluding Soviet influence from China on the other. This strategy was to be achieved through self-reliant struggles of revolutionary forces throughout the world and not by Chinese export of revolution through its own military forces. It called on the people of the world to "unite all the forces that can be united and form the broadest possible united front for a converging attack on US imperialism." The "principal contradiction in the contemporary world" was stated to be "between the revolutionary peoples of Asia, Africa, and Latin America and the imperialists headed by the United States." Lin's text outlined a strategy of developing the struggle to split up worldwide American military forces and destroy them piece by piece by means of revolutionary warfare in the third world. It had something in common with Che Guevara's concept of "One, two, three Vietnams."

Lin Piao's thesis of world revolutionary people's war stressed the importance of the principle of self-reliance and independence for each revolutionary struggle:

> "Adhere to the policy of self-reliance, rely on the strength of the masses in one's own country, and prepare to carry on the fight independently even when all material aid from the outside is cut off. If one does not operate by one's own efforts [. . . ] but leans on foreign aid—even though this be aid from socialist countries which persist in revolution—no victory can be won or consolidated if it is won."[32]

"Long Live the Victory of People's War" summarized the long experience of the Chinese Revolution in the hope that others might learn from it. The core of the lesson the Chinese had learned was to despise the enemy strategically while taking full account of him tactically. It was this combination of bold strategy and cautious tactics which had allowed the initially weak Chinese revolutionary forces to gain strength and finally defeat their stronger enemies. Within a few weeks after the appearance of the Lin Piao document, the militarist counterrevolution in Indonesia succeeded in its bloody extermination of the third largest Communist Party in the world. Clearly one of the largest massacres in modern times, the defeat of the Indonesian revolution came as a bitter blow to the Chinese and Vietnamese. They now knew that they would have to carry on their revolutions virtually alone, under siege from the immense forces of counterrevolution organized by the United States. In subsequent months, the revolutionary tide in the developing countries began to ebb. Everywhere, except for Cuba, Vietnam, and Algeria, nationalist and military regimes successfully opposed and restricted the forces of social and popular revolution. History raised the question of whether the Lin Piao strategy had come too late.

One day during that October, we stood at the window of our apartment in the Institute with one of our closest Chinese friends looking out on the brilliant autumn leaves and the last of the Evergreen Commune's golden wheat waiting for harvest. Speaking of Indonesia, she said in a somber voice, "They have suffered a defeat like we did in 1927, when Chiang Kai-shek nearly wiped out our Communist Party. Like us, it will take them a long time to come back." Whether or not Mao had foreseen this ebbing of world revolution, he was still determined, or perhaps even more determined, to carry out China's own domestic revolution "through to the end."

Five years later, in 1970, when Edgar Snow returned for his last trip to China and his final talk with the aging Mao, he asked the Chairman when he had decided that Liu Shao-ch'i must go. Mao replied that, in January 1965, the very month he had last talked to Snow, he had decided to get rid of Liu for two reasons. First, Liu was opposed to an internal cultural revolution which would "remove those in the Party in authority taking the capitalist road." Second, Liu Shao-ch'i desired to reactivate the Sino–Soviet alliance because of the American threat in Vietnam.[33]

Life in China was full of surprises, and we had little idea what to expect when we received a telephone call one evening in November asking us to prepare for a trip to Shanghai to celebrate Anna Louise Strong's birthday. It is true that the Chinese place importance on decade birthdays and particularly those of such a venerable age as eighty and that they feel great loyalty to old friends, especially those who have remained close to them when times were hard. However, Anna Louise was a very special old friend. When we walked with her in the parks of Peking, people who passed our slow procession, even young children, often recognized her as "Chairman Mao's American friend." She was the lady of the "paper tiger" interview, the first to use in English the Chairman's strange Chinese metaphor now so well understood throughout the world that even an American President felt called upon to state, "We are not paper tigers." She was one of the rare outsiders who took a message out from the caves of Yenan that few at that time were prepared to listen to—that Mao had led his troops on a strategic retreat not a defeat and was predicting from his Yenan base the victory that would follow in only a few years.

This woman, about to turn eighty, had begun her remarkable career very early. Receiving her Ph.D. from the University of Chicago at the age of nineteen, she turned first to the social problems for which her training as a minister's daughter had prepared her. With her sure feeling for the historically significant, she began her journalistic career by her coverage of the Seattle General Strike of 1919. She first went to Russia during the Revolution in her old role of social worker, taking part in the Russian and East European relief operation of The American Friends' Service Committee, but before long, she was also sending dispatches back to the *New York Times*. Her association with China began in 1925, when she was one of the few Western correspondents admitted to Canton during the Hong Kong strike. Two years later, she attended the first meeting of the revolutionary Wuhan government and witnessed the historic Hunan peasant uprising, predicted by Mao in his now classic work.

She made her home in Moscow for many years, departing whenever great events broke throughout the world. The Spanish Civil War was the center of her journalistic work in the Thirties, and, in the Forties, she returned to China for the Yenan interview. In 1948, when she attempted to explain Mao's strategy to the Russians, she was informed that on the basis of their scientific socialist analysis of China, a country lacking the necessary proletariat, the Chinese communists could never win. Although she was never told the reason for her arrest and deportation by Stalin later that year, she was always convinced that it was somehow linked to her relationship with the Chinese iconoclasts. Supporting evidence for this belief was the fact that Michael Borodin, representative of the Communist International in China in the 1920's and a friend of Anna Louise Strong, disappeared at the same time as her arrest and was never heard from again. She remained in America for the next decade. She was rehabilitated by Khrushchev in 1955 and invited back to Moscow by the Soviet Writers' Union, but it was to China that she went when she left the United States for the last time in 1958. It was in China that she felt the future of socialism would probably be determined.

In her comfortable apartment within the garden compound that in days past had been the home of the Italian Embassy, Anna Louise continued her writing. Although, with her great breadth of experience, she was interested in all world affairs, it was really the politics of America, China, and Russia that absorbed her. Although her memories were useful to her in understanding the present, she spent little time with them, having instead a remarkable enthusiasm for the new and creative political currents in the world. It was this freshness of spirit that was responsible for her passionate interest in the American student movement of the Sixties as well as the experimental quality of Chinese society where innovation was attempted in ways she knew from her own experience were impossible for the USSR.

The great lady of the community had efficiently coordinated the requirements of both her social and professional life into a weekly ritual. Each night of the week was regularly set aside for one or a couple of her friends who forever had their particular evening of the week closed off to other engagements. The Chinese in general regarded their invitations to foreigners to the theater, to meetings, or whatever as being an obligation almost diplomatic in nature. But one's dinner engagement with Anna Louise was understood to be sacrosanct, the only excuse that was instantly and respectfully accepted. We inherited Sunday evening dinner, a rite unchanged by events of any magnitude until Anna Louise's illness and slow decline in the last year of our stay caused it to be changed to Sunday lunch.

Formidable though she was, the *"lao t'ai-t'ai,"* as all referred to her in private, took pleasure in the sociableness of her evenings. There were many rituals. Unlike the rest of the puritanical city, she firmly continued to dress for dinner. In the balmy spring and autumn, we took annual and carefully timed walks to see the towering white lilacs beside the Temple of Heaven or the rose garden in one of Peking's ancient parks. But after dinners of creamed chicken and apple pie (As one of her dinner guests remarked about the bland cuisine of her household: "It takes years to train a Chinese to cook that badly"), Anna Louise conducted her work as a practiced journalist. She read widely and listened acutely. Evening by evening, we found ourselves the sounding board for her analyses. With skills developed by long experience, she asked perceptive questions, the important questions. From an evening of conversation, she would seize upon perhaps a single comment which had provided an insight which she regarded as valuable, and further developing her analysis, she would carry her own summation of Monday night over to Tuesday night and test it on the next evening's guest.

Her dinner guests contributed an interesting range of

talent and experience. Dr. Ma Hai-teh, who had arrived in China forty years before as the American Dr. George Hatem, was her own physician, bringing his reassuring conviction of the rightness of the Chinese society to which he had committed his life. Frank Coe and Sol Adler, both McCarthy victims, brought their impressive backgrounds as economists, their analyses of international affairs, their reading of the world press. Israel and Elsie Epstein, longtime residents of the Far East, were Anna Louise's editorial assistants when she felt she needed any.

There was no one more deeply a part of her long association with China than Anna Louise's "breakfast guest," her upstairs neighbor, Rewi Alley. Every morning he descended from his apartment, a veritable museum of Chinese porcelains, bronzes, and paintings collected for over thirty years, to share toast and Nescafé with her. Our boys, then eleven, thirteen, and fifteen, remember well the day he invited them to lunch when we were invited downstairs for the first time to lunch with Anna Louise. Rewi, shaped like a great boulder of his native New Zealand earth and dressed as always as if for a hiking trip, pulled open drawer after drawer filled with the jade, stone, and bronze remains of the awesome Chinese past and, as his excited young guests rushed from one thing to another, would only occasionally remind them, "Now then, try to be a bit careful. That thing you're stumbling over is two thousand years old, you know."

The bright star of the circle, the favorite of the "*lao t'ai-t'ai,*" on whom she, and indeed Peking's entire foreign community, leaned for information, expertise, and wisdom regarding China, was Sid Rittenberg. There will no doubt be eternal speculation in some circles as to who Sid Rittenberg really was, after his cataclysmic fall from power along with his important Chinese patrons in the Cultural Revolution. We knew him as a maverick of remarkable charm, a Southerner of distinguished Jewish family, who had gained his early radical experience in organizing Southern textile workers. He had learned his Chinese, as had so many others, almost by historical accident, in an army language program, and, finding himself in China in the late Forties, had decided to stay for the history that was being made there. He was a prodigious linguist, fluent in many dialects of Chinese. According to some of our Chinese friends, themselves impressive interpreters and translators, he was perhaps the finest Chinese-English interpreter in the world.

Along with his awesome erudition regarding all aspects of Chinese culture, he had the old-shoe warmth of the South and so performed to perfection the role the Chinese have for hundreds of years preferred to delegate to such a trusted and capable foreigner—that of their go-between in managing a community of idiosyncratic foreigners. It was a role virtually identical to the one played in the seventeenth century by those few intelligent and trustworthy Jesuits who mastered the language and the educational demands of the mandarinate and became the intermediaries from the Chinese court to their less civilized countrymen.

Sid materialized out of the Chinese mists to meet us only the day after we arrived in Peking. Arriving by bicycle and wearing the brown corduroy suit and disheveled tie that was his pre-Cultural Revolution uniform, he welcomed us with the combined graciousness of Charleston and Peking and evaluated us piercingly from behind his thick glasses. We were to see similar arrivals of the man in brown repeated many times in the next few years. Always the most popular of lunch partners at the Friendship Hotel, he was immediately surrounded by a group of Latin Americans, Arabs, or Africans, with each of whom he had a special relationship, for all understood him to be not only the most wise and sympathetic of counselors, but a man with an undefined mystique of power bestowed by "the Chinese."

When we all gathered in response to our birthday party invitations from Anna Louise, early one cold morning at the Peking Airport, we felt in the festive atmosphere a foretaste of the most munificent celebration of which this austere country was capable. Anna Louise, looking ancient and deceptively small in her winter traveling clothes—Chinese padded silk trousers and jacket—was the unmistakable doyenne, the animated center of a genial group of overcoated Chinese immediately distinguishable by that mysterious aura of power recognizable throughout the world. The impression was not misleading. This suave group of gentlemen included an assistant to Peking's Mayor P'eng Chen, the editor of the *People's Daily,* and other such powerful Peking figures. They, symbols of the official imprimatur upon this celebration and we, her circle of "dinner guests," symbols of international friendship, were about to depart together on what would be for all of us an historic week in Shanghai.

Accommodated in a gracious old hotel in the former French quarter of Shanghai, the American friends were comfortably settled on one floor. With that regard for rank so deeply imbedded in Chinese consciousness that it may indeed take 1,000 cultural revolutions to uproot it, Anna Louise was ensconced in the largest and most luxurious quarters at the end of the hall and her guests clearly, though of course unspokenly, lined up in order of status—we near the bottom. Although we all enjoyed the marvels of cuisine served in a private dining room and went off each morning and afternoon to a choice of Shanghai sights offered for our inspection, there was a feeling that this could not really be the entire point of such an unprecedented journey.

Our meeting with Anna Louise's old friend, the greatest of the Chinese iconoclasts, was announced to us very suddenly, as so many important events in China are. The reception hall to which we were whisked was only steps away from our hotel, and Mao Tse-tung and his wife, Chiang Ch'ing, making her first public appearance in many years, were already awaiting us in the manner of any other perfect Chinese hosts. Mao was surprisingly warm, almost grandfatherly in manner; but as he shook our hands, he paused significantly and looked penetratingly at each person, drawing back from memory what he knew of those he had seen before and, one thought, committing to memory forever the new faces. Chiang Ch'ing, unexpectedly small and reserved, gave one a light hand. She was so thoroughly the ladylike middle-aged Chinese matron that we forever found it difficult to associate her with the fierce patroness of Red Guards who was soon to emerge.

Mao, seated in the beige slipcovered armchairs of Russian vintage from which he seems to converse with all his guests, opened the conversation with remarks so startlingly casual that we took them at the time as an indication that he was Chinese host first, philosopher-statesman second. Within six months, we would understand that those remarks, like so many of his apparently informal comments, were fraught with meaning for those who could understand them. Those who could on this occasion were not the American guests, but the Chinese officials who had accompanied us from Peking. They remained discreetly silent as he directed his remarks to us, who, like Malraux and the French Ambassador a few months earlier, provided the screen through which his warnings were filtered to his colleagues. Lighting a cigarette, the Chairman, a longtime heavy smoker, remarked that although his doctors had recommended his stopping, he didn't intend to do so and invited the other smokers in the group to join him. When they had done so, he looked around the room in his methodical way and noted with interest that the non-smokers outnumbered the smokers. And then he added what we later understood to be the leitmotif of that prophetic meeting, that even though the smokers were in the minority, that should not concern them, that they should proceed in their own way nonetheless.

The Chairman seemed relaxed and calm that day, but not tending toward the philosophical wanderings that had characterized the meetings which he had had with Snow and Malraux. To Snow in the spring, he had spoken of his expectation to "meet God soon," the impossibility of predicting what the younger generation would do, and the chance that they might even want to bring Chiang Kai-shek back again. With Malraux, there had been little of that pessimism, but a conviction that things were not going as well as assumed with his revolutionary successors, that he must find the "others," and his final awesome remark that he was "alone with the masses." By November, his decision had been made. He had decided to fight, to risk civil war if necessary, and he had come to Shanghai to oversee the opening volley of the Cultural Revolution, the publication of Yao Wen-yuan's essay on Hai Jui. This task had already been successfully completed, so when he leaned comfortably back, cigarette in hand, and surprised us all by asking us our views on the world situation, one cannot guess whether he was opening the discussion in the way most fitting to his Socratic reputation or whether he was merely using up time gracefully on a day when his mind was on other things. Although he listened seriously, he did not seem overly interested in the half-dozen rather standard responses that he received. He remarked finally that since everyone's analysis was the same, the group must have met together to organize them and that it might have been interesting if someone had had a divergent view.

Our group that day included a Chilean and an Indonesian couple, all, like Anna Louise, guests of the Chinese Peace Committee, and, out of respect for the Indonesians and the significance of the recent catastrophic coup in Indonesia, Mao concentrated for a time on that subject. He asked if any of us had seen a small mimeographed paper put out by an obscure American Marxist–Leninist group which had blamed the defeat of the Indonesian Communist Party on its own revisionist policies. "It may be correct," he said, "but is it appropriate?" His words returned to our minds during one of those rare moments of the Cultural Revolution when the thoughts of Red Guards turned to foreign policy, and amid charges that Liu Shao-ch'i, Teng Hsiao-p'ing, or P'eng Chen must have been responsible for the Indonesian debacle, there suddenly appeared in the mimeographed pages of the Red Guard press an exquisite poem credited to Mao eulogizing the dead Aidit through the beloved metaphor of the early and prophetic plum blossom blooming in the snow. To Mao, respect not blame was the least that was publicly due to revolutionaries who had fallen in the struggle.

As he considered the number of Chinese-oriented Marxist–Leninist parties in the world, the Chairman was again

reminded of minorities and majorities. With an almost philosophical shrug, he asked rhetorically what one could do but
simply go on. Although he spoke with his customary long-
term optimism about the inevitability of the sunshine eventually coming out from behind the dark clouds, it was clear
that he was not unaware of the clouded state of the world
revolution. In a curious foreshadowing of future developments, he made no reference in this conversation with a
group of Americans to that central preoccupation of Americans, Vietnam. The target of both his wit and his wisdom
was the other superpower, the Soviet Union. He said to us
with some amusement that he had told Kosygin, "If you
call me a dogmatist, it's an honor" and "Although I am prepared to fight revisionism for ten thousand years, because
you are Premier of the Soviet Union, I will pay you the
courtesy of only fighting it nine thousand years."

In this casual conversation, in which we at the time saw
no indication of Mao's new shifts in policy, our retrospective
view shows that all was there: the decline of world revolutionary forces and the unsatisfactory development of a new
kind of vanguard party; Mao's assessment of the decreasing
threat to China from the US and the increasing one from the
Soviet Union, and his intent, clear to others in the room,
though not ourselves, to carry out the internal struggle
against revisionism regardless of his position in the minority.
Around him were Chinese who knew something of the reason for his Shanghai sojourn. The Party-controlled publications of Peking had refused to publish Yao Wen-yuan's
essay under the sponsorship of the father of the Revolution.
Peking, as the Chairman was later to remark, was closed so
tightly that "not even a needle or a drop of water" could
penetrate there. With us that day were Wu Leng-hsi, editor
of the *People's Daily,* and Yao Chen, staff assistant to P'eng
Chen.

Returning to more personal matters, Mao spoke to Anna
Louise about the Yenan days of the famous interview. She
finally had the opportunity to say to him what we had heard
her say privately many times, that she hadn't wanted to leave

when she was asked to deliver Mao's message to the out-side world, but had wished instead that she could have stayed with his armies to the end. Although she didn't say so, everyone understood that had she stayed, her arrest by the Russians, which was to cast a pall over her life and work for many years, would never have happened. Mao nodded and smiled, but replied that he himself had not realized that their victory would be as quick as it turned out to be.

We adjourned for lunch and awaited the arrival of the Chairman in a small and attractively furnished reception room. No one seemed to know what the next stage of pro-tocol would require, and our conversation ended abruptly as we all stood silently, expectantly, as he entered the room. He nodded absently, and then, as if there were nothing, no one there, as if he were quite alone in an empty room, stopped before an elegant bamboo carving decorating the wall and studied it with total absorption. It was one of a series of three or four, and he moved slowly and deliber-ately from one to the next and before each one spent what seemed like unending moments in the respectfully silent room. He showed the same concentration he had focused upon each face passing through his reception line that day, an intensity awesome and total. When he had completed his inspection of the room's art, he reemerged from his thoughts, and we found ourselves suddenly being ushered into lunch.

The meeting with Mao was the climax of that remarkable week, but with his usual perfect diplomacy, Chou En-lai, making his sole appearance, wound it down to a graceful but earthbound conclusion, a banquet complete with giant birthday cake. The guest list had been much expanded to include American residents of Shanghai, a large visiting Japanese delegation, and other distinguished persons who happened to be in Shanghai at the time. Anna Louise gave a remarkable and moving account of her life following the great historical developments of the twentieth century from her early journalistic coverage of the Seattle General Strike through the Chinese Revolution. It was not easy for her to remain so long on her feet. Because of the large number of Japanese guests, there was simultaneous interpretation of her lengthy speech into Japanese as well as Chinese, an ordeal for speakers far younger than she.

Seeing her growing fatigue, several of the Chinese officials seated nearby got up, obviously preparing to bring her a chair, but Chou En-lai sternly indicated his disapproval with only a glance and an almost imperceptible gesture of the hand. They sat down, and all of us sitting near her watched with growing uneasiness as she struggled to maintain her erect posture and firm voice. It was a triumph of the same will that had brought her to a productive eightieth birthday through wars, revolutions, and personal crises, and it was a triumph of which it would have angered her to be deprived. At the precise moment that she concluded her speech, Chou, legendary statesman and diplomat of exquisite sensibilities, rose and moved quickly to her side to seat her himself. It was a gesture we would often recall in the months and years to come, when millions of Chinese believed that he personally was the only man in that enormous country capable of solving the problems in which they all found themselves entangled. His long-tested skills as a negotiator and his capacity for political survival were put to daily tests, but what many people looked to him for was his understanding of their personal difficulties, his answers to their anguished letters, or quilts for their Red Guard children wandering through the cold of North China.

*Chapter V*

# Demons, Monsters,
# And Revisionists

THE AMERICANS at the birthday party were almost the last group of foreigners with whom the Chairman met before concentrating his attention on what would be his greatest and probably final attempt to move his enormous constituency into action against the enemy of internal revisionism. Before he met with us, the primary intent of his stay in Shanghai had already been accomplished—the November 10 publication of the literary essay "On the New Historical Play *The Dismissal of Hai Jui.*"

The "new historical play" was, in fact, not very new. It had been first performed on February 1, 1961 in Peking and had then been withdrawn after half a dozen performances. At that time, the allegorical significance of Hai Jui had undoubtedly been clear to many in higher Party circles, just as it was to become clear to all who read the newspapers in the months following November 10. The author of the play, Wu Han, a prominent historian, was the vice mayor of Peking under P'eng Chen. He had first begun to write on the subject that was to become the opening salvo of the Cultural Revolution as early as the summer of 1959, when he published an article in the *Peking Daily* entitled "Hai Jui Upbraids the Emperor." Hai Jui (1514–87) was an official of the Ming Dynasty famous for his honor and integrity. He had long been memorialized by the peasants of southern China, where he had held official posts, not only for his legendary impartiality in determining justice, but for

such social contributions as the initiation of an equitable
tax system and the project to harness the Wusung River.

The use of historical allusion as a means of political
attack is an ancient and familiar element of Chinese political culture. "Pointing at the mulberry and upbraiding the
ash" was a convention with which vice mayor Wu Han was
well acquainted. There can be little question that "Hai Jui
Upbraids the Emperor" pointed at the Ming Emperor Chia
Ch'ing and upbraided Mao Tse-tung. When Wu Han described the following confrontation between the virtuous minister and the dictatorial emperor, many Chinese understood
very well that he was attacking Mao.

> ". . . Hai Jui, then, in 1566, concerned with the prob-
> lems of the times, questioned the emperor and demanded
> from him reforms. He said in his memorial, 'In your
> early years you may have done a few good deeds. But
> now? You speak only of the ways of prolonging life . . .
> You live only in the West Garden . . . Officials have
> come to graft, and generals have grown weak, and peas-
> ants everywhere have risen . . . The country has been
> dissatisfied with you for a long time, a fact known by
> all officials of the inner and outer courts . . . So set
> on cultivating *tao,* you have become bewitched; so bent
> upon dictatorial ways, you have become dogmatic and
> biased."[34]

By the time Wu Han's next article on Hai Jui appeared,
in September 1959, the political climate had changed. Mao
had broken out of his isolation; Peng Teh-huai had been
dismissed at Lushan, and the balance of political forces
turned once again in the Chairman's favor. The new article
"On Hai Jui" seemed merely a scholarly analysis of Hai
Jui's historical role. The minister's lecture to the emperor
was reduced to a single sentence. In this second work, Wu
Han seemed to be disappearing into the mists of historical
research, but not without a parting shot. In language peculiarly like later admonitions to study Chairman Mao's Thought,
he urged the readers of the *People's Daily* to study Hai Jui.

Without knowledge of Wu Han's first article on Hai Jui,

it might be difficult to accept what came to be the general interpretation of his 1961 play "The Dismissal of Hai Jui." The play itself, read out of the context of the political struggles of the period, could be interpreted in any number of ways. The plot is a simple one. Imprisoned and tortured nearly to death for his audacious "upbraiding" of Chia-ch'ing, Hai Jui is pardoned upon the emperor's death and made governor-general of Kiang-nan, the fertile lower Yang-tze River plain. Arriving incognito, dressed in simple clothes and on foot, Hai Jui learns from peasants that the local officials and landlord gentry are extremely oppressive and corrupt. They exploit the peasants in the name of law and order, abduct their daughters, and confiscate their land with total impunity. When Hai Jui conducts an honest trial which clearly implicates the powerful local landlord, son of a retired prime minister, the combined forces of local and state power turn against him. However, before his final dismissal, he rules that the guilty local officials be punished and the land returned to the peasants.

While there was discussion as to whether the principal theme of the play was "return the land," "ridding the rascals," or "dismissal," for those who recognized Hai Jui as P'eng Teh-huai, the importance of primary or secondary themes was irrelevant. Of course, P'eng had struggled with Mao at Lushan over the organization of the communes; so "ridding the rascals" or "dismissal" simply represented the two possible political outcomes at Lushan.

There was a compelling political logic in Mao's choice of the Hai Jui matter for the opening battle of his Cultural Revolution, for there was no clearer symbolization of the post-1959 two-line struggle in the Party. In retrospect, the remarkable aspect of the Hai Jui debate was that it should have seemed esoteric to anyone, whether Western China-watcher or Chinese cadre. The response of powerful Party forces in Peking clearly indicates that its significance was not lost on them. Mao chose the September 1965 meeting of the Political Bureau Standing Committee to call for a criticism of "bourgeois reactionary thinking" in art and literature and suggested that a suitable target for criticism would be "The Dismissal of Hai Jui," unseen on the stage for over four years, but popularly available in printed form. No one picked up his suggestion. The reason was clear. This could not be simply another mass criticism like the anti-"middle character" campaign centered around *The Threshold of Spring*. Not only was Hai Jui P'eng Teh-huai, but the playwright, Wu Han, was vice mayor of Peking, close ally of Peking's powerful P'eng Chen. How many times in the Cultural Revolution were we to observe the ancient practice of attacking a subordinate in order to bring down his superior? With unerring instinct for their political culture, the question people always asked was, "But who is behind him?"

A mass campaign of criticism requires a major critical article in the press, and it was for this reason that Mao and his wife Chiang Ch'ing were spending the cold November in Shanghai. Sometimes called the most bourgeois of Chinese cities because of its history of Western commercial influence, Shanghai is also the most proletarian in the classical Marxist sense. The Chinese Communist Party was founded there in 1921, and for the rest of that decade, Shanghai was at the center of progressive intellectual ferment and working class struggles. That heritage of militancy remains alive. One could seldom visit a factory even before the Cultural Revolution without being introduced to honored veteran workers, who would tell their remarkable stories of highly organized trade union resistance to foreign entrepreneurs, local capitalists, the Kuomintang, or the Japanese.

In Peking, factories were a post-1949 phenomenon; and so, in general, was the working class itself. First-generation workers were children of the peasantry from the surrounding area. Theirs were the accomplishments of the new socialist industry, but they had few memories of the kind of trade union struggles familiar in Shanghai for decades. Peking was the capital city of party and government structures, heir to bureaucratic mandarinate traditions.

At Anna Louise Strong's Shanghai banquet, Chou En-lai had remarked, with the universal courtesy of politicians visiting other politicians' cities, that many people thought the capital of China should be moved to Shanghai. Whether his enthusiastically received remark hinted at his knowledge of the Chairman's reasons for visiting Shanghai is problematical; but there is no doubt that in Shanghai, unlike Peking, there were powerful political figures closely attuned to the Chairman's political line. As Mao said, "Why was the criticism of Wu Han started not in Peking but in Shanghai? Because Peking had no people who would do it."

The most prominent among Mao's supporters had been K'o Ch'ing-shih, the mayor of Shanghai from 1958 until his death earlier in 1965. He had been one of Mao's staunchest allies during the Great Leap Forward. Throughout the Cultural Revolution, Shanghai people often attributed the political sophistication and acuity characteristic of the Shanghai movement to K'o Ch'ing-shih's work there over the years. In any event, K'o was among the small number of powerful local officials throughout the country who had consistently stood with Mao in his inner-Party struggles. With K'o dead, Mao turned to two of the late mayor's key supporters. One was Chang Ch'un-ch'iao, a journalist and the Director of Propaganda in the Shanghai Party Committee. The other, Yao Wen-yuan, was the author of the November 10 essay on Hai Jui. Yao, a radical literary critic, had played a similar bellwether role in the anti-rightist movement of 1957.

We met Mao on November 28. By November 30, the impact of his Shanghai strategy was recognized in Peking. The *People's Daily* reprinted Yao Wen-yuan's article, but the editor's note was very explicit in stating that the debate at hand was an academic one involving the question of "How to deal with historical characters and plays." Newspapers everywhere began to carry letters from citizens, many of them exceedingly thoughtful and carefully reasoned. But since the *People's Daily* had successfully sidetracked the allegorical connection between Hai Jui and P'eng Teh-huai, the average reader was left with nothing but a problem of historiography.

To Party leaders, however, Mao was now quite prepared to spell the matter out, leaving not the slightest pretext for misunderstanding. To a meeting of the leadership in Shanghai on December 21, he said: "The crux [of the play] is the question of dismissal from office. In 1959, we dismissed P'eng Teh-huai from office. And P'eng Teh-huai is 'Hai Jui,' too." On December 30, the *People's Daily* published a self-criticism by Wu Han, in which he castigated himself for having taken a poor class stand, exemplified by his portrayal of the peasants as passive and helpless, dependent on the good will of an official of the ruling class, Hai Jui. He did not touch upon the question of "dismissal from office."

We returned to Peking to find our students occupied with this debate, but to us, and undoubtedly to most of them, it was neither more nor less significant than any of a dozen other debates and campaigns of the preceding year. It did not interfere with their language studies, nor did it really seem to grip them as much as the campaign to learn from Lei Feng still did. Indeed, of all the literary-historical debates of the early 1960's, the one which seemed to take hold of the imagination of the young most tenaciously was the debate over Li Hsiu-ch'eng, the last general of the Taipings. It was peculiarly relevant to the momentous events which would follow. Perhaps in the winter and early spring of 1966, it actually began to prepare these well-behaved young people for the task which they would soon inherit of toppling Liu Shao-ch'i, the Chairman of their country.

The Chinese Communists date the period of modern revolution back 100 years to the great Taiping peasant rebellion. Under the aegis of yet another Western ideology, Christianity, the Taiping forces swept over China demanding the division of the land, an end to foreign domination, the overthrow of bureaucratic officials, and equality of the sexes. For years, Taiping general Li Hsiu-ch'eng had been a venerated figure in Chinese Communist historiography. The fourteen-year rebellion (1851–64) ended in defeat, but historians had regarded Li's surrender not as a capitulation but as an attempt to buy time for the Taipings. In September 1963, a major article attacking this thesis had come out. It was written by Ch'i Pen-yü, like Yao Wen-yuan, a young radical critic who would rise to prominence during the Cultural Revolution. However, Ch'i's criticisms were not precisely those over which the students were debating. Ch'i had argued that Li's surrender was a betrayal of the peasant uprising and a sellout to the landlord class. His charge that Li had deserted the revolution for a class compromise was an affirmation of Mao's 1962 call not to forget class struggle. But, three years later, our students concentrated on a different point. What, they wondered, should be the historical evaluation of a person who had been a revolutionary all of his life, but betrayed his ideals at the end?

Perhaps it was the disturbing nature of the argument or their familiarity with Li Hsiu-ch'eng, but this was the debate which the students followed most avidly in the letters appearing in the *People's Daily* and which they brought with them into the classroom. The concluding argument regarding Li Hsiu-ch'eng came down on the side of absolutism. A final betrayal constituted a total obliteration of an honorable past. Li Hsiu-ch'eng must be regarded as a traitor. Thus, while the debate on Hai Jui quietly opened the public struggle over the Party's two lines, the debate over Li Hsiu-ch'eng provided a conceptual framework for the future overthrow of Liu Shao-ch'i.

Yet life at the school in the early months of 1966 had a singularly peaceful quality. We were by then well accustomed to the icy, early morning classes, and to teaching bundled up in padded jackets and overcoats. The students were always early, no matter how cold the weather. Red-cheeked and cheerful, they would see to it that there was a mug of hot water on the teacher's desk to help one get started on a dark morning. Hot boiled water, not tea, is the everyday drink in workaday China, and, although it took some getting used to, we finally became accustomed to drinking it even in the steaming southern Chinese summer. Any Chinese will tell you that it is far healthier than the icy drinks with which Westerners ruin their stomachs.

In the traditional way, the class always stood up when the teacher entered the room and chorused, "Good morning." It was one of many practices which they would criticize in the egalitarian air of the Cultural Revolution, but the warmth of the students, their simple manner, and their deep internalization of revolutionary concepts of equality had already divested this custom of its ritualistic severity.

One winter morning, when Nancy arrived at her eight o'clock class, breathless from running across the campus and up three flights of stairs, a student stood up to deliver a criticism in the name of the class. Stocky and broad shouldered, this young peasant student always wore a faded khaki jacket, a proud souvenir of time spent in the PLA. He had always displayed a great deal of shyness in speaking, but that morning, choosing his English words with care, he stated that their teacher had now been late three times in the semester. The class felt, he said, that she should make a greater effort to arrive on time. After all, there was a great deal of work to do, and if the students had the responsibility to get to class by eight o'clock, her responsibility was the same. In the customary way, it was a criticism interspersed with much praise. But also it was a demonstration of acceptance and camaraderie, an indication that the barriers of nationality, class, and culture could be overcome in a relationship based on equal responsibilities and shared duties. Of course, within the context of such confidence, it was impossible ever to be late again.

However, such normal life was already on the edge of the abyss. In February 1966, Peking's Mayor P'eng Chen had begun to prepare political counter moves against the campaign which Mao was clearly directing at him through the Hai Jui campaign.

In the fall of 1964, during the period when Mao was first developing his "guerrilla" attack on the Party hierarchy through the fields of culture and education, a five-man "Cultural Revolution Group" had been formed which included P'eng Chen. Its task had been to lead this revolution; but it had, in fact, never been active. At the time when Mao made explicitly clear through his Hai Jui remarks that he was prepared to move from oblique attacks in the field of culture into the open political arena, P'eng Chen prepared to move back into the field of cultural criticism.

It was a strategy consistent with the previous response of the *People's Daily* that Yao Wen-yuan's essay should be debated within the realm of scholarship, not politics. Under his direction, the "Cultural Revolution Group" prepared what came to be known as the "February Outline Report." It was an extensive study of the reform movement of the previous months in the field of art and literature and recommended that the same liberality be taken in the criticism of Wu Han that had been extended to intellectuals in the "Hundred Flowers" period. Since our students had been accustomed during the preceding few years to these discussions on revolutionary art and literature, it did not seem in any way illogical to them that P'eng Chen's group of five should be activated at that time. In reality, it was the beginning of the open battle between Mao and the political giants of the Peking Party.

Mao continued to intensify his own campaign through the propaganda work of the Army directed by Lin Piao. On January 18, the General Political Department of the PLA concluded twenty days of meetings during which it had made "a serious study of the important instructions given by the Central Committee of the Communist Party and Chairman Mao Tse-tung on building up the Army and its political work." Final reports at the conference were given by Premier Chou En-lai, Party General Secretary Teng Hsiao-p'ing, and Mayor P'eng Chen. Concluding reports on the work of the conference itself were made soon afterwards by Hsiao Hua, Director of the General Political Department of the PLA and Yang Ch'eng-wu, Deputy Chief of the General Staff of the PLA. Great emphasis was placed upon the familiar themes of the period: the "mass upsurge in the creative study and application of Mao Tse-tung's works, "regarding Chairman Mao Tse-tung's works as the highest instructions on all aspects of the work of the whole Army and putting Mao Tse-tung's thinking in command of everything." However, the conference report also stated:

". . . the decisive factor in putting politics first was Party leadership. The principle that military affairs should be run by the whole Party must be adhered to. The system of dual leadership by the military command and the local Party committee under the unified leadership of the Party's Central Committee must be resolutely enforced. The Army must come under the absolute leadership of the Party and the supervision of the masses in order to ensure that the line, principles, and policies of the Party are resolutely implemented in the Army."[35]

By early March, a document of a very different kind was in circulation. It was a letter from Lin Piao on the "creative study and application of Chairman Mao Tse-tung's works on the industrial and communications front." In the words which would soon become the bywords of the Cultural Revolution, it stated:

"China is a great socialist state of the dictatorship of the proletariat and has a population of 700 million. It needs unified thinking, revolutionary thinking, correct thinking. That is Mao Tse-tung's thinking. Only with this thinking can we maintain vigorous revolutionary enthusiasm and a firm and correct political orientation."[36]

There was not, in the brief document of March 11, a single reference to the Party.

The month of March was, for Mao, a decisive one. Utilizing in politics the strategic genius he had developed as a military commander, Mao placed great emphasis on winning the first battle in the phase of the strategic counteroffensive. He had written many years earlier, "The first battle must be won. The plan for the whole campaign must be taken into account. And the strategic stage that comes next must be taken into account. These are the three principles we must never forget when we begin a counteroffensive, that is, when we fight the first battle."[37] The first weeks of March served as a prelude to that first battle, when Mao would seize power from the Peking Party apparatus. Mao had made it clear that before any class can seize political power, it must first prepare public opinion. One of the most significant new revolutionary themes designed to raise the political consciousness of the people was the message and legacy of the historic Paris

Commune of 1871. "The Great Lessons of the Paris Commune," written by Cheng Chih-ssu in the March issue of *Red Flag* to commemorate the ninety-fifth anniversary of the Paris Commune, proved to be a prophetic article. Once again, an historical event was used as a basis for discussing current political controversies.[38]

As Mao came to concern himself more and more with the development of revisionism in the Soviet Union, he studied the Commune with increasing interest. The Chinese communists had long accepted the traditional Marxist-Leninist view of the principles of the Commune—direct election and recall of people's representatives, the combination of legislative and executive power in one representative assembly, and the principle that leaders should be paid no more than the wages of the average working man. In spite of its many positive characteristics, the Commune had been overthrown, and its failure has traditionally been attributed to the fact that the people had not maintained their armed strength in the face of the armed bourgeoisie. In his long writing career, Mao had referred to the Commune only a few times, and always his references pertained to its failures. But in the years 1957–64, during the polemics with the Soviet Union, the Commune began to suggest to Mao other historical lessons. In the article "Long Live Leninism," published in 1960 to commemorate the ninetieth anniversary of Lenin's birth, there is the contention (probably Mao's) first, that "the proletariat must use revolutionary means to seize state power, smash the military and bureaucratic machine of the bourgeoisie, and establish the proletarian dictatorship to replace the bourgeois dictatorship"; and second, that there is a logical line of succession from the Paris Commune through the October Revolution to the Chinese Communist Revolution.[39] In the last of the polemics, "On Khrushchev's Phony Communism and Its Historical Lessons for the World," published in the summer of 1964, not only is the Chinese Revolution seen as the last in the series of proletarian victories, but the deterioration of the Soviet Union into revisionism is seen as the last in the series of capitalist restorations.[40]

"The Great Lessons of the Paris Commune" emphasized the depth and efficacy of mass political participation and control, an aspect of the Commune experience which had not been dealt with in earlier Chinese writings. Much of the article concentrated, as previous ones had done, on criticisms of the Soviet Union's abandonment of the Commune principles; but, for the first time, there was a strong indication that Commune principles might be useful in maintaining the health of a proletarian dictatorship. It was the first public indication of an alternative to the hierarchical Party with which Mao had become so dissatisfied.

It was in the last week of March that Mao struck against P'eng Chen and the Peking Party organization. We were to hear later that Mao had declared at the time that the moment had arrived for the "monkey king" to brandish his "golden cudgel against P'eng Chen's imperial court." The Mayor of Peking was summarily overthrown sometime during the last few days of the month; the Peking Party Committee was dissolved; and the seizure of the *People's Daily* and the Peking propaganda machine by Mao's supporters logically followed. These decisive historical events were unknown to the general public until some weeks later, when Mao utilized his new strategic positions of power to launch the Great Proletarian Cultural Revolution.

The spring of 1966 proved to be a crucial period for China and the world. As Americans, our concern was focused on the rapidly escalating Vietnam War, which was threatening to spill over China's borders. The Chinese, both editorially and informally, had often reiterated their conviction that the American people, with their democratic history, would not become the Germans of the Sixties by giving their support to a barbarous war to which they had never consented. The Chinese attacks on Johnson and the Pentagon were fierce, but their confidence in the potential of the American people's opposition to the war seemed unshaken. It was a confidence that seemed to us remarkable in light of the increasing horror of the realities in Vietnam, and we wondered if much of the Chinese attitude was due to politeness or a dogma of revolutionary optimism. Whatever the case, all Chinese were enormously heartened when the predicted groundswell of the American people against the war began to take shape.

It was as a symbolic representative of millions of Americans that Nancy was asked to speak in the last part of March at a giant indoor rally at the Peking Worker's Stadium to support "the American people's struggle against the US war of aggression in Vietnam." The meeting was held in conjunction with the series of meetings and demonstrations of Americans in the spring mobilization against the war. Sixteen thousand Peking citizens crowded the stadium. It was one of those rare and moving moments when the sentiments of international feeling, so often verbalized, became realized in the bodies and solemn faces of the "distant" Chinese filling the bleachers and seated on the floor of an arena like those similarly filled in Berkeley or Cambridge.

On April 10, Premier Chou En-lai responded directly to the threat posed to China by American armies and aircraft approaching her borders. In an interview with a Pakistani correspondent, Chou forcefully outlined China's position in a succinct and powerful four-point statement. The first point stated that "China will not take the initiative to provoke a war with the United States" and was willing to continue negotiations with the Americans at Warsaw. Second, China affirmed her support for countries in Asia, Africa, and Latin America that were the victims of American aggression. Should such aggression expand into aggression against China, the Chinese would resist and fight to the end. The third point declared that China was prepared to fight no matter how many troops the US might send to China and whether it used conventional or nuclear weapons. Lastly, Chou warned the United States that if China was attacked, the war would have no boundaries. Countering "some US strategists" who wished to rely solely on an air and naval attack on China, Chou asserted, "If you come from the sky, why can't we fight back on the ground? That is why we say the war will have no boundaries once it breaks out."[41]

One week later, Dean Rusk, in a statement before the

House Subcommittee on Far Eastern Affairs, published on April 17 in the *New York Times,* stated among other things that "we want no war with China" and "we should continue our efforts to reassure Peking that the United States does not intend to attack mainland China." Both sides had now made their positions clear; Mao had gotten his military under control with the removal of Lo Jui-ch'ing, and Johnson had apparently restrained his generals from an invasion of North Vietnam and a war with China.

In retrospect, it is clear that two closely coordinated events on May 9 marked the beginning of a new revolutionary stage in Chinese history. The first was the publication of a fiercely worded editorial in the *People's Daily* titled "Open Fire Against the Anti-Party Anti-Socialist Black Line." The other was the announcement that China had successfully exploded her first hydrogen bomb. Together, these dramatic signals announced that China would not be deterred by either internal or external forces from carrying "the great socialist revolution through to the end."

With the Army, and now the central propaganda organs, firmly in his hands, Mao was ready to launch the greatest mass movement in the history of the People's Republic of China. The public campaign in the press during May laid the basis for the official condemnation of P'eng Chen and the Peking Party Committee as revisionists and anti-Mao "black liners." The attack was once again led by Yao Wen-yuan and joined by dozens of critics in the Peking and Shanghai newspapers.[42] According to Yao Wen-yuan, Wu Han, author of "Hai Jui Dismissed from Office" and vice mayor of Peking, was linked with Teng T'o, editor of the Peking newspaper *Frontline* and holder of a number of leading posts in Peking cultural and educational institutions. This anti-Mao political clique had existed for a long time and as early as 1961 had begun to publish a series of satiric and historical essays entitled "Evening Chats at Yenshan," which were clearly meant as an attack on Chairman Mao. The sponsor and protector of the anti-Mao group was none other than P'eng Chen.

In October 1961, Wu Han, Teng T'o, and Liao Mo-sha

together put out a series of essays entitled "Notes From the Three-Family Village." They were published in three Peking papers, *Frontline,* the *Peking Daily,* and the *Peking Evening News,* the intellectuals' favorite paper. In explaining how he decided upon topics for the essays, Teng T'o said: "I often thought of, saw, or heard things which struck me as problems, and these at once provided topics." The things which struck him as problems were indeed peculiar. He wrote on "Great Empty Talk," "Special Treatment for Amnesia," "Stories About Bragging," and "Learn More and Criticize Less." He wrote often about ancient officials dismissed from office. In October 1962, in the wake of the Lushan Conference, Teng T'o wrote to his readers, "I am discontinuing 'Evening Chats at Yenshan,' because I have recently turned my attention to other things in my spare time." His final essay, published on September 2, 1962, had been called "Thirty-Six Strategems" and concluded that, of the thirty-six, decamping or running away is the best. But although the series of "Evening Chats at Yenshan" was discontinued, the publication of "Notes From the Three-Family Village" continued until June 1964.

Yao Wen-yuan's criticism, and some of the more detailed ones that appeared during the same period, pointed out in precise critical explication the meaning of the "Three-Family Village" allegorical essays. The essays on empty talk, bragging, and amnesia, for instance, had to do with the exaggerated claims made for the Great Leap Forward. The dismissed officials of times past emphasized once more the P'eng Teh-huai affair, and others, "The Theory of Treasuring Labor Power" and "The Family Wealth Consisting of a Single Egg," were attacks on Mao's economic policies, the communes in particular.

Of all the debates which absorbed our students, this one was indeed the most elusive to us. With the issues buried deep in Chinese cultural history and the allusions of poetry and proverb, one could only listen with interest to the interpretations and accept them at face value. It was seldom that we felt cast in the role of visiting anthropologists, but the period of the discussion of these esoteric essays was one such time.

Stranger still was the reaction of everyone around us. By then we had experienced political debates by the dozen, but always they had been part of everyday life. They entered the classroom in orderly fashion and became part of English conversation lessons in which the use of the proper verb tenses was not inappropriate to their ingestion. Suddenly, the unthinkable had happened. Our Chinese students, who always came to class well prepared, who were always alert and enthusiastic, who always asked intelligent questions, began to assume the characteristics of their less exemplary scholar-cousins in other countries. They were unprepared. They stared off into space and did not hear the teacher's questions. They appeared in general bored to death with learning English. Anywhere else, the explanation would simply have been that this was a normal condition of the month of May, but in China this could not be the case. It was, in fact, a particular month of May, the one in which the eternal cycle of school terms would end, not to be resumed again for five or six years.

Nancy's teachers' group had completed a film on America accompanied by a commentary consisting of carefully graded vocabulary and sentence structure which would be used by the students in their language laboratory work. It had been a painstaking but pleasant job, and the teachers were pleased with their accomplishment. The first lesson was a disaster. No one could use the new vocabulary words; no one could use the structures. Such a thing had never happened before. The explanation was simple—no one was studying. The students' minds were on other matters. During class breaks, they buzzed about in small groups talking about the strange essays of Teng T'o. The impact of the accelerating events in Peking during the preceding weeks had not been lost on the university students. It could not be for nothing that the city's higher Party circles were suddenly undergoing a radical switch in personnel and that the major newspapers were functioning under new editorship. The attack on "Evening Chats at Yenshan" and "The Three-Family Village" pulled the events of the previous years together. Everything seemed clearer. It was suddenly obvious that there was something absurd in the idea of studies as usual.

As we, within the confines of our teaching responsibilities, tried to figure out how to motivate our formerly ideal students, the problem was resolved. In the middle of May, it was suddenly announced that the school term would end immediately so the students could devote themselves to the Cultural Revolution. The abrupt termination of classes left many questions. What about the unfinished courses? Would classes be resumed again in the summer? Would the students automatically go on to the next grade in the fall or how would that situation be handled? To all questions, we received what amounted to a collective shrugging of shoulders. No one knew the answers, and no one among this conscientious group of teachers and students seemed much interested. For them, the Cultural Revolution had at last begun.

Those among them who were Party members had also seen a document which would not be issued publicly until a year later, the "Circular of the Central Committee of the Chinese Communist Party" of May 16, 1966. It would later become known as the "May 16 Circular." In it was reported the dissolution of P'eng Chen's five-man Cultural Revolution Group and its replacement by "a new Cultural Revolution Group directly under the Standing Committee of the Political Bureau." Stating that the entire approach of the first group's outline report was fundamentally wrong, it went on in detail to analyze the reasons for this. "Proceeding from a bourgeois stand and the bourgeois world outlook, the report completely transposes the enemy and ourselves, putting the one into the position of the other, in its appraisal of the situation and the character of the present academic criticism."

But the most significant and startling paragraph in the May 16 Circular had been written as usual by Chairman Mao himself:

> "Those representatives of the bourgeoisie who have sneaked into the Party, the government, the Army, and various spheres of culture are a bunch of counterrevolu-

tionary revisionists. Once conditions are ripe, they will seize political power and turn the dictatorship of the proletariat into a dictatorship of the bourgeoisie. Some of them we have already seen through, others we have not. Some are still trusted by us and are being trained as our successors, persons like Khrushchev, for example, who are still nestling beside us. Party committees at all levels must pay full attention to this matter."[43]

The Party would soon have its opportunity to lead this novel movement, but, for the moment, Party members, like everyone else, were trying to get their footing in the fast-moving political atmosphere of Peking.

The gathering storm did not take long to break. With great historical consistency, it broke at the nodal point of many Chinese student movements, Peking University. Founded as the Imperial University in 1898, the most prestigious of China's universities had been in the eye of the storm throughout the great student protests which punctuated China's twentieth-century politics. China's original cultural revolution began there as the May 4 Movement of 1919. In the year just previous to this, the young Mao Tse-tung had been drawn from the lively student movement of his native Hunan to the even greater political activity of Peking University. He had worked there in the modest capacity of library assistant to Li Ta-chao, head librarian and professor of political economy, who was the scholar credited with having introduced Marxism to China. Again, on December 9, 1935, a date that continues to be celebrated today, the students of Peking University sparked the nationwide demonstrations against the capitulation of the Kuomintang to the invading Japanese. It was from the December 9 Movement that urban students were drawn to the new communist revolutionary base in the distant hills of Yenan. Many are the Chinese leaders who trace their political beginnings to that time and place.

Although the post-liberation Peking University (Peita) had changed in many ways, it had maintained its reputation as China's leading university and the starting point of political activism. In 1957, the first big-character poster (*ta-tzu-*

*pao*) of the "Hundred Flowers" movement went up in Peking University to signal the beginning of a nationwide campaign. In May 1966, the Cultural Revolution was to begin in the same way. In fact, the political battles of the Cultural Revolution had already been well under way there from the time of Mao's test run, the 1964 Socialist Education Movement. Although most work-teams of that movement had paid little attention to Mao's instructions to struggle against "those in the Party in authority taking the capitalist road," the team that went to Peking University had apparently followed the Chairman's orientation so accurately that they were sent away before their work was completed on the pretext that summer vacation was coming. Their departure was followed by a strange event. Lu P'ing, President of Peking University, sent about eighty Party members who had supported the work-team's approach to the International Hotel in central Peking, where, for seven months, the supporters of the administration tried to point out to them the error of their ways.

A few of the group of eighty did not recant. It was from this tough and politically knowledgeable group that the first rebel of the Cultural Revolution emerged. She was Nieh Yuan-tzu, a philosophy instructor, who had been chosen secretary of the philosophy department's Party committee over Lu P'ing's choice, the Party incumbent. She, like other Party cadres, had seen the May 16 Circular, and having already been involved in a highly sophisticated political struggle in which the connections of the Peking University administration to P'eng Chen's Peking Party Committee had become evident, she was undoubtedly clearer than most people, even in academic circles, as to what the meaning of it all was. On May 25, she and six members of the philosophy department, who had also been among the few tenacious resisters of the International Hotel group, posted a *ta-tzu-pao* in the dining room of Peking University addressed to Lu P'ing and several of his colleagues, to P'eng P'ei-yun, Assistant Secretary of the University's Party Committee, and Sung Shuo from the Municipal Committee's Universities Department.

"To hold meetings and to post big-character posters are mass militant methods of the best kind. But you 'lead' the masses by preventing them from holding meetings and putting up posters. You have manufactured various taboos and regulations. By so doing, have you not suppressed, forbidden, and opposed the mass revolution? We absolutely will not allow you to do so!

"You shout about 'strengthening the leadership and standing fast at one's post.' You still want to 'stand fast' at your 'posts' in order to sabotage the Cultural Revolution. We warn you that a mantis cannot stop the wheels of a cart, and mayflies cannot topple a giant tree. You are daydreaming!

"Now is the time for all revolutionary intellectuals to go into battle! Let us unite and hold high the great red banner of Mao Tse-tung's thought [. . .] resolutely, thoroughly, totally, and completely wipe out all monsters and demons and all counterrevolutionary revisionists of the Khrushchev type, and carry the socialist revolution through to the end."[44]

We did not hear about the events of those first days at Peking University until later that summer when similar events occurred in many places, including our own school. The first reaction of the Peking University students to the *ta-tzu-pao* seemed to be caution. Some criticized it by saying that the attack on the university administration was a diversion from the Hai Jui criticism. In addition, the writers of the *ta-tzu-pao* found themselves under heavy fire from the forces which smelled danger. No doubt there were storms of speculation among students throughout Peking—certainly in our own Peking First Foreign Languages Institute, Peita's neighbor in the heavy concentration of universities in Peking's western suburbs.

For those of us now temporarily removed from the world of students, the news of what Mao was later to call "China's first Marxist-Leninist big-character poster" did not come until a week later, June 1, when by Mao's specific authorization, the *ta-tzu-pao* was broadcast over the Central People's radio station, followed by a favorable commentary. A traditional all-night celebration began, and the drums and cymbals resounded through this huge student district. The tide turned rapidly. In the midst of student parades on the following day, a representative of the newly organized Peking Municipal Committee came to Peking University to announce the dismissal of P'eng Chen, Lu P'ing, and P'eng P'ei-yun. The Cultural Revolution had begun in accordance with a pattern which would be repeated a thousand times in the stormy course of its advance. There would always be this same apparently spontaneous correlation between the initiative of the masses and the fall of leaders. At the time of the first *ta-tzu-pao,* only Mao among the Party leadership was taking his side of the argument to the masses for their support, but it was not long before his opposition realized that they must do the same.

When the Chinese students and their teachers had vanished into study groups to discuss we knew not what, there were still a few students at the Peking First Foreign Languages Institute for whom there had to be studies as usual. These included a handful of North Vietnamese students who were ready to graduate and whose government expected them to complete their course of study and fulfill normal examination requirements. They were outside the politics of the moment, as we were, so the school administration asked us to assume the responsibility of seeing them through their work for the remainder of the term. They were charming students, full of the warmth so many Americans have been moved to find in the Vietnamese, and in some ways more flexible than their Chinese counterparts.

In the name of "English conversation," they told us many stories from Vietnam. The one that remains most vividly in our memories is the story of the elephants. In the war against the French, when the resistance forces had had very little mechanized equipment, they had relied heavily on elephants to do the work of trucks. Some of the elephants had been decorated as heroic animals and wore medals of honor about their great necks as they dragged and pushed their heavy burdens through the jungles. One such elephant had, in fact, become a national hero until he finally broke his perfect record by disobeying orders in a critical situation. In a ceremony quite as formal as the one in which he had been presented with his medal, he was stripped of it; and as it was removed, huge tears rolled down his wrinkled face.

Perhaps we remember the story so well because it seemed to epitomize a quality which we came to feel was characteristically Vietnamese—a spirit which, despite long decades of war, retained a gentle sentimentalism, a heroism both romantic and chivalric. Not that the concept of heroic animals was unknown to the Chinese. Across from the Peking Zoo, there was a refuge for retired revolutionary animals; and, as we passed on the bus, we sometimes saw a PLA horse of great age ambling about inside the fence. But that a heroic Chinese animal would weep was indeed unthinkable.

One June day, after the Vietnamese students had graduated, we all bicycled together out of the silent campus along the canal running beside pale green fields of rice to the Summer Palace Lake to spend a day of celebration and farewell. The weather was rather misty, as in classical Chinese paintings of boaters on such lakes, but we went rowing nonetheless. In spite of the fact that we felt it was their celebration, they insisted that it was for us and thus brought the lunch and did the rowing. They later wrote us from their cave classrooms outside Hanoi where they were teaching their students the English they had learned in Peking.

Toward the end of June, we were invited, together with some other foreigners, to attend a briefing on the most recent internal political developments by Liu Ning-yi, Member of the Party Central Committee, Vice-Chairman of the Standing Committee of the National People's Congress, and President of the All-China Federation of Trade Unions. For over four hours, Liu, in a most precise and thorough presentation, outlined to us in the style of a White Paper how it was that P'eng Chen, Lo Jui-ch'ing, Lu Ting-yi, and Yang Shang-k'un, had attempted to usurp political power in China and overthrow Chairman Mao. It was true, he told us, that P'eng Chen had played an important role at the famous

1960 Bucharest meeting with Khrushchev and that he had recently made important speeches in the name of the Chinese Communist Party in Indonesia. But, said Liu, these speeches were not his own. They had been prepared collectively, and P'eng Chen could not claim their authorship. In fact, P'eng had made a number of errors at Bucharest in not opposing Khrushchev firmly enough and even capitulating to some of Khrushchev's worst anti-China proposals. In Indonesia, according to Liu Ning-yi's account, P'eng Chen, representing the Chinese Communist Party, had succumbed to Sukarno's flattery and treated the Indonesian Communist Party as of secondary importance.

The second part of Liu Ning-yi's presentation dealt with the evaluation by the Central Committee of the Chinese Communist Party of Mao Tse-tung's contribution to Marxism-Leninism. It was an impressive summary of those areas of theory covering military strategy, the united front, party building, and the science of dialectics, to which Mao had made original contributions. While Stalin had listed four laws of dialectics, including the negation of the negation, transformation of quantity into quality and so forth, Mao had shown that there is only one dialectical law, that of the struggle of opposites within which all the others were incorporated.

Liu Ning-yi, a veteran communist of many decades, was later overthrown during the Cultural Revolution. We were later to wonder whether his summary had been prepared collectively or whether he had added a few concepts of his own and, like P'eng Chen before him, committed one or another mistake in his report to us. This was the beginning of a phenomenon which was to be repeated throughout the Cultural Revolution, as it has in every revolution, of a succession of leaders repudiating the "truths" of the overthrown leaders of yesterday. It was to create a difficulty for the new world left, as it had for the old in previous revolutions, of supporting today what they might condemn tomorrow. The truth which cried out after fifty years of twentieth-century revolution was that if revolutionaries chose to follow the earlier *Pravda* or the later *Peking Review* instead of the lifelong example of a Mao Tse-tung or a Ho Chi Minh, who followed their own independent lines, they did so with the certain result of the loss of credibility among their own people.

The great events at Peking University, followed by the famous early June editorials of the *People's Daily,* "Sweep Away All Monsters" and "We Are Critics of the Old World," sent out waves that were soon felt at the Foreign Languages Institute. A work-team arrived, sent by the Ministry of Foreign Affairs to channel this rebellion into the proper direction. Immediately, by their very presence, they became the dominant group in the small and privileged dining room in which we also ate our meals. That dining room was to be for us one of the first concretely comprehensible examples of what the Chinese man in the street felt the Cultural Revolution was all about. It was only a simple, one-story whitewashed building a few steps away from the apartment building in which we lived, but, like academic dining rooms the world over, its exclusiveness was determined by the status of its diners and the excellence of its cook. By means of a logic derived from the depths of their cultural history, the Chinese habitually classify foreigners among the privileged, a position both startling and uncomfortable for many of their foreign friends. As a result, we found ourselves assigned to the dining room habituated only by high Party cadres, administrators, deans, and senior professors.

It was a pleasant and relaxed place, where the few diners ate alone or with colleagues, and where others ordered meals which they carried home to their families. The food was simple, but in the proper Chinese fashion, individually prepared by a cook whom the epicurean Sid Rittenberg insisted was the best in Peking, an extravagant claim in a city of prestigious cooks, but quite possibly true, we thought. Everyone walked into the kitchen to choose a dish from the available meat, fish, and vegetables of the day and returned to his table to chat or read the paper until served by the cook's assistant, known to the English speakers as Miss Mulberry, a smiling, broad-faced young woman from a neighboring village whose inhabitants were the descendents of Manchu archers.

Our cook prided himself on his ability to cook Western as well as Chinese food. The president of our institute, a man of careful politics it would seem, had had a Russian wife, and when the Soviet advisors were at the Institute, the cook had learned to cook Russian food. By the time we arrived, the president had a new wife who was a member of P'eng Chen's Municipal Party Committee. But the cook still enjoyed using the skills he had learned in the old days. He baked the loaves of bread we and others took home for breakfast toast, and on holidays, made great piles of cookies and roast duck and chicken.

It was indeed distant in style from the crowded, cafeteria-style dining rooms where the students and junior teachers brought their own bowls and spoons to be served out of huge kettles of mass-prepared food. In only a few months, with the legitimization of the Red Guards, one of the first *ta-tzu-pao* to go up on the west side of the campus would appear on the door of our dining room stating: "Down With the Bourgeois Grandfathers' Dining Room!" And down it went, to remain closed for the entire Cultural Revolution.

In June, however, there was politics of another order, and the work-team obviously enjoyed their stay in the dining room. They took over the large round table in the back corner and consumed dish after steaming dish amid much lively talk and laughter. They were a formidable group of men, this work-team of senior cadres of the Ministry of Foreign Affairs, led by Vice Foreign Minister Liu Hsien-ch'üan. Ranging in age from mid-thirties through sixty, they had a collective look of toughness, intelligence, and confidence, and even in their informal shortsleeved white shirts and loose slacks, the summer uniform of Chinese men, they had a distinct air of authority. But in what seemed precise geometric relationship to the relaxed conviviality of the large table, the atmosphere of the rest of the dining room became increasingly subdued. Party secretaries and distinguished professors slipped quietly in, ate quickly, and slipped out again. They nodded briefly to each other and to us, but there were no conversations in the dining room except for those of the work-team.

The sudden shadow which these men, who greeted us so cordially, had brought to the dining room was then matched by a strange event. The gates of the east compound were locked. Our students, whom we had not seen since classes ended, were now mysteriously locked into their side of the campus. This information was conveyed to us with the customary Chinese grace and diplomacy, but it did not set well. We did not, of course, know that the same thing had happened throughout the city's universities. The flames emanating from Peking University were highly contagious, and the citywide policy of the work-teams was to keep them from spreading by isolating the students from each other and putting out the brush fires one by one.

The atmosphere of the Institute, in which we had come to feel so much at home, was suddenly strange. The students had vanished, and our teacher friends, busy, abstracted, and with their minds on matters unknown to us, were as good as vanished. Consequently, when the Chinese suggested that it just might be a good idea for us all to go to the beach for a while, both they and we were no doubt relieved at the timeliness of the solution.

There is in northern China just one beach to which foreigners go, to which Chairman Mao goes, and to which anyone lucky enough to go to the beach goes. It is Peitaiho, on the sheltered coast of the Yellow Sea, about 150 miles north of Tientsin, where one is suddenly returned, depending upon age, to the seaside holidays of one's childhood or to the nostalgic film landscapes of turn of the century beach resorts. It is a resort town frozen more in the time of World War I than II.

The six-hour train trip from Peking was festive in a way that a departure by camper or station wagon over hundreds of miles of freeway cannot be. Adults, as delighted as the children at this uncharacteristically frivolous expedition in a characteristically spartan society, wandered about the old-fashioned carriages, in which wooden seats for two facing each other over a table invited games and gossip. Straw hats, fishing poles, and oiled paper umbrellas filled the overhead racks, and baskets of every description overflowed with swimming suits, knitting, and the paperback detective stories beloved by the Peking foreign community.

The sleepy village of Peitaiho is perhaps what St. Tropez, Martha's Vineyard, Carmel, and Brighton once were. There is a main street of a few blocks with a public library, a dry-goods store stocked with the toothbrushes, plastic raincoats, and enameled washbasins standard to department stores throughout China, a few shops selling locally made baskets, straw hats, and mats, a small shuttered hotel which could as well be in southern France, and a tiny park with a statue of twentieth-century China's great writer Lu Hsün. The frequent summer rains bring an astonishing green to the landscape. The brilliant reds and oranges of the cannas and bougainvillea splash patches of color over the gardens surrounding the comfortable old summer homes. Their verandas and hammocks seem to have been left just as they were when their former owners—American missionaries, German businessmen, White Russian exiles—left China forever. This once-privileged refuge from the agonies of the old China has remained much as it had been, the great summer homes now converted into workers' sanatoria and conference places for high Party meetings. The old foreign community had been replaced first by Russian experts, for whom functional quarters were built, and now by experts from all over the world.

A large number of the foreigners then employed in China spent those first critical months of the Cultural Revolution in this Katherine Mansfield world, as distant from the real China as from the moon. We arrived at the beach in accordance with the custom of our particular group at routine hours of the morning and afternoon to lie on beach chairs or swim in salt water so limpid that it was probably quite impossible to drown in. If one knew where to find them in the early morning, it was possible to buy succulent local crabs from the fishermen and bring them back to be cooked for lunch and eaten with the ubiquitous Tsingtao beer. Anna Louise Strong was ensconced, along with other guests of high rank, in a spacious, veranda-enclosed summer hotel with a path leading down to a private beach. She presided in the same style which prevailed in Peking and soon had her summer schedule established.

Like the summer inhabitants of days past, we lived far away from the real China for those few months. Though we read the editorials emanating from Peking, they seemed strangely without life. Only one great event intruded, and that, too, took on the quality of fantasy that pervaded our never-never land. It seemed that Chairman Mao had taken a great swim down the Yangtze River. We all felt better about spending our days swimming. And we were reminded of a story told us by a teacher friend at the Institute. It seemed that Chairman Mao, since he wanted to be able to read the *New York Times* by himself, was studying English. When he came to Peitaiho, which he also liked to do in the summer, he used those unfilled gaps of time while floating on his back to practice conjugating English verbs. Like all of the personal stories which the Chinese people tell affectionately about Mao, its veracity is impossible to determine. But when we see his winter portrait, standing in his long overcoat and cap on the beach at Peitaiho, we are perversely reminded of a stout floating figure paying particular attention to the peculiarities of the English third person singular.

*Chapter VI*

# Make Trouble
# To The End

MAO TSE-TUNG'S historic swim across the Yangtze River at Wuhan on July 16 and his dramatic return to Peking two days later embraced all the elements from which reality is transformed into legend. Like Napoleon returning from exile on Elba, the seventy-three-year-old Chairman intervened once more in the politics of the Chinese Revolution. He had remained in the South, observing and waiting, while the leaders of the Party Secretariat took charge of the Cultural Revolution in Peking. Whether or not Mao's opponents walked into a trap deliberately set for them, they had consciously and decisively suppressed the mass movement, instituting what the students later were to label "the fifty days of white terror." Having enacted the symbolism of his poem *Swimming ("I care not that the wind blows and the waves beat; it is better than idly strolling in a courtyard")*, Mao presided over a hastily called meeting of Central Committee leaders on July 21 and 22.

Excoriating his senior colleagues for their suppression of the student rebellion, Mao declared: "Nieh Yuan-tzu's big-character poster of May twenty-fifth is a declaration of the Chinese Paris Commune for the sixth decade of the twentieth century. Its significance surpasses the Paris Commune." The linking of the Peking student rebellion with the 1871 uprising of the population of Paris now received the highest official sanction and laid the groundwork for the most radical interpretation of the goals of the Cultural Revolution. Continuing his attack on the Peking Party leaders, Mao told them: "After my return to Peking, I felt very unhappy and desolate. Some colleges even had their gates shut. There were even some who suppressed the student movement. Who is it who suppressed the student movement? Who opposes the great Cultural Revolution? The American imperialists, the Soviet revisionists, and the reactionaries . . . To cover over big-character posters which have been put up, such things cannot be allowed. This is a basic error of orientation. They must immediately change direction and smash all the old conventions."[45] The Chairman then scolded the Party leaders for fearing the masses and challenged them to undergo the test of socialism. He warned them to "be prepared for the revolution passing over your own head" and finally asked the big question, "When you are told to kindle a fire to burn yourselves, will you do it?" History was to answer that they would not, either as individuals or as an organization. "No person who suppresses the student movement," Mao declared, "will come to a good end," and he called for the withdrawal of the work-teams from the universities.

On the same day that Mao was lecturing the Peking high command, Liu Shao-ch'i proved that he thought other issues were more important than the student movement. Liu, as Chairman of the State Council, issued a statement declaring that China was ready "to undertake the greatest national sacrifices to support the Vietnamese people in defeating US imperialism" and that "China's seven hundred million people provide backing for Vietnam, and the vast expanse of China's territory is Vietnam's rear area." The statement was read to a million people gathered in T'ien An Men Square in a mass demonstration to "Aid Vietnam and Resist US Aggression." Liu's statement accused the United States of violating the 1954 Geneva Agreements and stated that the Chinese people would naturally, therefore, no longer "be restricted and bound in any way in rendering support and aid to the Vietnamese people." After affirming that "US imperialist aggression against Vietnam is aggression against China," Liu declared that the Chinese had made "every preparation to take such actions at any time and in any place as the Chinese and Vietnamese people deem necessary for dealing joint blows at the US aggressor."[46] It was Liu's last public statement in a revolutionary career which had lasted over forty years. Within a few weeks, he would be demoted to eighth place in the Chinese hierarchy. Within a year, he would be denounced as "China's Khrushchev" and later expelled from the Chinese Communist Party as a "renegade, traitor, and scab."

On August 1, Mao convened the Eleventh Plenum of the Eighth Central Committee of the Chinese Communist Party. When the delegates entered the Great Hall of the People on the fifth day of the session, they were confronted with Chairman Mao's own big-character poster, titled "Bombard the Headquarters." Accusing "some leading comrades" of having adopted the reactionary stand of the bourgeoisie and having "struck down the surging movement of the great cultural revolution of the proletariat," Mao's poster clearly stood as a manifesto of revolt.[47] It was immediately understood as a direct attack on the leaders of the Party Secretariat, Liu Shao-ch'i, Teng Hsiao-p'ing, and others who had defused the mass rebellion in June and July. Within a few days, Liu Shao-ch'i lost his position as vice-chairman of the Communist Party. Lin Piao was named as the only vice-chairman of the Party and officially designated as "Chairman Mao's closest comrade in arms and successor."

The triumvirate of Mao, Lin Piao, and Chou En-lai forged the leadership coalition responsible for carrying the great Proletarian Cultural Revolution "through to the end." These three, together with a new ad hoc leadership committee named the Cultural Revolution Group, would constitute what was soon to be known as the "Proletarian Headquarters." What the Mao-Lin-Chou coalition represented in the eyes of the masses was the Yenan tradition, and this is what gave it great strength as a leading force. The Eleventh Plenum allowed Mao and his supporters to recapture control of the decision-making centers of the country. Mao later admitted that "through discussion, I was able to secure the consent of slightly more than half of those present."[48] But that majority included a number of young rebels who had been invited to attend the meeting as voting delegates. However, Mao was not content with the Eleventh Plenum's drastic leadership reshuffle. He was determined to achieve the revolutionary politicization of the entire society by means of a massive revolt from below.

Soon the program of the Eleventh Plenum, known as the "Sixteen-Point Decision,"[49] flooded the country. Spelling out the rules, procedures, and goals of the mass movement, the "Sixteen-Point Decision" declared that the Cultural Revolution "is a revolution" whereby, "through the media of big-character posters and great debate," the masses "would argue things out, expose and criticize thoroughly, and launch resolute attacks on the open and hidden representatives of the bourgeoisie." Point Three stated emphatically that the "outcome of this great cultural revolution will be determined by whether or not the Party leadership dares boldly to arouse the masses" and that "the Central Committee of the Party demands of the Party Committees at all levels [. . .] that they persevere in giving correct leadership, put daring above everything else, boldly arouse the masses, change the state of weakness and incompetence where it exists, encourage those comrades who have made mistakes but are willing to correct them to cast off their mental burdens and join the struggle, and dismiss from their leading posts all those in authority who are taking the capitalist road, and so make possible the recapture of leadership for the proletarian revolutionaries." The cadres were divided into four categories: good; comparatively good; those who had made serious mistakes but had not become anti-Party, anti-socialist rightists; and "the small number of anti-Party, anti-socialist rightists." These last were to be fully exposed, overthrown, and completely discredited. Lin Piao, in a talk that was widely distributed at the time, made some interesting remarks about the question of the Party cadres. He said that some of the best cadres might not be the most popular, since they took the initiative, were not afraid of stepping on a few toes, and were courageous in stating the truth. Other cadres, acting like good politicians, got along with everyone and were essentially opportunists. Lin's words took on a deeper meaning as mass attacks on the Party cadres got under way. A special paragraph exempted the Army from a cultural revolution and mass movement within its own ranks or as a target from without. Since the Cultural Revolution was considered to be a revolution within the superstructure, meaning administrative, Party, and governmental bodies, it was essentially an urban mass movement and the peasantry was not officially involved. The peasants had been involved in the Socialist Education movement, which had ended prior to the Cultural Revolution. It was clear that the peasants were required to feed the cities during the movement, and this they did, increasing production every year during the Cultural Revolution. However, the Cultural Revolution was staged in the final analysis for the benefit of the peasantry, since one goal of the movement was to close the gap between the cities and the countryside.

It was clear that Mao and his supporters assumed from the beginning that this movement, like all the other movements in Chinese Communist history, would be led by the Party. This assumption that the majority of Party Committees and members would clear out revisionist leaders in their own ranks by mobilizing the masses against them was soon to be proved wrong. But, in the early stages of the movement, Mao was still attempting to reassure some of his worried colleagues at the central level who were beginning to have doubts that Party cadres throughout the country would ignite the fires designed to burn themselves. He told these leaders: "It doesn't matter if there are no Provincial Party Committees, we still have the District and Hsien Committees."[50]

Within a few months, it became evident that Mao did not have the district and county committees. Even more serious, the branch committees at every level ceased to operate. For the first time in the history of the Chinese Revolution, the politics of mass participation would not be led by vanguard units at the provincial, district, county, city, or branch levels;

the largest Communist Party in the world remained paralyzed for three years, while the masses in their millions monopolized the political stage. The Party organization showed little inclination to burn itself. On the contrary, the Cultural Revolution would prove that the Party as a whole was inclined to protect its own position of status and power with a great deal of ingenuity. Though statements were still issued in the name of the Central Committee, the majority of its members soon came under attack, and it, too, ceased to operate for the duration of the movement. The Central Committee, with the help of outsiders, had thus placed its stamp of approval on the Great Proletarian Cultural Revolution only to become a lame duck political organ waiting for replacement at the end of the movement. The power of the Central Committee was, in effect, delegated to an ad hoc committee, the Cultural Revolution Group, and the powerful Military Affairs Committee of the Central Committee under the leadership of Marshal Lin Piao.

Direct leadership of the mass rebellion was thus placed in the hands of leaders appointed or approved by Chairman Mao and named to membership in the Cultural Revolution Group. This small committee of thirteen members, soon to take its place at the center of national politics, was led by Ch'en Po-ta, Mao's former secretary, Party theoretician, and editor of the Party journal, *Red Flag;* K'ang Sheng, a Party veteran once in charge of Public Security; and Mao's wife, Chiang Ch'ing, who, until the early 1960's, had taken no part in public politics. The other ten members of the Cultural Group consisted of younger Party intellectuals, many of whom had been discovered by Chiang Ch'ing during the earlier movement in the literary and artistic field. They were new to the top levels of power, little experienced in leading mass struggles. The one thing common to all of the members was loyalty to Chairman Mao or to his wife. Mao's power now rested on a three-part coalition made up of Lin Piao representing the Army, Premier Chou En-lai, the chief administrator of the government ministries under the State Council, and the Cultural Group, acting in the name of the Central Committee of the Chinese Communist Party.

By the late fall of 1966, it was apparent that the "Sixteen-Point Decision" was already becoming obsolete as a guide for the mass movement. Within six months, it was hardly mentioned. The failure of the Party to act as the vanguard for the mass movement had undermined the effectiveness of the Sixteen Points. However, this failure allowed a popular revolutionary movement to develop in the classical tradition of all revolutions. With the suspension of the Party branches, rank-and-file workers and students found themselves on an equal footing with Party members. In every other movement, Party members had had automatic access to inside information not available to the ordinary citizen. During the Cultural Revolution, Party members, like everyone else, had to rely on the *People's Daily* and the *Red Flag* for political guidance. Often, ordinary citizens proved to be more prescient in the political struggle than many Party members, cast adrift in a political movement unprecedented in its complexity. History was to corroborate Chairman Mao's notion that some of those outside the Party were more revolutionary than some inside it. When the movement split into factions, Party members found themselves on opposing sides. Inner-Party struggle has become an affair of the masses.

The Great Proletarian Cultural Revolution brought the career of Mao Tse-tung full circle. His political life had begun in the upheaval of China's first cultural revolution, the May 4 Movement (1915–21); half a century later, he was ready to lead one last movement to consolidate the practice and experience of a new revolutionary belief system. It was an attempt to institutionalize the concept of uninterrupted revolution. The Cultural Revolution was, in fact as well as in propaganda, personally initiated and led by Chairman Mao. Yet unless the social basis for mass rebellion had actually existed, even a legendary leader like Mao would have been unable to spark a social explosion. Writing in 1936 on the strategy of revolutionary war, Mao stated: "The stage of action for a military man is built upon objective material conditions, but on that stage he can direct the performance of many a drama, full of sound and color, power and grandeur."[51] In 1966, Mao showed that the same was true for mass politics. Without a doubt, this new form of political rebellion was poorly understood by most, perhaps all, of the senior members of the Party. In a discussion with an Albanian military delegation visiting Peking in August 1967, Mao admitted that he had little support from China's top leaders for his campaign to launch a mass struggle against the revisionist and bourgeois power-holders in the Party. "At that time, most people disagreed with me. Sometimes I was all alone. They said my ideas were out of date."[52]

What, then, was Mao's concept of the Great Proletarian Cultural Revolution? During his discussion with the Albanians, he asked them what they understood to be its purpose. One of his guests replied that it was to struggle against the officials in the Party taking the capitalist road. Mao replied, "The struggle against the capitalist-roaders in the Party is the principal task, but not the purpose. The purpose is to solve the problem of world outlook and eradicate revisionism. [. . .] If world outlook is not reformed, although two thousand capitalist-roaders are removed in the current great cultural revolution, four thousand may appear next time."[53] In the broadest sense, then, the Cultural Revolution was meant to do nothing less than transform man's spiritual outlook. In practice, however, events were to show that it is not a simple matter to combine an ideological campaign with a political struggle for power. Certain political forces in the movement stressed class struggle and the seizure of power from Party officials; others stressed moral remolding and deemphasized class struggle for power.

Like the first days of the American and French revolutions, the early period of the Chinese Cultural Revolution generated public response through a nationwide philosophic debate which, though abstract, stirred passions as only revolutions are capable of doing. In the late summer and fall of 1966, the campaign to learn from the People's Liberation Army in order to turn the whole country into a great school of Mao Tse-tung's Thought swept everything before it. Like the words of the ancient sages, the Chairman's Thought was promulgated as the way to create citizens who would place the public interest before private interest, attack their own selfish interests as well as those of others, and construct a new society where leaders and officials devoted their lives to serving the people. The twentieth-century element which characterized the Chairman's Thought was the concept that the new harmony could be achieved only in the storms of the class struggle. If the Party apparatus refused to lead such a struggle, the movement would be guided by the higher principles embodied in Mao Tse-tung's Thought.

As the prestige of the Party organization waned, the combination of Mao, the Army, and the masses appeared unbeatable. Mao the symbol and Mao the man stood for the continuity of the revolution. His Thought was to the Chinese people what the American Constitution and its generalities are to the American people. Finally, if the Party was no longer the legitimate fountain of communist ethics and practice, who could doubt that Chairman Mao possessed the legitimacy and capacity to fill that role alone. Lin Piao was later to suffer for promoting the Mao cult during the Cultural Revolution, but the Chairman himself recognized its usefulness. He told a foreign visitor that, before the Cultural Revolution, the senior leaders of the country "treated me like a Buddha, but no one listened to what I had to say."[54] Now that he had power in his hands once again, without the organized backing of the Party, "there was need for more personality cult," as he told Edgar Snow in 1970.[55] It was needed, Mao said, to encourage the masses to break up the anti-Mao Party bureaucracy. To lay the foundations for this task, the newly reorganized Ministry of Culture announced in the fall of 1966 its plans to publish 35 million copies of Mao Tse-tung's *Selected Works*.

Whatever his ambitions, Lin Piao did lead the campaign to promote the "flexible study and application of Chairman Mao's works" and the massive effort to make Maoist theory the line that united "the entire Party, the entire Army, and the entire people." And it was Lin Piao who compiled "the little red book" of Mao quotations for the Army, an action which made Mao's Thought familiar to every soldier, then every Chinese, and finally millions throughout the world.

Lin was particularly revered in those early days of the Cultural Revolution by many of the middle school and university students for his reputation as a fearless soldier. Stories of his many campaigns, including the Long March, the famous victory over the Japanese at the battle of Ping-singkuan, the liberation of Manchuria during the final revolutionary war, and his service as the first commander of the Chinese Volunteers in Korea, were legion in Peking. He was never particularly popular among the foreign community, who considered him something of a sycophant, a wooden and austere man forever waving the little red bible of the Chairman's quotations. Yet the little red book was a unique and brilliant invention, which did for the Chinese people what Tom Paine's *Common Sense* had done for the Americans in the eighteenth century. Although it later led to dogmatic recitations, the pocket book of Mao quotes helped to provide, in the early period of the Cultural Revolution, the ground rules for the movement. There could be no question that the little red book was overdone during the great tumult of the Sixties, as much else was overdone, and many foreigners were disturbed by Lin Piao's statement that everyone should carry out Chairman Mao's instructions "whether you understand them or not." A Robespierre-like figure, Lin Piao labored to create the reign of virtue under the benevolent mantle of his revolutionary emperor. If, in the fall of 1966, some worried about his dogmatism, there were none to question his sincerity. Lin Piao, who had been at Mao's side since 1927, had been President of the model K'ang Ta Workers', Peasants' and Soldiers' University in Yenan, where the principles embodied in the "proletarian line of the Cultural Revolution" were forged. If Mao, as it was later stated after the Cultural Revolution, "saw through" Lin as early as 1966, it was the most closely-guarded secret of all.

The movement to overthrow the "four olds" (old ideology, old culture, old customs, and old habits) unfolded during the months when we were at the seashore. We got our first glimpse of young Red Guards sporting their military caps and red arm bands in the sleepy town of Peitaiho. In Peking, tens of thousands of middle school Red Guards poured onto the streets of the capital in their new assignment of "paying attention to state affairs."

Although Chairman Mao sparked much that was new in China, he also stirred up much that was deep in the Chinese tradition of rebellion. Taking their cue from one of Mao's poems, these youths of Peking chose the classical symbol of Chinese rebellion, the Monkey King, to express their new spirit of defiance:

> "Revolutionaries are Monkey Kings, their golden rods are powerful, their supernatural powers far-reaching, and their magic omnipotent, for they possess Mao Tse-tung's invincible thought. We wield our golden rods, display our supernatural powers, and use our magic to turn the old world upside down, smash it to pieces, pulverize it, create chaos, and make a tremendous mess, the bigger the better! We must do this to the present revisionist middle school attached to the Tsinghua University, make rebellion in a big way, rebel to the end! We are bent on creating a tremendous proletarian uproar and hewing out a proletarian new world."[56]

We heard reports of Chairman Mao's gigantic meeting with more than 1 million Red Guards in T'ien An Men Square, where he had put on a student's red arm band to legitimize their movement and told them, "Pay attention to state affairs and carry the Cultural Revolution through to the end." For more than two years, the youth of China would do little else.

When we returned to Peking at the end of August, we entered a dramatic and colorful world that had become a political festival of the masses. At the Institute, we found ourselves strangely unemployed. The gates to the school were now open, but the campus was almost deserted after ten o'clock in the morning as students and teachers disappeared into their intense study sessions, organizational meetings, and perusal of Cultural Revolution editorials and documents. Everywhere, on the walls of buildings, thousands of big-character posters stared out at us. We were now to live amid a sea of language, a lively world of large blue, red, and yellow ideographs. Freaks, monsters, demons, sinister soldiers, and gusts of evil wind were some of the charged phrases that energized a formerly tranquil atmosphere with the tension of conflict. No one could tell what the next morning might bring as new waves of words washed over the city. It was obvious to us that the revolution in our school had begun, but how far it had gone beyond the overthrow of the open vestiges of inequality was difficult to determine. In particular, it was not clear whether the walls of power had yet been breached.

Whatever the stage of the movement, the basic routine of political activity for the student population was now established for the duration of that movement. Students, teachers, and a few cadres would work late into the night, either individually or in groups, writing the posters which would then be pasted up the next morning. After breakfast, a great quiet reigned over this city of universities as the student population, numbering in the hundreds of thousands, silently read the posters of the previous night. And it was not only the students who participated in this orgy of writing and reading. Shop clerks, workers, office employees, and bus drivers somehow carried on their work while following the same basic routine as the students. It was a most impressive sight—the population of a country which only twenty years before had been 80 per cent illiterate conducting a national debate through the written word. Late in the morning and in the afternoon, the students and teachers would break up into study or strategy sessions, participate in demonstrations, or visit other organizations throughout the city to learn the latest news and read their posters. The formidable organization of the Chinese Communist Party, built up methodically over the decades, had been suddenly overturned and replaced by a communications and organizational network which embraced millions of ordinary citizens in a decision-making apparatus of their own. In the evenings, thousands of mass meetings occurred simultaneously throughout the capital. There, the latest political developments were discussed, analyzed, and acted upon.

Within six months, every wall in Peking was plastered with an outpouring of big-character posters. Hastily constructed fences lined with reed matting flanked the paths and walkways of every organization to provide additional space for the torrent of words and argument. When this space ran out, wires were strung across large dining halls and meeting rooms. As this deluge continued, it grew more sophisticated, and one quickly learned which posters were important and which could be passed by. All were signed by their author or authors, and unwritten rules stipulated how long they must remain before they could be taken down—usually two weeks. Undoubtedly, the traditional veneration of the Chinese for the written word and the fact that in the past it had been a crime to destroy written material—in each community, a man was specifically delegated to dispose ceremonially of all such paper—contributed to the respect shown the big-character posters during the Cultural Revolution. The posters varied in content, length, and style. Some consisted of one sheet of denunciation, affirmation, or analysis; others, twenty-five or thirty consecutive sheets, often containing a detailed history and evaluation of an institution and its leading groups. One or two each week became famous. Everyone talked about them, and many replies were made to the specific arguments of these key documents, which sometimes turned the movement from its previous course.

However, in the early fall of 1966, the movement was not yet off the ground. The spirit of rebellion was just beginning to work its magic in a population of university students who had for years been "the docile tools" of the Party apparatus. Some of the most interesting posters that we were invited to read were designed to foster critical attitudes among the young intellectuals toward old rules and regulations. Of these prods to student independence and initiative, among the most popular were the conversations between Mao Tse-tung and his niece Wang Hai-jung, which she had remembered and released to the public. She had been a student at our school, and one of the conversations with her uncle concerned her life at the Foreign Languages Institute. She had told the Chairman about a young man who did not listen attentively to the teacher's lectures, refused to do homework, read fiction during class, and slept through political reports. In addition, Wang Hai-jung told her uncle, this young man would leave school on Sunday and fail to show up for the scheduled political meetings that evening. Mao replied that students should be allowed to take naps in class, since teachers were often boring:

> "Teachers should lecture less and make the students read more. I believe the student you referred to will be very capable in the future, since he had the courage to absent himself from the Saturday meeting and not return to school on time on Sunday. When you return to the school, you may tell him that it is too early to return to school even at eight or nine in the evening; he may delay it until eleven or twelve."[57]

He further told his niece that, when she returned to school, she should set an example in rebellion and on Sundays shouldn't bother to attend meetings. She replied: "But I don't dare. This is the school system. All students are required to return to school on time. If I don't, people will say that I violate the school system."

Mao informed her that he didn't think she would be very capable in the future. The worst thing that could happen to her, he said, was that she might be expelled from school, but he believed that the authorities should allow students to rebel. After more protest from his niece that, as Chairman Mao's relative, she would be criticized for irresponsibility, the Chairman told her:

> "Look at you! You are afraid of being criticized for arrogance and self-content and for lack of organization and discipline. Why should you be afraid? You can just say that just because you are Chairman Mao's relative,

you should follow his instructions to rebel. I think the student you mentioned will be more capable than you, for he dared to violate the school system. I think you people are all too metaphysical."

At a later stage of the movement, when Wang Hai-jung took an active part in the mass movement in the Foreign Ministry, the ultra-left put up a big-character poster saying, "Mao Tse-tung Says Wang Hai-jung Will Never Amount to Anything," but the majority of the rank and file appreciated her spirit of self-criticism in reporting her conversations with her uncle.

Other unpublished speeches, conversations, and statements by Mao were posted all over the city in those early days. All these hitherto unpublished materials were only the first of a deluge of documents, secret reports, and internal government memoranda that were soon to flood the country, giving the Chinese people the most detailed and comprehensive information on the inner workings of a national political power structure that any people has ever had. Foreign Minister Ch'en Yi objected to the public posting of state secrets, some of which had been purloined from the drawers of high-ranking cadres by their own sons and daughters. But Mao, with his usual imperturbability, thought it couldn't do much harm. Once the door was opened, a long time would pass before it could be closed again. It was, of course, a windfall for the CIA and the swollen bureaucracy of the Hong Kong China-watching establishment, which paid large sums for Red Guard newspapers and leaflets smuggled out of China.

With all of the cries to destroy the four "olds," the early days of the Cultural Revolution were not without a sense of history, but the history with which the young Red Guards concerned themselves was the history of a revolution and, not surprisingly, with the living symbol of the Chinese Revolution, Mao Tse-tung. One crisp autumn afternoon, a few of our teacher friends asked if we would like to read a particularly interesting *ta-tzu-pao* pasted up on the exterior walls of the students' dining room. The students' side of the campus, which had been locked off during the previous summer, was now decorated with *ta-tzu-pao* as if for some surrealist carnival. We met students and teachers we knew. Their hands stuffed deep into the pockets of their padded jackets, chins buried in their wool scarves, they stood in the cold afternoon air reading soberly. They smiled and waved as we went by, but were not diverted from the seriousness of their occupation.

We stopped by the bulletin boards and "clothes lines" to read some of the controversy concerning the Institute, then we moved on to a huge, multi-paged poster which covered two adjoining walls. There were perhaps twenty people reading in the cold shadow of the walls, but they made room for a few more. We did our best to take notes with gloved hands as our friends began to read. According to the *ta-tzu-pao*, a group of Peking Red Guards had travelled to the region of Hunan Province, where relatives of Mao and his first wife, Yang K'ai-hui, still lived. They had asked them about the early lives of these legendary figures and brought their story back to the universities of Peking.

The story began with the young Mao Tse-tung's relationship with his Hunan Normal School professor, Yang Ch'ang-chi. Professor Yang, although a particularly distinguished scholar, was not unlike a number of intellectuals teaching in Hunan in the period between the 1911 Revolution and the May 4 Movement of 1919. Educated first in the Chinese classics, he had then studied in both Japan and Europe, and was thus well acquainted with both Western and Chinese thought. Like other progressive scholars, he was seeking the answer to China's dilemma. He reportedly said that if he could but find and train two great Chinese leaders, he would have made his contribution to saving China. One of the students he found was a serious young man of peasant background named Mao Tse-tung, who was soon included in the Sunday lunch and study group, where the professor discussed philosophy and the problems of the time with his best students. One of the other members of the group was Yang's daughter, Yang K'ai-hui.

Yang Ch'ang-chi believed not only in training the minds of his students, but their bodies as well; for he foresaw, at least in the abstract, the tests to which these political leaders would be put. So it was under his influence that Mao took daily morning baths in icy well water, tramped for days through the countryside eating the simple food he bought from the peasants, and studied his lessons in the din of the market place in order to train his powers of concentration. When the Yang family moved to Peking, Yang Ch'ang-chi's best student followed. While Mao was working in the library of Peking University, his old professor died. The young Mao helped the family collect money for the funeral and remained close to them during their period of bereavement. It came as no surprise when he and Yang K'ai-hui announced their intent to marry. Theirs was very much a modern marriage, a love match, not a traditional arranged marriage. Marriage was a subject of passionate interest to all young Chinese intellectuals of the period. Some of Mao's earliest political essays published in Hunan were written on the "woman question" and its inseparability from the tragedy of the arranged marriage. His marriage to Yang K'ai-hui is sometimes referred to as his second marriage, because as a young boy, his parents had arranged a marriage in traditional peasant fashion with a girl a number of years older than he. The marriage was never consummated, however, for in one of his youthful rebellions, the young Mao Tse-tung ran away from home and threatened never to return if his parents did not call off the marriage. They did.

Soon after their marriage, Mao and Yang K'ai-hui returned to Hunan. During this period, Mao organized workers' schools while serving as principal of a primary school attached to the Hunan Normal School, his alma mater, and did the pioneer organization of the peasants' associations. Yang K'ai-hui did political work alongside him, particularly among women. Sons were born. The *ta-tzu-pao* told of three. The official story in the precisely replicated model of the young family's Changsha home mentions two. When, several years later, we visited that home, the pictures on the wall and the careful account came alive for us from the popularized stories of the Cultural Revolution. The photographs were startlingly romantic, the couple movingly handsome. Within only a few years, Mao, photographed as a gowned intellectual with hair to his shoulders, would be in the mountains of Chingkangshan organizing his peasant army. From the very beginning, there was a price on his head. Yang K'ai-hui, at home in Hunan struggling to care for the children and continue the work she and her husband had begun, was given no peace. Finally taken prisoner by the KMT in 1929, she was tortured, while her older son was forced to watch, and at last beheaded.

The rest of the *ta-tzu-pao's* story was of the children. The aunt who took them under her care was constantly threatened by the authorities. Other relatives told her she was mad to take responsibility for children who would bring nothing but tragedy to those connected with them. She held on to them tenaciously, however, and continued to protect them until she was contacted by representatives of the underground Communist Party. They told her to deliver the children to a secret meeting place in Shanghai, where they would be taken to a school for the children of the young revolution's cadres. The connections were safely made, the children placed in the protection of the school, and it seemed that the years of agony for the small boys were ended at last. But the political fury of the times permitted them only a slight respite. The school was discovered by the KMT, violently broken up, and the children, according to the story of the *ta-tzu-pao,* "driven into the streets."

It is here that the story of the youngest child ends. According to the account the Red Guards brought back to Peking, he was smuggled out of the city and left with a peasant family. In later years, after decades of war and revolution, that family, like thousands of other families, had disappeared from the face of China. Perhaps this accounts for the discrepancy between the official story of Mao's children and the verbal stories of the Cultural Revolution. The youngest child's existence seems to have been incorporated into popular legend, for we remember hearing somewhere that he had finally been discovered, a man in his forties, working obscurely as a commune accountant. But this, too, may be apocryphal. The two older boys lived on the streets of Shanghai, begging, like thousands of the abandoned children of that fearsome city. At some point, they found refuge in a deserted temple, where they posted a sign saying, "We tell stories—one penny." Finally, they sold newspapers. It was during this period that one of them was said to have posted an anti-imperialist slogan on a lamp post and was beaten by a policeman. He suffered brain damage from which he never recovered.

When the two boys were finally found by the underground Party, they were sent to the Soviet Union, the older one to school and the younger to be hospitalized. It was in this world that they spent the long years of China's revolution. After the victory of 1949, the older son returned to China and to his father. He was, of course, fluent in Russian and became a translator; but it was only a short time before the new China was fighting a war in Korea. Mao's older son volunteered and was killed there. The younger son, who had long been institutionalized, was finally judged well enough to come home and live a quiet life with the aunt who had cared for him as a young child. But, just as the plans were complete, the aunt died, and her nephew suffered another mental breakdown. The story ends here. It is no doubt in reference to this son that P'eng Teh-huai's personal attacks upon Mao at the Lushan Conference included insults about his mad son.

Even when read in the lengthening shadows of an autumn afternoon from ragged poster paper on a brick wall, the story was enormously affecting, and the mood of the readers became increasingly somber as they moved from one sheet of the text to the next. Mao's role in relationship to the Chinese people could have been characterized in a number of ways: as revolutionary hero, philosopher-king, emperor-poet, or Buddha. But the tales of his personal tragedies had not been a part of the popular body of legend and story. In contrast to the cult of personality and his role as the "red sun," the cultural revolutionaries' search for their own history, embodied as they saw it in Mao, brought to the people a thousand such personal stories and anecdotes. His tragedies were the tragedies suffered in one way or another by millions of Chinese families through the decades of war, and the young Chinese of the peaceful post-1949 period now associated themselves with this individual and national suffering: "Every revolutionary must make sacrifices," the *ta-tzu-pao* said. It was the making of sacrifices for which the Chairman told them their generation now must also prepare.

The first to respond were the middle school students, who answered Chairman Mao's call for rebellion with an alacrity astounding to their elders. The outside world read the startling news of the young armies appearing on China's streets with wonder and alarm. Shouts of *"tsao-fan yu-li"* (Rebellion is justified!) resounded in every middle school in Peking. Two of our teenage sons found themselves swept into the currents of the youth rebellion at Peking University's Middle School. Chairman Mao himself had praised their classmate, P'eng Hsiao-meng, at the first great youth rally for being one of China's first young rebels. Most of the students from the middle school had taken the bicycle ride to Peking University to read the *ta-tzu-pao* there and had returned to their own school to emulate the attack on the school administration by the older students. But the complicated business of sorting out revisionism in the middle school authority structure was soon abandoned for the more exciting task of taking to the streets, where the real revolution might be found.

And so, by the thousands, they marched to ferret out hidden landlords, Kuomintang agents, and bad elements. The youngsters proudly changed the feudal names of ancient streets and shops, even though everyone continued to call them by the familiar names. One contingent actually suggested that red traffic lights should mean "go" rather than "stop," but after a talk with the Premier they agreed with him that perhaps it was not a practical proposal. It was these first creators of the "tremendous mess" that the Western press chose to represent as the essence of Red Guardism, labeling the movement a modern version of the medieval "Children's Crusade." Yet, despite some of their early and ludicrous excesses, the teenage Red Guards did succeed in unearthing a surprising number of old land deeds, KMT flags, bars of gold, and machine guns hidden by opponents of socialism living in urban obscurity while they awaited the return of Chiang Kai-shek and the victory of the counter-revolution. These trophies were promptly put on exhibit for the education of the rest of the population and hundreds of thousands came to take a look. The young masses were now in the process of educating themselves, and the Chairman, as an experienced revolutionary leader, understood that the first requirement of a people's movement is that it must move, and that premature criticisms by the leadership might halt it. Some of these early young rebels and their nationally prominent leaders would turn into elitist leaders before long, but no one during those early days thought of questioning their revolutionary spirit.

Peking seethed with revolutionary exuberance in that golden autumn of 1966. The lawfully proclaimed Red Guard organizations made full use of their rights to demonstrate in the streets. They marched in endless columns, their ubiquitous silk flags shining in the northern sun. Newspapers and revolutionary proclamations, published by mass organizations at government expense, were hawked on the street corners by the young activists. Rumors concerning the struggle among the top leaders of the country passed rapidly throughout the city and added to the general excitement and revolutionary élan. Everyone heard the story of an attempted February 1966 coup by P'eng Chen and Lo Jui-ch'ing. Lin Piao, it was said, had surrounded the city with troops loyal to Chairman Mao and had cancelled the orders for the divisions that had been instructed to seize the city. Transcripts of Lin Piao's May speech to the Central Committee warning of possible coup attempts by enemies of Chairman Mao passed from hand to hand and were eagerly read by thousands of ordinary citizens.[58]

By late September, massive numbers of "traveling" Red Guards from all over the country were arriving in the city daily, complicating what was already an extraordinary outburst of mass activity. The *"Ch'uan-lien"* (literally, to exchange experience) was one of the great social inventions of the Cultural Revolution. Young rebels on "Long Marches" and extensive travels throughout the vast country spread the revolutionary fever to all sections of the population. Free transportation for any who wished to travel in the name of the revolution soon preempted the country's railway network. The economic cost may have been heavy, but the youth in their millions came into contact with the larger society. Within a few months, these travelers, carrying their little red books, bedrolls strapped to their backs, penetrated every nook and cranny of China. Many learned more than they taught, and, despite some irritation at youthful intrusion into the ordinary workaday life of the adult population, the young Red Guards, at least in the early stages of the Cultural Revolution, were received with warmth and encouragement by the Chinese citizenry.

The population of Peking, spurred by Premier Chou's personal concern for the welfare of the crowds of visitors, saw to it that food, clothing, shelter, and medical care were provided for the youngsters who poured into the revolutionary Mecca to catch a glimpse of "the reddest sun" himself. It seemed as if every resident of the city was engaged in preparing the traditional northern steamed buns to feed the young pilgrims of the Cultural Revolution. Everywhere on the gray walls of the city was to be seen the famous quote from Chairman Mao: "The world is yours, as well as ours, but in the last analysis, it is yours. You young people, full of vigor and vitality, are in the prime of life, like the sun at eight or nine in the morning. All hopes are placed on you."[59] Mao Tse-tung had succeeded in tapping the roots of rebellion among the nation's youth. That elixir of revolution, that feeling of ordinary people that they are making history, had taken hold.

The famous mass meetings where the Chairman met with a million or so Red Guards in T'ien An Men originally had the purpose of mobilizing the youth. Soon such meetings became a necessity. Despite repeated instructions from the central leadership that the young people from afar could not remain in Peking and must return to their home provinces, the visitors refused to leave until they had seen Chairman Mao. No sooner had a million boarded the outgoing trains after their meeting with the Chairman than another million would arrive. When the giant square of the revolution could no longer contain the flood, Mao rode throughout the city in a jeep and so accommodated the hopes of 2 or more million youngsters at one stroke.

Observers in the West, who shuddered at the thought of turning the youth loose on any country, failed to realize that, in the long run, the march of the Chinese youth during the 1960's contributed to the unity of a nation which had long been geographically fragmented. The experience of the wandering Red Guards helped to undermine the parochial notions characteristic of a people just emerging from a past shaped by the peasant village. How many times had we urged our own students to seek out the museums and parks of Peking on a Sunday and how many times had they decided against venturing out of the school gates? Many of them had turned the walls of their universities into new villages. It seemed that only their Chairman was able to convince them to go out into the larger world in order to learn that all of China was their home.

We were surprised, but should not have been, at some of the retrograde social forms emerging from the new revolution. Our two sons came home one day from Peita Fu Chung (Peking University Middle School) to inform us with some indignation that a number of the students at their school, sons and daughters of the nation's elite, had themselves formed an exclusive organization. Called the Lien Tung (United Action), this group was organized by the offspring of senior military officers and national Party officials. Restricted membership in United Action was determined by the "five reds," meaning that only the children of workers, poor peasants, Party cadres, Army men, or revolutionary martyrs were eligible to join. Needless to say, the sons and daughters of workers and peasants, a decided minority in the organization, were not the ones who either led or set the policy of United Action. The "five reds" concept was in essence a feudal blood line test adapted to the conditions of revolutionary China, and the organization which adopted it soon exuded an arrogance formerly associated with the Kuomintang.

Military in organization and style, the Lien Tung rapidly created a hierarchical command system which separated the commanders, who wore silk arm bands, from the rank-and-file soldiers, who wore cotton ones. According to our sons, who, like the majority of students, had naturally been excluded from the organization, the Lien Tung leaders and many of its members possessed large sums of money presumably obtained from their parents. For a few months in the fall of 1966, the United Action, by virtue of its superior discipline and organization, usurped the leadership of the Peking middle school Red Guard movement and attempted to arrogate to itself the sole right to act in the name of the revolution. Utilizing brutality and violence, this numerically small organization was soon exposed as a "conservative" organization mirroring the efforts of senior Party officials to control Mao's new revolution. This ugly phenomenon, which we had not dreamed could exist in the China we had come to know, served to substantiate Mao's assertion that elitism existed in important sectors of China's youth. It was indeed empirical evidence that the old exploiting mentality which remained entrenched in high circles in the Party, if not checked, could result in the transformation of a revolutionary party into a fascist party. P'eng Hsiao-meng, the young woman who pinned the Red Guard arm band on Mao at the historic August youth rally, became a leader of the Lien Tung at our sons' school, and before long they would be attending "struggle meetings" against her. Within six months, the United Action was outlawed as a counterrevolutionary organization, one of the few so designated. Its leaders were placed under arrest for a short period of time and then released.

The students at our Institute debated the theory of "natural redness" all during the long summer and early fall of 1966. They argued fiercely over the validity of the saying propagated by the conservative Red Guards: "If the father is revolutionary, the son is a hero, and if the father is a reactionary, the son is a bad egg." This concept came to be known as the "T'an Li-fu Line," named for the young Red Guard who was Chairman of the Cultural Revolution Preparatory Committee at the Peking Industrial Institute. T'an, the son of the Deputy Procurator of the State Council, became famous for his advocacy of the struggle of the "five red categories" against the "five black categories" (bourgeoisie, landlords, rich peasants, counterrevolutionaries, and bad elements). Leadership of the Cultural Revolution in the early days was monopolized by the sons and daughters of high officials. Nepotism, that old scourge of traditional Chinese politics, rooted as it was in the powerful Chinese family structure, continued throughout the course of the movement. It was a practice not only among the anti-Mao forces, but the Mao forces as well. Just as the wife of Liu Shao-ch'i became a political force on Liu's side, the wives of Mao Tse-tung and Lin Piao also rose to positions of national leadership in the all-out struggle for power. The rule that when the husband went down, the wife went with him, operated with statistical regularity. However, the Maoists firmly opposed the theory of "natural redness." Ch'en Po-ta, the nationally recognized leader, deriving his power from the Cultural Group and its assignment to formulate policy and directives for the orientation of the mass movement, proposed rephrasing the saying about the sons of revolutionaries and the sons of bad eggs into: "If one's father is a revolutionary, his son should try hard to be a hero, and if one's father is a reactionary, his son should rebel." Realizing that the "five red" categories were being utilized as a device by the Party conservatives to exclude the masses and potential rebels from politics, the Mao forces denounced this theory as a feudal legacy.

Nevertheless, for a long time, the theory of blood and class origin served to split the mass ranks despite repeated pronouncements that this was an erroneous and potentially counterrevolutionary theory. Long after the demise of the Lien Tung, Lin Piao and other leaders were still attempting to counter the ideology of the theory of "natural redness." Lin placed the emphasis for the determination of who was to be considered a revolutionary on "performance." At the beginning of the Cultural Revolution, he said in one speech that the theory of blood relationships and parental origins had split the revolutionary youth, "causing them to look at one another from a great distance on the two banks of the heavenly river and almost leading to the premature death of the movement." He then stated definitively, "All our youths, of whatever origin, should enjoy equal treatment."[60]

The movement of the middle school Red Guards was soon played out, as the great majority of the students, including one of our own sons, deserted their schools to embark on long marches to distant provinces and revolutionary shrines. It was in the universities that the real mass politics of the Cultural Revolution began to evolve. During the period immediately following the withdrawal of the work-teams, the school Party organization attempted to continue the policies of the work-teams in everything except name. Although the work-team had been withdrawn, its spirit and influence lingered on. The school Cultural Revolution Committee, made up of "responsible" Party members and, in fact, a creature of the work-team, continued to follow what soon came to be known as the "bourgeois reactionary line." Instead of directing attacks against "those persons in the Party in authority taking the capitalist road," the Cultural Revolution Committee still concentrated its efforts against the "bourgeois academic authorities" and so-called counterrevolutionaries among the masses.

We were invited one day to a "struggle meeting" organized by the Cultural Revolutionary Committee against three of our former colleagues labeled as "bourgeois academic authorities." The meeting was led by young teachers and older students whom we recognized as stalwarts of the school Party bureaucracy. They ruled over a tribunal which was distinguished by its atmosphere of grim self-righteousness. After a few rather perfunctory and uninspired speeches on the necessity of the Great Proletarian Cultural Revolution, the three academic "monsters" were led down the center aisle, between the seats of the assembled students and teachers, to the front, where they were forced to mount three stools and stand with heads bowed facing the audience. Two were Party members. Two we knew very well; all had for many years been leading professors in the English Department. One of the targets was indeed a remarkable man. The scion of an old and wealthy Chinese family, he had done his graduate work in English literature at the University of Chicago. He had also worked as a translator for the Chinese People's Volunteers in Korea, and as an interpreter on Chou En-lai's staff at the 1954 Geneva Conference on Indochina. In 1965, at the age of fifty, he spent six months with others from our Institute in barren Shansi Province helping to direct the Socialist Education movement in the countryside. He was an active and apparently dedicated Communist Party member, but the question raised against him was whether a man with such an upper-class background should have been admitted to the Party in the first place. The whole charge was just another version of the blood line theory then causing havoc throughout the city.

It seemed to us that our colleague stood on his stool with a great deal of composure while under attack for his class background, a factor hardly new, since neither he nor anyone else had ever made a secret of it. His skill as a master calligrapher, a product of his privileged past, had often been eagerly sought by anyone in the school in need of perfectly brushed characters on documents or scrolls. We would learn later that the attitude of many at that meeting coincided

with our own, which was that this attack was a diversion
from more serious issues. Unfortunately, although the majority of students and teachers did not really believe that
this man was an enemy, an active minority continued to
consider him one for the duration of the Cultural Revolution. In the terminology of the period, he was "set aside,"
that is, his case was left to be determined later. During those
long years when he was exiled to gardening chores around the
school, he remained cheerful and in good health, read all the
big-character posters, and continued to maintain an unflag-
ging interest in the politics of the day despite his position as
a political pariah. At the end of the movement, he was fully
reinstated, apparently none the worse for wear; and, in
1974, we had a pleasant visit with our former colleague as
he was passing through San Francisco as a member of a
delegation of Chinese linguists touring the United States on
a professional visit.

The other academic "enemy," standing with fists clenched
and face contorted with ill-concealed rage, embodied a
more complex political question. Having studied and taught
at Oxford, he was an established scholar of English literature, and upon returning to China in the 1950's, had been
given the post of Dean of the Institute's English Department. There was no doubt that he had hoped to turn this
language school into an Oxford of the Far East nor that he
had succeeded for a time, with the help of others, in establishing a curriculum of English classics and formal grammar
beyond the ken of most students not from bourgeois backgrounds. But the facts were that this orientation had been
thoroughly rejected by 1964. This non-Party professor was
no longer the dean, and he had recently worked well with
the new program by volunteering to teach first-year students,
most of whom were peasants. No longer in a position of
power and possessing little authority, if he were, in fact, taking the capitalist road, he might find it a little difficult to
march down it all by himself.

At this meeting, he was accused of having once been an
officer of the Kuomintang, but this, too, had been known for

years and thoroughly aired during the anti-rightist campaign of the 1950's. Reworking the evidence of previous movements was not the pathbreaking direction called for by the Great Proletarian Cultural Revolution, and surely these men were not the main targets of a movement designed to remove those in the Party in power taking the capitalist road. The meeting left a bad taste in our mouths.

Within a few months, it would be clear that it had indeed been a diversion designed by those who wished to protect the status quo at the Institute. The masses at the school, having "educated themselves," would soon reject this bureaucratic style of work. The Cultural Revolution Committees were dissolved, and those Party members who had been loyal to the work-teams, seeking to preserve their reputations in the new circumstances, set up their own mass "rebel" organizations. These were quickly labeled "royalist" organizations by the rebels and were soon discredited.

Formation of mass rebel organizations proceeded in stages. Once students recognized their rights to form revolutionary organizations, both students and teachers got together in small groups on the basis of friendship, mutual interest, or academic departments. By the fall of 1966, more than seventy separate revolutionary organizations were established at Peking University, and the situation was more or less the same in other schools. Within one to four months, however, these small factions coalesced into two or sometimes three major mass rebel organizations.

All during the fall and early winter of 1966, the national argument centered on the wrong policies initiated by the work-teams and whether or not those who opposed those policies constituted the real revolutionaries representing Chairman Mao's "proletarian revolutionary line." Those who had supported the work-teams were soon to find themselves having to account for that support. The issue was more or less settled, at least in theory, by November 1, with the publication of the famous No. 14 editorial in *Red Flag*, "Victory for the Proletarian Revolutionary Line Represented by Chairman Mao."

We were invited by a group of young teachers to study the editorial with them and for the first time began to understand fully what the struggle of the preceding months had been all about. The young teachers were quite elated that the editorial confirmed the position they had been taking for months. Even after the work-teams had been withdrawn, the mass of the Party members still clung stubbornly to the line that the real enemies were those non-Party members trying to usurp the leadership of the movement and pick its targets. Some of our friends, who had been attacked by the work-teams as being anti-Party and forced to make self-criticisms, naturally felt vindicated by the withdrawal of the teams. They, in turn, were quick to criticize those students and teachers who had supported the reactionary line of the work-team sent to the First Foreign Languages Institute. *Red Flag* No. 14 agreed that the real rebels had been correct: "The struggle between the two lines has all along centered on the question of one's stand and attitude toward the masses." In the past, rectification movements had been led by the Party, and the Party leadership in each unit, not the masses, had determined who would be the targets of attack. A few of our friends had had the audacity to suggest that the First Party Secretary of the school and other leading Party cadres deserved criticism, and now it was clear that Chairman Mao agreed with them. According to the editorial, the proletarian revolutionary line represented by Chairman Mao called for trusting the masses, relying on the masses, respecting their initiative and "allowing them to educate and liberate themselves." In other words, the movement was not to be guided by elite Party members in the old way but allowed to proceed on its own course. The bourgeois reactionary line was defined thus:

> "Certain representative personages who have put forward this line are against the masses educating themselves. In dealing with the masses, they resorted to 'tutelage' practiced by the Kuomintang; they treat the masses as if they were ignorant and incapable and look upon themselves as men of wisdom and resourcefulness;

they suppress the masses and stifle their initiative; they
shift the targets of attack and direct their spearhead
against the revolutionary masses, branding them as
'counterrevolutionaries,' 'anti-Party elements,' 'Rightists,' 'pseudo-revolutionaries,' 'pseudo-leftists but genuine
rightists,' and so forth."[61]

As each sentence was read, there were loud exclamations
and interruptions while either students or teachers listed the
names and actions of school associates who had committed
the exact errors listed by the editorial as constituting the
"bourgeois reactionary line." The editorial admitted that "a
great amount of work is needed before the evil influence of
the bourgeois reactionary line can be eradicated." Moreover, it was stated, this line "had a certain audience inside
the Party, because there exists the handful of persons who
are in power and are taking the capitalist road, and who
regard this erroneous line as their protective talisman." Another reason given for the power and persistence of the
erroneous line was that "a considerable number of muddleheaded people inside the Party whose world outlook has not
been remolded" follow it. In fact, these "muddleheaded people" appeared to make up a majority of the Party leaders
and members in most organizations. "Muddlehead" became
a favorite word among the rank and file in our Institute.
However, the more serious implication of the appearance of
the bourgeois reactionary line rested on the fact that the
Chinese Communist Party as an organization would not, or
could not, lead the Cultural Revolution on the local mass
level of action. The mass uprising had brought the people
into collision with the Party apparatus.

The result of the *Red Flag* editorial was the collapse of
the conservative and "royalist" organizations which had
acted as surrogates for the work-teams. All now rushed to
join any rebel group which would accept them and thus
remove the stain of the bourgeois reactionary line. True conversion to the rebel spirit was often hampered by the conservative label which was attached to those who had supported the work-teams and their reign of "white terror." A

sizeable section of the young Party members were now attracted to ultra-left positions to compensate for past errors.

At the beginning of the movement, the conservative Red Guard organizations had set up exclusive citywide coordinating centers called the First and Second Red Guard Headquarters. Since September, the radical Red Guards had set up the Third Headquarters. By November, this center had become the most powerful rebel apparatus in Peking. Premier Chou and the Cultural Revolution Group gave full support to the Third Headquarters and established direct connections with it. The Maoist forces were at last creating a network to oppose the old Party organization now working in a clandestine manner and supported by individual Party cadres' instinct for self-preservation. Red Guards from the First and Second Headquarters, viewing with alarm the ascendency of the new and powerful Third Headquarters, complained bitterly that Premier Chou and the Cultural Group were refusing to deal with them and were, in fact, discriminating against them. They were right. Bypassed and isolated, the First and Second Headquarters by the end of the year had lost all their former influence.

The real politics of the movement began to unfold once the guidelines were at last clearly understood by the majority of participants. By the closing months of 1966, the political interests of various groups fighting for power were hidden under a cloak of left phraseology. The new opposition was labeled as "those who wave the red flag to oppose the red flag and use Mao Tse-tung's Thought to oppose Mao Tse-tung's Thought." By definition, the Cultural Revolution was a left social movement. All groups, if they hoped to survive, had to pronounce allegiance to the same social goals.

By December, the great majority of rank-and-file participants in the great movement had come to understand the meaning of the "bourgeois reactionary line." It was clear that that line had been designed to protect the old Party cadres by directing the attack against the masses rather than upon "those in the Party taking the capitalist road." But the masses were slower to realize that the opposition to Mao had taken a new form, one that later was to be labeled as "left in form, but right in essence." The old Party apparatus and its multi-million membership was suspended, but those members had melted into the mass movement and, behind the scenes, experienced and skilled Party cadres, trained by decades of mass movements, took advantage of every new directive from Chairman Mao's Headquarters to manipulate the mass organizations in their own interest. At the end of the year, the *Red Flag,* in a new editorial, warned that "our Party will not allow anyone to attack the revolutionary masses or bombard the proletarian command posts under the pretext of 'opposing the bourgeois reactionary line.' "[62] The opposition was once again accusing the revolutionaries of following the wrong line! In many units, according to the new editorial, the spearhead of struggle was being directed "not against the handful of persons within the Party who were in authority and were taking the capitalist road, but against the revolutionary left." Oppositional forces were proving themselves adept at "hoodwinking the masses" and "inciting one section of the masses to fight against another." Since every organization considered itself the true left, the problem remained of how to determine which was the real left and which the false.

There had been no method whereby Mao or any other national leader could have divined beforehand the actual power of the old bureaucracy or the tactics that would be used to obstruct the mass movement in order to protect the holders of power. As was his practice, Mao learned to swim by swimming and directed revolution by allowing it to proceed under its own momentum. Mao recognized, however, the inherent difficulty of conducting revolutionary politics under the leadership of those who had already achieved power through a successful revolution. After observing the unique politics of the Cultural Revolution for some time, the Chairman observed:

> "In the past, we fought North and South; it was easy to fight such wars. For the enemy was obvious. The

present Great Proletarian Cultural Revolution is much more difficult than that kind of war. The problem is that those who commit ideological errors are all mixed up with those whose contradiction with us is one between ourselves and the enemy, and for a time it is hard to sort them out."[63]

In many areas it proved impossible to sort them out, and the definition of the enemy was to change more than once before the movement was over. In the end, even some of the most prominent leaders of the movement were consumed by the fires they had lit.

We were told that after a period of extremely complex factional struggle in the Cultural Revolution, someone had asked Mao how one determined which side is correct. He had replied, "The side that wins." This was reminiscent of Napoleon's remark on great military battles: "You commit yourself and then you see." But the remark reflected more than sheer pragmatism; it stemmed from Mao's belief that new ideas need testing in practice. He wrote in his essay "Where Do Correct Ideas Come From?" (published in 1963) that in social struggle, "the forces representing the advanced class sometimes suffer defeat, not because their ideas are incorrect, but because, in the balance of forces engaged in struggle, they are not as powerful for the time being as the forces of reaction; they are therefore temporarily defeated, but they are bound to triumph sooner or later."

The Chinese genius for political infighting, acquired from a 1,000-year-old dedication to the art of bureaucratic politics, added to the complexity of a widespread struggle for power in thousands of organizational units. Describing the tactics of his opponents in classical literary terms, the Chairman warned his followers of the cunning of the opposition and what they must expect:

"When in a predicament, those who represent the exploiting classes usually resort to the tactic of attack as a means of defense, to preserve themselves today so as to grow tomorrow. In short, they are always considering what tactics to use against us and 'spy out the land,' in order to employ their tactics successfully. Sometimes they play possum waiting for a chance to counter-attack."[64]

These "serpents," asserted Mao, infesting "most of China, big or small, black or white, baring their poisonous fangs or assuming the guise of beautiful girls, are not yet frozen by the cold, although they sense the threat of winter." Such descriptions might have come from the *Romance of the Three Kingdoms* or from the chronicles of the great dynasties.

The First Foreign Languages Institute in Peking was a microcosm of the larger movement. Functioning as a key unit in the Foreign Ministry complex (Wai Chiao Pu), this large university stood at the base of a crucial organizational structure led by Foreign Minister Ch'en Yi under the direct supervision of Premier Chou En-lai. Moreover, Chairman Mao always maintained a special interest in foreign affairs, and what went on in the Foreign Ministry was of special concern to him. The fate of the rebel organizations in the First Foreign Languages Institute was directly related to the struggle among key national leaders for control of the Foreign Ministry. We found ourselves situated in the eye of the hurricane. It would take many years before the power equation in our Institute was finally determined, and then it would reflect the final settlement of the struggle among the highest leaders in the nation.

Hung-ch'i Ta-tui (Red Flag Battalion) embraced the overwhelming majority of students in our school and quickly assumed leadership of the Cultural Revolution during the early fall of 1966. The June 16 Independent Rebel Corps, often signing its posters 6-1-6, contained about 100 members, who followed an ultra-left line during the whole course of the Cultural Revolution. Opposed to Premier Chou En-lai from the very beginning, June 16 was led by Liu Ling-k'ai, an early rebel and young firebrand who was to become notorious as an ultra-leftist. June 16 was very successful in winning over a number of the workers in the school. These included some of the cooks, including the master chef from our dining room, groundsmen, and drivers. We attended only a few of its meetings, because it soon became an extremely closed and secretive organization devoted to clandestine research on the Premier and other leaders of the State Council. Their public meetings often were for the purpose of publicizing some alleged or real atrocity perpetrated against individuals claimed to have been victims of the bourgeois power holders. These meetings were extremely grim and military in nature, with each speaker formally saluting the portrait of Chairman Mao with his back to the audience before proceeding to speak. The affinity between rightist organizations like Lien Tung and the ultra-left June 16 was startling. Similar behavior on the part of participants attracted to the two political poles of the Cultural Revolution was a phenomenon appearing with remarkable consistency throughout the course of the great rebellion.

The Red Flag Battalion, on the other hand, was informal and lively in style and reflected its mass character. As the leading rebel body in the school, it took up as its first order of business the criticism of the work-team and its "bourgeois reactionary line." Rebels who had been denounced by the work-team as "anti-Party elements" and "counterrevolutionaries" were rehabilitated. These victims were now acclaimed as heroes and received the proud designation of "early rebels," an honor due only to a minority of cultural revolutionaries. Those who followed the line of the work-team were in turn denounced and had to admit their mistake of line and orientation. "Royalists" who had collected "black materials" (incriminating dossiers) on the rebels were forced to turn over this material, and much of it was publicly burned before the cheering masses. After protracted negotiations with Premier Chou, the rebels succeeded in forcing the return of the withdrawn work-team to undergo criticism for its erroneous line. Liu Hsien-ch'üan, Vice Foreign Minister, head of the work-team, and veteran of the Long March, came back for a long stay at the Institute under circumstances quite different from those under which he and his team had arrived at the beginning of the summer. We were invited to attend a mass criticism meeting against him and, with the rest of the faculty and students, filed into the largest meeting hall in the school to witness an interesting drama.

For the first time, we were able to see the historic confrontation between the new youth and the Party organization. In this case, the Party was represented by one man with a flawless revolutionary record who had become a symbol of bureaucracy. The atmosphere of this meeting contrasted sharply with the grim discipline and obedient passivity of the "struggle meeting" conducted by the Party stalwarts against the academics some months earlier. For once, we "honored foreign guests" were welcomed to sit anonymously on the floor in the very back of the auditorium among the youthful, militant, exuberant mass of students and teachers who at last were running something by themselves. As the young rebel leaders, wearing the red arm bands of their organization, conferred in small groups at the front of the hall, adjusted microphones, and arranged their crimson banners, flags, and slogans on the stage, the audience chatted, joked, and exchanged rumors and ideas. Humor livened an atmosphere of overall purposefulness.

Finally, the meeting was called to order by a handsome and dynamic young man who proved proficient both as an orator and parliamentarian. Quotes from Mao on the mass line were read, everyone joined in revolutionary songs, slogans were shouted, and then the main purpose of the meeting was at hand. Liu Hsien-ch'üan, Vice Foreign Minister and head of the work-team, was escorted to the stage amid the absolute silence of the audience. Liu was a formidable figure, whose huge head sat like a rock on his stocky frame. He stood in the middle of the stage with his legs apart and his arms clasped behind him, facing the crowd with an unflinching gaze. One had the impression from the beginning that he thought that, whatever might be forthcoming, it could not be any worse than the Long March. A series of young men and women then began to read over the microphone an indictment and bill of particulars against the work-team and its record in the Institute. It was a factual presentation quite accurately detailing the persecution of the rebels, the locking of the school gates in early June, the protection of the senior Party officials in the school from just criticism, and other "crimes" which had, in effect, derailed the mass movement. After each charge was read and enlarged on, the audience would shout, "Down with the bourgeois reactionary line!", "Long live Chairman Mao's proletarian revolutionary line!" and other appropriate slogans. When the indictment of the work-team's activity had been presented, a new prosecutor took over the microphone and directed questions to Liu Hsien-ch'üan.

"Who was responsible for the policy adopted by the work-team?" Liu, standing like a bull in an arena, replied, "I was responsible." "Didn't Foreign Minister Ch'en Yi supervise the work-team and its policy?" Liu answered without a blink, "Ch'en Yi sent the work-team, but I was responsible for its policy." Despite every effort to force from Liu the admission that Ch'en Yi was ultimately responsible for the mistakes made by the team, he did not budge from his position that he alone was responsible for all the mistakes flowing from an incorrect orientation and that he was willing to account for them. He said that he had conducted a reactionary policy because, over the years, he had become separated from the masses and did not understand Chairman Mao's Thought well enough.

The Vice Foreign Minister remained at the school for some weeks while the masses spent hundreds of hours "correcting the orientation" of the movement and exposing the bureaucratic work style of the Party. In the 1970's, after we had returned to the United States, we read that Liu Hsien-ch'üan had been appointed China's Ambassador to the Soviet Union. Remembering the formidable figure standing alone as the shouts of "Down with the bourgeois reactionary line!" washed over his head, we felt that a tough man had been chosen for a tough job.

During that tumultuous autumn, the Red Flag Battalion set up an exhibit depicting the history of the two-line struggle in the school since the beginning of the Cultural Revolution. Premier Chou En-lai came to see it. After his inspection, he objected to some of the material containing harsh attacks on Foreign Minister Ch'en Yi. After the objectionable material had been removed and other leaflets and documents relating to the formation of the Red Flag Battalion had been added, the Premier suggested that the exhibit be sent on a tour throughout the country for the education of the masses outside Peking. At this point, an argument broke out among the student rebel leaders over whether or not the exhibit truthfully portrayed the history of struggle in the Institute. One faction asserted that, as it now stood, the exhibit constituted a whitewash of Foreign Minister Ch'en Yi, who had overall responsibility for the bourgeois reactionary line in the Institute and the work-team which had carried it out. When no agreement could be reached, the anti-Ch'en Yi faction withdrew their own materials from the exhibit, thus destroying its effectiveness. As a result of these and other disagreements, the Battalion split as some of the early rebel leaders swiftly set up a new organization called the Red Flag Rebel Detachment (Hung-ch'i Tsao-fan T'uan). It denounced the old Hung-c'hi as conservative, denounced Foreign Minister Ch'en Yi and the head of the work-team Liu Hsien-ch'üan as enemies who should be overthrown, and began an internecine struggle which would not end until the Cultural Revolution itself faded into history.

Chairman Mao's headquarters, referred to by all as the "Proletarian Headquarters," consisted of the Chairman, Lin Piao, Premier Chou, and the thirteen-member Cultural Group. By attacking Premier Chou, the Rebel Battalion had come into conflict with one of the members of the "Proletarian Headquarters." Within six months, the Rebel Battalion would be a part of a citywide alliance headed by key members within Chairman Mao's appointed Cultural Revolution Group, whose goal was the overthrow of Premier Chou and his deputy ministers in the State Council, plus the replacement of senior generals in the Army. It is hard to say whether this split in the revolutionary ranks occurred first at the top or the bottom, or whether it occurred at every level throughout the country simultaneously. But a similar kind of split did occur in every organization and institution throughout the country.

Now the nation was confronted in every administrative, educational, and economic unit with two and sometimes three mass popular revolutionary organizations, each proclaiming that it alone was the true representative of Chairman Mao's revolutionary line. The situation was complicated because Party members, like everyone else, were split into two camps. "True rebels" belonged to every organization. Former conservatives wishing to avoid the stigma of past errors rushed to join the most left-sounding group. "Bad elements," those who for one reason or another had never come to terms with socialism and had never been ready to make the sacrifices necessary to build a modern, non-exploitative society, melted into the new mass organizations with all the rest. The new situation was as startling to us as it must have been to millions of others. We had thought that perhaps this movement would unite 90 per cent of the people who supported Mao Tse-tung against the 10 per cent who did not. Now if we wished to participate in the movement, and in China there was nothing but the movement, we would have to make a choice. Every Chinese, including Chairman Mao, would have to choose one of the sides during the key crises that would arise during the next few years. The future would prove that those choices were difficult to make and often less than satisfactory. Mao reflected precisely that ambivalence when he was said to have asked a senior colleague, "Do you have a dual character?" and before he could answer, stated, "Well, I do."

*Chapter VII*

# The Best Of Times,
# The Worst Of Times

OCTOBER 1, National Day, 1966. Millions of young Chinese, no longer wearing the scarves of Young Pioneers, but their new Red Guard arm bands and Mao badges, poured across T'ien An Men Square in straggling groups, waving their little red books and shouting, "Chairman Mao, Chairman Mao." They infected each other with the emotion that characterized all of their T'ien An Men meetings with the Chairman, and along with their shouting, there was hysterical weeping. It was a far cry indeed from the orderly parades of past years, with their perfectly orchestrated formation marching and paper flower montages.

Our third Peking winter was beginning. Like the rest of the city's foreign working community, we were thrown into a strange new universe, a world far different from the one to which we had gradually become accustomed. During our first autumn we had been cast into the role of "new international friends." Taken to view the accomplishments of old and new China, given a thousand courteous explanations, we were dazzled by the events of each day. By our second autumn, we had begun to assume some of the attitudes of the "old China hands" of the 1960's. Well settled in our teaching routine and living at our Institute, our children having completed a year of intensive Chinese and now attending regular Chinese schools, we felt that we knew what to expect of life in Peking. We began to take for granted certain privileges extended to the foreign experts whose length or kind of stay qualified them as "old hands." The more desirable of these were not material privileges so much as the possibility of visits to interesting places and talks with interesting people. The American group, personified by Anna Louise Strong with her long and special ties to China, was regarded as being especially favored in this regard. However, the second of our winters seemed to spin toward a social crescendo for Peking's entire foreign expert community. Even Christmas was celebrated in grand style, as the experts danced around a giant Christmas tree in the ballroom of the Friendship Hotel.

Western-style dancing, along with potted flowers, goldfish, and brightly-colored clothing, would be among the high visibility frivolities most rapidly designated "bourgeois" by the Red Guards, but, in fact, the waltz and foxtrot had an honorable revolutionary association in China. Anna Louise and George Ma reminisced with pleasure about the regular Saturday-night dances of the old Yenan days. She had written a description of the dancing styles of the leaders of the revolution which, twenty years later, was still delightfully perspicacious. Chou En-lai was the most polished of waltzers; Chu Teh, Mao's great military partner, led his partner on another Long March; Liu Shao-ch'i was precise and methodical. With Mao, she said, you could never quite understand where you were going, but he and his partner somehow always stopped exactly in time with the final note. For a number of years after 1949, the tradition of the Saturday-night dance had been continued at the Peking Hotel, but the demands upon the elegant Chou in particular were said to have been overwhelming. The new requirements of state power soon swept away this pleasant pastime of simpler days.

The period from Anna Louise's November 1966 birthday to the closing of the winter social events was the end of an era. It was, as our children came to call it, "the last winter of Liu Shao-ch'i." In the first winter of the Great Proletarian Cultural Revolution, there was none of the previous year's social activity. The revived puritanism of the revolution began to infect the foreign community as quickly as it did the Chinese. Sid Rittenberg, whose connoisseurship of Chinese food was unparalleled and whose apartment was furnished with fine Ming period antiques, was a bellwether in this regard, as in every other ideological current of the Cultural Revolution. We received with some astonishment his enthusiastic announcement that he had begun a regimen of cold baths and jogging. His past role as guide par excellence to the restaurants of Peking and erudite interpreter of classical Peking opera disappeared with those same restaurants and operas. We were soon to hear instead fantastic rumors, including one that his favorite Szechuan restaurant, also the favorite of the Peking Party Committee, had been closed, not so much for its "bourgeois" food as for the cache of machine guns found stored in its cellar.

However, Rittenberg had truly grasped the symbolic drama requisite of Chinese political movements. We were later to decide that all urban Chinese must keep in their trunks one faded and patched suit of blue clothes reserved for political movements. Many of the young Shanghai women with whom we taught had attended the parties of the preceding winter in the simple but very well put together costumes of the fashionable Chinese woman—their wool trousers slim and well cut by excellent Shanghai tailors, cashmere sweaters under padded jackets, and neat leather moccasins or Maryjanes. Now they appeared in faded and patched blues. For those foreigners who had not yet adopted ordinary Chinese clothing there was no way of dealing with the change in fashion but to buy a new Chinese cotton suit, and many were the chic Latin American women who suddenly abandoned their Chinese silk print mini-dresses for blue proletarian costumes.

The atmosphere of the city was one of crackling excitement. Undoubtedly, there were certain periods during the Watergate affair when those close to power or sources of information felt the same kind of excitement, when every day, sometimes every hour, brought new revelations, new struggles, new shocks. But, in the Peking of the first winter of the Cultural Revolution, the entire people felt intimately involved, particularly those who were in any way connected with the student movement which dominated the mass politics of the period. Liu Shao-ch'i and Teng Hsiao-p'ing, in the eyes of the masses, were as good as downed, and the students began to look critically at every cadre in power, just as those same powerful figures cast about for student support. The debacle of the work-teams dictated that this movement would operate according to new rules.

In December 1966, there was an interesting change in the embellishment of Peking's omnipresent walls. The messy but lively *ta-tzu-pao* covered with vigorously painted characters and decorated with caricatured demons and monsters were suddenly replaced by neatly lettered quotations from Chairman Mao. They began in one corner of the wall and extended to the other and around them were firmly designated boundaries of fresh paint. There was, somehow, on the endless walls of the ancient city, not an inch of space for the spontaneous criticisms of the people. There were red suns and red flags painted in profusion, but gone were the angry denunciations and the wildly scampering stick figures of Liu Shao-ch'i. It was the "Sea of Red," a deliberate attempt to shut out the criticisms of the people by pre-empting the wall spaces of the city. It was one of the first of repeated attempts by besieged Party officials to turn the revolutionary spirit of the day into self-defeating idiocy. The Cultural Revolution would produce unending creativity in similar oblique methods of "waving the red flag to oppose the red flag." Although the "Sea of Red" and other forms were uniquely Chinese, we, the "outside persons," were not the only ones bewildered by their strange variety. The Chinese themselves again and again staggered out of the latest "smokescreen" to denounce the perfidy of those so ingeniously trying to shield themselves.

The "Sea of Red" itself was the creation of T'ao Chu, a powerful national Party leader. It was Rittenberg who alerted us to the importance of T'ao Chu's political rise long before we would otherwise have known of it. He came from a powerful base as First Party Secretary of the heavily populated south central region and, after the political eclipse of Liu Shao-ch'i and the Peking Party Committee, became the most important voice of the Party organization. Attempting, like many Party officials, to straddle both sides of an increasingly unsteady political fence, he assumed the critical post of head of propaganda, a position that was to be a primary goal of each successive wave of power-seekers during the course of the entire movement. In the absence of the old structures, those in a position to interpret the line coming from the top —presumably from Mao and his "proletarian headquarters" —were the only ones who could centrally influence the actions of the millions looking for orientation in this unrehearsed drama. It was from the authority of this position that T'ao Chu was able to initiate the "Sea of Red," setting up the "left in form, right in essence" thrust of the period. "Doubt everything and overthrow everything" was a characteristic slogan in the repeated efforts of officialdom to protect itself through the diversion of the movement into mass chaos.

However, T'ao Chu was in too delicate a position to attempt such maneuvers. Although he had been politically astute enough to attach himself as an advisor to the new organ of legitimacy, the Cultural Group, that relationship, as virtually all of the members of the sacrosanct Group would discover, was a poor guarantee for political longevity. It was later claimed that members of the Cultural Group had been suspicious of him, saying that he made decisions behind their backs, but Mao stated that it was the masses who uncovered T'ao Chu. He fell in January 1967 under a mass attack on his policies in Kwangtung Province and on articles which had appeared under his jurisdiction as head of propaganda. T'ao Chu's fall signified the end of the brief period of half a year in which powerful Party bureaucrats would hold positions enabling them to direct the Cultural Revolution in a relatively open way. From the winter of 1966–67 on, the power game would be played by very different rules, of which T'ao Chu's "feint to the left to attack from the right" was but a forerunner.

The Cultural Group, which remained at the storm center of the Cultural Revolution from beginning to end, reflected as well as initiated the shifts in strength and policy which racked the million-person political armies of this strange war. It was the Chairman's attempt to put together a leadership coalition of undisputed authority for a movement whose goal was to dispute authority.

Although such a goal was revolutionary in China's political history, the structure of this leadership group was not. One fascinating aspect of the Cultural Revolution is the degree to which this monumental event which temporarily shattered so many familiar structures of Chinese society brought back time-honed institutions of the past. To the foreign observer and sometime participant, it was difficult at the time to sort out the old and the new. Editorials and the conversation of ordinary people were filled with references to the need to destroy the "four olds," and the novelty of Mao's basic theoretical concept of the movement was so great that the population of China was deeply convinced of the historical originality of their task. In that assumption, they were not mistaken. The profundity of Mao's assertion that only through the continuous struggle of the people against those who oppress them, under any social system, does mankind progress, will undoubtedly continue to reverberate through the modern bureaucratic world long after the last word has been written on the Great Proletarian Cultural Revolution. However, history does not give to any people at a particular moment of their national life an infinite choice of political structures.

By the end of 1966, the Chinese Communist Party, having brought to China a political culture which had radically transformed the country's institutions, was paralyzed. Its leaders and members would continue to struggle for policies and personal political survival, but the Party could no longer continue to lead the Chinese people, and least of all in the very movement directed against itself. The Cultural Group, Mao's personally appointed committee for the direction of the movement and, as was generally assumed until splits within the group became endemic, his spokesman, was a structure invoked from the distant past by the needs of the moment. China's emperors, when blocked by the opposition of their cabinets, had circumvented them by the creation of an Inner Court, answerable only to the ruler. Perhaps when Mao stated, "Very few people understood what I wanted to do. Sometimes I was practically alone,"[65] he gave tacit admission to the fact that only another "inner court" would lend itself to the task he envisioned.

Thus, there was an inescapable logic in the make-up of this singular group. Their primary qualification was loyalty to Mao and commitment to his revolutionary plans for the Cultural Revolution, and, consequently, it is not surprising that familial connections should have had some importance. Chiang Ch'ing, the Chairman's wife, was a woman of no public political experience except for her recent involvement in cultural reform in the fields of art and literature; and Ch'en Po-ta, Mao's secretary and speech-writer of many years, was an intellectual ideologue, not a public leader. The group was heavy with radical intellectuals, several of whom came from leading editorial positions on the Party theoretical organ, the *Red Flag,* Wang Li, Kuan Feng, and Lin Chieh; Mu Hsin, former editor of the *Kuang ming Daily;* and Ch'i Pen-yü, the radical historian who set off the ideological campaign against Liu in the spring of 1967 with his article "Patriotism or National Betrayal?" Perhaps the best known was Yao Wen-yuan, writer of the Hai Jui essay that had constituted the Chairman's opening salvo of November 1965. The Chinese deny his relationship by marriage to one of Mao's daughters or nieces, but the speculation is not surprising considering his ability to retain power when the entire preceding group of radical intellectuals fell. All were essentially untried performers on the political stage of China and, interestingly, in a movement which stressed the primacy of actual revolutionary experience as opposed to empty theory, most had made their mark in the area of theory. They were to perform their parts on this central and much-exposed stage lacking not only the extensive experience in politics which many of their opponents enjoyed, but without a political or social base from which they could draw support. The Red Guard movement was the Cultural Group's original base, but its fragmentation would both reflect, and be reflected in, the disintegration of the Cultural Group itself.

There were a few important exceptions to the political rootlessness of the majority of Cultural Group members. K'ang Sheng, a formidable figure of the old Party machine, former head of the Bureau of Security, made the delicate adjustment to the shifts in the Cultural Group, maintaining his pro-Maoist position with skills tempered in many struggles. Chang Ch'un-ch'iao was a veteran of Shanghai's sophisticated and dynamic politics, whose practical abilities would very soon be proved, and whose position, even now, is seen as evidence of the importance of his Shanghai base and his skill in speaking for that powerful constituency. Finally, there was Hsieh Fu-chih, a veteran revolutionary who would play a key role in Peking's turbulent politics as head of the new Peking Revolutionary Committee. These, then, were the members who made up the Chairman's revolutionary "inner court."

The months of December 1966 and January 1967 were a period of great chaos in China. Red Guards crisscrossed the country in the millions and continued to pour into Peking. Inspired by the editorials of the day, they rushed on in their search for class enemies. From the time it became clear that the Cultural Revolution was, in the Chairman's words, a "class struggle," the masses turned to past struggles for a form which fit the realities of this one. The primary class struggle of the people's experience or knowledge was the land reform movement, and it was from this struggle against China's landlords that so many of the forms of the Cultural Revolution were derived. So, when students began to attack either "bourgeois reactionary authorities" or Party officials, they fell back on the archaic forms of earlier struggles or simply on China's long historical tradition. Enemies were paraded through the streets wearing dunce hats and signs around their necks, a strange contemporary manifestation of the traditional Confucian "rectification of names." Criminals in early imperial China had been branded with a mark which indicated not only the nature of their crime, but their class status. The Communists themselves, before being executed by the Kuomintang, had been forced to wear signs defining them as "bandits."

The tendency to replicate the past was intensified by such mass study campaigns of the early Cultural Revolution as the one to reread Mao's 1927 classic analysis of China's class structure, "Report on the Investigation of the Hunan Peasant Movement." In it, Mao, describing the mass rising of the peasants, said, "At the slightest provocation they make arrests, crown the arrested with tall paper hats, and parade them through the villages saying, 'You dirty landlord, now you know who we are!'" In 1927, Mao, more than other revolutionaries, understood the historical necessity and indeed inevitability of the Hunan peasants' violent wrench with a past of subservience and class fear; but in 1966, he had no wish to preserve such methods. Stressing the difference between the recommended "struggle by reason" (*wen-tou*) as opposed to the emerging "struggle by force" (*wu-tou*), Mao wrote to Chou En-lai a little later that winter:

> "Recently, many revolutionary teachers and students and revolutionary masses have written to me asking whether it is considered struggle by force [*wu-tou*] to make those in authority taking the capitalist road and freaks and monsters wear dunce caps, to paint their faces, and to parade them in the street. I think it is a form of struggle by force [*wu-tou*]. These goals cannot achieve our goal of educating the people. I want to stress here that, when engaging in struggle, we definitely must hold to struggle by reason [*wen-tou*], bring out the facts, emphasize rationality, and use persuasion before we can reach our standard of struggle and before we can achieve our goal of educating people."[66]

However, new forms do not easily evolve. Although the use of hats and signs gradually began to diminish, what they symbolized was never entirely absent from the Cultural Revolution.

Quite by chance, on a December shopping trip to downtown Peking, we became aware that another social force had erupted onto the streets of the capital. On this bright, cold afternoon, the thousands of Red Guards seemed completely overshadowed by the ominous intensity of new arrivals, the contract workers. Everywhere, mature men and women walked down the main shopping street, reading the *ta-tzu-pao,* standing about in groups, talking and watching, their faces angry and sullen. It was a Chinese population which we had never seen before and which we would never again encounter. Thousands of workers with grievances from a hundred parts of China were now finding that they shared the same wage inequities, insecure employment, and lack of social and political rights. They were a strangely quiet crowd, but their felt injustice hung menacingly over the city.

In our many visits to factories, large and small, in various parts of the country, we had been deluged with statistics regarding worker welfare—old-age pensions, medical care, sick and maternity leave, and, most significantly, what amounted to a guarantee of the right to work. The millions of contract workers had none of this. In a system rising out of the temporary, migratory needs of construction projects, and then the flexible manpower requirements of the Great Leap Forward, they were hired on the basis of individual contracts which specified the nature and duration of each job and the wage to be paid for it. In addition to the lack of fringe benefits, these workers could be hired and fired at will. Factory managers had no responsibility for housing them as they did for other workers nor for seeing to it that the state supplied them with grain.

There had been various ideological explanations of this contract system—that it helped mitigate the differences between city and countryside by bringing commune members into industry for brief periods of time; or that it permitted urban workers to spend part of their working time in the countryside. In reality, this contract system meshed perfectly with Liu Shao-ch'i's Soviet-oriented concepts of how China should develop economically. Factory management, as he and his Party supporters saw it, should place increasing importance on profitability. The contract system more and more became an institutionalized part of Liuist plans to increase the level of state capital accumulation and cut down on state costs. This was startlingly revealed by the fact that the Party stated in its third Five Year Plan that it planned to hire no more permanent workers after 1967 and that demobilized soldiers and many school graduates would be funneled into similar contract worker status. This situation did reflect the harsh limitations of China's economic possibilities and the grim difficulties involved in employing a population of 700 million, but it also appeared to run counter to Mao's emphasis on a gradual decrease of inequities rather than the creation of more.

On December 26, the leading contract workers, representing their rebel group, the All-China Red-Worker Rebels' General Corps, met with Chiang Ch'ing, Ch'en Po-ta, and others of the Cultural Group and received official approval. Chiang Ch'ing opened the meeting by stating, "Chairman is backing you up!" In their speeches, the worker representatives placed careful stress on the political inequities of the contract system.

> "The present contract labor system divides the working masses into two brackets, creates differences, causes dissension among the ranks of proletarian revolutionaries. Not only does it harass the revolutionary activism of the working masses, but it obstructs the development of the productive forces of society, besides that it spreads the seed of revisionism and becomes a hotbed for the restoration of capitalism. The handful of capitalist roaders in authority within the Party, by means of this revisionist system, have deprived completely millions of millions of workers of their political rights. The system was instituted after Liu Shao-ch'i's report on his inspections made in the various parts of the province of Hopei

in March 1964. On the basis of this report, the Ministry of Labor drew up the contract and temporary labor system for enforcement throughout the nation."[67]

However, Chiang Ch'ing's responses tended to stress the economic inequity which, in fact, was at the basis of the workers' grievances. "The whole thing is capitalist—to keep a number of hired workers, so as to cut down expenses on the part of capital." She urged the workers to take immediate and radical steps to end the contract system: "You just wipe out all the offices of labor distribution in the country."[68] The meeting was reported to have been an extremely emotional one, with all the members of the Cultural Group in tears, and "even the receptionists in the Assembly Hall cried bitterly."

The same mood of rage and bitterness characterized the subsequent public meeting in the Workers' Stadium which David attended. Workers and soldiers packed the big indoor stadium, and the storm of emotion which we had first felt in the streets of Peking now took on a heightened intensity as worker after worker told angry personal stories of harsh working conditions and inadequate housing, food, and clothing. The impassioned recitation of atrocities seemed not merely an exposure of the crimes of the "capitalist road," but an indictment of the entire socialist system. The crowd responded with sympathetic fury, and, halfway through, the meeting was abruptly adjourned to permit the entrance of further thousands of workers who had torn down the fence outside to force their way into the building.

Within a week, a selected group of foreigners was invited to a special meeting with the contract workers' leaders arranged by Sid Rittenberg. Although neither of us attended it, we realized from what friends told us that these workers suffering from concrete economic grievances had struck a chord in the consciousness of every American who heard them. Their stories, familiar to Americans who had been involved in our labor movement, were empathetic in a way that some of the complaints of the Red Guards had not been.

A film was made of this "historic" meeting of the contract workers and the "foreign friends"—by whose jurisdiction it was not clear, but undoubtedly through whatever connections Rittenberg enjoyed with the Cultural Group.

Within a few weeks, it was clear that the Cultural Group, in its search for social forces that would fight the Party bureaucracy, had opened a Pandora's box. The arrival of the thousands of contract workers in Peking had, of course, not been entirely spontaneous. Like all of the sudden surfacings of various social groupings throughout the Cultural Revolution, their emergence represented a combination of real grievances among the population and the attempt on the part of those in leadership to manipulate those grievances into a politically expedient force. However, it was soon obvious that these workers, "sponsored" by certain members of the Chairman's leading committee, were not raising the problems in the superstructure which he saw as the targets of this revolution but the problems of the economic base. And just as it had not been possible to deal with all the economic inequities in the past, so it was not possible now. Fundamental to the difficulty was not just a struggle of two lines, but also the struggle of a poor country facing formidable obstacles in employing its huge population.

The contract workers' brief prominence cast into a sharp perspective the dual possibilities of the Cultural Revolution. On the one hand, the movement opened the possibility for people to air their grievances; on the other hand, it also contained the ever-present potentiality for those grievances, especially if they represented the interests of a particular social group, to be utilized by the various political forces in the society. As the outcry of the contract workers spread, it became increasingly economic in character, and did become an indictment of "seventeen years of revisionism," not just "those in the Party taking the capitalist road." There was a fine line between criticizing the errors of the past seventeen years and throwing the baby out with the bath water. When the leadership of the contract workers crossed that line, they condemned their organization to banishment beyond the bounds of permissible participation. Certain concessions were made, including the right of individual contract workers to full participation in the Cultural Revolution, but the Cultural Group, their original patron, outlawed their organization as counterrevolutionary, one of the very few mass organizations so designated.[69]

Although the prominence of the contract workers' movement was shortlived, it did indicate a new stage in the revolution, the shift away from the students to widespread worker participation in the Cultural Revolution. The entrance of workers into the movement was the culmination of a much slower process than the one which had catapulted the students into action, but one that would have an almost immediately profound effect. Shanghai, the base from which Mao had launched the Cultural Revolution, a year later generated the new revolutionary forces which ushered in the great events of January. When the Peking Red Guards, spreading the fires of revolt to the rest of the country, arrived in Shanghai, they found an independently organized workers' movement there to greet them. It was a workers' movement light years in distance from that of the contract workers. Probably it could have arisen only among a working class possessing the militant tradition, experience, and revolutionary maturity nurtured among the Shanghai proletariat for nearly half a century. As the contract workers had perhaps represented the consciousness (and the real problems) of peasants entering the working class, so the Shanghai workers represented its most advanced sector.

The nucleus of a citywide rebel workers' organization had existed as early as the summer of 1966. Together with rebel students, a core of young journalists on the daily newspaper *Wen-hui pao,* and a number of Party cadres like Wang Hung-wen (who was to become one of the highest ranking leaders in the nation after the Cultural Revolution), the workers gradually expanded this rebel organizational network. By December, they were able to rally 60,000 workers under

Nancy Milton at the Temple of Heaven park, Peking, 1968.

Two sons, Grant and Mark Lupher, on the Great Wall, 1966.

David Milton, Peking, 1968.

Nancy Milton's second-year English students at Pei Hai Park, Peking, May 1966.

David Milton's fifth-year newspaper-reading class, 1965.

Students of the Peking First Foreign Languages Institute working on canal construction, Western Suburbs, Peking, 1965.

Basketball game between Chinese and foreign high school students, Peitaiho, summer 1966 (Christopher Milton, *far right;* Mark Lupher, *next right*).

Nancy Milton addressing meeting to support the American People's Struggle Against the War in Vietnam, Workers' Stadium, Peking, March 1966.

Workers' Stadium Meeting: Chu Teh, Nancy Milton, Kuo Mo-jo.

Mao Tse-tung and Chiang Ch'ing receive Anna Louise Strong and friends on her eightieth birthday, Shanghai, 1965.

Anna Louise Strong greets Red Guards, May Day, 1967 (Sidney Rittenberg, *rear center*).

Christopher Milton with Red Guards, T'ien An Men Square, after return from 1,000-mile march, winter 1966.

Red Guards from all over the country await Chairman Mao's arrival at T'ien An Men rally, fall 1966.

Army men singing at National Day Parade, T'ien An Men,
October 1, 1967.

Cadres of the First Foreign Languages Institute and the
Foreign Experts' Bureau, parade reviewing stand, T'ien An
Men, National Day, 1967.

Revolutionary committee, transistor radio plant, Shanghai, August 1967.

Shanghai dock revolutionary committee, Shanghai, 1967.

the banner of the Workers' Rebel Headquarters. The local Party, led by Ch'en P'ei-hsien, First Secretary of the East China Bureau as well as First Secretary of the Shanghai Municipal Party Committee, and Ts'ao Ti-ch'iu, the Mayor of Shanghai, fought back, organizing tens of thousands of workers in the city loyal to the Party. These "hoodwinked" workers, as they were called by the rebel opposition, were organized by professional Party functionaries to support the citywide alliance of "royalist" Red Guards. Their organization was officially recognized by the Municipal Party Committee, while the Workers' Rebel Headquarters was denied official sanction and branded as outlaw.

In December, 2,500 rebel workers seized a Peking-bound train at the Shanghai railroad station, determined to make the journey to Peking to report to Mao on the counterrevolutionary suppression in Shanghai. The train was sidetracked by alert Party officials at Anting, a small town outside Shanghai, and every effort was made by the Shanghai authorities to persuade the workers to return to production. Suddenly, Chang Ch'un-ch'iao arrived from Peking as an emissary from Mao. He signed the demands of the workers, supported their rebellion against the Shanghai Party Leadership, and gave Peking's official support to the Workers' Rebel Headquarters. After the Anting incident, the student conservative organizations collapsed, and the city Party machine organized its own conservative "Workers' Scarlet Guards for the Defense of Mao Tse-tung Thought." After a number of bloody battles, the largest fought out between thousands of workers at Kunshan, a Shanghai suburb, in late December, the rebels defeated the Scarlet Guards. The organization collapsed when the population as a whole realized that Mao and the leaders in Peking supported the Workers' Rebel Headquarters.

It was at this point, in January, that the old Party machine, its functionaries in the Shanghai Municipal Party Committee, district party chiefs, and plant managers counterattacked with methods that took Mao and the Peking leaders of the Cultural Revolution completely by surprise.

The Party bureaucrats initiated a citywide strike, organizing a walkout by cadres, technicians, and thousands of workers who had been prodded to transform a political struggle against Party officials into a struggle for wages, bonuses, free travel to Peking, and other economic demands. At the same time, officials opened up the city's financial and industrial coffers for wholesale grants of wage increases, bonuses, and cash handouts in a gigantic attempt to buy off the Shanghai working class. (Henry Ford would have applauded this use of the technique with which he had tried to stave off the organization of his plants in the 1930's.)

Rank-and-file workers and students, under the leadership of the Workers' Rebel Headquarters, and the central leadership's representatives, Chang Ch'un-ch'iao and Yao Wen-yuan, responded almost intuitively to the crisis. The city faced total paralysis from the cutoff of water and electric power, the disruption of the transportation system, the shutdown of the docks and major industrial plants, and the state of anarchy introduced into the city's financial institutions. Rebel workers and students rushed to emergency posts at the power stations. Volunteers poured down to the docks to get the docks into operation. Students manned ticket booths at the railway stations, and workers all over the city began to stand double and triple shifts in the understaffed factories.

With the approval of the central leaders in Peking, a group of reporters and staff workers seized control of the influential newspaper *Wen-hui pao* on January 3, 1967. On the fifth, they published a historic "Message to All the People of Shanghai." Signed by the Workers' Rebel Headquarters and eleven other mass organizations, this manifesto called on "comrade revolutionary workers" to restore production in the city. To those followers of the Workers' Scarlet Guards who had deserted their plants, the proclamation asked, "Whose interest are you serving? By acting in this way, whose hearts, after all, are you gladdening and whose are you saddening?" The manifesto implored those who had been deceived to "wake up quickly, return to your posts in production, and return to the proletarian revolutionary line."[70]

Chairman Mao, who followed the events closely, declared to the Cultural Revolution Group on January 9, "The leftists have now seized power at the *Wen-hui pao* [. . .] this direction is fine [. . .] this stands for the overthrow of one class by another; it is a great revolution." Exulting over the developments in Shanghai, the Chairman told his colleagues that "the seizure of power in the two papers [*Wen-hui pao* and *Chieh-fang Jih-pao*] is a question of national significance and it is necessary to support their rebellion. [. . .] The rise of the revolutionary forces in Shanghai has given hope to the whole country. The impact is bound to be felt in the whole of East China and all provinces and municipalities in the whole country."[71] As Chang Ch'un-Ch'iao was to confirm at a later date, it was Chairman Mao who defined their actions as a seizure of power. Chang said:

> "We submitted a report to the Center on the situation in Shanghai and what steps we had taken. Chairman endorsed our actions, telling us that the seizure of power was wholly necessary and correct. This is how we came to use the term 'seizure of power' as suggested by Chairman Mao."[72]

Once again, Mao had drawn theoretical conclusions from unfolding historical events. His method of "dissecting a sparrow," the use of the successful experience of a single unit to provide the general formula for the whole, was applied to Shanghai. The "January Revolution" was to provide a new form of struggle designed to meet and overcome the obstruction and deflection of the mass movement by the old Party organization. The new form was "the seizure of power from below."

However, the Shanghai formula never achieved the same success in the rest of the nation. As a result, Shanghai and its January Revolution in many respects marked the apogee of the Great Proletarian Cultural Revolution. The reasons were many. The Shanghai workers had a long revolutionary tradition, organizational know-how, discipline, and, perhaps most important, an able and united leadership. Factionalism and anarchism existed in Shanghai as they did in every other part of the nation, and five consecutive power seizures were necessary before the new leadership was consolidated, but Shanghai's inhabitants were second to none in overcoming these obstacles. Shanghai provided the perfect backdrop for the struggle to work itself out in the classic fashion of the great modern revolutions.

The difference between revolutionary and reformist politics lies in the ability of people to transcend their immediate interests and make sacrifices for national or universal goals. In so doing, they transform both themselves and the world around them. This is what Marx meant when he said that, by liberating themselves, the proletariat would liberate mankind. Proof of the remarkable revolutionary consciousness of the Shanghai proletariat was the fact that, within a few months, 95 per cent of the money dispensed by the old Shanghai bureaucrats was voluntarily returned by the workers who had been "hoodwinked." Mass meetings were held throughout the city, at which officials guilty of bribery were forced to stand with bowed heads as the workers showered them with paper money until they stood knee-deep in the shameful currency. It was this element of revolutionary consciousness which distinguished the Shanghai workers movement from the interest-oriented struggle of the nation's contract workers; quality as opposed to quantity, long-term transformation versus short-term gains. These have always separated the politics of revolution from economic struggles.

Two factors were to work against the Shanghai power formula in the rest of the country. Opposition forces changed their tactics, manipulating the lessons of Shanghai in their own interest, and the old feudal political culture and practices inherited from the past were stronger in the rest of the country than in Shanghai. In Peking, for example, the factional students who dominated the movement came under the influence of the Byzantine maneuvers characteristic of the ancient Chinese bureaucracy. The situation proved even more difficult in those provinces where conservative power-holders in league with the powerful provincial army commanders utilized old customs, traditions, and superstitions to rally popular support and isolate the revolution forces. Szechuan proved to be the Vendée of China, and in Kwangtung, the royalist groupings not only refused to collapse, but remained in the majority from the beginning until the end of the movement.

"World history," Marx once said, "would indeed be very easy to make if the struggle were taken up only on conditions of infallibly favorable chances." Mao, recognizing that the rest of the country might not provide as fertile ground for revolution from below as Shanghai, was still determined to push the power seizure as far as it would go. However, trouble was beginning to appear at home. The members of the Chairman's Proletarian Headquarters, while celebrating their victory in Shanghai, immediately divided over what it all meant. For Chiang Ch'ing, Ch'en Po-ta, and the young intellectuals in charge of the nation's propaganda organs, the Shanghai experience was nothing less than the reenactment of the 1871 Paris Commune. This time, however, in new, more favorable historical circumstances, the Chinese would be able to achieve what the less fortunate Parisians had not. For Premier Chou, with his forty-five years of experience in leading revolutionary struggles, the power seizure in Shanghai was far from inaugurating the millennium of people's rule which the commune principle represented. The January Revolution thus stands as a decisive turning point which forced Chairman Mao and the central leaders to make judgments on the historical limits of the revolution which they had set in motion. In the final analysis, that decision would determine the combination of forces that would rule the country.

One day in January, while bicycling into the city, we met Sid Rittenberg. He told us that he was working with Nieh Yuan-tzu and Peking Red Guard leaders together with Chiang Ch'ing and the Cultural Group to set up the "Peking Commune." It was the first we had heard about plans for a Peking Commune, or even that it was on the agenda. However, on January 26, Premier Chou told a meeting of representatives of rebel organizations that the demand for the implementation of the Paris Commune universal election and recall system was historically premature. According to Chou, the conditions necessary for putting into practice the Commune election were "integration of the revolutionary organizations with the masses of the people; the elimination or transformation of the rightists and the isolation of the ultra-left"; and the rebels would have to unite "with ninety-five per cent of the masses and ninety-five per cent of the cadres." Chou then bluntly stated: "We are far from having reached that stage at this point."[73]

Apparently, the Cultural Group in control of the propaganda organs disagreed with the Premier, because, on January 31, the *People's Daily* published an editorial which once again promulgated the model of the Paris Commune, cited Mao's statement that Nieh Yuan-tzu's *ta-tzu-pao* stood as a declaration of a "Peking Commune of the Sixties of the twentieth century," and emphasized the necessity of smashing the old organs of state power. The next day, Chiang Ch'ing and Ch'i Pen-yü met with revolutionary rebels of the Central Documentary Film Studio. In the course of their talks, Chiang Ch'ing exclaimed: "Don't become an official. The title 'chief' is to be smashed to pieces. There will be no need for 'chiefs' in the future. We will have the people's commune."[74]

On February 6, Chang Ch'un-ch'iao and the Shanghai leaders, after skillfully handling serious factional disputes in Shanghai, announced the formation of the Shanghai People's Commune. Four days later, Red Flag, the Red Guard organization of the Peking Aviation Institute, and one of the most radical and politically mature rebel groups in the country, published an editorial entitled "Long Live 'Peking People's Commune.'" In those heady months, the concepts of people's rule through universally elected organs of government were sweeping away the older tradition of rule by the vanguard party. The editorial by the Aviation Institute's Red Flag organization proclaimed enthusiastically:

"Peking's revolutionary rebels, who are united, have wrested power from the Party people in authority who took the capitalist road and are now deliberating on, and making preparations for, the establishment of 'Peking People's Commune.' All revolutionaries clap their hands for joy and proclaim: 'Very good indeed!' "[75]

Asserting that the "Peking People's Commune" would emerge as "a brand new state apparatus," the editorial went on to argue that this new development was dictated by the class struggle and the new development of "productive forces" and "is a natural product of historical development." Red Flag declared that Chairman Mao had foreseen the "inevitable emergence of this magnificent new thing in the world." The Peking Commune was described as a "form of state power led by the working class, based on the worker–peasant alliance and formed jointly by workers, peasants, revolutionary cadres, revolutionary intellectuals, and other revolutionary masses. The revolutionary masses may take part directly in the administration of the state."

From February 12 to 18, Mao held three meetings with Chang Ch'un-ch'iao and Yao Wen-yuan, who had come to Peking to report on the complex situation in Shanghai. Despite the victory of the revolutionary forces there, the city was still troubled by anarchy and factionalism. Learning that rebel organizations in Shanghai had called for the "elimination of all chiefs," Chairman Mao declared:

"This is extreme anarchism; it is most reactionary. Now they do not wish to refer to anyone as the chief of such and such; they call them orderlies or attendants. In reality this is just a matter of appearances. Actually there will always have to be chiefs; it depends on the circumstances."[76]

It would not be the last time that the masses would take the brunt of criticism for echoing the statements, concepts, and policies of leaders of the Cultural Group.

For the first time, the Chairman faced squarely the growing practical and theoretical assault on the disintegrating Communist Party. There is little to indicate that he ever wished to do more than again root the Party in the social forces which it was designed to represent, but its resistance to this new social movement threatened the Party's very existence. It is not clear just what the Chairman had meant by "the Chinese Paris Commune of the Sixties"; perhaps he had just floated the idea, waiting to see how things would develop in practice. But when forced to choose between the Commune and the vanguard Party, he chose the latter. In a discussion with the leaders of the Cultural Revolution, he put his finger on the key dilemma confronting them all:

> "If everything were changed into the Commune, then what about the Party? Where would we place the Party? Among Commune committee members [in Shanghai] are both Party members and non-Party members. Where would we place the Party committee? There must be a party somehow. There must be a nucleus, no matter what we call it. Be it called the Communist Party, or social-democratic party, or Kuomintang, or I-Kuan-tao, it must have a party. The commune must have a party, but can the commune replace the party?"[77]

In his thinking, obviously not, and consequently he announced his decision on the matter in unequivocal terms:

> "Many places have now applied to the Center to establish people's communes. A document has been issued by the Center saying that no place apart from Shanghai may set up people's communes. Shanghai ought to make a change and transform itself into a revolutionary committee or a city committee or a city people's committee. Communes are too weak when it comes to suppressing counterrevolution."[78]

On February 27, the Shanghai People's Commune was renamed the Shanghai Municipal Revolutionary Committee. Perhaps the general assumption that the Chairman agreed with the political principles of the Commune was not correct. Six months later, he told a visiting Albanian military delegation:

> "Some people say that election is very good and very democratic. I think election is only a civilized term. I myself do not admit that there is any true election. I was

elected People's Deputy for Peking District, but how many people are there in Peking who really understand me? I think the election of Chou En-lai as Premier means his appointment as Premier by the Center."[79]

The Chairman rejected the commune concept of mass power seizure against a background of mass uprisings and turmoil which broke out all over China in the month of January. This crisis period in turn produced a major struggle at the top between the Cultural Group and Premier Chou over the definition, form, and strategy for the new seizure of power. While Ch'en Po-ta and his allies argued that the new power seizures were in truth a revolution surpassing that of 1949, the Premier viewed the new stage of power seizure as a much more limited operation, necessary for transforming only those administrative units led by officials clearly defined as capitalist-roaders. A debate that we heard often during those months was whether or not the Chinese state organs were completely in the hands of the revisionists and whether or not the seventeen years of communist rule had been tarred with the brush of revisionism. How could one explain Chairman Mao's leadership of the revolution if that entire revolution were called into question? This dilemma posed serious theoretical problems which the Cultural Group found hard to handle. Suddenly, all the leaders and the millions of participants in this vast social movement had to confront for the first time the compelling question: Just what does this revolution seek to accomplish in practical terms?

Some of the Peking-based leaders of the Cultural Group, who had never before led a revolutionary movement, had, in an excess of zeal, unleashed some troublesome genies from the bottle. They had embraced the revolt of groups before knowing what it was these groups represented and found themselves attached to interests they would later be forced to renounce. In addition to the "All-China Red Worker Rebels' General Corps," which embraced the contract and temporary workers, there arose a national organization of students who had been sent to the countryside prior to the Cultural

Revolution. Calling themselves the "National Revolution Rebel Corps of the Educated Youth Going to Mountainous and Rural Areas to Defend Truth," they claimed that they were all victims of the revisionist line and demanded the right to return to the cities. Then there were the ex-army men, organized into the national "Red Flag Army" and the "National Revolutionary Rebel Corps of Army Reclamation Fighters." Representatives of these new "armies" poured into Peking in December, all brandishing concrete grievances and all directing their attack at the State Council and the national government. Using bricks and iron bars, these angry rebels broke into the offices of the State Council, smashed into arsenals, and invaded offices containing confidential documents. Although their grievances may have been just, these were not the forces destined to transform private interest into public interest through the process of removing power-holders taking the capitalist road. Within a few months, all these organizations were outlawed by official decree as counterrevolutionary.[80]

It was in response to these political developments that Chairman Mao, rejecting the Commune principle, came down on the side of Premier Chou. In place of the Commune, he suggested a new formula for power seizure from below based on the recent seizure of power in Heilungchiang Province in the Northeast—a three-way division of power among revolutionary Party cadres, representatives of the People's Liberation Army, and representatives from the mass organizations. By supporting the principle of the seizure of power from below, the Chairman underlined the legitimacy and continuation of the Cultural Revolution. By ordering the Army "to support the broad masses of the left," he ended the Army's former neutrality and brought it directly into the movement, guaranteeing it a share of political power.[81] By including the Party cadres in the new organs of power, Mao moved to undermine the opposition of the Party functionaries to his revolutionary policies. Apparently, even the members of the Cultural Group realized that the Commune principle was unworkable, for they also supported the new triple alliance. Of course, they, like the other political forces involved, would make their own interpretation of how that power was to be shared. The *Red Flag* editorial No. 3, published on February 1, summed up the experience of the January Revolution and explicitly outlined the new model of power seizure now applicable to the whole country. Titled "On the Proletarian Revolutionaries' Struggle to Seize Power," it was to be the last of those stirring public documents which linked the Chinese people to the great revolutions of history. *Red Flag* No. 3 was a strategic document; the documents which followed were tactical responses to events no longer shaped by an all-encompassing vision. The numerous revolutionary proclamations issued in the succeeding years never quite achieved the elevated and universal tone characteristic of all those great popular documents of history which have assimilated the aspirations of a particular people in their attempt to "storm the heavens."

Containing sections written by Mao Tse-tung, the *Red Flag* declaration announced:

> "Proletarian revolutionaries are uniting to seize power from the handful of persons within the Party who are in authority and taking the capitalist road. This is a strategic task for the new stage of the great proletarian cultural revolution."[82]

Calling on the people of the country to study the experience of the January Revolution in Shanghai, it announced that the January Revolution was "now sweeping the country" and then went on to spell out the methods necessary for completing the revolutionary seizure of power in a nation of 750 million people. It called upon the revolutionary mass organizations to forge a great alliance and warned them that without such an alliance, the struggle to achieve power "cannot be completed successfully. Even if some power has been seized, it may be lost again." The most significant departure from the commune principle, and the one signifying a retreat for the Cultural Group, was the statement concerning the role of the revolutionary cadres in the struggle to seize power. They could not only take part, but "can become the backbone of the struggle to seize power and . . . can become leaders in this struggle."

The mass character of the Cultural Revolution was, however, maintained. The statement made clear that the seizure of power from capitalist-roaders "is not effected by the dismissal and reorganization from above, but by the mass movement below, a movement called for and supported by Chairman Mao himself. Only in this way can the leading organizations of our Party and State [. . .] be regenerated and the old bourgeois practices be thoroughly eradicated."

The line on the cadre question was, nevertheless, pounded home. The reason that they had to be included in the new power formations, and perhaps even depended upon to lead the struggle, was because "they are more experienced in struggle, they are more mature politically, and they have greater organizational skill." Chou En-lai told some revolutionary rebels that Chairman Mao himself wrote the following sentence in the editorial:

> "Cadres who have made errors should be treated correctly and should not be overthrown indiscriminately. *They should be allowed to correct their errors and be encouraged to make amends for their crimes by good deeds, unless they are anti-Party, anti-socialist elements who persist in their errors and refuse to correct them after repeated education* [italics added]."[83]

Both Shansi and Heilungchiang Provinces, where successful power seizures had been completed, were now advocated alongside Shanghai as the model to follow. P'an Fu-sheng, a leading party cadre in the Northeast, had led the struggle for power in Heilungchiang and so became the highly publicized symbol of the new role for revolutionary cadres.

One of the concluding sections of the editorial referred to the Paris Commune and the Marxist axiom that the proletariat must not only take over the existing bourgeois state machine but "must thoroughly smash it." This was followed by the pronouncement that "a number of units, where a handful of Party people in authority and taking the capitalist road have long entrenched themselves, have become rotten." Therefore, "smashing the existing state machine must be put in practice in the struggle for the seizure of power in these units," and again, in these places "we must smash them thoroughly." Thus the new manifesto contained a little something to support the hopes of all the disparate forces. Each would seize upon those paragraphs favorable to its own cause.

In subsequent months, we heard rumors in Peking that Ch'en Po-ta had smuggled back into the editorial the concept of smashing the state machine and that the Chairman was angered by this. Whether or not this was a fact, many mass organizations came to the conclusion that their particular unit was the most rotten of all, requiring a clean sweep of all those in power.

Every shift in line or orientation from the Proletarian Headquarters now produced a crisis, a pattern that was to continue throughout the course of the movement. As a result of the new line on the cadres, the old Party leaders, mainly the Vice Premiers in the State Council who had been under severe attack, struck back. This "Adverse February Current" in turn produced a new upsurge of revolutionary activity at the bottom. At a high-level meeting on February 16, attended by members of the Cultural Group, the Premier, and a phalanx of prominent government leaders, the Vice Premiers led an attack on the Cultural Group. These top level State and Party leaders included the old marshals (Chu Teh, Yeh Chien-ying, Ch'en Yi, Nieh Jung-chen, and Hsu Hsiang-ch'ien), the Vice Premiers of the State Council and heads of ministries (Li Hsien-nien, T'an Chen-lin, Ch'en Yun), and others. T'an Chen-lin, a prominent veteran from the Kiangsi guerrilla period and Minister of Agriculture, led the attack. He was reported to have said that he had made no mistakes and then stated, "I need no protection from others. Veteran cadres have been struck down." "He added bitterly, 'I should not have lived for sixty-five years, should not have joined the revolution, should not have joined the

Party, and should not have followed Chairman Mao in making revolution for forty years.' "[84] Premier Chou was upset by this attack on the Cultural Group and when Mao heard about it he was reported to have said that anyone who opposed the Cultural Group would be opposed by "us," meaning himself, Lin Piao, the Premier, and the Cultural Group itself.

However, the new counterattack by these prominent State and Party officials drew forth a series of Central Committee decrees which, under the guise of attacking excesses in the mass movement, in effect questioned the legality of the revolutionary mass organizations. Official prohibitions against seizing government offices and ministries, against physical assaults on cadres, and bans on the seizure of government files (threatening legal action against violators) were posted throughout the country. These prohibitions were aimed at severely restricting the activities of the Red Guards. *Red Flag*'s editorial No. 4 came out carrying the line that the cadres must be included in new power seizures and that if they were not it would be "impossible to establish a powerful core of leadership." Exclusion of the cadres from leading organs of power, it was asserted in a characteristically Chinese simile, would "result in something like a group of dragons without a head dragon."[85]

A determined effort was made by the central authorities to restore "law and order" and reestablish the functioning of the old state administration. Mass organizations were ordered to criticize their shortcomings and institute rectification movements within their own ranks. Ideological aspects of the Cultural Revolution were given priority, while the attack on the capitalist-roaders was deemphasized. Most of our friends disappeared into interminable meetings to which we were not invited.

During this period, we were told that Foreign Minister Ch'en Yi had repudiated his self-criticism relating to his conduct and attitude at the beginning of the Cultural Revolution. Marshal Ch'en Yi's self-criticism had no doubt been accepted with sighs of relief by the Chairman and the Premier and had apparently met with the qualified approval of the members of the Cultural Group. Now the crusty old soldier had returned to square one. This news dismayed our rebel friends in the Red Flag Detachment (Hung-ch'i Ta-tui) at our Institute and enraged the Rebel Regiment (Tsao-fan T'uan). The latter quickly claimed that Ch'en Yi's retraction of his self-criticism was final proof, as if any were needed, that their attack on the Foreign Minister was a justified and revolutionary action from the beginning. But, despite the rage of the radical Red Guards, the campaign to temper the attack on Party cadres continued. The daily press sternly reproached those guilty of "doubting all, suspecting all, and overthrowing all." The masses were reminded that the goal of the Cultural Revolution was not the dismissal of cadres, but the transformation of world outlook so that China would not change color.

In the second week of March, our students invited David to march with them to the Agricultural Institute, less than a mile from our own Institute, where a mass rally against Vice Premier T'an Chen-lin was taking place. Thousands of students from all over the city were massed at the Agricultural Institute, and the new arrivals sat on the grass in front of the main building to listen to the boisterous and angry speeches pouring forth from loudspeakers. For hours, the crowd intently listened to the reports of how T'an Chen-lin had engineered a false power seizure in all the administrative units and schools under his jurisdiction. T'an, it was asserted, was a "reactionary and a fascist" who had brutally suppressed the revolutionary mass organizations by labeling them counterrevolutionary. It was, the students claimed, a return of the whole work-team "white terror" tactics. As a result, the mass movement erupted with a force which turned the whole city once more into a political battleground. The new spring campaign against the "Adverse February Current" was officially inaugurated by the Red Guard Congress, and the main editorial in *Red Flag* No. 5 appeared with a warning against the exclusion of the masses from the new revolutionary three-way alliances.

As a result of the new revolutionary wave set into motion by the "Adverse February Current," two well-defined city-wide factional alliances emerged. They were named, in the classical and historical Chinese fashion, the Heaven faction and the Earth faction—Heaven led by rebels (Red Flag) from the Aviation Institute and Earth led by their opposite numbers (The East Is Red Revolutionary Rebels) from the Geology Institute. A citywide struggle for control of the Peking Red Guard Congress and the Peking Revolutionary Committee, which was to replace the old city Party Committee, commenced as the two great alliances emerged in organizational formations. Once more, big-character posters against Premier Chou appeared declaring that he was behind the reactionary policies of the "capitalist-roaders in the state ministries" and was protecting them from the just attacks of the masses. The whole moderate policy of power seizure was soon labeled as a creature of the Adverse February Current and simply a device of the Party leaders to restore themselves to a position of undisputed power. The conservative cadres "jumped out," as the rebels put it, in February. Now, as the air warmed and the first spring flowers thrust up their shoots, the students, making up the legions of foot soldiers in the cause of the Cultural Group, took their stand. The Army, in the meantime, was preparing to make its own power felt at times and places of its own choosing. The three-way alliance was turning into a three-way struggle for power.

## Chapter VIII

# Factions Foreign
# And Domestic

THE LIVES OF our Chinese friends and neighbors at the Institute were by now almost totally absorbed in the Cultural Revolution, intricate as the traditional ivory balls within ivory balls. There were, of course, a few who attempted to remain at a safe distance from the widening whirlpool; and some even succeeded in doing so. We thought of the cool teacher, one of the "red mandarins," as we privately named his group, who told us that when he had seen crowds of Red Guards approaching his dormitory building during the work-team period, when intellectuals were under attack, he had simply ducked out the back door and headed for the canal, where he spent every day of several weeks peacefully fishing. "I knew there was nothing wrong with me," he said calmly, "and I knew that they would realize it sooner or later. Meanwhile, why go through all that?"

However, as the intensity of the Cultural Revolution mounted, one current or another inexorably drew everyone into the swirling center, transforming reticent observers into passionate participants. Domestic life somehow continued, and, in fact, there were any number of young teaching couples who decided that this period without a regular work schedule would be a good time to have a baby. Within a few years, the number of Peking toddlers in their customary broad-brimmed white hats would indicate that it was a decision made rather widely. But the passions of factional loyalties were the inescapable center of everyone's lives, and we, too, were becoming more and more closely attuned to these emotions and concerns.

After our school's Red Flag Detachment (Hung-ch'i Ta-tui) had split and produced the Red Flag Rebel Regiment (Hung-ch'i Tsao-fan T'uan), we discussed the issues in the Institute with members on both sides, for our students and fellow teachers had gone in opposing directions. There were now three rebel groups in the school. (The June 16 Independent Rebel Regiment, with its small band of about 100 militants had maintained its own separate existence from the beginning of the movement and would continue to do so until it was denounced as a counterrevolutionary organization in the summer of 1967.) After a short period of investigation, we soon concluded that there was a recognizable pattern between the two main organizations that would finally determine our own decision. For no one could participate in this great historic event, as it was daily referred to, except by the choice of sides. Most of David's fifth-year students became members of Tsao-fan T'uan (Rebel Corps). His class, partly because of its senior status, contained a large number of Party and Youth League members, who maintained a spirit of discipline and took very seriously their political leadership of the younger students. Nancy's second-year students, most of whom were peasants, beneficiaries of the recent Foreign Ministry policies requiring increased worker-peasant enrollment in the Institute, tended to join Hung-ch'i (Red Flag). We had teacher acquaintances on both sides, but a greater number of those to whom we were closest were Hung-ch'i supporters. The majority of the senior Party cadres in the school became either members or behind-the-scenes supporters of Tsao-fan T'uan.

The central question in every factional struggle on every level was the determination of "enemies." Chairman Mao had repeatedly stated that 95 per cent of the cadres were good and that only the bad 5 per cent, a "tiny handful," were the targets of the movement. The problem that was to rack the nation, from government ministries to the smallest workshop, was how to determine that tiny handful. Once all of the cadres understood, as they did very early, that they could avoid being labeled "bad" only by organizing their own mass "troops," the problem became just about insoluble. However, neither we nor anyone else understood this at the time. In that first exhilarating winter of the Cultural Revolution, everyone considered himself to be one of the "pathbreakers" described in the impassioned newspaper editorials and assumed that in this "great debate," all of the hidden facts would eventually come out and those who had been deluded would finally be won over to the side of the triumphant majority.

The Institute's two Red Guard organizations had very early decided who they felt were the tiny handful of persons in power taking the capitalist road. Tsao-fan T'uan's targets were three men, none of whom had been in positions of power in the school for several years, but who, the Rebel Corps said, had been responsible for setting the "revisionist" line that had continued after them. One was a young and brilliant former Party Secretary of the English Department who for two years had been working in the Middle East section of the Foreign Ministry, where he was said to have shown great promise. The second was a former First Party Secretary of the Institute who had been living on the campus for the past few years in virtual retirement, on indefinite sick leave because of a nervous breakdown. The third, also a leading Party cadre, had been transferred two years earlier to the presidency of the Institute's neighboring school, the Peking Language Institute, where foreign students were trained in Chinese. In the familiar Chinese manner of neat sloganization, the triumvirate became known from their surnames as Liu-Hao-Shih. On the other side, Hung-ch'i's two targets were the current First Party Secretary of the Institute and one of the Second Party Secretaries. In accordance with the same system, the two were code-named Shui-Yang.

The merits and demerits of these five were to be questioned from the beginning to the very end of the movement, and in the fall of 1966, they were asked by both Red Guard organizations to participate in an open debate. Its avowed purpose was to enable the student-teacher masses to reach their own conclusions about certain contested events involving the cadres' connections with the now discredited Peking City Party Committee. It was a meeting that did much to confirm our remarkably ingenuous view that the historic event we were observing was a debate of exceptional proportions.

The question of "connections" was to play an increasingly important role in the cadre debate. In a Party structure in which the implementation of central directives was the responsibility of all cadres, it was extremely difficult to assign blame for cadres who had carried out instructions from above. For this reason, judgments of impossible subjectivity began to appear. Had the cadre carried out "revisionist" policies "enthusiastically" or merely "obediently," Mao's line "actively" or "passively"? In many places, arguments continued for years on such matters without ever reaching a clear determination. In Peking, however, it was assumed possible to establish real organizational ties to the P'eng Chen City Committee, whose record indicated a conscious and consistent opposition to Mao's policies, no matter what degree of "red flag waving" had necessarily accompanied it. Thus the essence of any debate became the establishment or refutation of such organizational ties.

The innovative aspect of the particular meeting we attended was not its rather standard content, but its open debating form. Contrary to the practice in "struggle meetings," where the accused cadre was not permitted to state his own case, the two groups of cadres in this meeting debated with each other in a parliamentary fashion seldom seen in China. There was little interference or direction from the mass organizers of the meeting. It was our first public introduction to the young cadre who had voluntarily returned from the Foreign Ministry to face his accusers in his former organization. He gave such clear proof that day of his ability that his Tsao-fan T'uan opposition would not risk influencing its constituency again by permitting him further freedom of speech.

It was an impressive meeting, rational, dignified, without the hysteria and unsubstantiated evidence of so many of the meetings which were to occur during the long course of the Cultural Revolution. It was one of the few meetings we attended which conformed entirely to official instructions, which stated: "When there is a difference among working masses of a unit or a locality or among workers' organizations, discussions should be held by presenting facts and persuading through reasoning [. . .] without creating a situation of confrontation." Because of our own political and philosophical background, we undoubtedly saw it to some degree as a revolutionary application of the great traditions of Anglo-Saxon law, but the rest of the audience seemed as impressed as we with this novel meeting. Within a few months, however, it was to be denounced by both sides as a "black" meeting for having permitted each other's enemies the right to speak. The definition of the Cultural Revolution as a class struggle negated the possibility of a social movement conducted through debate.

To us, the relative "correctness" of each Red Guard faction began to seem fairly clear—in fact, even simple. While the overwhelming majority of the Party cadres supported one organization and focused their attack on three men who held no power in the Institute, the majority of students and ordinary teachers joined the other organization, which had as its targets the two main Party persons in authority. The logic of it all seemed quite obvious. We became Hung-ch'i members. Upon joining, we wrote our only big-character poster contribution to the Cultural Revolution at the Peking First Foreign Languages Institute, in which we explained our choice of sides, placing most emphasis on the fact that we did not see how a movement against "those in the Party in authority taking the capitalist road" could be conducted against cadres not in authority. We closed our *ta-tzu-pao* with the customary Chinese courtesies, stating that these were our modest conclusions and that we would be glad to have them corrected if inaccurate. Foregoing the formalistic polite denials that usually follow such statements, several of David's Tsao-fan T'uan students had no hesitation in telling him that they considered his decision to be quite wrong.

For any student organization in Peking, there were external as well as internal issues to be dealt with. The Peking First Foreign Languages Institute was under the jurisdiction of the Foreign Ministry, so the struggle in that Ministry attracted far greater student commitment and concern than the far less exciting issues of our own campus. From the very beginning, the key political issue in the Ministry centered on Ch'en Yi. It had been the contention of Tsao-fan T'uan that Ch'en Yi and, obliquely through him, Chou En-lai, should be among the major targets of the Cultural Revolution. Hung-ch'i, firmly behind Premier Chou, was always uneasy about the campaign against Ch'en Yi, for Hung-ch'i members were clearly aware of its real aim. At the same time Hung-ch'i also had reason to criticize Ch'en Yi for his conservative stance in the Cultural Revolution. Consequently, it attempted to maintain a delicate and sometimes impossible balance of "Criticize Ch'en Yi, but don't overthrow him." June 16 took one of the most extreme positions of any university group in the city and consistently maintained open opposition to Premier Chou himself.

These questions would bring the First Foreign Languages Institute into the storm center of the top-level power struggle later in the Cultural Revolution. However, the issue of Ch'en Yi's leadership always had a local use as well. Predictably, whenever pressure against the school's two Party Secretaries became particularly heavy, Tsao-fan T'uan would mount a great campaign against the "crimes" of Ch'en Yi, and the local issues would be swept aside.

The campaign simmering against Premier Chou reached a dramatic crescendo on January 7, 1967, when June 16 posted a *ta-tzu-pao* in T'ien An Men Square titled "Chou En-lai, what do you want?" Security forces came to the school and arrested the June 16 leaders, of whom the best known was Liu Ling-k'ai, for having gone beyond the bounds of permissible revolt. As might have been expected, the uproar was overwhelming. Some thousand new posters, approving and protesting the arrests, appeared overnight. Loudspeakers broadcast the stridently stated views of the contending sides. However, in a week, the offenders had been released and were back at school to continue their revolution, but with the clear understanding that this would no longer include *ta-tzu-pao* against the Premier in the most official of all Chinese public places.

The seizures of power arising from the January Revolution produced the same ramifications at our Institute as elsewhere in China. Hung-ch'i, numerically the larger of the two main organizations, seized power in the First Foreign Languages Institute. Although its members, including ourselves, enjoyed a brief moment of triumph, it was never more than symbolic. Rather than solving the power problem, the Hung-ch'i coup only increased the polarization within the school. It was a typical Cultural Revolution phenomenon that the two factions would disagree over the fundamental question of who should be removed from leadership in their particular organization. Each saw the other side's enemies as their own heroes. This was the situation, repeated in most of the thousands of institutions in China, that would finally undercut the meaning and effectiveness of the seizure of power from below.

In the foreign community, too, as among the Chinese, differing interests and attitudes produced similar factional splits. Within our own community, existing both inside and outside Chinese society, these splits reflected real differences in social and political relationships. From the beginning, those who were teachers found it difficult to remain aloof from the events that absorbed the lives of the students of Peking. Engrossed though the students were, they welcomed many of us to their early meetings, gave us briefings on the latest editorials, took us to see the newest big-character posters, and let us know that they felt responsible for our education in this greatest of all Chinese political movements.

After full-scale factional divisions appeared, one's own faction took on similar responsibilities, while for those who remained outside the factional boundaries of the movement, there was no longer any possibility of participation.

For the foreign experts who worked in offices, mostly doing language "polishing" for the Chinese foreign languages publications or foreign language broadcasting at the Peking Radio, relationships in this strange new period were more difficult and formal. Unlike the schools, which suspended their classes, these offices continued their work. Normal hours were observed, and there were no free and enthusiastic students to draw one into their political lives. Still, the "foreign friends" were sometimes invited to meetings and, depending on their degree of closeness to their professional colleagues, often learned something of what was going on in their work unit.

Although few of the foreign guests verbalized their feelings about the historical continuity of internationalist participation in young revolutions, this was undoubtedly an underlying assumption shared by these guests from around the world and, at that stage of the Cultural Revolution, by many of the hosts. Foreign participation had been a factor in all the great modern revolutions, from the American to the Chinese, and the Cultural Revolution seemed in its early stages to have a close affinity with those historically brief moments of international fraternity. The Paris Commune, whose egalitarian traditions were a legacy of the Western world, had become one of the thematic rallying points of this anti-bureaucratic battle of the Eastern world. In the first year of their power, the Red Guards played the "Internationale" interminably over their loudspeakers and, for the first time in our experience in China, permitted their foreign friends the democratic privilege of sitting on the floor or standing in the back of the meeting instead of having the best seats in the house.

Historically, the question of citizenship had worked both ways for revolutionary allies. The National Convention of the French Revolution had conferred the rights of citizenship on a long list of distinguished friends: Bentham, Priestly, Washington, Hamilton, Paine, Kosciuszki, and Anarchis Cloots, among others; while Paine, the greatest propagandist of the American Revolution, never became an American citizen, retaining his birthright as a British subject in order to function as a "citizen of the world." There were no Tom Paines in Peking, but an impressive representation of "world citizens" who saw no reason not to take their place, insofar as that was possible, next to the Chinese rebels.

There was one group of foreigners who actively advised against following this path. These were some of the true "old hands" who had been in China for up to thirty or forty years and who were in some cases Chinese citizens themselves and in a few cases even Party members. They warned that this great battle was strictly a Chinese affair. Being both "Chinese" cadres and elders of the foreign community, they spoke as people who had a permanent commitment to China, no matter how the battle came out. Another group of foreign "cadres" took the course of intense involvement in the Cultural Revolution. Like their Chinese counterparts, the "old hands" moved in various ways, some hoping by calm responsibleness to avoid the worst of the storms; others, by intense, often ultra-left engagement, to come out on top of whatever new power coalition should appear. As foreigners, they would have both protections and vulnerabilities that Chinese cadres did not share.

There were other long-term foreign residents who, either by choice or imposition, did not share this elite status. Several had for years struggled to divest their lives of the special privileges which the Chinese impose on all foreigners; others, the foreign wives of Chinese, had long suffered a two-edged discrimination. Being neither foreign nor Chinese in a culture in which one's social and political definition determines the boundaries of participation, they took part in the life of their adopted country with neither the rights of Chinese nor the privileges of foreigners. It was this segment of the foreign community which most closely paralleled the aggrieved sectors of the Chinese population. It was logical, then, that within the foreign community, some of their spokesmen should appear as "early rebels" with what became known as "The Four Americans' *Ta-tzu-pao*." Titled in proper Chinese fashion, "What Monster Is Driving Us Down the Road to Revisionism?", it attacked the Party authorities in the Foreign Experts Bureau for their imposition of high salaries, superior living conditions, and privileges of various kinds, thus undermining the revolutionary will expected of everyone else in China.

Everyone in Peking's American community agreed that the privileged position of foreigners was a problem. Many had long ago insisted on at least a cut in salary. But this *ta-tzu-pao*, in its total stress on the external influences on consciousness, was very typical of other rebel posters of the same period, which placed overwhelming stress on outside forces. The other side of the dialectic would not be brought to prominence until later in the Cultural Revolution, when every person would be urged to "Fight self; repudiate revisionism" and to make "self" the target of the revolution. The *ta-tzu-pao* debate in the American community raised many of the questions which similar small Chinese groups throughout the country were also debating. In Chinese society, we were guest observers, regardless of our factional partisanship; but in our own small community, we began to learn at first hand about the laws of the Cultural Revolution. It was finally agreed that, whatever its weaknesses, the four Americans' *ta-tzu-pao* was a revolutionary statement. Later, it became clear that certain leaders of our small community, soon to throw themselves into the storms of ultra-left politics, were aware that Chairman Mao himself had written a note, his "*p'i-shih*," stating his opinion that this was a "revolutionary *ta-tzu-pao*." This, however, was but another affirmation that the laws determining the struggles in Chinese society would also determine ours. As in the Chinese struggle, leaks from the top would influence the mass movement, but not determine it, for the political issues we debated were ones which truly involved the practical realities of our everyday lives.

Chairman Mao's "*p'i-shih*" on the *ta-tzu-pao* would be announced by Ch'en Yi in a dramatic meeting for all the foreigners, but the day before his meeting, another event occurred which would bring together into one Red Guard organization the several social groupings among the foreigners. Foreigners as foreigners came into the Cultural Revolution just as some of us individually had already done in our Chinese organizations, by invitation of the rebels. We, and a small number of others, considered ourselves fortunate to be able to live within the precincts of our organization; but the great majority of foreign experts from all countries were residents of the cavernous Friendship Hotel, built to specification for the former thousands of Russian experts. A sprawling complex of apartments, offices, meeting halls, an Olympic-sized swimming pool, and unending hallways, it was embarrassingly luxurious by Chinese standards. The staff was large. It included not only the mysteriously invisible functionaries of the Foreign Experts' Bureau and their busy interpreters and helpers, but cooks, drivers, and domestic workers of all kinds. Like every other working unit in China, it was filled with rebels. Having their own grievances against the Experts' Bureau, a delegation of rebels came to foreigners whom they knew to be sympathetic to the Cultural Revolution and asked for their support. And so there came into existence the first and last Red Guard organization of foreigners, the Bethune-Yenan Regiment, drawing its name from the symbolism of the internationalism of Dr. Norman Bethune and the Maoist revolutionary spirit of Yenan.

The prime movers and first leaders of Bethune-Yenan were the foreigners whose involvement in the Cultural Revolution was rooted in the internationalist participation common to all revolutions. Their main concern, therefore, was not so much reform of their own position in Chinese society, but support for the Chinese revolutionaries. Their concept of this role was symbolized in the decision to have a five-member coalition leadership representing five continents. Those, on the other hand, who associated themselves primarily with the position of the American *ta-tzu-pao* also joined Bethune-Yenan and assumed from the beginning that the position of the *ta-tzu-pao* was the primary policy position of the organization. It was this fundamental divergence in opinion regarding the real function of the organization—whether it was to support the Chinese rebels or to fight for integration of the foreigners—that caused internal battles as furious as any which rocked its Chinese counterparts. The five members of the first leadership group—from South Africa, New Zealand, Belgium, Brazil, and the US— were ousted within six months, the opposition shouting "conservatism" and demanding in the words of one of its more extreme spokesmen, a position for Bethune-Yenan "in the vanguard of the Chinese Cultural Revolution."

Chairman Mao's "*p'i-shih,*" characteristic of his political style of awaiting the appearance of social phenomena and then commenting favorably on those which he believes to represent positive trends, was a comment of approval, just as his comments on Nieh Yuan-tzu's *ta-tzu-pao* had been. In addition to remarking that the four Americans' *ta-tzu-pao* was revolutionary, he also stated that all "revolutionary foreign experts" who wished to do so might participate in the Cultural Revolution. In his presentation of the "*p'i-shih*" to Peking's entire foreign community, Foreign Minister Ch'en Yi added that there were among the foreign residents in Peking different groups with different interests. He specifically mentioned the difference in interests between long-term residents and those who would stay and work in China for a more limited period. The American *ta-tzu-pao* supporters, taking the position that there should be but one revolutionary policy affecting all foreigners, within days attacked the Foreign Minister for his "bourgeois world outlook," an attack which would begin to move them into the same sphere as the Chinese organizations whose target was also Ch'en Yi.

By the spring of 1967, the rigid factionalism in Peking's First Foreign Languages Institute, as in every unit in the country, had intensified dramatically. It had been a long time since one side had shown any willingness, not to say interest, in hearing the views of the opposition; but the antagonism continued to mount as each devoted monumental research efforts to proving the case of "its" cadres. Students and teachers spent days in libraries, pouring over old records and newspapers, and others formed investigation teams to track down the political and personal histories of both friends and enemies. They traveled for miles to remote villages and distant cities to talk with relatives, childhood acquaintances, military comrades, and political coworkers—and returned, not surprisingly, with opposing evidence. Perhaps this was best epitomized by a student who announced to us triumphantly that, although the opposing faction had interviewed a former village neighbor of his side's cadre and received some negative information, he had learned quite the opposite from the man's mother.

One case that absorbed both factions for a considerable period of time concerned the early career of one of the deputy Party secretaries at the Institute, now important for what his political background might mean in his "links" with a higher target. The man in question had in 1937 left Peking University, where he had joined the Party as a student, to work on a Sian newspaper run by the Young Marshal Chang Hsueh-liang. The paper was published by the Kuomintang and, in the customary terminology of the period, referred to the Communists as "bandits." At the same time, it was strongly advocating the policy of a united front with the Communists when they themselves were devoting major efforts to the implementation of a united-front policy. The question that arose thirty years later was: Had the cadre become a traitor and gone over to the KMT, or was he working, as he claimed, as an underground Communist to further the Party's main political program of that period? Both sides made line-by-line analysis of the old newspapers. It was soon discovered by the Hung-ch'i investigators that the editor in chief of the newspaper was himself an underground Communist. We were impressed with the meticulousness of the research and the down-to-earth nature of Hung-ch'i's conclusion, which argued that one could not judge the policies of the past by those of the present and affirmed that the cadre had served the revolution well in his role of underground journalist regardless of the practical necessity which required him to bend to the political terminology of the day.

Such research, however useful it might have been as a substitute for school, contributed little to the resolution of the power struggle, for neither side was influenced by the conclusions of the other. To an increasing degree, the researchers were engaged in convincing the convinced. The factional splits dating from months earlier had been hardened rather than modified by the events of January, when the revolutionary masses had been called upon to seize power, and February, when they had been instructed to include cadres in the three-in-one revolutionary committees. The test of legitimacy in both cases was the question of who among the masses and the cadres constituted the true revolutionaries. It was now a definition of life and death importance, for it would determine who would hold power and who would be smashed. Neither side could afford to yield positions already taken.

It would appear that Mao decided at important meetings of the Political Bureau and the Military Affairs Commission in March 1967 to turn the direction of the Cultural Revolution at this point against Liu Shao-ch'i and Teng Hsiao-p'ing in an obvious attempt to direct the embattled forces on top and among the masses against a clearly defined target. *Red Flag* came out with its No. 5 edition in the first week of April, containing a major article devoted to launching the new campaign. It took the form of a return to the cultural criticism so prominent in the opening stages of the Cultural Revolution, but the recondite quality characterizing the Hai Jui debate was no longer in evidence. In "Patriotism or National Betrayal?—On the Reactionary Film 'Inside Story of the Ch'ing Court,'" Ch'i Pen-yü, one of the radical intellectuals of the Cultural Group, attacked not only the film itself, but its support by the man now called "the top person in authority taking the capitalist road." Liu Shao-ch'i, still unnamed, was repudiated for crimes even more serious than taking the capitalist road; he was branded for national betrayal as well. Ch'i Pen-yü tied these general crimes to the specific difficulties of the Cultural Revolution itself:

> "The fact that this top Party person [Liu Shao-ch'i] so bitterly hates past revolutionary mass movements enables us better to understand why, collaborating as he did with another top Party person in authority taking the capitalist road (Teng Hsiao-p'ing), he put forward a bourgeois reactionary line in the current great proletarian cultural revolution in a vain attempt to extinguish the revolutionary flames lit by Chairman Mao himself, why he confused right and wrong and turned things upside down, organized attacks on the revolutionaries, suppressed the masses and carried out a White Terror, and why he tried in a hundred and one ways to boost the arrogance of the bourgeoisie and crush the morale of the proletariat."[86]

Theoretically, almost everyone had something to gain from a campaign against Liu and Teng. For the Party cadres, some of the pressure would be removed from themselves; for the Cultural Group, the attack on Liu-Teng-T'ao (T'ao Chu was linked to the others as the third main enemy) meant a continued attack on revisionist policies. The preceding quotation clearly indicates the hope that the warring Red Guards would see Liu Shao-ch'i as the cause of their conflicts and transfer their attack to him, but that hope indicated an illusory view of the Red Guards' concept of the immediate political realities. Liu was, they knew, a "dead tiger." While some argued that the struggle against Liu-Teng was the ideological heart of the movement, we were to hear again and again battle cries against the "living tigers."

The major ideological aspect of the struggle against Liu centered around criticism of his book *On the Cultivation of a Communist Party Member,* originally written in 1939 and reprinted in 1962 with certain important revisions and its more contemporary English title, *How to Be a Good*

*Communist.* The editorials of the period laid particular stress on several fundamental points of political difference between the 1962 version and the Thought of Mao. One was Liu's stress on ideological training through "self-cultivation" versus Mao's "ideological remolding" through study of his works and involvement in actual class struggle:

> " 'Self-cultivation' is a book concentrating on self-cultivation by communists. However, it departs from the reality of class struggle. It does not talk about the seizure of political power and the dictatorship of the proletariat, but only about the bourgeois self-cultivation of the individual. This is the reactionary nature of 'self-cultivation' in which its essence lies."[87]

The absence of reference to the dictatorship of the proletariat was taken as particularly important proof of Liu's spirit of "capitulationism"—such references in the 1939 edition were removed in 1962. A *People's Daily* editorial of the time said: "Would not self-cultivation of this kind simply cultivate philistines who would avoid revolutionary war and the seizing of political power by armed force?", thus continuing to raise in this ideological campaign the still acutely delicate question of the seizure of power.

Criticism of what was termed Liu's concept of "slavishness" fed the continuing flames of revolt against Party cadres. Editorials frequently cited these words of Mao:

> "Communists must always go into the whys and wherefores of anything, use their own heads, and carefully think over whether or not it corresponds to reality and is really well founded; on no account should they follow blindly and encourage slavishness."[88]

The Chinese people were reminded constantly that "Erroneous leadership, which brings harm to the revolution, should not be accepted unconditionally, but should be resisted resolutely." However, none of these concepts of Mao's was new to the ideology of the Cultural Revolution or held out the real possibility of resolving outstanding problems. Recited thousands of times by every Red Guard in China from his or her little red book, they had been the philosophical base from which had arisen the early cries of "Tsao-fan yu-li" (It's Right to Rebel).

Although conscientious teachers and students at the First Foreign Languages Institute, in compliance with central directives, tried earnestly to organize meetings and study groups to repudiate Liu's book, they were in general greeted with great indifference. A few of the more classically-minded intellectuals among our Chinese friends became absorbed in scholarly exegesis of the book's Confucian elements, but it appeared to us in our conversations with them that the more intense the analysis the more delicate the political problems. Mao, as well as Liu, demanded discipline of Party members and the subordination of the minority to the majority. Informed by friends and editorials that the campaign against *How to Be a Good Communist* would go to the heart of the struggle between the two lines and the two roads, we waited and watched expectantly. But the movement against Liu's book quietly disappeared, and only the formalistic references to the evil influences of Liu's "black book" remained.

By the spring of 1967, the assiduous printing presses of the Red Guards, whose news many citizens found far more exciting than the official editorials of the day, were busily turning out copies of a particularly interesting document on Liu. Titled "Premier Chou Talks About Why Firepower Must Be Concentrated on Criticizing the Party's Top Person Taking the Capitalist Road," it was typical of the thousands of internal speeches published and circulated rapidly by Red Guard groups "in the public interest" and often the interests of their own faction. These frequently had an enormous impact on the struggle down below. In this one, Premier Chou addressed a question which must have occurred to most reasonable persons: "Some people ask why Liu Shao-ch'i was not criticized earlier since he has committed so many mistakes. Why is he criticized only now?" Basing his argument on historical analogy, beginning with Marx's position regarding the First International and continuing through examples drawn from the Paris Commune, Lenin's role in the October Revolution, and the later "correct" and "incorrect" line of Stalin, he elaborated one fundamental theme: "All political mistakes develop gradually. It took more than twenty years to observe Teng Hsiao-p'ing and Liu Shao-ch'i." Chou then described those critical periods during which Liu had made mistakes, corrected by Mao—his capitulationist interpretation of the wartime Chungking Negotiations with Chiang Kai-shek, his erroneous position on the role of the national capitalists following liberation; on the formation of cooperatives; his view that the country's principal contradiction was between relations of production and productivity ("Liu Shao-ch'i's political report and Teng Hsiao-p'ing's organizational report at the Eighth Party Congress"). Liu's errors culminated finally in his policy on the implementation of the Socialist Education Movement. Chou completed his speech with a comparison which, in retrospect, is truly arresting:

> "In short, it is not that Chairman Mao did not criticize Liu Shao-ch'i; several criticisms were in the written form, the most severe one being the drawing up of the Twenty-three Articles during the 1964–65 Four Liquidation Movement [more commonly translated as the "Four Clears" or "Four Clean-up Movement"]. At that time, Chairman Mao nearly lost all hope in Liu Shao-ch'i. All the help to him in more than twenty years was to no avail. At this time, our Deputy Commander Lin Piao had won confidence everywhere. After several decades of fostering, tempering and leadership, it was proved that Comrade Lin Piao was the first one to hoist high the great red flag of Mao Tse-tung's Thought. In recent years, despite all interferences of Lo Jui-ch'ing, Comrade Lin Piao personally led the Liberation Army in studying Chairman Mao's writings, establishing an indelible record [. . .] We have a leader who has been tested. Why don't we confirm the fact according to law. Therefore the 11th Plenum was convened last year, and the problem was solved. On the one hand, the one who has committed mistakes could not do it despite all the rescue work. On the other hand, the tested successor to

Chairman Mao, trusted by the entire Party and entire Army, should be elected."[89]

This document makes strange reading several years after the "tested successor" was also discovered upon the eve of his succession to have an unhappily flawed history, and the whole nation has devoted its political energies to criticism pairing the marshal of "indelible record" with the philosophical father of all that is regarded as authoritarian in Chinese culture—Confucius. However, at the time no one paid much attention to the final paragraph of Chou's speech. It was simply affirmation of what every man and woman in the street already knew, that Chairman Mao had chosen a new successor, and this time it was one of whom he was sure. What those who perused the speech did find interesting was the historical documentation of Liu's revisionism, a documentation decidedly less esoteric than the criticism of his book.

However, the aspect of Liu Shao-ch'i's repudiation that generated the most feverish excitement among the students of Peking was the huge Tsinghua University "struggle meeting" against his wife, Wang Kuang-mei, certainly not a "living tiger," but a living surrogate for her husband. It was a meeting prohibited to foreigners. Busloads officially dispatched from the Friendship Hotel were as officially turned back on the road leading to the university. Only Sid Rittenberg, operating at the heart of Peking politics, attended that meeting, where, apparently because of his close connections with certain members of the Cultural Group, he sat in an honored place on the main platform.

It was a meeting one could hardly regret missing. Although Wang Kuang-mei had played a political role of her own in her direction of the Socialist Education Movement and in her leadership of the Tsinghua University work-team, the grueling day-long meeting was primarily a symbolic attack on Liu Shao-ch'i. Personally, Wang Kuang-mei presented some all too obvious "enemy" attributes. She was the daughter of a wealthy Tientsin capitalist, and to her more recent role as the wife of China's president she had brought an aristocratic elegance and style which became the delight of the Cultural Revolution's young caricaturists. They emphasized this aspect of her "problem," by forcing her to wear a silk dress, high-heeled shoes, and a necklace of ping-pong balls satirizing her pearls. All in all, the promoters of the meeting generated a distasteful pettiness which was somehow communicated even, or perhaps especially, to those like ourselves who knew of the proceedings only through hearsay.

The "struggle meeting," from the early advent of the work-teams, had been accepted as the ritual form through which the superstructural revolution would be concretely carried out. Like other phenomena of the Cultural Revolution, the "struggle meeting" had been derived from the methods used in thousands of Chinese villages during the land reform period, when accused landlords or traitors stood with bowed head before the people (just as the people in the past had stood with bowed head before officials) to admit their crimes against society. The struggle meeting had thus not generally been a means of determining guilt, but of providing political education and mobilizing the peasants to understand the nature of their centuries-long oppression. It was meant to turn their fear and passivity into a weapon for radical social change. Such meetings were not tribunals so much as a means of mass mobilization. It was for this reason that the now time-hardened practice arose which forbade the accused the right to reply.

The problems of the Cultural Revolution were very different from those of the land reform period, when the identification of class enemies had been fundamentally clear. Now, the enemies were by no means agreed upon, but the struggle meetings held by all factions proceeded on the assumption that the cadre being "struggled against" was *the* enemy. As a result, not only did the struggle meetings not bring the masses into closer unity with each other, as had been their purpose in earlier periods, but they served to further exacerbate hostility, for each group was incensed at the harsh treatment of its own "good" cadres. We did not attend any of the huge citywide Red Guard struggle meetings against such officially approved targets as Wang Kuangmei and P'eng Chen, but our two older sons, being middle school students of the Red Guard age group, did. Clearly, such officially sanctioned meetings did little to provide a constructive example for lesser units embroiled in struggle over the question of just who the enemy actually was.

Peking's "living tiger" in the late spring of 1967 was Ch'en Yi. For the ultra-left groups, Chou En-lai was the *"hou-t'ai"* (the backstage power) behind all of the government ministers; but, in order to reach him, these ministers would have to be knocked down first. Because of his role in sending the work-teams to the various units under the Foreign Ministry, including the Peking First Foreign Languages Institute, Ch'en Yi had had from the beginning a particular vulnerability among certain student groups, including Tsao-fan T'uan. He had openly indicated his impatience and displeasure with the Red Guards, often in a sardonic way. Months before, for instance, we had heard of his insistence on wearing the dunce hat imposed on him by Red Guards to lunch in the students' dining room, because, he said, he had come to like the hat. He had scolded Red Guards for turning against their parents and for "burning the bridge" of China's revolution by smashing those who had brought the country into socialism. When the Cultural Revolution was still in its early months, we had met Ch'en Yi at Anna Louise Strong's home and listened to the two old veterans debate the propriety of naming this political revolution a "cultural revolution." Ch'en Yi argued that the term used by Lenin was a proper one. However, despite his approval of the nomenclature, his actions and remarks over the months clearly indicated that he was less than enthusiastic about its content. He made no secret of his disapproval. It was precisely because of his courage and his honesty that Marshal Ch'en Yi had long been one of the most popular men in China.

Under the worried prodding of Mao and Chou, he had made the necessary self-criticisms for his misunderstanding of the Cultural Revolution, but his repudiation of that criticism and his role in leading the revolt of the Foreign Ministry cadre in the February Adverse Current had finally brought him into conflict with even those Red Guard groups which had stood by him in earlier months. Those who had opposed him from the beginning now cried "Overthrow Ch'en Yi," while others, like the Institute's Hung-ch'i, now chimed in with "Criticize Ch'en Yi." "Liaison Stations" to coordinate the criticism of Ch'en Yi sprouted throughout Peking, and the students busily propagandized the townspeople, many of whom were hardly pleased with this particular campaign. A Hung-ch'i student, distributing the group's "Criticize Ch'en Yi" paper in front of the city's main department store, was asked by an indignant citizen, "Why are you students attacking our old general?" and was only slightly mollified by the reply that this organization was not attacking but criticizing.

However, fearing that in the revolutionary fervor of the time, they had indeed become as conservative as their opposition accused them of being, Hung-ch'i students broke into the Foreign Ministry on May 13 and, in the usual melee of violence and destruction of property, broke into files of classified documents shouting, or so it was said, "To hell with state secrets." This first was also the last of Hung-ch'i's violent forays in the Foreign Ministry struggle, but Tsao-fan T'uan would continue to "rush in" in similar ventures until the final August 1967 debacle at the Foreign Ministry. In their invasion of May 29, Tsao-fan T'uan had new and surprising support within the Ministry itself in the person of a rising cadre named Yao Teng-shan. The chargé d'affaires of the Chinese diplomatic mission in Indonesia, Yao had courageously defended the Chinese Mission against the attacks of violent mobs and then, when the Chinese diplomats had been expelled from Indonesia, returned to Peking to a hero's welcome. He made full political use of his sudden fame. On May 1, he had been received by Chairman Mao, and when the customary formally posed portrait of the Chairman and his visitors appeared on the front page of the

*People's Daily,* it showed a broadly grinning Yao with his arms linked firmly with Chairman Mao's on one side and Chiang Ch'ing's on the other. The uncharacteristic nature of the pose caused a buzz at the time it appeared, for in hundreds of such pictures Mao had never been seen linking arms with any of his guests, and in this one, he appeared to be far from enthusiastic. After the May 29 raid on the Foreign Ministry, we were surprised to hear that, unlike Hung-ch'i, which had been harshly reprimanded for its similar raid, our opposition had instead been led in their raid by one of the most important men in that Ministry. Clearly, Yao was hoping to become an even more important man by his utilization of the student ultra-leftists, and it was from Sid Rittenberg that we were to hear that Yao Teng-shan could be expected to be China's next Foreign Minister.

Since the foreigners' own Cultural Revolution had begun six months after the Chinese one, its progression was always a few steps behind the national model. At the time when every organization in China had split into factions, the Bethune-Yenan Regiment was still enjoying a state of early unity. Its first three months of existence were quite successful. It reached a membership of ninety people from every area in the world, providing a forum of activity and discussion for non-Chinese who were searching for a constructive role they might play in an historic social movement. Everyone was pleased when the regiment was officially recognized by the Chinese press in the winter of 1967 as a respected revolutionary fraternal organization like all the other myriad rebel groups in the nation's capital. In those first heady months of January, February, and March 1967, the regiment was invited to march in support of Chinese rebel organizations at the various departments where the foreigners worked. It was soon apparent that the young Chinese rebels in the universities also hoped to use the prestige of the foreign regiment by inviting its representatives to speak and share the platform at mass meetings and rallies. Thus the foreign regiment found itself operating on three fronts: supporting the rebels in the Foreign Experts' Bureau;

answering requests for support from Chinese groups at the
press and the various schools where the various foreigners
worked; and meeting demands of university Red Guard
organizations for speakers from Bethune-Yenan in the effort
by these groups to indicate to all concerned that their cause
had acquired world-wide significance.

After the initial euphoria had begun to wear off, a number of us involved in this international revolutionary con-
glomerate began to have a few apprehensions about the
purpose, direction, and political effect of the organization
we had founded. It was a feeling, a dim perception, that
perhaps we might be used by political forces over which we
had no control and about which we had little understanding.
Appropriately in this rebellion of the young, it was our sons
and daughters from Asia, Africa, Europe, and North and
South America who were the first to articulate the pitfalls
which confronted an organization of enthusiastic outsiders
entering the thickets of Chinese politics. In a *ta-tzu-pao*
beginning with the Chairman's quotation "No investigation,
no right to speak," they warned their parents and elders that
they were naïvely lending themselves to Peking's complex
factional battles by permitting themselves to be used as
speakers by organizations of which they knew nothing. Already, they said, members of Bethune-Yenan had spoken
under the sponsorship of politically questionable Red Guard
groups. Our community of teenagers, far more capable in
the language than most of their parents and as active in
circulating through the streets and schools of the city as
their Chinese peers, were knowledgeable evaluators of
Peking's political currents.

We were reminded of Ch'en Yi's warning in January, that
the foreign friends had the right to form their own rebel
organization, but that they should be careful not to support
counterrevolutionary Chinese groupings. It was a warning
that the foreigners who were later to take over leadership
of Bethune-Yenan chose to ignore. But those who had
founded the regiment were inclined to heed the prescient advice of the young people by advocating a cautious stance

for foreigners in the Chinese Cultural Revolution. For this, they were soon overthrown as conservatives and replaced by a radical leadership who proceeded to involve themselves in a larger politics which proved to be their undoing.

Even less prepared than the Chinese for the division of the movement into irreconcilable factions, the foreigners soon found themselves in a difficult position. Except for Rittenberg and perhaps a few others, the foreign supporters of the Cultural Revolution were not involved in the larger citywide politics determined by the struggle between the Heaven and Earth factions for control of the Peking Red Guard Congress and the Peking Municipal Committee. Those of us who had been invited to participate in the movement at our places of work came to a recognition that the factional struggle involved much more than local issues long after the Chinese had taken this fact for granted.

For the foreign participants, as perhaps for the Chinese also, some of the most rewarding results of their participation in the Cultural Revolution consisted of public recognition of the validity of their concrete criticisms. For instance, there were few foreigners working for the various branches of the Chinese press who had not repeatedly protested the way in which Chinese articles were translated into unreadable versions of their native languages. Their criticisms had always been politely received, but over the years, there were few changes made in the baroque style of foreign language periodicals. So when a lengthy *ta-tzu-pao* posted by foreign experts working at the New China News Agency drew the following "Directive on External Propaganda Work" from Chairman Mao, there was general delight.

> "Some foreigners have offered suggestions on the external propaganda conducted by *Peking Review* and Hsinhua News Agency. In the past, they did not proselytize the fact that Mao Tse-tung's Thought has developed Marxism, but now, after the Great Cultural Revolution, they are doing it with fanfare, and there is such boasting that it is hard to swallow. Why must one say some of the words by one's self? We must be modest,

especially toward outsiders. In being a little modest toward outsiders, naturally we must not lose our principles. In yesterday's communiqué on the hydrogen bomb, I deleted Great Leader, Great Teacher, Great Commander-in-Chief, and Great Helmsman. I also deleted "limitless flame." How could there be limitless flame in the world? There is always a limit, so I deleted it. I also deleted "10,000 per cent" from the phrase "mood of 10,000 per cent joy and excitement." It was not 10 per cent, 100 per cent, or 1,000 per cent but 10,000 per cent. I didn't even want to have 1 per cent, and so I deleted it entirely."[90]

But, like the Chinese, the foreign propaganda workers would also learn that the leap from "struggle-criticism" to "transformation" was indeed the longest and most difficult leap of all. Throughout the Cultural Revolution, there were repeated references to the slogan "Tou-p'i-kai" (struggle-criticism-transformation). But, since the first two stages could never be satisfactorily completed, the third was constantly being postponed.

Sometime in the late spring, Rittenberg told some of us in the regiment that a remarkable new star named Ch'en Li-ning had arisen in the Chinese political skies. This man, it seemed, had been committed to a mental institution for his political beliefs after it had been discovered by the revisionist Party apparatus that he was making a political study of the works of Liu Shao-ch'i, systematically analyzing their incorrect content, and carefully recording all his findings in a series of notebooks. Our immediate reaction was that this was shocking confirmation of the parallels between the methods of Liu Shao-ch'i and those of his Soviet counterparts. Ch'en Li-ning, we were told, was not a madman but a political genius who had been discovered only when the Cultural Revolution had liberated him and allowed his voice to be heard. He was now speaking all over Peking and was eagerly sought as a star performer at various rallies. Rittenberg suggested that Bethune-Yenan might make a great contribution if it could sponsor a mass meeting with Ch'en Li-ning as the main speaker. All agreed that the sponsorship of the "revolutionary madman," an appellation that might have given us pause, was a worthy project for our rebel regiment of foreigners.

An arrangement was subsequently worked out with the Red Rebels of the Foreign Languages Press for a mass meeting jointly sponsored by their organization and Bethune-Yenan to denounce "China's Khrushchev" (Liu Shao-ch'i), at which Ch'en Li-ning would be billed as the main speaker. On the appointed day of the meeting, David was among those delegated the task of picking up the celebrity at the Iron and Steel College, where Ch'en made his base, and delivering him to the Press in time for the meeting. We were aware that the Iron and Steel College was a stronghold of the citywide Earth faction, but at the time this fact did not appear to us to have any relevance, since we lacked the awareness of almost all Chinese that every political action possessed symbolic and factional significance. The small delegation arrived at the Iron and Steel College and located "the madman of the new age" (as Ch'en Li-ning was later to be called in order to link him with the classic story "A Madman's Diary" by the great revolutionary writer Lu Hsün). There we also found a delegation from our Institute's ultra-radical June 16 organization. It was soon made clear that June 16 had scheduled a meeting at the same time as ours and that the "madman" had promised to speak to them, too. After some rather tense negotiations with the June 16 delegation, it was agreed that the Bethune-Yenan committee would bring Ch'en to the Foreign Languages Institute, where he could meet his commitment to the scheduled June 16 meeting, that we would wait until the meeting was over, and then deliver Ch'en to the Press, even though this might mean that the meeting there would be delayed.

We carried out our end of the bargain, delivered Ch'en to the Foreign Languages Institute, and waited patiently for him to give his speech to the masses assembled by June 16. After more than an hour had passed and Ch'en Li-ning did not reappear, we decided to go to the site of the meeting and remind him that a sizable crowd was anxiously awaiting his arrival at the Press. The June 16 rally was being held on a playing field, and when we foreigners arrived at the platform, for the first time since the beginning of the Cultural Revolution, we found ourselves in a decidedly menacing atmosphere. While we reminded the June 16 leaders that they had promised to share Ch'en Li-ning with us, the crowd, which included some of David's students, began to shout, "Down with the Red Flag's foreign supporters!" As we tried to extract Ch'en Li-ning from the clutches of June 16, who were reluctant to allow him to leave, we began finally to understand that the "madman" belonged to them, that he was their symbol, and we had no right to him.

Ch'en gave his speech to the Press meeting under our sponsorship. It was highly emotional and, some of us thought, rather demagogic. There was a question whether Ch'en Li-ning was revolutionary, mad, or perhaps neither. Clearly, to the Chinese, he represented something rather different from the Soviet parallel which came to the minds of so many foreigners. In fact, there is no evidence in China of political incarceration in mental institutions, either before or after the Cultural Revolution. Perhaps in the minds of many who heard him, something echoed from the depths of Chinese history when political dissidents had sometimes feigned madness as a shield for their opposition. When it was revealed several months later that not only had Ch'en corrected the works of Liu Shao-ch'i, but had critically annotated the entire corpus of Mao's works as well, the public fury was of a pitch we had seldom encountered in those years of outrageous events. The people had been defrauded in a manner which enraged them by one whose title "The Madman of the New Age" was an audacious attempt to purloin the most honorable of literary symbols, Lu Hsün's madman, a revolutionary dissident. Ch'en Li-ning was officially denounced as a fraud and linked to the May 16 organization, later declared counterrevolutionary.

For the foreigners, the strange encounter with Ch'en Li-ning had a special significance. One day after Ch'en's meeting at the Foreign Languages Press, June 16 at the

Foreign Languages Institute put out a leaflet attacking the Red Flag (Hung-ch'i) "for enlisting the support of 'foreign devils.'" For those of us who had entered the Cultural Revolution because of its historic and international links with the American, French, and Russian revolutions, it was now necessary to face the fact that we had also encroached on the intimate world of a family fight.

## Chapter IX

# The Three Kingdoms:
# Left, Right, And Middle

"EMPIRES wax and wane; states cleave asunder and coalesce"—so begins the Chinese classic *The Romance of the Three Kingdoms*. It would be difficult to find a Chinese who has not in some way internalized the political and historical concepts expressed in this most popular of all Chinese novels. The notion of politics as a process, an ebb and flow of power constellations, an unending struggle leading to splits, consensus, and coalition remains firmly rooted in the Chinese consciousness. By the spring of 1967, after one year of uninterrupted revolution, millions of ordinary citizens had entered a realm of power which for thousands of years had been restricted to the elites.

After nearly a half century of experience in political struggles, Mao had come to the conclusion that "apart from uninhabited deserts, wherever there are groups of people, they are invariably composed of the left, the middle, and the right. This will be the case for ten thousand years."[91] Yet, he added, while a clear left, right, and center rapidly emerge at the beginning of a social movement, in the course of time the early left may well degenerate and transform itself into the right. Thus, in Maoist theory, the three political categories are not fixed but changing, and the true left is formed and consolidated only through a process of protracted political struggle. After observing the complex politics and patterns of the Cultural Revolution for more than a year, Mao reached a deceptively simple formulation of one of the main laws of the movement: "There is one main tendency in a given period, and it may cover up the other tendency. While opposing the right erroneous tendency, the left erroneous tendency appears; while opposing the left erroneous tendency, the right erroneous tendency may appear."[92]

Our lives, like those of all the citizens of the capital city, were now governed by the ebbs and tides of a social movement which had in time assumed an elemental ambience. It was as if the posters, the marching columns, and the blare of loudspeakers had always existed. Riding our bicycles down the back road leading to the Institute, we were no longer startled by the sight of the once flat, now upturned, white granite slab marking the grave of the renowned painter Ch'i Pai-shih. The gravestone had been set askew by youthful rebels long ago and would no doubt in calmer times be restored to its original place so that the children could once again play ping-pong on its smooth broad surface.

The division of the half-million student population of Peking into the Heaven and the Earth factions was both a demographic fact and a way of life. Even the foreign community, following the social law of the movement, divided like an amoeba under the microscope. Our students who belonged to other factions no longer spoke to us nor invited us to their meetings, and we learned of their activities only through the filter of our own faction, which kept a close watch on the activities of its opponents. Despite the new political concepts and ideas which flooded the society, it was clear that the ancient Chinese adage "He who wins power becomes a king; he who loses power becomes a bandit" had not lost its grip on the popular consciousness. There was no one among the 3,000 students at the Foreign Languages Institute who did not know that the fate of the Red Flag Battalion was inextricably tied to the fate of Premier Chou En-lai. If Chou went down, so would Hung-ch'i. Having taken on a life of its own, the mass movement below was one star in a galaxy of forces made up of the Army, the Cultural Group, the State bureaucracy, the now inchoate but latent power of the Party apparatus, and the immense peasantry which watched from the sidelines, all revolving in a system held together by that final arbiter, the "red sun," which was Chairman Mao.

During the hot summer of 1967, a state of semi-anarchy prevailed in the most populous country in the world. Work went on, the buses ran, there was no interruption of water and electricity, but administration had virtually ceased. The whole middle organizational level had been wiped out. There was only the very top and the bottom. No ordinary official dared to give orders. Even orders issued by the highest officials in the land, including Premier Chou, Vice Chairman Lin, the Military Affairs Commission, the State Council, and the Cultural Group, were often ignored. The command to desist from marching cadres around in the streets in paper hats was ignored, as was the order prohibiting storming into public buildings and rifling state documents. Although the Red Guards were told not to go to Sinkiang and Tibet, they went anyway.

On June 16, *People's Daily* published an article entitled: "Masses Demand Stop to the Use of Broadcasting Vans and Deafening Loudspeakers." Reporting that the loudspeakers were making "such a big noise" that people were unable to sleep, the article condemned the use of high-pitched amplifiers as weapons in a civil war between mass organizations. The peasants of the Evergreen Commune next to our school sent a delegation to register a complaint with our rebel organizations stating that the commune members were unable to sleep because of the night-long cacophony from the school loudspeakers. By the time the Red Guards were ready to turn them off in the early hours of the morning and go to bed, the peasants were just about ready to get up and begin their day's work. But the direct protests of the masses, the *raison d'être* of the Cultural Revolution, had no more effect than any others.

Ch'en Po-ta told some Red Guard leaders that he was thinking of leaving town because he could neither sleep nor get any work done and that the noise was even disturbing

Chairman Mao at his home in Chungnanhai. All to no avail. The war of the loudspeakers intensified regardless of the fact that in the battle of drowning out the other side neither could be understood. It seemed strange that the Chinese, on the whole a quiet people, could go to such extremes. But there was method in the madness. It was all part of a struggle for power played for very high stakes, a conflict which the Proletarian Headquarters itself had termed "a life-and-death struggle."

An atmosphere of extraordinary freedom and purpose existed in those days, an intensity of life which has been noted in all the great revolutions. People talked about everything, speculated endlessly, and read everything they could get their hands on; ordinary folk had become political philosophers contemplating the years to come. It was a time when everything came to the surface—the past, the present, and the future all jumbled together. When one of our students came to our apartment one day to borrow *Moby Dick*, we had a long discussion about China and the world. He asked us whether we thought the Americans would land on the moon and when we replied we did, he said that that was all right, since the Americans were part of the human race and could represent it there. Our young friend, possessed by the speculative mood of the time, told us that he thought there would always be factions in China now that they had emerged during the Cultural Revolution. We asked whether this meant a two-line struggle or a two-party system. He simply replied that he did not know how the system would operate, but that factions would continue to exist. It was evident that at least one Chinese rebel in the summer of 1967 was toying with the idea of institutionalizing the struggle between the left, right, and middle that the Chairman said would exist for 10,000 years.

One thing seemed clear. The struggle in Peking, like that in Paris almost two centuries earlier, would decide the fate of the nation. In the France of 1791–93, a whole nation followed the arguments of the Jacobins, the Feuillants, the Cordeliers, and the Enragés through a vast informal network of communication which radiated out from the capital. In the Peking of 1966–68, of course, it was the arguments and positions of the "East Is Red" of the Geology Institute, the "Chingkangshan" of Tsinghua University, and the "Red Flag" of the Aviation Institute that stirred the passions of the masses. Throughout the vast reaches of China, the youth anxiously perused the revolutionary tracts disseminated by Peking rebel organizations so that they could emulate the orientations, policies, and lines of the Peking factions.

The popular level of Chinese urban society was linked together by a new network of people's organizations, liaison stations, Red Guard Congresses, and informal alliances which made themselves known by thousands of Red Guard newspapers, published at government expense. The result of this proliferation of organization was the politicization of hundreds of millions of people. Once, when the leaders of the Cultural Group heard that a workers' delegation from a distant province had arrived in Peking and they could not locate them, it was found that the workers were living in the dormitories at Tsinghua University. When the irritated national leaders asked the workers why they did not stay in the quarters arranged for them by the center, the workers replied, "Because we learn more here."

The Earth faction provided the battalions of political troops called into action on every front by Ch'en Po-ta, Chiang Ch'ing, and the younger team from the Cultural Group consisting of Wang Li, Ch'i Pen-yü, Kuan Feng, Lin Chieh, and Mu Hsin. Elation spread throughout the ranks of the Earth faction and dejection in the army of the Heaven faction in April, when the entire Cultural Group arrived at a meeting of Red Guard representatives wearing the red arm bands of the Earth faction. In the summer of 1967, when the formerly obscure intellectuals of the Cultural Group began their all-out offensive against the Deputy Ministers of the Government serving under Premier Chou En-lai and what they termed the "handful of reactionary power-holders in the army," they were able to command the allegiance of a formidable group of Red Guard organizations.

The Earth faction, which followed the line of the Cultural Group, was led by the East Is Red of the Geology Institute and regiments bearing the same name at the Peking Postal Institute, the Agricultural College, the Institute of Science and Technology, the Forestry Institute, Mathematics Institute, Teachers Institute, Hydroelectric Institute, Nationalities Institute, and Industrial Institute. Tung-fang Hung (The East Is Red) was a favorite name of the organizations making up the Earth faction, but there were a few by that name belonging to the Heaven faction as well. Hung-ch'i (Red Flag) was one of the most popular organizational names in the Heaven faction, although the Red Guard group at the Agricultural Machine Institute belonging to the Earth faction also called itself Red Flag. Earth also boasted the support of the Peking Commune of the Petroleum Institute, the Politics and Law Commune of the Political Science and Law Institute, the 729 Corps of the Light Industry Institute, and many others. At our own First Foreign Languages Institute, of course, the radical June 16 Independent Rebel Regiment (known throughout the city as Liu-i-liu or 6-1-6) and the Red Flag Rebel Corps (Hung-ch'i Tsao-fan T'uan) were key components of the Earth faction.

A concrete analysis of the social composition, political interests, and coherent ideology of the two major citywide Red Guard factional alliances during the Cultural Revolution faces formidable obstacles. However, it was clear that the Earth faction organizations supported the political goals of the Cultural Group, while the Heaven faction opposed, for the most part, the overthrow of the vice ministers of the State Council and looked to Premier Chou for leadership. While the Earth faction was rooted in the technical institutes, the Heaven faction found its support in prestigious universities such as Peking University, Tsinghua, and our own Institute, which was a training ground for the Foreign Ministry. Without a statistical breakdown of the membership of all the Red Guard organizations—data which probably will never become available—a definitive answer to the social and political composition of the two main Peking factions may be impossible. Political struggles among students and intellectuals are always more complex than those among clearly defined social groups, as the People's Liberation Army men were to find out when they entered the schools. If the Earth faction had been a clear reflection of the forces of the Cultural Group struggling for power, then one would have expected to find its membership made up of those who, for one reason or another, had been excluded from positions of power and status; were not from peasant or worker background; and had the most severe grievances against the Party organization. The Heaven faction, on the surface the more conservative of the two factions in relation to the goals of sweeping power-holders out of office, might have been expected to have more Party members and a membership less disgruntled with the status quo. Whatever the case may be, this pattern did not fit the First Foreign Languages Institute.

Perhaps our Institute, and the Foreign Ministry generally, was not a typical unit of the Heaven faction, but the fact was that our own Red Flag contained the younger students, many of whom came from worker-peasant background, fewer Party members, and fewer former "royalists" who had supported the work-teams than did the Rebel Regiment. Even more important, the overwhelming majority of Party cadres in our school supported the Rebel Regiment and opposed Red Flag. It was clear to us that many of the supporters of the Rebel Regiment whom we knew had been conservatives at the beginning of the movement had, in order to atone for their political sins, taken an ultra-left stance and joined the Rebel Regiment. The small but radical June 16 Independent Rebel Corps, on the other hand, had won over virtually all the manual workers in the school including the cooks and drivers. Many of these, however, did not have "good" political backgrounds. (A chauffeur in China who did not receive his training in the Army had frequently been a driver for the Chiang Kai-shek regime in the old days.) The ultra-left then, during the Cultural Revolution, was a mixed bag of sincere militants and rightists posing as leftists, and it was hard to sort them out. But there was no lack of clarity on the political issues which divided the rebel groupings in our school. Red Flag supported Premier Chou; the Rebel Regiment and June 16 worked night and day to topple him from power.

This basic split between Peking's Red Guard organizations had grown out of the earliest struggles between the Geology Institute's East Is Red and the New Peking University Commune when the two organizations fought for leadership control of the 3rd Red Guard Headquarters. The rift between the two groups widened with time, forcing every student organization in Peking to support one side or the other. Nieh Yuan-tzu of Heaven and Wang Ta-pin of Earth commanded the loyalty of tens of thousands of Red Guard "fighters."

Despite the prominence of Nieh Yuan-tzu, the main author of the famous big-character poster which began the Cultural Revolution at Peking University, it was Red Flag of the Aviation Institute, and its dynamic young leader Han Ai-ching, that provided the ideological and organizational leadership of the Heaven faction. He commanded a remarkably disciplined organization which was able to unite students, teachers, and cadres behind a coherent political line. Apparently, the Aviation Institute rebels came close to mastering Chairman Mao's fifth requirement for revolutionary successors: "They must be proletarian statesmen capable of uniting and working together with the overwhelming majority. Not only must they unite with those who agree with them, they must also be good at uniting with those who disagree with them and even with those who formerly opposed them and have since been proved wrong."[93]

Aviation's Red Flag was able to organize a solid Revolutionary Committee in May without any opposition. However, while it seemed able to solve the contradictions within its own unit, it was unable to do so in the citywide factional struggle because of that struggle's close relationship to the split at the very top. Before the revolution was over, unity at the top was achieved only by overthrowing the members of the losing faction. On the bottom, unity was achieved by dissolving the student factions in that vast ocean of the peasant-dominated countryside.

While the Tung-fang Hung (East Is Red) of the Geology Institute maintained close relations with Wang Li, Kuan Feng, and Ch'i Pen-yü of the Cultural Group, Red Flag of the Aviation Institute supported the man the Earth faction labeled as "the behind-the-scenes backer of the handful of power-holders taking the capitalist road" in the State Council and national ministries. That man, as everyone clearly understood, was Chou En-lai. The Red Flag of the Aviation Institute and our own Red Flag stood in the forefront of the struggle to protect "our most beloved Premier Chou" as a member of the Proletarian Headquarters. In the opinion of the Heaven faction, "the handful of bad eggs" who were attempting to "incite bad feelings between Premier Chou and the Cultural Revolution Group" would "come to no good end"—the threat was among the most powerful one Chinese can make to another.

Although we were never to come across statistical proof, our impression at the time was that the two citywide factions were more or less equal in numerical strength. Besides the Red Flag of the Aviation Institute, Nieh Yuan-tzu's New Peking University Commune, and our own Hung-ch'i, the Heaven faction boasted the support of the prestigious Chingkangshan of Tsinghua University (led by the popular and later notorious K'uai Ta-fu), the Three Red Banners of People's University, the K'ang-ta Commune of the Nationalities Institute, the East Is Red of the Mining Institute, the 88 Corps Group of the Finance Institute, and the Red Eagle Combat Corps of the Peking Light Industry Institute, plus a number of other organizations in the Foreign Ministry Complex and other administrative units and schools.

Peking's five most prominent Red Guard student organizations produced five nationally known leaders, who for a time carved out independent kingdoms of power for themselves. Nieh Yuan-tzu of the New Peking University Commune, K'uai Ta-fu of Tsinghua University's Chingkangshan, and Han Ai-ching of the Aviation Institute's Red Flag all belonged to the Heaven faction. Wang Ta-pin of the Geology Institute's East Is Red and T'an Hou-lan of the Ching-kangshan at the Peking Normal School were the leaders of the Earth faction. All five had been early rebels and had without exception contributed to the collapse of the conservative 1st and 2nd Red Guard Headquarters as well as the consolidation of the 3rd Headquarters. For this, they had all received the blessings and support of the Cultural Group. All, except Nieh Yuan-tzu, who was a teacher and cadre, were students in their early twenties. Sweeping like comets across the heavens, these young leaders, who elicited the love and hatred of tens of thousands of students, would within a year fall from power and face political disgrace. But in the summer of 1967, they were still in charge of massive armies, complicated organizational networks, broadcasting stations, and printing facilities which allowed their influence to extend from China's Northeast to the farthest reaches of Sinkiang and Tibet.

When, in the spring of 1967, the split within the 3rd Headquarters between the Geology School East Is Red and the Peking Commune hardened into the citywide Heaven and Earth alliances, the fight for power centered on control of the Peking Red Guard Congress, the Peking Revolutionary Committee, and its propaganda organ the *Peking Daily*. While the Heaven faction won control of the Red Guard Congress at the outset by electing Nieh Yuan-tzu as Chairman, the Earth faction was able to win control of the Peking Revolutionary Committee under the leadership of a member of the Cultural Group, Hsieh Fu-chih, who served as Chairman. By June, the Earth faction had won control of all three centers of power, but theirs was a Pyrrhic victory, since none of these power centers could control the member organizations, and all were equally powerless when it came to resolving the factional warfare which paralyzed the operations of city government.

All through the spring and summer, reports of bloody conflict poured into Peking from the provinces, fueling the fires of the ultras, who called for drastic action to stem the counterrevolution which, it was asserted, threatened to drown Mao's revolution in blood. Something like civil war had been taking place in the major cities of Szechuan for months, and violence was reported in Honan, Kiangsi, Kwangtung, and Yunnan. Delegations from these provinces and returning Peking Red Guards swarmed into the capital with atrocity stories. Many of these were dramatically embellished and exaggerated, but enough bloody shirts were displayed in street exhibits to convince anyone that at least some must be proof of the narratives that accompanied them.

When our oldest son returned from his three-month-long march to the Yellow River, he casually stacked three bayonets and a number of huge knives under his bed. He argued that this was standard equipment for rebels, and it took some weeks of disagreement before the equipment was jettisoned. The disposal of the weapons presented something of a problem, since there was no proper authority to receive them, and these were highly inflammatory symbols in a world of factions. We finally smuggled them out of the house and pitched them into a nearby irrigation canal.

If it had not been apparent before, it was now, that the Cultural Revolution was, as the Sixteen-Point Decision affirmed, indeed a "revolution" and that the masses had taken literally Mao's quotation posted on walls throughout the city:

> "A revolution is not a dinner party, or writing an essay, or painting a picture, or doing embroidery; it cannot be so refined, so leisurely and gentle, so temperate, kind, courteous, restrained, and magnamimous. A revolution is an insurrection, an act of violence by which one class overthrows another."[94]

Struggles precipitated by the February Adverse Current accelerated the pendulum swings from right to left. A pattern of oscillation set in, which, if not brought under control, threatened to shatter completely the political machine. Turning points in the history of revolution frequently occur when the organized counterrevolution acts decisively to polarize the population, thus forcing revolutionary leaders to forge new and crucial policies. It was the mutiny of the Ninth Independent Division of the People's Liberation Army at Wuhan in the summer of 1967 which finally polarized the Chinese polity and brought China to the brink of civil war.

One day toward the end of June, as we strolled through the Institute courtyards looking at the new posters, we ran into some of our students whom we had not seen in months. They told us that they had been in Wuhan, the great industrial complex situated at the confluence of the Han and Yangtze Rivers. The ingenuousness of our question, "How are things going there?" must have surprised them, since every student in Peking was undoubtedly aware that Wuhan was racked with turmoil. Sporadic fighting between the two main mass organizations in the city had been under way for weeks, and our students told us they had been lucky to escape with their lives. Thousands of combatants armed with spears, crowbars, and homemade swords clashed daily, as attacks and counterattacks turned one of China's largest cities into a swirling battleground.

The conservatives, our students told us grimly, had organized themselves into a citywide organization colorfully named the "One Million Heroic Troops," and these had instituted a rule of white terror which encompassed both sides of the Yangtze triple-city complex of Wuhan-Hankow-Hanyang. The "Million Heroes" consisted of some 500,000 office employees, skilled workers, and militiamen and had the backing of the Party organization in their murderous assault on the minority of rebels enlisted under the banner of the Wuhan Workers' General Headquarters. The latter organization, a coalition composed of workers from the Wuhan Iron and Steel Company, the bulk of the University and middle school students, and a contingent of Peking Red Guards, were under a permanent state of siege, and the reactionaries, according to our usually reliable and calm students, were threatening to annihilate them all. They had themselves witnessed a full-scale battle between the two armies when the conservative Million Heroes stormed across the Yangtze River bridge in commandeered trucks to assault a radical stronghold in Hankow. Hundreds were killed in a battle which then spread to all parts of the city. Appalled by this report, we asked our young informants why the Army hadn't intervened. "But the Army has intervened," they told us. "The Army, under the command of 'fascist' General Ch'en Tsai-tao, is openly backing the Million Heroes, providing the 'bad eggs' with trucks and even weapons to wipe out the revolutionary rebels."

It had been apparent for some time that the Army was having difficulty in executing its orders "to support the left," and in some cases had supported conservative organizations, but the general assumption was that this was attributable to the Army's lack of experience in domestic politics. But now in Wuhan the People's Liberation Army, that "Great School of Mao Tse-tung's Thought," was, under the leadership of the commanding general of the Wuhan Military District, spearheading the counterrevolution, smashing with force the very rebellion that Mao Tse-tung had initiated and was personally leading (as the press reminded us every day). How was one to account for this turn of events?

Perhaps it is only in retrospect that the role of the Army in the Great Proletarian Cultural Revolution can be properly assessed. At the beginning of the movement, the PLA established itself as the fountainhead of the Maoist orientation and line in opposition to the policy and work style of the old Party machine. The Army newspapers played the leading role in disseminating Maoist ideology. With the suspension of the Party organization in the fall of 1966, the PLA emerged as the only viable organizational structure possessing a monopoly of coercive power. Assigned the contradictory tasks of maintaining law and order, promoting production, and supporting the revolutionary left organizations in their seizure of power, the Army soon found itself in the position of supervising factory and administrative management at every level of authority. Since the task of supporting the left proved to be the most elusive of goals, the others were given priority, and an organization committed to radical ideology soon found itself in a functionally conservative stance, often wedded to the preservation of the status quo.

Historically, the PLA, the instrument of peasant revolutionary war, had served as the organizational vanguard of a vast movement of social transformation. Political power in the Chinese Revolution had indeed "grown out of the barrel of a gun." In those long years of revolutionary war, it was hard to determine whether the Party organized the Army or vice versa. From the very beginning, Mao recognized the distinction between the two organizations when he stated that the Party commands the gun, while the gun should never command the Party. Nevertheless, despite the fact that, during the Cultural Revolution, it was the Army which played the historic political role and not the Party organization, it was a long time before the Chinese would admit that the People's Liberation Army had developed its own unique power interests.

The official position on the legitimacy of the Army's political stance during the Cultural Revolution was stated by Premier Chou En-lai in response to a 1970 suggestion by Edgar Snow that perhaps there was a tendency toward military dictatorship in China:

> " 'Absurd,' says Premier Chou. 'How could that be?' The PLA is an instrument of the Party and the servant of the proletariat. 'The Army is loyal to the Party; the Party within the Army has always held leadership through its own organizations right down to the company level.' Chou added: 'We are all connected with the Army.' Chairman Mao had himself organized the Army, and Chou had also been a general, therefore it was wrong to make distinctions between military and non-military individuals in positions of leadership."[95]

While the Army supported Chairman Mao against his political opponents in the Party in the early stages of the Cultural Revolution, it remained outside the tumultuous political process, protected from a Cultural Revolution within its own ranks by the Sixteen-Point Decision. All this changed in February 1967, when Mao ended the Army's neutrality and thrust it into the political process with paradoxical instructions to preserve order and promote revolution. Army officers forced to meet the political struggle head-on faced three options: They could support the Party structure and its political following; they could replace the Party bureaucrats with their own Army cadres; or they could support radical mass organizations in the seizure of power from below. In the provinces, where the generals had close organizational and personal ties with the Party structure of authority, they often supported the conservative mass organizations; in other instances, they took power themselves and, in a few cases, supported the radicals.

From the point of view of the masses, if the Army was now entering the political arena of the Cultural Revolution (and, in fact, too often supported the conservatives), then why should the Army itself not be subject to the Cultural Revolution within its own ranks? This was the issue which the Wuhan Incident would fan into a political prairie fire. An obvious fact, clear to Chairman Mao, and one that should have been clear to everyone else, was that if the Army ever split, a civil war became inevitable. One question confronting historians of the Cultural Revolution is whether the mutiny at Wuhan represented the revolt of a local Army commander against the Peking leadership or whether the action of the Wuhan mutineers was symptomatic of a larger conflict between the Army as a whole and the Cultural Group. Whatever the case, fault lines were beginning to appear in the coalition of leaders responsible for carrying the great rebellion "through to the end." Soon Chairman Mao would have to decide whether the whole Cultural Revolution movement had not transgressed the outside limits of political acceptability.

Our sons brought us further news of developments in Wuhan. They had read the posters in the center of the city put up by the followers of the Wuhan Workers' General Headquarters, which claimed that the PLA had disbanded the Workers' Headquarters and arrested its leaders. The rebels were demanding the release of those arrested and the restoration of their organization. The Army command in Wuhan ignored orders from the Central Cultural Group in Peking to admit its mistake, free the arrested rebel leaders, and recognize the legitimacy of their organizations. In April, the Military Affairs Commission of the Central Committee had issued a ten-point order to all military units in the country prohibiting them from firing on any mass organization, from disbanding any organization, from arresting any member of a mass organization, or from taking any action concerning the mass movement without prior instructions from the Center. In April, General Ch'en Tsai-tao and the Army Command in Wuhan disregarded the Ten Articles, as they were called, and in July, during the mutiny, Ch'en Tsai-tao again refused to comply with Premier Chou's telephone instructions to desist from attacking the mass rebel organizations.

Responding to the crisis in one of the country's key industrial cities, a delegation headed by Hsieh Fu-chih and Wang Li of the Cultural Group was sent to Wuhan to transmit personally the orders from the Center. Wang and Hsieh arrived in the triple city on July 14 and immediately declared their support for the three main revolutionary organizations in the city—the "San Kung," "San Hsin," and "San Lien." They also announced that the case of the Wuhan Workers' General Headquarters would be reopened. General Ch'en Tsai-tao responded to these demands from Peking by stating:

> "While the case of the Workers' General Command may be reopened, the Million Heroic Troops will not permit this thing to happen. Since the Million Heroic Troops are in control of Wuhan's economic lifelines, such as communications, water supplies, and electricity, any attempt at reopening the case of the Workers' General Command may result in the cutting off of power and water supplies."[96]

On July 19, Wang Li, as Peking's representative, delivered a four-point directive from the Cultural Group to military cadres at or above division level of the Wuhan Military Region Command, reiterating all the orders and demands from the Center. The reaction on the part of General Ch'en Tsai-tao and the Million Heroes was immediate and violent. General Ch'en is reported to have questioned the rank of Wang Li and his right to speak for the Party Central Committee. The Million Heroes painted slogans on the main streets declaring: "Both Wang Li and Hsieh Fu-chih are Persona Non Grata!" "Get Out of Wuhan, Wang Li and Hsieh Fu-chih!" and "Hang Wang Li!" This warning was quickly followed by the sudden, dramatic, and outrageous kidnapping of Wang Li by the mutineers. A revolutionary rebel view of the July 20 kidnapping in the steaming city of Wuhan, a city referred to by all Chinese as "one of the country's three furnaces," reveals the fervor unloosed in Chinese breasts by this event:

". . . In the stifling heat which engulfed Wuhan in July, a counterrevolutionary act of abducting central leaders began. In the wee hours of July 20, Lei Jung-hua, the Number One leader of the Tunghu detachment of the 'One Million Heroic Troops,' led other bandits to kidnap the central leaders. When the truckload of bandits stopped at the entrance to the Tunghu Guest House, the guards of the '8201' unit at first pretended not to let the bandits in. However, these bandits simply surged forward and got through without any difficulty. But both Vice-Premier Hsieh Fu-chih and Comrade Wang Li were not caught unawares; they faced the pack of 'wolves and jackals' firmly. In a firm voice, the Vice-Premier said to them: 'I am Hsieh Fu-chih. Kidnap me or kill me as you please.'

"Directing the mutiny were army officers carrying revolvers. After entering the Guest House, they pointed machine guns and pistols at the central leaders. To avert bloodshed and loss of lives in the event of an armed clash, the guards of Vice-Premier Hsieh and Comrade Wang Li had to put away their revolvers. Seizing the opportunity, the screaming bandits surged forward and began to take away Comrade Wang Li, Chairman Mao's emissary, a member of the Central Cultural Revolution Group, and Assistant Editor-in-Chief of *Hung-ch'i Journal*."⁹⁷

Then the account describes the terror unleashed by the 8201 unit:

> "Brandishing pistols before the unarmed masses, the killers went on a rampage, throwing spears and other lethal weapons all over the river city. The whistle of fire engine sirens was mingled with the rumble of nearly a thousand vehicles carrying members of the 'One Million Heroic Troops' and the detachments of the 'San Ssu.' The loudspeaker vans of the 'One Million Heroic Troops' blared reactionary slogans, plunging the entire city of Wuhan into the horrors of war."

Soon "the Yangtze River Bridge and Chiang Han Bridge were closed, navigation along the Yangtze River was stopped, communication routes, main thoroughfares, major buildings occupied, the airfield surrounded, and railway stations seized. Running amuck in Wuhan, members of the 'One Million Heroic Troops' and the small bunch of rotten eggs of the '8201' unit did as they pleased—attacking, kidnapping, brutally beating people, and even killing young revolutionary fighters and the revolutionary masses." Wang Li was beaten, and clumps of his hair were torn out by "ranting and raving hooligans of both sexes."

When the Peking leaders learned of the kidnapping of their representatives, they acted decisively. Three infantry divisions and an airborne division were dispatched to Wuhan, while Navy gunboats sailed up the Yangtze to recapture the city lost to the counterrevolution. Premier Chou flew into the city, narrowly escaping capture when his plane at first sought to land at an airfield surrounded by Ch'en Tsai-tao's tanks. Street rumors in Peking claimed that the Chairman himself had gone down to Wuhan to negotiate an end to the crisis. In any case, Wang Li and Hsieh Fu-chih were rescued in a daring rebel operation and smuggled out of the city, returning to Peking on July 22. General Ch'en

Tsai-tao and his commanding officers finally capitulated, and the mutiny was brought under control. Ch'en and the other officers were taken to Peking under arrest, as the Wuhan Military Region was put into the hands of officers loyal to Mao, Lin Piao, and the leadership of the Cultural Revolution. How ironic, yet characteristic of the politics of revolution, that, after the Cultural Revolution, the mutineers at Wuhan were treated with a greater leniency than were many of the political leaders of the movement that was designed "to touch people to their very souls," as the editorials of the day put it!

As news of the great mutiny spread, Peking reverberated to the tocsins associated with the French Revolution, except that loudspeakers rather than church bells sounded the alarm. Heterodyne waves of sound thundered over the tiled roofs of the ancient Chinese capital: "Down With Ch'en Tsai-tao!", "Long Live the Revolutionary Victory in Wuhan!", "Smash the Dogs'-heads of the Counterrevolution!"

On July 25, our students marched en masse from the western suburbs to T'ien An Men to take part in a great Welcome Home rally for Hsieh Fu-chih and Wang Li, the revolutionary heroes of the Wuhan incident. Every able-bodied citizen of Peking joined the entire national leadership, excepting Mao, in welcoming these martyrs and celebrating the defeat of counterrevolution in Wuhan. A left wave of tidal proportions washed over the capital as the Cultural Group escalated its drive for power. Led by Chairman Mao's wife and his personal secretary, Ch'en Po-ta, the leftist drive for power appeared to many to have the backing of Chairman Mao himself. Could it be possible, the radicals argued, that Chiang Ch'ing was not the most reliable of those who claimed to represent the Chairman? On July 22, in response to the crisis in Wuhan, Chiang Ch'ing made her famous speech putting forth the slogan "Attack with Words, Defend with Force," which rebels all over the country took as the signal for an offensive. Mao's wife told the "young generals": "They [the conservatives] do not lay down their arms and are raising rifles, spears, and swords against you, and you lay down your arms. This is wrong. You will get the worst of it. This is what is happening at the present in Wuhan."

The intellectuals and propagandists who made up the core of the Cultural Group chose the summer of 1967 to summon their Red Guard armies for an assault on the two strongest bastions of power in the country—the People's Liberation Army and the State bureaucracy led by Premier Chou. The July crisis, brought about by the actions of the Army, proved, as had the February crisis, brought about by the Party cadres and the Ministers of the State Council, that the triple alliance concept formulated after the January Revolution was failing as a mechanism to unite the country. Each time one of the three elements of the alliance was in the ascendant—whether the old cadres, the Army, or the mass organizations supported by the Cultural Group—that element attempted to crush, not unite with, the other two political forces. During the January storm, the working masses had prevailed in Shanghai; during February, the Party cadres marched back to restore their lost power; in June and July, sections of the Army moved to consolidate control under their own aegis, and in midsummer, the Cultural Group and its student battalions launched their own drive to seize power at the center. In Peking, as elsewhere in the summer of 1967, the three component parts of the proposed alliance came together with implosive rather than bonding force.

The Wuhan mutiny only fueled the fires of an ascendant "ultra-left" drive that had been under way in Peking for months. This new upsurge had accelerated in response to the signal provided by the symbolic publication of the May 16 Circular, the inner Party document which had started the Cultural Revolution one year earlier, on May 16, 1966. The publication of the heretofore restricted May 16 Circular was understood as a signal for the renewal of the attack on the capitalist-roaders. Regardless of whether or not there was an internal struggle over its publication among the nation's leaders, the immediate effect was to weight even more heavily the power side of the Cultural Revolution equation over the ideological side. At every turning point of the movement, one faction stressed power and the other ideology.

On the very day of the publication of the May 16 Circular, the ultra-left June 16 of our Institute put up a big-character poster which caused a sensation in the city. Entitled "Unmasking a Big Conspiracy," the poster directly branded Premier Chou as a "counterrevolutionary double-dealer," accused him of supporting conservative organizations and of "maintaining his faltering reactionary rule." On May 30, a number of rebel organizations held a meeting in T'ien An Men Square which launched the slogan "Pulling down Vice Premier Li Hsien-nien." One of the speakers was reported to have said, "If we hold the meeting only when the Premier permits us, we are not genuine rebels."

By June, the Earth faction had succeeded in gaining control of the Capital Red Guard Congress. The Peking Revolutionary Committee already under the control of the Earth partisans had stepped up its attack on the Vice Premiers of the State Council and, through them, the Premier. In terms of the rules of the movement laid down by the 11th Plenum of the Party Central Committee, Mao, Lin, and Chou, plus the Cultural Group, constituted the Proletarian Headquarters, authorized to lead the Cultural Revolution. An attack on any of these constituent elements of command could therefore be argued as an assault on Mao's own headquarters and therefore a counterrevolutionary action. Such an attack could be viewed as a stand that was "left in form and right in essence," and this is just what the Heaven faction proclaimed from every rooftop.

It was perhaps no coincidence that at the very time the Earth faction was seizing control of the Capital Red Guard Congress, the "ultras" took power in the foreigners' Bethune-Yenan Regiment. Those of us who had founded the regiment resigned after a prolonged attack, in which our leaders were branded as "conservatives." A group made up primarily of American long-term residents in China, who shared the opinion of the Earth faction that Foreign Minister Ch'en Yi had a "bourgeois world outlook," elected Israel Epstein to lead Bethune-Yenan in a more "revolutionary" direction. Rittenberg, who had taken no organizational role in Bethune-Yenan but had always shown great interest in the organization, at first supported the old leadership and then at the height of the battle characteristically switched his support to the challengers. Soon the Chinese masses would consider Bethune-Yenan to be Rittenberg's organization. Most of the rank-and-file members of this foreign rebel group knew very little and understood less of the Peking Heaven and Earth Red Guard armies which stood in the shadow of civil war. We ourselves were finding the struggle at our own Institute, where we knew something of the participants and the issues, more comprehensible than the conflict generated by a band of well-intentioned foreigners floundering in a social movement not of their making.

During the last ten days of July, in response to the Wuhan incident, members of the Cultural Group launched a new offensive "to drag out the handful in the Army." The new doctrine, promulgated by Lin Chieh, a prominent member of the Cultural Group and an editor of the *Liberation Army Daily,* was a logical extension of Chiang Ch'ing's slogan "Attack with Words, Defend with Force." *Red Flag* editorial No. 12, "The Proletariat Must Take Firm Hold of the Gun," spelled out the new concept by calling on the mass organizations to seize arms, because "the proletarian revolution cannot succeed" without control of the gun. The new manifesto was, in the final analysis, nothing less than a call for civil war. Weapon seizures by rebel organizations throughout the country followed within hours of the new call being put out over the radio. All in all, the new program constituted a declaration of war on many of the top leaders of the People's Liberation Army.

Under rather strange circumstances, Nancy had encountered the new slogan "dragging out the handful in the Army" in the early spring and, as with so many of the kaleidoscopic incidents of the Cultural Revolution, promptly forgotten it. Having accepted a request from the New China News

Agency (Hsinhua) to work as an English-language "polisher," she had spent a number of months there, red penciling the ever-shifting editorials and attending a few of that organization's Cultural Revolution meetings, which remained inscrutable through her lack of acquaintance with the main cast of characters. There, too, however, there were memorable moments. One was the cold night when the whole staff rushed from their desks at 1 A.M. to greet the new chief of propaganda, none other than the famous member of the Cultural Group, Wang Li. A handsome man, stout in his khaki padded overcoat, his suave bankerly appearance seeming strangely out of place amid the admiring swarms of excited Red Guards, he spoke briefly, promising to bring the factions together. Nancy, like the rest of the staff, was never to see him again. A number of weeks later, however, under the new management, an editorial passed across her desk which, for some reason, was then withheld from publication. Not until July did she know why. That editorial, which did not appear in the spring, had laid out the line "to drag out the handful in the Army." Whether it had been determined that the time was not ripe or whether the editorial had been short-circuited by opposing forces is one among many unanswered questions.

Not surprisingly, the first time we heard the new slogan was in a speech Sid Rittenberg gave to some foreigners in the last week of July on the situation in Wuhan. He told us that the top handful of capitalist-roaders had been pulled out of the Party and that the next stage of the movement would be devoted to dragging out the handful in the Army. Rittenberg spoke with the authority of one who was firmly established in the top leadership of Peking's Earth faction. Indeed, there were many Chinese in the city who believed that he was actually a functioning member of the Cultural Group.[98] But the Earth faction and its supporters on the Cultural Group would find, within a matter of weeks, that by their dual attack on the Army leaders and Premier Chou's state bureaucracy, they had badly miscalculated the power realities of the nation.

Just as the Peking political cauldron was reaching its boiling point, our whole family departed for that vibrant but stable center of revolution, Shanghai. We had collectively reached the decision that the time had come for our oldest son, who had just passed his eighteenth birthday, to return to his own country, itself in a storm against US involvement in Vietnam, so that he could participate in that critical period of American history. We had arranged for him to take a final trip to the Northeast with one of our most dynamic students, a Red Flag activist. For three weeks in July, the two young men, one Chinese and the other American, traveled on trains packed with Red Guards, workers, and PLA men touring Harbin, Shenyang, and Ch'angch'un, the major cities of the Northeast.

They joined the endless debates on the trains continued around the clock by a people participating in revolution, observed the growing violence between the factional armies in China's great Northeast industrial cities, and talked to countless members of revolutionary committees. They were no different from the other millions of young people during that summer of 1967 who argued the same points from the highlands of Tibet to the cities of Inner Mongolia.

Our two younger sons were to join us later in Shanghai, traveling alone from Peking by train, the staff insisting that they sit in isolated splendor in the dining car, safely quarantined from the miasmas of the revolution. We parents, as always the privileged foreign friends, missed all the hurly-burly by means of a quiet plane trip, during which the only politics consisted of the stewardesses reading the quotations of Chairman Mao. The five of us met in Shanghai for the sendoff.

During the second summer of the Cultural Revolution, Shanghai exuded an atmosphere of busy confidence and purposefulness that was lacking in Peking. Walking the streets, watching the crowds, and talking to the activists, one immediately had the feeling that here were people who had not only tasted the elixir of revolution, but knew where they were going. The city, of course, had the same problems of factionalism, anarchism, individual ambition, and pressure from interest groups as did the rest of the nation; but it was clear that they could solve these problems and any others that might arise. It is true that they had the best newspaper in the nation, the *Wen-hui pao;* probably the most mature, disciplined, and politically advanced Army units; and the best mass leaders to be found. Perhaps these were enough to account for the success; yet it was the people from below, who had somehow surfaced to administer offices and factories, who impressed us the most. Once it was known that we weren't exactly foreign visitors, but teachers and even honorary participants in the great rebellion, we were able to talk informally with all those to whom we were introduced.

We went one day to a steel mill across the Huang-p'u River and were introduced to the revolutionary committee, whose average age hardly exceeded twenty-six. As we settled in our chairs expecting the usual formal tea offering, the young man who was supervising one of the biggest steel mills in the largest industrial city in the country asked if we would like frozen ice bars. For Americans who had never fully adapted to the Chinese conviction that steaming tea is more cooling in midsummer heat than the icy concoctions with which Westerners were believed to ruin their stomachs, this was indeed a delightful turn of the revolution. Seeing our surprised expressions, our host explained that since the work of the mill was so hot, the new committee had decided to make their own popsicles at the plant, an innovation which had proved to be very popular with the workers. Following the informal and comfortable style of the rebel managers, we were all soon sitting with our legs over the arms of the chairs munching on our popsicles as we launched into an intense discussion of the Cultural Revolution in their factory, a discussion which ranged from the most serious to the most humorous. These were the youth whom the Chairman had compared to "the sun at eight or nine in the morning."

Their counterparts were everywhere, and our visits to docks and factories gave us the impression that Shanghai was being run by its revolutionary successors. It was on a visit to a Shanghai dock that we understood that we really were seeing those elusive "others" of whom Mao had spoken to Malraux. The revolutionary committee that greeted us were again only in their late twenties, a group of young men exuding energy, confidence, and enthusiasm. The old formalism of such official visits was gone, and although we did have tea around a large table, the discussion proceeded in bursts and rushes, spontaneous, and filled with the concrete details in which it seems all such workers in the world really do talk. As middle school graduates, considered "intellectuals" in the contemporary Chinese definition, they had answered a 1963 call from the Shanghai Party to become dock workers. They had brought with them a worker-intellectual mentality which fitted Mao's theoretical concept of China's future man. Before the Cultural Revolution, they had continued their studies, taking university extension courses at night, and could now not only repair all the machinery used on the docks, but had begun to design their own. However, politically, they had not succeeded in their new careers. Openly critical of Party bureaucrats who never got out of their offices and down into the holds of ships, they had been chided by the older longshoremen, who told them that if it hadn't been for the Party, they, the less fortunate, less educated workers would long ago have died the grim death of all waterfront coolies. Although the young worker-intellectuals had applied for membership in the Party or Youth League, none had been accepted. "We were called 'juvenile delinquents,' before Chairman Mao recognized us," they told us with merry laughter and very little humor in their eyes.

So they had been the rebels on their dock, fighting not for personal interests, but for a new and different political direction. Through their own experience, they had a clear idea of what that direction should be. Once in power, they had revolutionized the administration of the dock. One aspect of their revolution was the fact that they, the new administrators, spent only one hour a day in the office, and for the rest of their long and intense day's work, were out on the wharves, participating in the work and the workers' problems. It was a concept of worker management which organizational theorists might regard as absurdly utopian in a world of increasing technological complexity. We often wondered to what extent the young rebels were able to continue it. They were operating their committee without any Party cadres. That question was still not settled, they said, but introduced one tentative candidate for reinstatement, a tough and burly man in his fifties, as stereotypical of a Shanghai Party dock official as they were not. He sat quietly listening to the entire discussion, not adding a word to their explanation of the situation past and present.

It was these young leaders who seemed to us then, and still do today, to represent the true rationale of the Cultural Revolution and the fulfillment of its purpose. It has often occurred to us since that if one were to test the final success of the Cultural Revolution, it would be necessary to apply the litmus to this same Shanghai dock and the present position of its first revolutionary committee.

During a day-long visit to the P'eng P'u housing development, a huge workers' living complex in the Shanghai suburbs, we received a casual, but obviously heartfelt, invitation to return when our boys arrived and spend a few days, or as long as we liked, with a family we met. We accepted with pleasure, and it was during our visit there that we became acquainted with that important and influential stratum of urban activists, the women of the neighborhood committees.

In spite of the fact that they still called themselves housewives, many of those we met were skilled administrators, actually the cadres which the community considered them to be, responsible for the management of a complex web of community services, including nursery schools, family counseling, the dissemination of health and birth control information, mending and tailoring shops, and the entire range of social services necessary for this active 50,000-person community of working-class families. We met with a group of these leading women, and the most dynamic and sparkling among them, forty-year-old Comrade Chang, became our invaluable guide to the sprawling P'eng P'u world. She, a Party member, though not a paid official, had been at the other end of the Cultural Revolution dialectic from the young rebels we had been meeting elsewhere.

P'eng P'u, like any community, had its share of disagreements and dissatisfactions over government policy and its local implementation by these community workers. This current movement for criticizing Party leaders had released an outpouring of grievances. Women such as Comrade Chang were perhaps among the least bureaucratic of any local Party leadership, for they were not "career" communists, and the nature of their community responsibilities dictated their following a mass line. Nevertheless, they, like Party cadres everywhere, were attacked for policies which they had not determined. However, confident as they were of their local links with their community, they were unafraid to defend those policies which they still believed to be correct, even in the face of a powerful interest group attack. Comrade Chang told us of her own difficulties in standing up for one such policy, which she said she had felt both earlier and at the present time was a good one and which should not be included in a criticism of "revisionism."

It had been a matter of policy before the Cultural Revolution, and is now once again, to send thousands of young Shanghainese to settle the western lands, primarily in the huge frontier province of Sinkiang. Sometimes the policy had been carried out well and sometimes badly; some of the young people have gone to the frontier enthusiastically and others bitterly, for Shanghai people, like New Yorkers, Londoners, and Parisians, never really seem to be happy away from their own crowded city. But there are few people who will not tell you that the policy is undoubtedly the only practical solution for the largest city in the world, bursting at the seams with its population of 10 million, as it concomitantly is for the gigantic undeveloped frontier, desperately lacking educated manpower for its agricultural and industrial development. Nevertheless, angry parents generated a storm of attack against Comrade Chang for her role in making arrangements for their children to leave home and family for the western provinces. She had listened to them and then disagreed with them, one of the few cadres we met who dared to take such a stand. She apparently had something of the traditional Chinese capacity for bending like a reed in the wind, for her combined gaiety and firmness were clear indication that she had come out of it all psychologically intact. Her overall role of service to the people was too well known for her neighbors to have any wish to "overthrow" her, and though the irate parents had not changed their view nor she hers, she was on the job as usual, the indispensable community organizer.

The workers of P'eng P'u were employed at a number of large nearby factories, one of which was a major electric motor plant. On one steamy evening, we met with that plant's new revolutionary committee to hear a remarkable Cultural Revolution story. Once again, our hosts across the table were young and energetic, but seated with them this time was an equally dynamic middle-aged cadre, not a silent observer as at the docks, but the reinstated plant manager and member of the revolutionary committee. He was a man who had come up through the ranks in the most honorable of ways. A worker in this same plant before 1949 under both the KMT and the Japanese, he had joined the Party in the hard and dangerous days of the underground organization. After liberation, he had thrown himself into the enormous tasks faced by this key factory and had clearly earned the managerial position he eventually attained. So when he, a man who often worked a sixteen-hour day plus weekends and took his problems home with him late at night, became the factory's main target of Red Guard attack, he was, he told us, not so much upset as enraged. The young workers criticized him for spending too much time in the office, for devoting himself entirely to increasing production without any sense of what the purpose of it all was, of knowing nothing about the workers themselves. They were, he was convinced, "young punks," who knew nothing of suffering, of the exploitation of labor, of work, and the importance of production in a plant that was a key link in the national defense system. They did not change their position; nor did he. They held forty "struggle meetings" against him, and his only reply to his accusers was that if they wanted to run the factory themselves, he would resign his post as manager and become an ordinary worker again. Instead, they demanded that he remain in his post under their "supervision," and it was then that both sides learned something of the other. He found that these 'punks" were working double shifts to keep productivity to normal, even with their Cultural Revolution activities, and were struggling manfully with technical problems. When, after a period of watching with interest and increasing sympathy, he began to offer some modest expertise, the walls of suspicion on both sides started to come down and there began to evolve the sort of new worker-management relationship which the young rebels had been talking about. He joined them on the work floor, attended their study sessions, and realized that these youngsters were more political than he, since he had not had time to study politics for years.

Within a few months, having decided that he was indeed the best man to manage the factory, they had returned him to his former position, but with an altered concept of what that position entailed. This story, which they told together, the young rebels giving their side of it and the plant manager his, was clearly the prototypical account of what the Cultural Revolution was supposed to be about, a success story of criticism leading to enlightenment rather than to factional hatreds. Although, two years later, in the summer of 1969, we met with dozens of three-way committees, very few of them were marked with the same enthusiasm and success as this early committee created by the masses and their cadre, who had worked things out themselves, without the compromises and pressures imposed by the Army and worker teams which, in so many cases, had to forge revolutionary committees out of factional chaos.

The man who put all that we had seen of Shanghai's political success into theoretical terms was a member of the Municipal Revolutionary Committee. He was one of the relatively young Party cadres who had been incorporated in that three-way organ of power and proved to be a living example of those revolutionary leading cadres whom Mao had insisted on including in the new power arrangements, because "they are more experienced in struggle, they are more mature politically, and they have great organizational skill." He frankly admitted that the situation in Szechuan, Kwangtung, and many other provinces was quite chaotic, that violence was occurring on a large scale, but that this should not frighten one. "Didn't Marx teach us that, through motion and struggle, new things appear? The thing that should disturb us most is stagnation. When a pool or river is stagnant, you can't see the bottom, but when the water rushes swiftly, all the submerged rocks and things below the surface become visible." This was what the Cultural Revolution had achieved, he stated. It had allowed all the social forces to surface, and this was a good thing if one really cared about charting new progress and wished to examine carefully all the obstacles which must be overcome for a new historical advance. He had read everything of Mao's before the Cultural Revolution, but claimed that he had not understood much. Now, he said, after one year of struggle he had learned something about dialectics, the stages of a social movement, and the difficulty of leading masses who were already in motion—a test, he indicated, that would either make one or break one as a leader.

After putting our son on the plane for his trip back to the United States, we returned to Peking exhilarated by the Shanghai experience, having almost forgotten that we had left Peking in the midst of its most serious crisis of the Cultural Revolution. Back at the Foreign Languages Institute in the second week of August, we found ourselves immersed in a sea of sound. All of the Rebel Corps' (Tsao-fan T'uan) loudspeakers were blaring at once, as if one tidal wave of sound would sweep the detested Red Flag Battalion and all its minions away for ever. The deafening message was filled with menace: "The Red Flag is now on its last legs! Finally it has been proved once and for all that the Red Flag's protection of Ch'en Yi shows that they are a conservative organization which should be disbanded immediately!", and so on. This was rather standard fare, but it seemed more insistent, more confident than usual, and it was evident that something important had happened. We set out in search of the young Red Flag teachers who could tell us something about the latest developments. We found one of them who told us rather gloomily that things looked bad for Red Flag: "It looks as if the Cultural Group has turned against us completely." From his canvas bag, he pulled out a sheaf of paper which, he told us, was the transcript of a talk by Wang Li at the Foreign Ministry on August 7, and we all sat down under a tree to read it.

On the night of August 7, Wang Li, the hero of Wuhan, and Yao Teng-shan, that other hero who had stood up against the violent mobs in Indonesia, had received representatives of the ultra-left Foreign Ministry Liaison Station. Wang Li had his foot in a cast, a token of his bravery in Wuhan. The Red Guards, viewing him perhaps as the young had viewed Danton or Marat in 1791, asked him anxiously about his health. Curtly dismissing this solicitude, Wang Li proceeded directly to the business at hand. Informing the radicals that he had been assigned by the Cultural Group and Chairman Mao to take charge of the movement in the Foreign Ministry, he said that he had called them in because "the resistance to the movement is strong in the Ministry of Foreign Affairs. Diplomacy is turned into an awe-inspiring and important affair that is beyond the means of other people. Is diplomacy really so difficult? To my mind, the internal problems of Red Guards are much more complicated than diplomacy." He reproached the young firebrands and the ambitious Yao Teng-shan for not having seized functional power in the Ministry. "How could you make such a revolution without touching the setup?" When the Red Guard representatives told him that they had previously been criticized for going too far in the seizure of power, Wang Li replied:

> "You are wrong. If the personnel power of the cadre department in the Foreign Ministry cannot be touched, then would it not mean that the Organization Department of the Central Committee must be reinstated? It wields the biggest personnel power. I think you wield no power now. An awe-inspiring reputation presupposes some power."[99]

He added that the "leftists" must do more than supervise the work of the top cadres in the ministry, suggesting that they should seize total power themselves. In August 1967, such a statement could only have one effect—that of throwing gasoline on a fire.

Wang Li next referred to the citywide criticism of Yao Teng-shan for having initiated the slogan of "Down with Liu, Teng, Ch'en" and exclaimed, "Why not shout this slogan?" The reason up to this point had been quite clear. The Cultural Group had definitively declared this slogan to be incorrect, since Ch'en Yi was to be criticized but not overthrown. Legitimacy had been granted only to the slogan "Down with Liu Shao-ch'i, Teng Hsiao-p'ing, and T'ao Chu." Slogans could not be changed without a major change in line, but Wang Li, a prominent member of Chairman Mao's Headquarters, was indicating that the line had changed. There could be no other interpretation. It was for this reason that Tsao-fan T'uan had opened their exuberant loudspeaker offensive and our rebel friends in Hung-ch'i had fallen into their corresponding gloom. This was indeed a crucial turning point, for the division between the two organizations rested on the fate of Ch'en Yi. It was hard not to be infected with our friend's despondency when he said, "Perhaps we made a mistake. Maybe we should have been tougher on Ch'en Yi. He really has taken a reactionary position, you know." Feeling that they had been deserted by the top leaders in the country, our confident Hung-ch'i friends were beginning to doubt themselves. Our colleague was still sitting under the tree with Wang Li's speech in his lap as we left.

The loudspeaker war reached a new crescendo, as the ultras, the June 16 rebels whom Wang Li had praised in his speech, joined Tsao-fan T'uan in the din of denunciation of the Red Flag Regiment, which was, according to the new blast, "tottering on its last legs." Suddenly, we remembered a recent conversation with Rittenberg, who had told us that Yao Teng-shan had been his guest for dinner and that Yao just might end up as the new Foreign Minister. We had dismissed this as nonsense and quickly forgotten about it. We were, of course, convinced that our Heaven sources of information were sounder than his Earth sources. Rittenberg had often informed us of new developments, but those new developments had just as often turned into mysterious debacles like those involving the contract workers and the "revolutionary madman." And since "our" Institute belonged to the Foreign Ministry, we were sure that our friends were more knowledgeable about that particular struggle than he could possibly be.

We knew, for instance, that Wang Hai-jung, Mao's niece, a Peking First Foreign Languages Institute graduate, had become very active in the Ministry and had posted a number of *ta-tzu-pao* (which everyone was certain were inspired by the Chairman himself) in defense of Ch'en Yi. In July, Wang had posted a sixteen-character slogan which everyone believed originated with her venerable uncle and represented Mao's opinion of Ch'en Yi. In essence, the slogan stated that Ch'en Yi was honest, he was loyal, he was not a double dealer; however, he talked too much and therefore got in trouble. Later, Wang Hai-jung and her colleagues put up a three-part slogan, "Struggle against Ch'en Yi, criticize Ch'en Yi, protect Ch'en Yi," followed by an underlined blank, understood by all in that guessing game which is never quite absent from Chinese politics, and which the Chinese love, to mean "Liberate Ch'en Yi."

The pieces now began to fall together into a pattern of political consistency. For more than a year, foreign policy had remained in limbo, the country being so completely embroiled in its domestic affairs, that, except for the new upheavals in Hong Kong sponsored by Chinese radicals, one would hardly have known that a real world existed outside of China. Yet the Chairman had not forgotten the external factor. Students told us that, in a recent meeting in Peking, Mao had said that he had never agreed with Teng Hsiao-p'ing's 1965 analysis that America had shifted its strategic interests to the Pacific and Vietnam. It was reported that Mao believed that the United States' major interests were in Europe and the Middle East and would remain so. Thus, the Chairman, following his own methodology, so carefully worked out in his military writings, that a commander must occupy himself not only with the present battle and campaign but the succeeding strategic stage, had his eye on the future. The next strategic stage after the Cultural Revolution would involve the Foreign Ministry, and since that Ministry involved one of the Chairman's own special preserves, those intervening in this area ran the risk of a confrontation with the supreme commander himself.

In those August weeks of crisis, we began to see clearly what many of our Chinese friends had seen for some time. The split in the revolutionary ranks had become so serious that sooner or later the Chairman himself would be the only one who could resolve it. One of our students a few weeks back had criticized what he called a terrible editorial in the *People's Daily* and replied to our comment that it must have been written by the Cultural Group, "But don't you know that the Cultural Group is split?" By the second week of August, it was apparent, even to us, that a major section of the Cultural Group had launched a two-pronged attack first on the Army and secondly on the Premier and the Deputy Ministers on the State Council. The radicals on the Cultural Group were making a concerted effort to seize control of the propaganda organs, Peking Radio, and the Foreign Ministry. Sid Rittenberg, after a complex and involuted series of power seizures and counter power seizures at the Radio, had been appointed head of a three-man committee which was actually running the Radio. We also heard at this time that the Rebel Corps from our Institute and June 16, who had been camping outside the Foreign Ministry, had stormed the besieged fortress and, together with other student armies from the Earth faction and the radical Foreign Ministry Liaison Station, seized power, putting Yao Teng-shan in control. Mao's niece, Wang Hai-jung, was said to be in a difficult position. The ultras had even put up a poster saying, "Chairman Mao Says Wang Hai-jung Will Never Amount to Anything!"—a reference to her earlier published conversations with her uncle, in which he had criticized her as an insufficiently rebellious student.

It did not take us long to find out why we had seen some of the Tsao-fan T'uan students from our Institute walking down the peaceful, tree-lined road beside the school one hot August morning carrying cans of gasoline. With the happily expectant air of summer picnickers, they were on their way to burn down the British Chargé d'Affaires Mission, an action in line with the new foreign policy orientation of Yao Teng-shan and his young radical supporters who had taken over the Ministry of Foreign Affairs. This action was ostensibly in opposition to British suppression of the masses in Hong Kong, who had started their own cultural revolution in the crown colony, but in reality to keep up the ultra-leftist offensive in the Foreign Ministry. Predictably, Premier Chou ordered the young Chinese ultras not to enter the British diplomatic quarters and, just as predictably, they ignored him and burned the place down. Those around the world who already thought the Chinese had gone mad were confirmed in their views; but like all the madness of the time, it was simply politics of another order. The target of the attack was not really the British, but Chou, who was placed in precisely the embarrassing and difficult position designed for him. Faced on the one side with rebels who claimed to be "carrying the revolution through to the end" and on the other with China's delicate, albeit suspended, foreign relations, his position was now quite dependent on Mao's evaluation of this left pendulum swing and of Chou himself.

Sensational new posters began to appear in the city, put up by the new and mysterious May 16 rebel organization. The broadsides openly called for the overthrow of Premier Chou En-lai. It was during this period that the Heaven faction held its long and carefully prepared meeting in the Great Hall of the People to criticize Ch'en Yi. The strategy was to criticize Ch'en Yi, then accept his self-criticism, and thus end the affair once and for all, removing the whole issue as a bone of contention between the two warring factions. We were greatly honored by our Red Flag friends with an invitation to attend. On the morning of the meeting we received a telephone call from Rittenberg. He said that he had heard that there was to be a meeting to criticize Ch'en Yi and wanted to know if it was still on. We replied that as far as we knew it was, but thought it strange that this was the only reason he had called.

For the first time in our years in China, instead of sitting on the main floor of the Great Hall, we sat up in the huge overhanging balcony. Every one of the 10,000 seats was taken by Red Guards from every organization under the Heaven banner in Peking and, as far as we could see, we were the only foreigners present. It was one of those rare occasions when we felt ourselves a part of the masses—no longer "outside persons," but at home in a joint endeavor, surrounded by our friends and colleagues. The slogans had been carefully prepared under the personal supervision of the Premier to call for repudiation and criticism of Ch'en Yi's mistakes, not for his overthrow. We waited for more than four hours, but neither the Premier nor Ch'en Yi appeared, much to the consternation of the audience. We learned later that Ch'en Yi had not appeared because armies of the Earth faction numbering tens of thousands had surrounded Chungnanhai and thus, the old Marshal, under a state of siege at his home, had been prevented from appearing before the Heaven meeting.

When we heard what had happened, we were reminded of Sid Rittenberg's morning phone call and wondered whether there was a connection between the two events. A few days later, Premier Chou himself was surrounded at his office in the Hall of the People by hundreds of thousands of enragés who, he later told Edgar Snow, wished to break in and seize the files of the Central Committee. Chou was blockaded for two days and nights until, by skillful negotiation, he persuaded the crowd to disperse. Lin Piao then moved in with the Army to take control of the situation. During this turning point of the revolution, our Red Flag friends disappeared into strategy meetings, for clearly this was the moment that would determine the fate of Premier Chou En-lai's consistent defenders.

Then, one day in the final week of that incredible August, we met one of our young Red Flag teacher friends walking through the grounds of the Institute. He was the gentlest of young men, unchangeable throughout the storms of those years. He dearly loved Peking opera and would burst into song at any happy provocation. On this day, he was humming to himself, but even his serene personality and love of music seemed inadequate to explain his smiling face when he greeted us. "Well, everything is all right again," he said in his customary calm way, with only his shining eyes betraying his excitement. Then he told us the whole dramatic story of how the Premier had taken back control of the Foreign Ministry and thrown out Yao Teng-shan. He said that Chou En-lai had called the radical seizure of the Foreign Ministry "the four-day dream" (after a Chinese folk story which tells of a man who fell asleep, dreamed he was the emperor, and then awoke to find that he was just an ordinary mortal). Chairman Mao had intervened as directly as at any time in the whole Cultural Revolution, writing in the margin of Wang Li's now notorious August 7 speech: "This is a big, big, poisonous weed!" On Lin Chieh's editorial calling for dragging out the handful in the Army, the Chairman wrote, "Save our Great Wall!"—his term for the People's Liberation Army. So once more, the Chairman had come down on the side of the popular and indispensable Premier. But in order to do so, he had had to subdivide his three categories of left, right, and middle. He had come out, he later admitted, a "center-leftist." It was a grouping which had few other representatives.

## Chapter X

# "One Cultural Revolution
# May Not Be Enough"

AFTER EXACTLY one year, Mao Tse-tung's experiment with his historic new concept of continuous revolution had revealed its limitations. At the end of the crisis month of August, Mao was ready to sum up. During an extended talk with a visiting Albanian military delegation, he told them that China was paying a very high price in the current Great Cultural Revolution and added: "The struggle between the two classes and the two lines cannot be settled in one, two, three, or four cultural revolutions." It would take at least fifteen years, he said, to consolidate the present movement while two or three of these revolutions should be carried out every 100 years. There could be little doubt that Mao was disappointed in the students and was beginning to look to other sectors of the population for successors:

> "It was desired to bring up some successors among the intellectuals, but now it seems a hopeless task. As I see it, the intellectuals, including young intellectuals still receiving education in school, still have a basically bourgeois world outlook, whether they are in the Party or outside it. This is because, for seventeen years after the liberation, the cultural and educational circles have been dominated by revisionism."[100]

Although he admitted that the "revolutionary spirit of the revolutionary young generals is very strong," he asserted that they were not yet ready to take over the reins of power: "If you (the young rebels) go up on the stage today, you will be kicked off it tomorrow." He apparently also had in mind some of the intellectuals that either he or his wife had appointed to top positions in the Cultural Group, since, at the time of his talks with the Albanians, Wang Li, Kuan Feng, Mu Hsin, and Lin Chieh had been toppled from power and were under arrest at ultra-left counterrevolutionaries.

Noting that the historic May 4 Movement of 1919 had been started by intellectuals but finished by workers, peasants, and soldiers, Mao characterized intellectuals as possessing quick perception and having the ability to change course quickly, but said that they also have natural limitations, "lack the will for thorough revolution, and very often show a wavering character." By example, he pointed out that, while it was the intellectuals and students who had first seen through the bourgeois reactionary line at the beginning of the present movement, it had been the workers, whom he was to call the "masters of our time," who had accomplished the January Revolution and seizure of power in Shanghai. Mao went on to explain to his Albanian visitors why "the broad masses of workers and peasants and the backbone of the Party and the Young Communist Youth League have been hoodwinked in the course of criticism and repudiation of the bourgeois reactionary line." It was because the workers, peasants, and soldiers "are practical workers and so, naturally, they know little about those in the upper levels." Another reason given by the Chairman for confusion in the ranks of the ordinary people was their "unbounded love for the Party and its cadres" and the fact that the capitalist-roaders "hold up a red flag to oppose the red flag." But even though the masses had been deceived for a long time, Mao was convinced that once they understood the issues they would change and "be the main force again with the intensification of the movement." Key decisions having been made in August to effect a new direction, line, and orientation for the movement he had set in motion, Mao, after his philosophical talk with foreign visitors, set out in September on a tour of the provinces to seek an answer to the most serious problem facing the nation—factionalism.

The August crisis and the Chairman's response to it resulted in a series of decisions leading toward centralization of power at the center, a decline in the influence of the Cultural Group, and the imposition of controls on the mass movement. These new policy decisions would be implemented through the cooperation of Premier Chou and the Army under Lin Piao, these two men being assigned the leadership tasks for the next stage of the Cultural Revolution. As early as August 9, only two days after the Wang Li speech at the Foreign Ministry which Chairman Mao had characterized as a "poisonous weed," Lin Piao had delivered a major speech to senior Army commanders to sum up the disastrous experience at Wuhan:

> "Chairman Mao has told us that bad things may be turned, under given conditions, into good things. [. . .] The Wuhan incident is a very bad thing [but its] educational significance is tremendous."[101]

Stating that "the solution to a problem will be blunted if it gives us no pain," Lin went on to say that not only was Ch'en Tsai-tao's reactionary line exposed but the Wuhan incident had revealed the "complexity of the class struggle." "Upheaval," according to Lin, was not "something to be feared," rather it was "necessary and normal." Attempting to accentuate the positive, he declared that the "victory of the present Great Cultural Revolution is very great. The price we have paid is the smallest, smallest, smallest, but the victory we have gained is the greatest, greatest, greatest."

There were only two conditions which Lin listed for the success of the movement. The first was the "Thought of Mao Tse-tung and Chairman Mao's lofty prestige" and the second was the strength of the People's Liberation Army. Perhaps it was an augury of the future that Lin listed no other forces which might contribute to the success of the Cultural Revolution other than Chairman Mao and the Army. Lin did order his generals, however, to make no decisions without checking with the Center. Perhaps the most important sections of the speech, seen in retrospect, were Lin's comments on the necessity to build a new state machine and his remarks concerning political power:

> "The old leadership group of power-holders was incapable of becoming a state machine, fell, and has been taken over by the military. Our State machine has many things which are capitalist and revisionist, and its fall does not do any harm. Let it fall."

Lin called upon the Army to learn from its mistakes, in which case the generals would not fall and, instead of "being dragged out," might find themselves exercising State power. It became apparent, if it had not been before, that in August 1967, when each element of the three-way alliance looked into the mirror, it saw only itself. Each force of the tripartite group which made up Chairman Mao's headquarters consistently produced competing policies, lines, and ideologies. However, since Lin was the designated "successor" to Mao, it was not illogical that he should seek to build a power base for himself. Apparently, that is what he was seeking to do, and the Army was the logical place to build it.

The most popular section of the Lin Piao August 9 speech, quoted by everyone at the time, was his analysis of the "four kinds of upheaval":

> "1. Good people struggling against bad people.

> "2. Bad people struggling against bad people. We make use of such struggles in an indirect way.

> "3. Bad people struggling against good people. This has happened in Peking, in the Navy, the Air Force, in the Headquarters of the General Staff, and in the General Rear Service Department. The good people come in for attack, but this has also done them some good.

> "4. Good people struggling against good people. This is, of course, not good, and some damage has been done. But this is a contradiction among the people, and it can be easily resolved."

The only kind of upheaval that "we don't want to see," said Lin, "is the third kind—bad people struggling against good people." But, although everyone was pleased with the formula, no one quite knew how to make it work, since the definition of who was bad and good was always in dispute.

On August 11, only two days after Lin Piao had outlined the new orientation for the Army, Ch'en Po-ta and Chiang Ch'ing, bending to new pressures from above, repudiated the line emanating from their own Cultural Group and directed against the Premier. They did so by attacking the mysterious May 16 secret organization which had surfaced during the summer to direct open attacks against Premier Chou. Later, all those who went down in the August policy dispute over the direction of the Cultural Revolution would be linked with May 16, which was to become the convenient catchall category for those associated with ultra-left counterrevolution. Chiang Ch'ing declared at the August 11 public meeting: "Such an organization as the May 16 will not be tolerated. It is an act of sabotage." She referred to a number of provocative handbills which had been distributed on Wangfuching Street bearing "peculiar names" such as "Hidden Dragon," "Hidden Road," and "Hidden Tiger" and declared that "they seemed to have been put out by secret agents and might have something to do with May 16. This is an act of sabotage and must be clearly explained to the masses."[102] Within two weeks, May 16 was officially labeled as a "counterrevolutionary organization."

We had heard a great deal about May 16 from our student and teacher friends all during the summer. They had speculated that one of the headquarters of that clandestine organization might well be the fifth floor of the main building of our Institute, where Liu Ling-k'ai and his June 16 band of militants had barricaded themselves. This later turned out to be correct. Naturally, as soon as the "problem" of May 16 was exposed by national leaders, Hung-ch'i made the most of it. Immediately, the most brilliant investigative researchers were put to work on the history and connections of May 16. It was already known that Wang Li's niece was a member of Tsao-fan T'uan. This fact, previously an asset, turned into a liability. The Hung-ch'i research team obviously wished to find out whether the niece had been a conduit for the policies of the uncle and to uncover the connection between Tsao-fan T'uan and its ally, June 16. Throughout the city, similar research was carried out by energetic investigators of the Heaven faction, all of whom labored to unravel the ramifications of the May 16 conspiracy. For these Chinese rebels, who had learned long ago how to trace lines upward, it had become an automatic reflex to follow a trail as far and as high as it would go. In those hot weeks of August, there were hundreds of the most experienced young sleuths at work exploring the roots and connections of May 16; it was an investigation which threatened to lead into the Cultural Group itself. The students were all determined to probe the key question: "What did they know and when did they know it."

It was, however, in the interests of Chairman Mao's Proletarian Headquarters that the investigation not proceed too far. Even the Premier, the target of the conspiracy, was energetic in attempting to heal the breach which his opponents had opened up in the command center of the Cultural Revolution. The Premier was well aware that if the gap were not closed, the slumbering rightists, the deposed cadres, and the enemies of the Cultural Revolution itself, would come thundering through. Consequently, he issued an order imposing four conditions regarding the treatment of the May 16 question:

"1. The problem should not be expanded.

"2. Only a few bad leaders need be arrested.

"3. Those who had been hoodwinked should be liberated.

"4. The rightists should be prevented from fishing in troubled waters."[103]

The Premier could afford to wait. It was in his and the Chairman's interest that Chiang Ch'ing not be discredited, and the future would prove that, in the long run, almost all of the Premier's most deadly opponents would fall from power.

Our Red Flag students, however, could not refrain from exploiting their victory over leaders who in May had refused to recognize them, and so, at a late August meeting in the Hall of the People, they harassed Ch'en Po-ta in a typical Chinese manner. Ch'en Po-ta spoke Mandarin with such a heavy Fukienese accent that it was difficult for northerners to understand him, and for this reason he had quite often employed Wang Li as his interpreter. On that late August evening, Ch'en Po-ta appeared alone and, after his speech, one of our Red Flag rebels rose to his feet and asked Ch'en where his interpreter was. Ch'en was furious and retorted. "What's the matter with you people? Don't you understand Chinese?" But the students had made their political point.

All of the major actors in the Cultural Revolution performed during the August crisis. Each sought to upstage the others, and even the tightly knit team of foreign veterans—Sidney Rittenberg, Michael Shapiro, and Israel Epstein—became involved in a major ultra-left plot in Tientsin which soon achieved nationwide notoriety. The three, acting in the capacity of representatives of Bethune-Yenan (but without the knowledge of the membership), took part in The National Forum of Fighters of Literature and Art for Workers, Peasants, and Soldiers in Tientsin. This August conference, later to be denounced by the national leaders as a "counter-revolutionary black meeting," was apparently an attempt by the followers of the big four on the Cultural Group, Wang-Kuan-Lin-Mu, to establish a national organizational network under the guise of literary and art work. The highlight of the affair was the production of the play *Madman of the Modern Age,* based on the life of Ch'en Li-ning.

Rittenberg had been promoting the new play for weeks and was actively seeking to get this epic translated into many languages for distribution throughout the world. There were even reports that he had attempted to get Chiang Ch'ing's support for his project. He had arranged for a special performance for the foreigners, which, for some reason not related to political foresight, we failed to attend. As a result, we missed the "reactionary black play" staged at what was later to be termed the "counterrevolutionary" National Forum in Tientsin, in which Rittenberg, Epstein, and

Shapiro had somehow become entangled. It was all quite as bizarre as the fraudulent "madman" Ch'en Li-ning himself.

By the end of August, our friends from the Heaven faction were euphoric over the recent political developments which they believed had proved once and for all the correctness of their political line. The young teachers, politically more experienced than the students, felt that this was a propitious time to hold out the hand of reconciliation to their opponents in the Rebel Regiment and settle the factional differences in the school. Such an action, they argued, would be in line with Chairman Mao's teaching to seek unity even with those who had opposed you in the past. But the Hung-ch'i student leaders would have none of this. They were determined to crush the opposition by exposing and discrediting the Rebel Corps' leaders, a strategy they were convinced would bring about the complete capitulation and conversion of the membership. We agreed with the analysis of our teaching colleagues that the 180-degree turn of the political compass opened the possibility of reconciliation among factions, foreign as well as Chinese. It was in this spirit that we went one afternoon with our British colleague, David Crook, to have a talk with Sid Rittenberg.

We had been hearing startling reports about the movement at Peking Radio. Hung-ch'i students and teachers maintained close connections with rebel groups at Peking Radio, where Sid worked, and from our friends' recent visits there to read the *ta-tzu-pao,* we learned that a mass repudiation campaign against Rittenberg had begun with the fall of his patron, Wang Li. We were also aware that a representative of the Cultural Group had gone to the broadcasting station at the end of August to announce that Sid no longer held any official position there and was awaiting assignment to other work. Most of the foreign, and particularly the American, community, who knew Rittenberg as the most reliable transmitter of information from "the Chinese," still did not, or would not, understand that his information reflected the factional position of one group of Chinese and took at face value his own assurances that the Cultural Group's announcement presaged a promotion. In reality, as the weeks passed, he remained in limbo, vulnerable to the attacks of an angry rank and file.

Sid Rittenberg was in a position qualitatively different from that of other foreigners like ourselves. Regardless of our factional loyalties, our involvement in this social revolution was regarded by the Chinese as so irrelevant that they permitted us to wander amid their battles with the immunity of so many Pierres at Borodino. However, since February, Sid had held a position of great power; he was, in effect, the head of Peking Radio. It was indeed a remarkable fact that control of one of China's key propaganda organs should be in the hands of an American, and *Pravda* was not the only foreign newspaper to call attention to this anomalous situation.

By January 1967, Rittenberg had become a leader of the Mao Tse-tung Thought Combat Corps, which had seized power at Radio (as it was familiarly called). By the middle of January, there was a counter power seizure, and after several weeks of confusion, both within the Cultural Group and among people working at Radio as to which seizure should be supported, Rittenberg suddenly switched sides, turning against his own group to support the second power seizure. The resulting revolt by the Combat Corps against the new power seizure was crushed, but hardly resolved, when Wang Li, then the Cultural Group's man in charge of the Broadcasting Bureau, denounced the errors of the Combat Corps, ordered it to conduct a rectification movement within its own ranks, and appointed a three-person rectification committee to direct the movement. The committee, consisting of Rittenberg, a young man, and a very young woman, soon exercised control not only over the rectification movement, but actually assumed supervisory and executive power over the day-to-day operations of Peking Radio. The power relations of the triumvirate were described as consisting of the brilliant Rittenberg who made policy, the not at all brilliant young man who put the policy in writing, and the very inexperienced young woman who read the decisions aloud to the assembled masses in her beautiful Peking dialect. They became known as "the brain, the scribe, and the voice."

Now, with the fall of Wang Li, all this had been turned upside down. Hung-ch'i's Heaven allies, the Radio Combat Corps, had taken the offensive, just as our own students were doing. Arriving at the Radio apartment building where Sid lived, we, the two Davids and Nancy, made our way through the once tranquil hallways, now busy with rebels hurrying about their organizational business, their hands full of sheaves of paper as always. They observed our direction with guarded curiosity, but were neither friendly nor unfriendly as we approached the apartment of their "living tiger." Perhaps Sid was already under "mass arrest," a hypothesis which, within a few weeks, was shown to be fact. However, he welcomed us at the door in his shirtsleeves and with his customary confident warmth. It had been a long time since we had been to this sunny apartment where we had enjoyed Sunday lunch and long afternoons of conversation with Rittenberg, his Chinese wife, and the stream of fascinating guests who were forever dropping by. Everything looked a bit stripped down—we sat on kitchen chairs instead of their Ming predecessors—but it seemed that we, the worried visitors, were the ones who had changed, not the urbane pourer of tea. He listened to our account of the attack against him, and only his eyes, always intense behind his thick glasses, gave any hint of his concentrated attention. He waved aside our concerns about his exposed position, assuring us that the poster attack was simply the work of a small group of reactionaries and would soon be straightened out. He talked more than we, and most of the afternoon was taken up with his complicated account of the events at the Radio. When we at last interjected to ask the key question—how had he ended up in supreme supervisory and executive control of Peking Radio?—he replied with his usual disarming frankness that he really didn't know. Perhaps he had been assigned by the Cultural Group, or perhaps it was the masses who had appointed him. It wasn't at all clear. His display of ingenuousness was indeed impressive, but the masses at Radio understood very well that Rittenberg had been put in power by none other than Wang Li. Sid dismissed as alarmist our urgings that he should clarify what he knew about the August plot to overthrow the Premier and particularly its connections with his position at Radio in a full disclosure to the workers there and make a self-criticism if it was appropriate to do so. At the end of our afternoon's long and inconclusive conversation, he walked us to our bicycles in the traditional manner of all good Chinese hosts, and, as he waved us off, said, "Wait and see. Wang Li will be up on T'ien An Men with the rest of the leaders on October first." It was obvious that he felt he still had powerful supporters on top.

By September 1, with the overthrow of key radicals in the Cultural Group, the ultra-left offensive in Peking had been contained, and the new leadership coalition led by Premier Chou and Lin Piao was ready to publicize the new policy lines worked out for the next stage of the Cultural Revolution. Chairman Mao had departed for his inspection trip of the southern provinces, where extensive violence and a small-scale civil war were spiraling into chaos. The Premier condemned the May 16 counterrevolution in a major speech on September 1 and outlined the new orientation of the movement, which demanded discipline and a new respect for the Army.

But it was Chiang Ch'ing's speech on the 5th that was utilized most extensively by the central leaders to publicize the new political line flowing from Chairman Mao's headquarters. The Chairman's wife, who had become famous as the fiery spokesman for the Red Guard revolution, was the most logical choice for a major effort by the new leadership to convince the "young generals" that the line they had received from the Cultural Group encouraging an attack on the Premier and the Army was not only wrong, but even counterrevolutionary. Appearing before a meeting of rival delegations from Anhwei in the Great Hall of the People, Chiang Ch'ing revealed that she had been pressured to speak:

> "Greetings to you all, comrades!" (Loud shouting: "Long Live Chairman Mao! A Long, Long Life to Him!")

> "I have come rather hurriedly, and I have no idea
> what is going on here. Venerable K'ang [K'ang Sheng]
> just dragged me here. Nor have I prepared for the few
> words which I shall say here."[104]

After preliminary remarks on the excellent situation of the
Cultural Revolution "taking the nation as a whole," she
came quickly to the main point concerning the new orientation desired by the center. It was that the Central Committee, meaning Chairman Mao, Chou En-lai, and Lin Piao,
had decided to concern themselves with "the problems
province by province and city by city in the case of those
large cities." This was the signal that the emphasis was shifting
from Peking to the localities. Except for the struggle against
Liu Shao-ch'i, the leadership hoped to avoid any more mass
campaigns directed at the personnel connected with the central command headquarters. Then Chiang Ch'ing attempted
to quench the fires that she herself had helped to light:

> "Comrades, I am not in favor of armed struggle
> [*wu-tou*], and you must not think I like it, because I am
> firmly opposed to it. I resolutely support Chairman
> Mao's call for peaceful struggle, not armed struggle.
> What I mean is [referring to her slogan of July]: 'Attack
> with words, defend with force.'
> "When the class enemies attack us, how can we not
> afford to have an inch of iron in our hands [that is, re-
> main unarmed]. This is the situation I have in mind, but
> at present we need not have that kind of armed struggle.
> "Armed struggle always hurts some people and dam-
> ages state property. [The slogan] 'attack with words and
> defend with force' must not be deprived of its class con-
> tent; it must not be viewed in isolation from definite cir-
> cumstances and conditions. It would be bad if, on your
> return, you stirred up fights by wearing fighters' helmets
> and raising spears."

(At this point, K'ang Sheng interrupted to exclaim: "Not
spears. We now have machine guns." He was referring to
reports from all over the country that real weapons, including
artillery in Szechuan, were now being used in factional
fights.)

The Chairman's wife next referred to that painful subject of the May 16 conspiracy, with which some of her closest associates in the Cultural Group had been involved:

> "The May 16 assumes an 'ultra-leftist' appearance; it centers its opposition on the Premier. Actually, it has collected black material to denounce every one of us, and it may throw it out in public at any time. It is a very typical counterrevolutionary organization, and we must raise our vigilance against it."

Chiang Ch'ing further warned the young rebels: "You cannot steal weapons from the Army. On the national defense front we are going to lay down a stern penalty. The Central Committee has already passed it. I want to warn soldiers that if anyone wanted to take away my weapons I would certainly retaliate. Of course, opening fire would be wrong." But the implication was that if the person were bad she would, and this statement was quoted extensively all over the country. The last point of this most publicized speech concerned the new revolutionary committees which Chiang Ch'ing described as a "new provisional organ of power." Not only was "an evil gust of wind" (meaning "bad" people) attacking the Central Committee headed by Chairman Mao or the People's Liberation Army, but they were also attacking the new revolutionary committees, and she implied that this would not be tolerated.

In short, the new line called for the rapid establishment of revolutionary committees province by province and city by city based on compromise between competing mass organizations, an end to armed struggle, support for the PLA, outlawing of May 16 and organizations like it, and an end to attacks on revolutionary committees already set up.

On the same day, September 5, a Party and Government Circular was issued by the CCP Central Committee, the State Council, the Central Military Affairs Committee, and the Central Cultural Revolution Group. The order, addressed to all Provincial and Municipal Revolutionary Committees, Military Control Committees, Military District Commands, and all Revolutionary Mass Organizations, bore the notation

"Seen. Take action accordingly. Mao Tse-tung. September 4" and was a manifesto in support and praise of the Chinese People's Liberation Army. Stating that the PLA is a "peerless people's army [. . .] personally formed and led by our great leader Chairman Mao and commanded by Vice Supreme Commander Lin Piao," the order referred to the duty of the Army to support the revolutionary left and called attention to the campaign launched in the press on August 25 for Support-the-Army and Cherish-the-People; but the crucial clauses laid down strict new prohibitions against interference with the Army. All mass organizations were strictly forbidden to seize arms, ammunition, and equipment anywhere in the nation and prohibited from occupying command organs of the Army. A time limit was set for return of arms already stolen. If the new order was violated, the Army, in the last instance, was given permission to open fire in self-defense.[105] In effect, the new instructions paved the way for the Army, the only remaining viable organization in the country, to fill the vacuum created by the demise of the nationwide Party apparatus. Chairman Mao turned to the Army in those critical autumn months of 1967 because it was the only organizational weapon he possessed.

The reaction by the Hung-ch'i leaders and membership at the First Foreign Languages Institute to the new policies and political line of the central authorities conformed to the pattern of response which marked all the turning points of the Cultural Revolution. Now that the tables had turned, it was the Hung-ch'i loudspeakers which blared through the night in a continuing counterattack on Tsao-fan T'uan, accusing its leaders and followers of attempting from the "left" to "topple the proletarian dictatorship and resist the great cultural revolution." Hung-ch'i exultantly demanded that Tsao-fan T'uan criticize its "ultra-left" excesses, just as three weeks earlier Hung-ch'i had been confronted with the demand to confess its rightist tendencies.

On the day following Chiang Ch'ing's public condemnation of the May 16 ultras, September 6, dozens of trucks bearing Red Guard fighters from all over the city arrived at our school to participate in the storming of the "counterrevolutionary" June 16 fortress on the fifth floor of the main building of the Institute. (June 16 was considered to be the headquarters for the mysterious citywide May 16.) As these shock troops massed in front of the school under their customary red banners and crimson silk flags, we joined the crowd to find out what was going on. All of the young people, quite naturally belonging to the Heaven faction, were in high spirits as they organized the assault squads to break into what they termed "one of the principal headquarters of May 16" in the country. The operation took a number of hours, since the June 16 rebels had barricaded the stairway to their fifth-floor redoubt with heavy wooden beams and planks. But finally, amid cheers from the onlookers, the assault force broke through with axes and battering rams, overcame the outnumbered defenders, and captured the stronghold. The "black leaders" of June 16 were led away and turned over to the security police. According to a leaflet triumphantly distributed by the victors, "an abundance of reactionary propaganda and other sinister materials and fifteen hard-core elements of the June 16 Corps were captured."[106] The news that June 16 had been collecting a file on the Premier was hardly news, since they had been doing that from the first day of the Cultural Revolution.

Although we did not know Liu Ling-k'ai, the notorious leader of June 16 who was placed under arrest, we had heard him speak and were interested to know what his fate might be. One young teacher told us that Liu Ling-k'ai had been one of the first real rebels in the movement, was extremely stubborn, and refused to admit that he was wrong, despite a number of "struggle meetings" held against him. Like his counterpart, K'uai Ta-fu, the famed leader of Chingkangshan at Tsinghua University, Liu Ling-k'ai appeared to represent the persistent Chinese cultural current which, over the millennia, had produced that minority of recalcitrants always referred to by those in authority as "bandits." Mao himself had been such a student, and perhaps it should not have surprised him that there would be those among the Chinese youth who would take literally his advice to "rebel to the end."

Hung-ch'i, with its membership of 2,000 students, now

outnumbered Tsao-fan T'uan by two to one. Although the Rebel Regiment had never been as outspoken against the Premier as June 16, it was felt by the Red Flag leaders that the programs of the two organizations had been essentially the same and all that would be necessary for final victory would be to prove the links between the two. Similar thinking generated similar actions by Red Guard leaders in every organization controlled by the Heaven faction in Peking. The Earth faction was thus put in the position of fighting for survival, and it adapted accordingly by taking up arms in a desperate defense of its cause. The result could only be, and was, more violence between the two sides.

Whatever the strategy now pursued by the Peking Red Guards, it had little effect on the national leaders, who were firmly committed to their decision to wind down the movement and centralize control once again at the top. A stream of policy pronouncements flowed from the center to achieve these goals. Editorials advised the students to spend their time criticizing the capitalist-roaders and "to conduct well the struggle, criticism, and transformation" of their own units. Discussions were begun on rebuilding the Party and the convening of the Ninth Party Congress, and a public execution took place in Peking of four "counterrevolutionary murderers" to remind all concerned that indiscriminate violence would no longer be tolerated. In the meantime, the Chairman was touring China's strife-torn south, central, and eastern provinces, visiting Honan, Kiangsi, Chekiang, Hunan, Hupeh, and Shanghai. During this September trip, Mao turned his full attention to that hydra-headed monster of the Cultural Revolution—factionalism—and the way to overcome it.

We heard from our Chinese friends that, to be able to read the big-character posters in Shanghai, Mao walked the streets in disguise, wearing one of those face masks commonly worn by Chinese as a protection against cold germs and fine dust. We had heard before that he used to ride around Peking at night so that he could read the latest slogans posted on the walls of the city. On this trip, the Chairman was particularly anxious to determine why it was that everywhere in the country the Party cadres had been hit so hard by the masses. We were told that he spoke to hundreds of cadres and of each he asked, "Do you lecture people all the time?" and "Do you listen to what other people have to say?"

In Kiangsi, Mao met with some political leaders and, after hearing reports of the violent turmoil throughout the Yangtze River basin, stated, "Some people say there is no civil war in China. But I think this is a civil war. It is not a foreign war. It is a violent struggle." He soon came to his old conclusion, derived from his long revolutionary experience, that the more one side was suppressed, the more it would resist. He told rebel representatives in Hunan, "We ourselves are the product of Chiang Kai-shek's suppression. After the great revolution, we had only several tens of thousands of men. Chiang Kai-shek's suppression gave us hope. His suppression produced at once three hundred thousand Party members." Mao told the local leaders in Kiangsi that during the long revolutionary guerrilla war there had been many mountain strongholds and isolated bases of operation, but they had all been united by common principles. All great political movements, he said, produce factions. "It simply does not work if there is only one faction." Moreover, he asserted, the left as well as the right needed education, and, if not educated, the left would become the ultra-left. It was in times of tension, he said, that problems unveiled themselves and became easy to resolve—"How can problems be resolved without tension?"

It was reported that, on his way back to Peking by train, he called in both factions of the train crew and helped to arbitrate their differences. When he heard the good news that a great alliance had been concluded between the three factions within the railway system, he told the railway workers, "Congratulations. May I present you with four characters: *Tou-szu, p'i-hsiu* (Struggle against private interest, criticize revisionism)." This was to become the slogan for the next stage of the movement.[107]

When the Chairman returned to Peking before National

Day, he summed up his inspection tour by saying, "We should expand our educational front and reduce our attack front, should use the formula of unity—criticism and self-criticism—unity to solve the contradictions among ourselves." He had added the term self-criticism to the "unity—criticism —unity" slogan which the Chinese Party had used for decades. We were told that Mao, after studying the question of splits in a social movement, had come to the conclusion that all people at one time or another feel oppressed, either by others or by a situation. Therefore, there is a universal tendency for individuals to gravitate toward a group in opposition, seeing in that opposition a chance to right their own particular grievances. It was an insight which spoke to the human condition. One of the ways to prevent a social grouping from polarizing, Mao thought, was for the majority to accept the demands of the opposition. For example, if the opposition wanted representation or seats on a leading committee, they should be given those seats. Thus the grounds for conflict would be removed, and the feeling of opposition would melt away. If the opposition demands were not met, the minority would soon attract a larger and larger number of individuals who identified their own feeling of powerlessness with the group that was shut out. If each faction refrained from criticizing the other and devoted all its efforts to making a self-criticism of its own mistakes, a sincere basis for unity would be laid. Mao had long believed that even enemies must be given a way out; otherwise they would fight to the death.

Chairman Mao's theoretical summary of his inspection trip was formulated in his statement that "under the dictatorship of the proletariat, there is no reason whatsoever for the working class to split into two big irreconcilable organizations." This conclusion of Mao's was repeatedly broadcast to the whole nation during the last three months of 1967. His trip to the South resulted in the formulation of what was to be called "Chairman Mao's Great Strategic Plan."

The new orientation stressed ideological work in every organization in the country and called for uniting the factions, correct treatment for cadres, and the need for mass organizations to establish proletarian discipline. Self-criticism for all became the order of the day, and a campaign to combat anarchism and "small-group mentality" was launched on a nationwide scale. The "Great Strategic Plan" included the instruction which resulted in the establishment of Mao Tse-tung Thought study classes in thousands of organizations. Every organization was now officially referred to as "revolutionary," but people would not quickly forget the organization with which each had once been identified. Finally, Mao threw his support to the Army. Recognizing the difficulties confronting an army assigned contradictory tasks, he stated:

> "It is unavoidable that the Army should make mistakes in undertaking for the first time the large-scale fighting task of supporting the left, supporting industry and agriculture, and carrying out military control and military training. The chief danger is that some people wanted to knock down the PLA."[108]

For over forty years, Mao Tse-tung has been associated with extremely bold and daring undertakings. Yet his success has also depended upon caution and unending patience. Throughout his career, he has shown contempt for adventurism, that tendency to fight battles one cannot win. Whatever his sympathies for the Cultural Group, it was clear that they had bitten off more than they could chew. The Premier, Mao's alter ego and administrative genius, was an indispensable ally, while the problems of the Army required delicate and skillful handling to avoid ultimatum and confrontation.

Although many of the ideas associated with the "ultra-left" could be attributed to the Chairman himself, he was a student of Lenin's admonition that "every truth, if carried to excess [. . . ] if it is exaggerated, if it is carried beyond the limits within which it can actually be applied, can be reduced to absurdity, and [. . .] is even inevitably converted into an absurdity."[109] Mao, one day in 1964, when reminiscing with Anna Louise Strong about the early days of the Chinese Red Army, told her, "Some commanders forgot that soldiers must walk, soldiers must eat, and bullets kill people." It was the Chairman's way of saying that the commanders had planned battles too far away for all the troops to get there in time, that they had failed to provide supplies for the campaign, and had underestimated the firepower of the enemy. He had come to the conclusion in the summer of 1967 that the Cultural Group no longer had the political resources to support its bid for power and so Mao ordered a retreat, sacrificing in the process not a few of the advanced guard.

Mao's strategic plan was promulgated by the new leadership coalition presiding over the October 1 National Day celebration. Lin Piao moved to the center of the stage once more, and the Peking central authorities worked frantically to guarantee that the annual parade, consisting of massive contingents of marching youths, continue as a national symbol of unity rather than turning into a riot. On the day of the great parade, Wang Li was not atop the T'ien An gate with the rest of the leaders, nor was Rittenberg in the stands with the rest of us. Instead, occupying positions of prominence next to Chairman Mao were all the old marshals, many of whom had been denounced by the radical Red Guards in previous months: Chu Teh, Ch'en Yi, Hsu Hsiang-ch'ien, Yeh Chien-ying, and Nieh Jung-chen. The regional commanders, who had long been targets of attack in their various provinces, also occupied commanding positions on the imperial gate: Huang Yung-sheng, the Army commander in Kwangtung and Canton; Hsu Shih-yu, commander of the Nanking Military District; and Ch'en Hsi-lien from the Northeast. Together with the Vice Ministers like Yu Ch'iu-li, the Minister of Petroleum, who had been a key target of the Earth faction for more than a year, the Army leaders, led by Vice Supreme Commander Lin Piao, who gave the main speech, symbolized to the nation that the new line was in effect. Mao's "closest comrade in arms," Marshal Lin Piao, emphasized the new slogan for the last stage of the Cultural Revolution: "Struggle Against Self-Interest! Criticize Revisionism!"

Stressing the theme of ideological remolding as the major goal of the movement, Lin declared to the assembled masses: "Only when private interests have been struck down thoroughly can one thoroughly proceed to struggle against the revisionists." In short, the masses would now have to complete rectification of their own record and behavior before they could proceed against the power-holders. Everyone was told to "make himself the target of the revolution." After a year in the background, Lin Piao was apparently ready to claim his position as "successor."

A huge effort had been exerted to guarantee that the parade went off without a hitch. The authorities were faced with the problem of convincing hundreds of thousands of citizens who were irreparably divided into hostile factions to march together. Army teams had been sent to all the schools to drill the students in contingents combining members from all factions. The task was not an easy one, but somehow the parade took place, and hundreds of thousands of politically divided citizens, in an outward semblance of coordinated unity, marched with heads held high past the reviewing stand commanded by Chairman Mao. Nevertheless, the next day, factional strife erupted anew on every campus as the partisan armies prepared for new levels of violence which would be curbed only after another year of intensive struggle. It would take a while before the youth would realize that rebellion was no longer justified.

Although the official propaganda organs were placing renewed emphasis on the Cultural Revolution as an ideological campaign devoted to struggling against private interest and promoting the public interest, the factions continued their politics dedicated to power. The Heaven faction, taking advantage of its new victories, redoubled its attacks on the Peking Revolutionary Committee under the leadership of Hsieh Fu-chih and opened a new front against the Party theoretical organ *Red Flag,* which had in effect become the house organ of the Cultural Group. On our own campus, as on other campuses, the Earth faction Red Guard organizations, now on the defensive and temporarily deprived of effective political arguments, turned to violence in an effort to survive. Beatings, kidnapping, and physical assaults increased as the student population of each university turned in on itself.

The Rebel Corps at the Institute took over one of the dormitory buildings and turned it into an impenetrable fortress. Red Flag, on the other hand, since it possessed a two-to-one majority of students, could afford to be more relaxed, and its members, although steering clear of Rebel territory, came and went at will. Resorting to ingenious stratagems, the rival factions in this arena of micro-war attempted to outflank, outmaneuver, and outfox the opposition "commanders" and their squads of "fighters." As the level of combat increased in the succeeding months, Red Flag, which controlled the school dining halls, sought to deny their opponents access to these vital facilities. This action naturally led to increased levels of violence.

The chief of Tsao-fan T'uan's "security section" had been a student at our school in the early Sixties and, having failed his exams, had returned to his Hupeh village. Once the Cultural Revolution was under way, this former student announced to the peasants in his village that he had been unjustly dismissed from the Institute by revisionists who had persecuted him for his class background. But now, he asserted, he had been summoned by Chairman Mao to Peking in order to lead the Cultural Revolution in his former school. Reaching into the vast store of traditional Chinese physiognomic lore to give substance to his claim to a remarkable fate, he pointed to the mole on his chin as a sure augury of fame. It was a sign well known to the peasants in his village, whose homes, like all the others in China, contained the omnipresent picture of the Chairman—with just such a mole carefully included. The peasants took up a collection to send the young hero off to the capital in style. The "Mole" then, a terror of the campus, led the Rebel Corps security squads for many months, and the Red Flag fighters took care to stay out of his hands. The day came, however, when he was sent back to his village as a "reactionary fraud."

Marx once observed that men make their own history "not under circumstances chosen by themselves, but under circumstances directly found, given, and transmitted from the past." Before our very eyes in that beautiful autumn of 1967, our students, who had seemed to us so fresh, modern, and future-oriented, were now "conjuring up the spirits of the past" and appearing in fantastic costumes and insignia. Wearing bright crimson sashes, many became the proud possessors of iron spears from which hung the red tassels associated with the great peasant rebels of history—the Taipings, the Yellow Turbans, and the Red Eyebrows. The iron picket fence that had once surrounded part of the campus had recently been uprooted and dismantled to provide the armoury for the warriors of the two rebel factions. Although the violence at the Institute never reached the degree of civil war which turned Tsinghua and Peking Universities and the Nationalities Institute into surging battlegrounds, one great medieval battle was fought when the Rebel Corps and Red Flag formations confronted each other on the main playing field and on signal charged each other with their spears. Miraculously, no one was killed, but a number of students were hospitalized with serious wounds. That was the sole major battle; the ensuing conflict then de-escalated into a series of minor sieges, skirmishes, and guerrilla assaults.

One day while bicycling back to the school, we stopped on the side road to watch a Hung-ch'i guerrilla group besieging the Tsao-fan T'uan stronghold. Atop the fifth-floor roof of an adjacent building, a small squad of Hung-ch'i "fighters," consisting of three young women and two young men were hoisting brick and stone missiles up from the ground. Another small group on the ground loaded the lowered baskets. When a sufficient pile had been stacked on the roof, the two young men took up positions on the side of the roof nearest the rebel stronghold. The three women, in their white blouses and neatly braided hair, served as a transport crew. With the sure-footed gait one always associates with the traditional peasant shoulder poles, the young women delivered the bricks to the men, who then slowly and deliberately elevated them high over their heads and sent them crashing through the windows of the next building. None of the actors spoke or uttered a sound. All was quiet except for the shattering of glass.

On the ground, about 100 feet in front of the Rebel Corps Headquarters, another group of Red Flag fighters gathered around a Tibetan student who was famous for his accuracy with a slingshot. The group pointed to the top of the roof of the rebel building, and it was immediately apparent to us that the target was a loudspeaker perched on the edge of the roof five stories from the ground. The small group slowly spread out, and the Tibetan now stood alone in the middle of the circle. He armed his sling with a stone the size of a baseball, twirled it in great arcs around his head, and finally loosed the missile with tremendous velocity toward its target. He scored a direct hit on the loudspeaker, which fell to the ground. Again, there was not a word spoken. Meanwhile, a woman walked calmly down the road carrying a net bag of fresh fish, looking neither left nor right. Further away, two students played ping-pong on a makeshift table under the plum trees. It was as if we had intruded upon a silent movie or a surrealist dream. Coming from a rather violent culture ourselves, we had in our lifetimes witnessed riots, strikes, and fights at home, but these were always accompanied by jumping, running, frenzied cursing, and shouting. This silent, slow vengeance, which had been progressing for days before we had arrived on the spot, was beyond our ken, and we realized once again the degree to which culture, that immeasurable factor, shapes and bends every political process.

It was in this period of officially proclaimed unity, but actually growing tension, among the Cultural Revolution's myriad participants that our friend, teaching colleague, and next-door neighbor David Crook was kidnapped by the Rebel Corps. He had been attending a meeting of the Red Flag teachers' group when, hearing some commotion outside the building, he went out to see what it was all about. Finding a melee of students from both sides engaged in a fracas, he ingenuously waded into the crowd shouting, *"Yao wen-tou, pu-yao wu-tou!* (struggle with reason, not with force!),"* and was immediately "captured" by members of the Rebel Corps and carried off to their bastion. A few hours later, the Rebel Corps broadcasting station blared forth that the headquarters of Tsao-fan T'uan had David Crook, "a British agent and spy," under arrest. There was no way of freeing him except by storming the building, and Red Flag had no intention of doing that. Remembering the "Mole" and concerned for David's welfare, we and two Belgian teachers took the step which every Chinese citizen considered when faced with an insoluble problem—we wrote a letter to Chou En-lai. Stating that David Crook, a resident in China for many decades, a veteran of the Spanish Civil War, a teacher at the First Foreign Languages Institute since its founding in the Liberated Areas during the third revolutionary war, had been illegally kidnapped by a mass organization, we hoped that the Premier would look into the matter.

Late that night, we drove to the State Council building situated just behind the Winter Palace in the old Imperial complex which makes up the nerve center of China. It was one of those dark, brisk Peking autumn nights when the moon shines quietly on the old trees and high red walls of the Forbidden City. The streets were deserted, but as the car lights lit up the huge brass-studded gates of the State Council and the People's Liberation Army soldiers guarding it, we saw row after row of human bundles wrapped in their quilts sleeping in front of the great gates. They were people from all parts of the country who like ourselves had petitions to deliver or were seeking to see the Premier personally to report to him the calamities, injustices, and problems occurring in the far-flung provinces of the nation. In that moving and consistent tribute which we had observed so many times both before and during the Cultural Revolution, millions of people felt that if they could only manage to get a message to their omniscient minister, all problems would be solved. We presented our letter to the ever-smiling and courteous PLA men, who assured us that it would be given to the Premier personally and then we drove away down the ancient imperial streets, inhabited only by the guards and those sleeping figures who had come from afar to see Chou En-lai.

A few days after Crook's kidnapping, a small Army investigation team arrived at the Institute, and since no one, including his family, had any idea what had happened to him, we devised a stratagem for determining what the PLA's role in investigating the matter might be. Isabel Crook packed a small bag with personal effects and books, and she, David Milton, and our Belgian teacher friend set out across the battle-wracked playing field toward a solitary soldier standing unarmed amid the debris. A large group of Red Flag students joined us, adding their support to the little mission, while the rebel warriors, wearing their bamboo construction helmets, peered suspiciously down from the fifth-floor redoubt of their besieged fortress. The soldier responded politely but noncommittally to our account of the illegal kidnapping, explaining that since the Army had just arrived at the school, he knew nothing of the case. The Hung-ch'i students were furious, but the shouting condemnations that they heaped upon him for the Army's inaction in the face of "fascist atrocities" did not seem to disturb him. In fact, there was in his light, almost amused comment to us that this was "only a mass organization," a kind of paternalism new to us, but one of which the students would often complain. Unperturbed or not, however, he was finally forced to go off in search of a superior officer. The deputy commander of the Peking Garrison with whom he returned, after listening to our impassioned retelling of our story, agreed to accept responsibility for the delivery of the bag, although he, too, said that he had not as yet been able to investigate the case. With solemn formality, he gave Isabel Crook a receipt for all the items in the bag. The Army had entered the case.

Within a few days, we learned that Crook had been turned over by the Rebel Corps to the Peking Garrison Command, and a few months later was transferred to the jurisdiction of the Bureau of Public Security. He had become entangled in the larger politics of the Cultural Revolution, a pawn of the increasingly fierce struggle for power. For this, he would be held in prison for five years. In 1973, Premier Chou En-lai, apologizing in the name of the Chinese Government and Party, made clear that David Crook had been framed and was innocent of all charges made against him. Who was responsible for this shocking injustice? Perhaps the forces behind the Earth faction were determined to bring down at least one of the foreign supporters of the Heaven faction in return for the group of Anglo-Americans on their own side who had become involved in the Wang Li plot. Secrecy, the universal handmaiden of all politics, may prevent us from ever knowing the full story.

Both David and Isabel Crook, who was herself placed under house arrest during those long and bitter years, have resumed their teaching positions at the Institute where, for so many years, they have played an important and respected role. Like many of their Chinese counterparts, they displayed an awesome toughness, resiliency, and confidence in the face of injustice. We had a long talk with David Crook in Los Angeles in the late summer of 1974. He looked quite the same as he had some seven years earlier and was remarkably philosophical, showing little bitterness over his years of unjust imprisonment. For David and Isabel Crook and thousands of Chinese, the Cultural Revolution was indeed not "a dinner party or painting a picture or doing embroidery." But some among those thousands, who did not find within themselves similar reserves of strength, or were unwilling to suffer further assaults on their dignity, when condemned as enemies by their former friends and colleagues, took their own lives.

In the aftermath of the Crook kidnapping, we decided that our continued involvement in the movement at the Institute was no longer an asset to our Hung-ch'i friends and might, in fact, prove to be a problem, since Tsao-fan T'uan, with their backs against the wall, were forever seeking new targets. And what could be more sensational than digging up more "foreign spies?" In the light of this conclusion, we moved out of the Institute and back into the foreign community at the

Friendship Hotel. We, the foreigners, were just one of the many social groups which had, one after another in dizzying succession, marched on and off the stage of a great social movement and then were seen no more. Premier Chou explained much later that a decision to remove the foreigners from the movement was taken by the Central Committee in January 1968, because "some had supported this faction and some that" in a situation where "bad people were stirring up trouble."

In the meantime, the campaign at Peking Radio against Rittenberg was growing, and the reputation of Bethune-Yenan was declining as the masses in Peking increasingly associated the organization with him. Although he held no official position in Bethune-Yenan, he was declared to be its "*hou-t'ai*" (real power and behind-the-scenes backer). We saw Rittenberg at a friend's house one evening during this period, and for the first time he appeared shaken, because he had heard of a big-character poster put up by students at Tsinghua University calling him an American spy. He told us angrily that this was the work of those "irresponsible students" we had supported in the Heaven faction.

The campaign against Ch'i Pen-yü, the last representative of the ultra-left on the Cultural Group (except for the most important figure of all—Ch'en Po-ta, who was purged after the Cultural Revolution), was reaching its conclusion. When Ch'i Pen-yü was overthrown in January, it was only a few weeks before Rittenberg would be placed under arrest by the central authorities. During those last tense months of 1967 and the beginning of 1968, a number of signals had been sent from the top to indicate that Rittenberg was now considered an enemy, signals which all the Chinese read very well, but which some of the foreigners refused to believe. In December, a picture taken at the Asian, African, and Latin American Writers Conference, including members of the Cultural Group, was published in *China Pictorial,* and the faces of Wang Li, Kuan Feng, Mu Hsin, and Rittenberg were all crudely blacked out. Rittenberg told his friends that it was the work of reactionaries in the press. Soon afterward, we learned from our Red Flag colleagues that a new, huge thirty-five-page big-character poster stretching around the whole courtyard at the Radio had appeared. Its title read: "How Is It That An American Adventurer Seized Red Power at Peking Radio?" Ch'en Po-ta, as the senior representative of the Cultural Group, came to Radio one midnight at the end of December and in his speech to the assembled masses said that he was very pleased with the political level of the rebels at Radio and praised their excellent writing ability. He gave as an example the title of the aforementioned big-character poster, and the people at Radio understood, by one of those masterpieces of indirection so admired by the Chinese, that Rittenberg was doomed. We passed on this information to Israel Epstein, thinking that it might help him disengage Bethune-Yenan from the impending disaster, but he only listened intently, went away, and came back in a week to tell us that he had checked out the information and found it to be incorrect. He had, of course, checked with Rittenberg. That was the last conversation we were to have with Epstein before he, too, was swept up in the net.

One day in early February, we all learned that Rittenberg and his wife had been "taken," as the Chinese put it, and his apartment closed off by the chilling official Chinese paper seals stretched across the doorway announcing official confiscation and control of the premises. Some weeks later, the foreigners working at Radio were invited to a mass meeting held by the Rebel Organizations in power and attended by the PLA control team to hear a report on the Rittenberg question. It was announced there that Rittenberg had been associated with an American Army Intelligence unit during World War II, that he had come to China in 1945, and worked as an interpreter at the Executive Headquarters in Peking during the ceasefire in the civil war, had later gone to Yenan, and was subsequently arrested by the security organs. Placed under house arrest in 1948, he was later reinstated. According to the report given to the foreigners at Radio, Rittenberg had been arrested in 1948 on information provided by Stalin, but that Lo Jui-ch'ing, then head of the

State Security Ministry, and later to become Chief of Staff of the Army, and An Tzu-wen, the Moscow-trained head of the Chinese organization department of the Central Committee, who had been overthrown as part of the P'eng Chen clique at the beginning of the Cultural Revolution, had cleared Rittenberg of all charges and removed the files of the case in order to enlist him in their future conspiratorial causes.

If the story was correct that the information on Rittenberg had been forwarded by Stalin, then it would seem likely that the evidence against him in the late 1940's was his association with Anna Louise Strong, who had taken him to Yenan as her interpreter in 1947. Stalin had arrested Anna Louise Strong in 1948 on false charges as an American agent. In any case, according to the report given to the mass meeting at Peking Radio, Rittenberg had come to the Broadcasting Bureau in 1953, had worked ever since indebted to Chairman Mao's opponents in the Chinese leadership, and, more remarkable still, had been made a member of the Chinese Communist Party. It was never clear how "official" this explanation of the Rittenberg case was, but, in 1973, he was singled out by Premier Chou as a "very bad person." One thing is clear: he was involved in a high-level conspiracy to topple the Premier of one of the world's major nations—a most injudicious project for anyone, let alone an American in China. Rittenberg remains, as the title of one Red Guard leaflet of the time put it, "A Mysterious American."

The rank and file of Bethune-Yenan, consisting of about fifty of the foreign experts still remaining in China, decided that the organization should have been dissolved long ago. Consequently, over the protests of the leadership, they called a meeting to effect this purpose. In a stormy session, the membership voted overwhelmingly to dissolve Bethune-Yenan and then walked out, leaving the leaders and a small band of followers, including those who had written the famous "four Americans' big-character poster" praised by Mao, standing alone in an empty hall determined to carry on their revolution all by themselves. A few days later, the Chinese national leaders, as if they had held off until the foreign community itself had taken some action, moved in and arrested Israel Epstein and his wife Elsie Cholmeley and Michael Shapiro and his Chinese wife, who was a delegate to the National People's Consultative Congress and active at the Earth faction's stronghold in the National Academy of Science. Their apartments were sealed, and none was seen again until, together with David Crook, they were all released in the winter of 1973. Premier Chou apologized to them all for the long time it had taken to clear up the case and implied that they had been hoodwinked by "bad elements," namely Sidney Rittenberg. In the winter of 1968, the foreign community, in a state of shock, found itself removed from a politics which only the Chinese could resolve. It would take another six months before the Red Guard movement itself was summarily suspended from the top.

Far more important than the demise of the foreign contingents in the Great Cultural Revolution was the decline of the leading committee of that revolution. Suffering from the decimation of its ranks and a decline in its political fortunes, the Cultural Group was, by the end of 1967, in a state of virtual eclipse. *Red Flag,* the theoretical house organ of the Cultural Group, had been the instrument through which the political leaders of the great movement disseminated orientation and line to the rebel organizations. It had, in effect, replaced the Party organization as the communication channel delivering policy directives from top to bottom. With the arrest of some of its key editors, the authoritative journal had come under increasing attack by mass organizations, despite all the efforts of Chiang Ch'ing and Ch'en Po-ta to protect its staff, premises, and influence. But the damage had been done, and the journal, after putting out its November issue, suspended publication. Around the same time, Chiang Ch'ing, who was "mentally exhausted," retired temporarily for a rest at Hangchow. The Premier told a meeting of Red Guards that "arduous struggle" had undermined her health. Chou En-lai now devoted all of his considerable efforts to around-the-clock negotiations to unite the unruly factions and bring about the great alliance of revolutionary mass organizations in each province, city, and key administrative unit.

From the very beginning, the Cultural Revolution as a political process was plagued by the amorphous nature of its political targets. By the end of 1967, an attempt was made by those at the very top, including Mao himself, to redefine the targets of the movement, a decision which, in the last analysis, meant changing the rules of the game. In the beginning, Mao and his followers fought to make "those in the Party in authority taking the capitalist road" the main targets —counterrevolutionaries, "bad elements," landlords, former rightists, and bourgeois academics being subordinate targets. After more than a year and a half of tumultuous struggle, it was decided to reverse the priority of these targets, a shift which sought to turn the movement onto the path of the familiar rectification movement, which traditionally had cleansed the Chinese Communist Party of "bad elements." On November 8, at a meeting of opposing factions from Canton in the Great Hall of the People, Chou En-lai attempted to clarify the issue:

> "Recently, the Chairman issued a directive on what constitutes demons and monsters. He said that these referred to those landlord, rich, conterrevolutionary, bad, and rightist elements who had not been successfully reformed, and *not to those in the Party taking the capitalist road*. [Authors' italics.] Special agents and rebels who have wormed into the Party should be cleared out. The editorial of the *People's Daily* last year entitled 'Wipe out the Demons and Monsters' referred to those landlord, rich, counterrevolutionary, bad, and rightist elements in society who had not been successfully reformed."[110]

The reason for this change in emphasis and priority undoubtedly lay in the fact that it had proved to be extremely difficult, in some places impossible, to determine just who those taking the capitalist road might be, and who, in fact, was waving the red flag sincerely and who was waving it "to oppose the red flag." Rightists, former landlords, and the traditional types of counterrevolutionaries would prove to be much simpler to root out. Not a few of these turned out to be the resurrected targets of earlier historical rectification movements, and these were dragged out again, as if their cases were new. Since the rules were being changed, the remaining members of the Cultural Group would soon try to label those they believed to be capitalist-roaders as "traitors, spies, and renegades," but, in the case of Teng Hsiao-p'ing, the officially designated "Number Two capitalist-roader" in the nation, and other high officials, their efforts would prove unsuccessful.

China, having produced a language replete with double negatives, was in the process of producing a similar politics. What had been termed a reversal of verdicts in 1967—that spring adverse current produced by T'an Chen-lin and the other Vice Ministers of the State Council—was, in 1968, to become a "reversal of the reverse verdict." No matter how strenuously the Chairman and the Premier tried to wrench the political process from the well-traveled and rutted path it had established, the pattern of interaction among the various forces which were to constitute the "three-way alliance" was now more or less set. Soon after the fall of Ch'i Pen-yü, the "right erroneous tendency" began to emerge. It was a repetition of the right upsurge in the winter of 1967 after the January Revolution in Shanghai, although, this time, the relative strengths of the opposing forces had been reversed. Then the Cultural Group had been on the ascendancy; now it was following a downward curve. The Army and senior cadres in the top ministries proved to be more formidable opponents than those deputy ministers who had fought back defensively in the "adverse February current" of 1967.

On February 13, ninety-one section heads and ambassadors of the Foreign Ministry put up a big-character poster with the title "Expose the Enemy! Fight and Defeat Him Thoroughly! Criticize the Reactionary Slogan 'Down With Ch'en Yi!' " The professional cadres, feeling that the exposure of the adventurer Yao Teng-shan and the fall of Wang Li had vindicated their position, were now ready to reassert what they felt was their rightful power. They hoped to sweep out all those rebels who had the audacity to attack Foreign Minister Ch'en Yi. Moreover, the Foreign Ministry professionals probably sensed that the strength of their position lay in the Chairman's special concern for the preservation of a sensitive ministry which would be essential in forging new policies in the post-Cultural Revolution period. The Premier, on the other hand, recognizing that this overt resurgence was fraught with danger, ill conceived, or at the least ill timed, struck back immediately. On March 5, he issued a three-point instruction to the Foreign Ministry. Beginning with a curt "Your big-character poster has three mistakes," Chou went on to list them. First, he said, "to protect themselves, ninety-one cadres have come out to show their faces. They pretend to protect Chief Ch'en while actually protecting themselves. This is unbearable." He softened the blow by stating that "some of you will remold yourselves well in the future." Point Number Two was perhaps the key to the reasons for the Premier's anger. This was no time, said Chou, to give ammunition to the radicals, and if the goal was to protect Ch'en Yi, it was the wrong way to go about it. "By protecting Ch'en, you have actually helped the enemy." Who that enemy might be was not specified. The third point constituted a stiff lecture to cadres who "stand opposed to the masses," and warned: "What is serious is that you are discontented with, and bear a grudge against, the Great Proletarian Cultural Revolution." Then Chou cautioned the elite of the ministry that "the present is no time for giving assistance and protection [to Ch'en Yi]. You must first make criticism. You can convince other people only by criticizing yourselves. Criticism must be made on the basis of self-criticism by the Party Committee."

It was clear that the Party Committee in the Ministry had been reinstated to power and was now returning to its old work-style. A week earlier, Ch'en Yi, undoubtedly prodded by the Premier, had written a letter denouncing the ninety-one cadres' big-character poster. After a long *mea culpa,* Marshal Ch'en ended his letter by stating: "If they resolve to correct their mistakes, they will have the support of all."[111] This episode opened one last round in the three-way struggle for power that would result in a temporary victory for the Army, followed by the return of that formidable and apparently indestructible instrument, the vanguard Party.

The question of which forces would control the Party remained open. Campaigns similar to the one mounted by the ninety-one cadres in the Foreign Ministry sprouted all over the city. On March 8, Fu Ch'ung-pi, the Peking Garrison Commander, accompanied by a truckload of armed soldiers, attempted to force his way into the offices of the Cultural Group, presumably to arrest Ch'i Pen-yü or some of his followers. When Chiang Ch'ing stopped him from entering, Fu Ch'ung-pi is reported to have asked her, "What is your rank?", but she prevailed, and the soldiers went away. During the same period, attacks were made on those revolutionary committees dominated by the Earth faction in an attempt to associate key individuals with either Ch'i Pen-yü or the May 16 counterrevolutionaries. By the middle of March, big-character posters went up all over the city attacking General Hsieh Fu-chih, who was a member of the Cultural Revolution Group as well as chairman of the Peking Revolutionary Committee. Hsieh was a key figure, since it was he who was in charge of making preparations for the convening of the Ninth Party Congress, and the contending political forces had already begun to focus their efforts on winning control of the Party Congress that was to herald the end of the Cultural Revolution.

Chairman Mao had placed his weight behind the new policies of consolidation and restraint of the mass movement, but he did not wish to jettison the Cultural Revolution itself, to see all his efforts overturned by a victory of the "right erroneous tendency." Therefore, Mao once more attempted to rejuvenate the Cultural Group and restore its authority and prestige so that it might steer the great rebellion to a successful conclusion. Chiang Ch'ing reappeared at the end of January and began to meet with representatives of Rebel Groups from Peking and the provinces. In the middle of

March, she set forth the new line from the center, which amounted to a counterattack on the rightists. Meeting with leaders from Szechuan on March 15, she stated that "at present in the entire country, the rightist reversal of the verdict is the principal danger."[112] A few days later, she told some delegates from Chekiang that "rightist splittism has raised its head somewhat from last winter to the present."[113] On March 22, Mao made another of his crucial decisions by ordering the removal and arrest of Yang Ch'eng-wu, Acting Chief of Staff of the Army, Yü Li-chin, Political Commissar of the Air Force, and Fu Ch'ung-pi, Commander of the Peking Garrison.

Chairman Mao, perhaps disturbed by the speed with which the Army was substituting itself for all other constituted authority, and concerned with the manner in which Mao Tse-tung's Thought was being utilized as a cover for authority other than his own, sent out one of his periodic signals as early as December 17 in a letter to Lin Piao, Chou En-lai, and the Cultural Group. Among other things, the letter called attention to three points:

"1. The way in which absolute authority is presented is improper. There has never been any single absolute authority. All authorities are relative. All absolute things exist in relative things, just as absolute truth is the total of innumerable relative truths, and absolute truth exists only in relative truths.

"2. The talk about 'establishing in a big way' and 'establishing in a special way' is also improper. Authority and prestige can be established only naturally through struggle and practice. They cannot be established artificially. Prestige established artificially will inevitably collapse.

"3. The Central Committee of the Party banned birthday celebrations a long time ago. The entire nation should be notified of the reaffirmation of this ban."[114]

The Chairman was referring to major editorials written by Acting Chief of Staff Yang Ch'eng-wu, calling upon the nation to "establish the absolute authority of Mao Tse-tung's

Thought in a 'big way and the biggest way.' " The "serious theoretical mistakes" committed by Yang Ch'eng-wu were promoting the erroneous slogan "establish the absolute authority of Chairman Mao and his Thought," but the unforgivable actions undoubtedly involved the raid on the offices of the Cultural Group, the insults to Chiang Ch'ing, and the attempt by the Army to destroy completely the power and authority of the Cultural Group.

We were told at the time than Lin Piao had personally arrested Yang Ch'eng-wu on the stage of the Hall of the People in the presence of 10,000 PLA officers. Chiang Ch'ing, who spoke at one of the many meetings called with leading army men during this period, asserted, "I am by no means one who is always right." She admitted that she had made mistakes and certainly had a lot of faults, but emphasized that she was not connected with Wang Li, Lin Chieh, and Kuan Feng. In fact, she told the Army officers, these "black hands" had refused to ask for instructions from the Cultural Group and had acted behind its back. It was the Cultural Group itself, she claimed, which had "dragged them out and hung them up and did not allow them to interfere with Chairman Mao's strategic plan. However, somebody attempted to utilize this situation in order to deny the victory of the Great Proletarian Cultural Revolution and deny the achievements of the revolutionary masses and revolutionary small soldiers." The "somebody," of course, referred to the Chief of Staff of the Army, Yang Ch'eng-wu, Commander of the Peking Garrison, Fu Ch'ung-pi, and Yü Li-chin, Political Commissar of the Air Force. Chiang Ch'ing explained her implied protection of Ch'i Pen-yü as an attempt to separate his case from that of Wang Li and Kuan Feng, because his method was different, "so that he revealed himself at a different time."[115]

Chiang Ch'ing, after renouncing all connections with the May 16 ultras, went on to accuse Yang Ch'eng-wu of attempting to seize control of the Army's *Liberation Daily,* the *People's Daily,* and the Broadcasting Bureau, and attacking the Cultural Group for its "idealism" and "denying the leadership of the Party organization." She further asserted that Yang had attempted to overthrow Hsieh Fu-chih in order to take over the Peking Revolutionary Committee.

Chou En-lai was a little less explicit, accusing Yang Ch'eng-wu of utilizing Mao's Thought for his own personal ambition. Lin Piao accused Yang of attempts to build an independent kingdom of power and for his bad connections with Lo Jui-ch'ing and other followers of Liu Shao-ch'i. Lin was particularly anxious that the attacks on Yang not be expanded to an attack on Yang's friends and subordinates in the Army. The pattern now followed by all the actors in the top coalition of power was to attempt to contain an attack by any one faction by not letting that attack spread beyond a few victims, who were always made to appear to represent no one beyond themselves. It was the same pattern followed by the Premier and Chiang Ch'ing in trying to limit the repercussion of the May 16 conspiracy in the summer of 1967. The fall of Yang Ch'eng-wu, Fu Ch'ung-pi, and Yü Li-chin obviously constituted a counterattack by the Cultural Group on the Army for its attempt to exploit the victory over the Cultural Group brought about by the exposure and fall of Wang, Kuan, and Ch'i. The center hoped to end this round of trade-off purges by linking all the overthrown figures together; in other words, to claim that Wang Li, Ch'i Pen-yü, Yang Ch'eng-wu, and his generals were all part of the same group. However, all of the various contending forces knew better.

This attempt to link all overthrown power-holders in the same category became a common practice of the center in its effort to prevent retaliation by followers. Thus, a blurring of political categories of right, left, and center was effected in order to obscure the actual political line that a fallen leader might have represented. Moreover, it was the common practice of the faction to which a fallen leader belonged to claim that he was not really associated with that faction but was in reality a hidden representative of the opposing faction. The masses were getting a profound education and coming to the realization that the political arena, especially the Chinese political arena, was no place for the naïve.

For the last time, the Cultural Group tried to exploit a victory and regain its lost prestige. Chiang Ch'ing was once again referred to as "the great leader and standard-bearer of the Cultural Revolution," and the formula "to support or to oppose the Central Cultural Revolution Group is a question of fundamental standpoint and a major question of right and wrong" was revived. The Earth faction poured out of their redoubts to launch what had become an annual spring offensive, this time to attack Lin Piao. A notorious big-character poster of the period was the "Thirty-Four Whys" put up by the "East is Red" of the Geology Institute, which attempted to link Lin Piao with Yang Ch'eng-wu. But the Peking Red Guards were no match for the powerful Army organization, which had become entrenched in positions of power in the revolutionary committees throughout the country. Only Chairman Mao could take on the Army, and he desperately needed it to rebuild a politically fragmented country.

On March 30, the central leaders met with representatives from Hunan to hammer out the provisions for finally setting up the Hunan Provincial Revolutionary Committee. At this meeting and others throughout April, attempts were made to restore the Cultural Group, the symbolic representative of the mass organizations, to its rightful place in the most important three-way alliance in the country—at the very top. If the three-way alliance at the top was unbalanced, what could be expected on the lower levels? Chiang Ch'ing in her remarks to the assembled delegates could not have made the issues at stake more explicit:

> "To reverse the verdict on the February adverse current is to abolish the Central Cultural Revolution Group. Some people do not put the Central Cultural Revolution Group in the most important place in their minds. This is a serious rightist and conservative idea. The young fighters don't negate the Central Cultural Revolution Group. If they negate the Cultural Group they will be negating themselves."[116]

Premier Chou had, for over forty years, acted as the gyroscope of the Chinese Revolution, keeping the ship, set in its course by the great helmsman Chairman Mao, from capsizing in stormy seas. He now devoted all his efforts to strengthening the weakened position of the Cultural Group. The three-way alliance was shifting every day in favor of the Army. At every opportunity during the spring of 1968, Chou attempted to rebuild the political reputation of Chiang Ch'ing—"Comrade Chiang Ch'ing takes a firm stand. She holds the most positive banner. She sees questions most sharply. We must learn from Comrade Chiang Ch'ing."[117] However, all the considerable skills of the Premier were not enough to completely erase the stains on the reputation of the Cultural Group. It was difficult to convince everyone that "the few bad elements who had sneaked into the Cultural Group" had, in fact, been "dragged out and hung up" by the Cultural Group itself, even though the Premier, who had been the main target of attack of the May 16 plot, stated that this was indeed the case.

As new provincial, city, and local revolutionary committees were being forged under relentless pressure from above, the masses intuitively sensed that this spring offensive might be the last round in a struggle to achieve mass representation in the new organs of power. The remaining core of radicals in the Cultural Group exerted all their efforts to retain for themselves the right to determine the main targets of the movement. If the rules had changed, then the same targets would be attacked under the new rules as under the old. "Venerable K'ang," as K'ang Sheng was always called, the Party veteran in the arcana of security work, no longer attempted to define capitalist-roaders by reference to philosophic world views, but by facts that would brook no dispute among the masses. Referring to the major national leaders who had become the targets of the Cultural Revolution, he stated in one speech in the spring of 1968:

> "What are these people? They boast of being 'veteran revolutionaries.' They are found to be veteran counter-revolutionaries, veteran renegades, and veteran secret enemy agents!"

The implication was that they were no longer to be considered Chinese, but representatives of that hostile outside world.

"Liu Shao-ch'i had been arrested four times. He surrendered to the Kuomintang in Hunan in 1925; he surrendered to Wang Ching-wei in Wuhan in 1927; he surrendered to Japan in Shenyang in 1929; he again surrendered to Chiang Kai-shek of the KMT in 1936. His wife, Wang Kuang-mei, is a diehard secret agent of the United States, Japan, and the Kuomintang who has sneaked into our organization.

"T'ao Chu is a big renegade. P'eng Chen is a big renegade. P'eng Teh-huai is a traitor. Ho Lung surrendered to the Kuomintang. Lo Jui-ch'ing is a secret agent who never joined the Communist Party. Lu Ting-yi is a US Chiang secret agent. All these people are representatives of the US Chiang reactionaries in the Communist Party.

"In exposing these people, we are struggling against the representatives of the Kuomintang and imperialism."[118]

At the close of this startling indictment of some of China's former top leaders, Chiang Ch'ing interjected with the shout, "Down with Teng Hsiao-p'ing." Venerable K'ang then added "Teng Hsiao-p'ing was a deserter. It is still necessary to expose him continuously." History would prove, however, that Teng would have more staying power than K'ang Sheng.

Chairman Mao appeared to put his imprimatur on the task of simplifying the targets of the Great Proletarian Cultural Revolution in the spring of 1968 by issuing a redefinition of the Cultural Revolution itself. The new definition simplified the struggle considerably by making the targets an organizational question:

"The Great Proletarian Cultural Revolution is in essence a great political revolution under the conditions of socialism made by the proletariat against the bourgeoisie and all other exploiting classes; it is the continuation of the prolonged struggle between the Chinese Communist Party and the masses of revolutionary people under its leadership on the one hand and the Kuomintang reactionaries on the other, a continuation of the class struggle between the proletariat and the bourgeoisie."[119]

This new definition was interpreted by people with whom we came into contact to mean that, in order to overthrow a cadre, one must prove organizational ties with the KMT, the Japanese, the comprador bourgeoisie, the big landlords, or the intelligence agencies of the foreign imperialists (which now included the Russians). The President of our own Institute was thus arrested as a Russian agent, as was a teacher at our school, the Russian wife of Mao's famous opponent of the 1930's, Li Li-san. We were to hear that Li Li-san himself committed suicide in the Northeast during the Cultural Revolution. With the help of the masses, agents of all types who had burrowed into the Party and other organizations were uncovered. However, those days, when all foreigners became suspect, were rather bitter ones for the "foreign friends" in China. It was a period for which the Premier would later apologize personally in the name of the Chinese State and Party.

Since the arrest of Rittenberg and other foreign "old hands," the foreigners had been excluded from the Cultural Revolution and from Chinese life. No one was officially notified, but invitations to meetings were no longer extended, and the non-Chinese, though fed and paid as usual, were largely left to fend for themselves. The end to the period of internationalism that had marked the first year of the movement was manifested most dramatically during the giant Chinese demonstrations in support of the May 1968 Revolution in Paris. No foreigners, French or otherwise, were asked to participate. For the moment, even the international revolution had become a Chinese affair.

Although we saw our Hung-ch'i friends less frequently, they considerately continued to brief us on the movement. An Army team of thirty men had come to stay at the school and study the movement there. Tsao-fan T'uan students had rushed to greet them, attempting to win the favor of the PLA men by weeping that the members of their "revolutionary organization" who came from worker and peasant background were being persecuted by "the bourgeois intellectuals in Hung-ch'i." Evidently, these theatrics swayed the Army team, since, in a few months, it delivered an official report which, in effect, supported the position of Tsao-fan T'uan in the school's movement. The report was literally howled down by the majority of the students who supported Hung-ch'i, and the Army team was withdrawn. Four more teams were sent to the school over the succeeding years. All supported Tsao-fan T'uan, and all were rejected by the students and teachers. Apparently, the Army, like all armies, had a direct interest in the Foreign Ministry of the nation, but the young rebels at the First Foreign Languages Institute were no longer easily intimidated by authority. In the end, the Hung-ch'i main line was thoroughly vindicated, although its excesses had often been as great as those of its opposition. In the spring of 1968, it was difficult for us to comprehend the issues at stake in the new struggles between the Heaven and Earth factions, and our friends manifested ambivalence on the rights and wrongs of the matters under dispute. It was as if a thick fog had settled on a great battlefield. The combatants continued to charge and retreat, though it was no longer clear who belonged to what side.

Weariness now began to set in. Too many mistakes had been made by all sides, and no flag remained untarnished. By the summer of 1968, the students were, for the most part, holed up in their various schools, each faction barricaded within the walls of its own "territory." None of the offensive or defensive strategies of these deadly serious student armies had any further effect on national politics. Devoid of any coherent political orientation, factional strife among the students had taken on a life of its own. The majority of students had deserted their campuses. Many returned to their home provinces for a visit with family and relatives; others stayed in their dormitories making transistor radios or carving traditional Chinese stone seals. The hard-core remnants of the student legions devoted all their time to perfecting the art of tunneling under the enemy's buildings or to constructing ingenious siege machinery—catapults made out of truck inner tubes that could fire bricks hundreds of yards, scaling ladders, and other paraphernalia of positional warfare.

Armed civil war broke out anew at Peking University when the Earth faction, led by Geology's East Is Red, together with its allies, "Peking Commune" of the Petroleum Institute and the "Yenan Commune" of the Nationalities Institute, stormed onto the campus in support of Nieh Yuan-tzu's opposition—Peita's "Chingkangshan." These armies, energized and sustained by the battle cry "Down with Nieh Yuan-tzu, the Black General of the February Adverse Current!", assaulted the broadcasting station and the cadres' dormitories run by the "New Peking Commune." When Nieh, the author of the manifesto "The Chinese Paris Commune of the Sixties," and Li Chung-ch'i, Deputy Commander of the Peking Garrison, arrived together to stop the fighting, Nieh was stabbed in the back of the head, and Li was severely beaten. By the summer of 1968, the Chinese Cultural Revolution was beginning to devour its own children, the "small generals" as well as the large, and Chairman Mao was ready to close the long drama of mass politics. The lessons would have to be studied and summed up for many years so that the next cultural revolution might be as different as this one had been from all other mass movements in Chinese communist history.

The students had been the full-time professional rebels of a vast social movement, and though many were the victims of "petit bourgeois factionalism," egoism, and "small-group mentality," they had served loyally the causes of political leaders suffering from the same diseases. They had enjoyed the heady excitement of "participating in state affairs," had taken advantage of their own power, and had been used by others, both kings and pawns in a great game. But their role was over, the people were sick of the din and enraged at the destruction of state property and equipment in privileged institutions, paid for by the sweat of the workers and peasants. It was under these circumstances that Chairman Mao sent the workers, those "masters of our time," by the thousands into the schools to restore calm and thus end the great "*luan*" (chaos). In the last week of July, when Mao sent the massive "Workers' Mao Tse-tung Thought Propaganda

Teams" into the universities, a sudden blissful silence settled over the city. For the first time in more than two years, the incessant din of loudspeakers ceased. Peking, a city of some 4 million souls, breathed a collective sigh of relief. The workers saw to it that the students went to bed at ten o'clock, an accomplishment that drew applause from a grateful populace.

But, at Tsinghua University, one last tragedy marred what had been an historic social movement. The diehard rebels under their student general, K'uai Ta-fu, who were armed to the teeth with submachine guns, rifles, and even a makeshift tank, opened fire on the unarmed workers, killing five and seriously wounding fifty. It was a bloody ending to the record of the "little generals," who had spread the flames of social revolution to hundreds of millions. K'uai himself proclaimed to any who would listen that it was a "black hand" which had sent the workers to smother his "revolution." A courageous and skilled young leader, he had crossed the line into political madness.

The Peking Red Guards had been the children of Chairman Mao and his proletarian headquarters. He himself had conferred the mantle of his revolutionary legacy upon the rebel offspring with his symbolic adoption of their red arm band in the distant August of 1966. But the young rebels, in the way of most progeny, had not fulfilled their parents' wishes in the way in which the older generation had intended. On July 28, Mao presided over an historic council, to which were summoned the famous Red Guard leaders of the Heaven and Earth factions, representatives of those potential successors who had become shipwrecked in the storms of the revolution.

The gathering of his inner court and his heirs presumptive around the aging ruler evokes a scene strangely like the opening moments of *King Lear*. The time of testing, of watching and waiting, had come to an end. The father of the Chinese Revolution, moving closer to death, had determined his disposition of the kingdom, and he had called his younger children together to tell them it could not be turned over to them. It was a decision that he wished to convey directly and personally.

The symbolism of this confrontation between the two generations, this gathering of the family to hear the verdict on the youthful experiment in politics, must have been apparent to all. Here sat Mao Tse-tung, Marshal Lin Piao, and Premier Chou En-lai, all veterans of the Long March and for forty years leaders of one of the greatest revolutions in world history. Ranged alongside were the division chiefs of the Cultural Revolution: Ch'en Po-ta, Chiang Ch'ing, K'ang Sheng, Hsieh Fu-chih, Yao Wen-yuan, Lin Piao's wife Yeh Ch'un, and the new Army Chief of Staff, Huang Yung-sheng. It was they whom their Chairman had determined would be his successors, although, within two years, Mao, like Lear, would decide that some of these were themselves wicked usurpers. On the occasion of this great Chinese drama of power, however, all assumed the role of judgmental elders.

Into the council came the "young generals": Nieh Yuan-tzu, leader of New Peking University Commune and Vice Chairman of the Peking Revolutionary Committee; T'an Hou-lan, the young woman leader from the Peking Normal School; Han Ai-ching, the leader and strategist in command of the Aviation Institute's Red Flag; and Wang Ta-pin, the commander of the Geology Institute's Red Guards and titular head of the Peking Earth armies. K'uai Ta-fu, the charismatic leader of Tsinghua University's Chingkangshan and commanding general of the battles still raging there, had been invited but had not accompanied the other four. It was an absence commented upon immediately by the Chairman as he shook hands with the other Red Guard leaders. To Mao's rhetorical query as to whether K'uai had not been able to come, the several generations rushed forward with their interpretations. Hsieh Fu-chih stated pointedly that he was afraid K'uai had been unwilling to come, but K'uai's student ally Han Ai-ching protested: "No! At this moment, if he knew that there was a meeting with the Central Cultural Revolution Group, he would weep because he missed the chance to meet the Chairman." But Mao knew his little generals. "K'uai Ta-fu wants to capture the black hand," he said wryly, referring to K'uai's use of the familiar Chinese idiom for an evil behind-the-scenes manipulator. And continuing to use K'uai's own words, Mao went on, "So many workers were sent to the schools to 'suppress' and 'oppress' the Red Guards." With a great apparent consciousness of the dramatic moment, Mao turned to the four commanders of Peking's antagonistic armies of Heaven and Earth, whose battles had been contained by the worker-soldier *deus ex machina,* and said,

> "Who is the black hand? You still haven't captured him. The black hand is nobody else but me. K'uai did not come. He should have come to arrest me. It was I who sent the workers of the Hsinhua Printing Plant, the General Knitwear Mill, and the Central Police Department. I asked them how to deal with the fighting in the universities, and told them to go there to take a look . . . ."[120]

The decision to end his own student revolution by sending in the workers must have been a bitter one for Mao. It had been delayed long past the time when the Peking man and woman on the street thought it should have been taken. In front of the young leaders, Mao began to muse aloud about the possibilities which he had felt were open to him. Perhaps he was explaining his decision to them; perhaps also, he was reviewing it for himself. "How do you deal with fighting in the universities?" he asked rhetorically. "One way is complete withdrawal. Leave the students alone. Let everybody fight if he wants to. In the past, the Revolutionary Committee and the Garrison Command weren't afraid of the disorder created by fighting in the universities. They didn't interfere, didn't get upset, and didn't put it down. I still think this was right."

Another way to solve the problem, the Chairman said, was to give the students a little help. The dispatch of workers and soldiers to the universities was meant to accomplish this and " . . . has won the support of the workers, the peasants, and the majority of the students." Mao pointed out that, although there were more than fifty institutions of higher learning in Peking, fighting was severe in only five or six. If they couldn't handle the problem, he told the four student leaders, then the military under Lin Piao or Chief of Staff Huang Yung-sheng would have to handle it. Although he spoke in the language of possibilities, it must have been quite clear to all present that Mao had already decided that the young leaders couldn't "handle the problem."

> "You people have engaged in the Great Cultural Revolution or struggle-criticism-transformation for two years. But now, one, you are not struggling; two, you are not criticizing; three, you are not transforming. Struggle is struggle, but what you are doing is armed struggle. The people are not happy. The workers are not happy. The peasants are not happy. Most students in your schools are not happy."

Nieh Yuan-tzu had been the earliest star of the Cultural Revolution, author of the manifesto which had started it all. The only teacher and cadre among the student leaders, she had most firmly established her place in the new political hierarchy through her position as Vice Chairman of the Peking Revolutionary Committee. But she remained the central figure amid Peking University's violent factionism and had begun to have the reputation of being something of a tyrant. Her Peita opposition referred to her as the "Old Buddha." "Even within the faction that supports you there are people who are unhappy. Can you unite the whole country this way?" Mao asked her. "Don't tell me that there is nobody against you in the New Peking University Commune [Nieh's faction] and among the cultural revolutionaries in the schools. I don't believe that! They may not say anything in front of you, but they will say devilish things behind your back.[. . .] I say, you, Old Buddha, had better be a little more farsighted. There are several thousand people in Peking University's Chingkangshan [the opposition faction]. If they were released like a torrential flood, they would wash the Dragon King's temple away."

As he continued his ironic criticism, perhaps most harsh to the eldest of his intended successors, the Chairman suggested his third solution to the problem of the fighting.

> "Don't live in one city. Separate one into two. Either you or 'Chingkangshan' move to the South. If one is in the South and the other is in the North, you won't see each other and won't be able to fight. Each one puts his house in order, and then everybody will be united. Otherwise, you will be afraid. They might launch an attack on the Old Buddha's nest. You won't be able to sleep. You'll be afraid. They will be afraid, too."

Mao had followed the battles of Heaven and Earth meticulously. It was said that, in accordance with his method of "dissecting a sparrow," he had chosen Tsinghua University as his case study in analyzing the student struggle and that he had read every leaflet, every *ta-tzu-pao* printed there. So when he directed his withering sarcasm at the war which, to the students, had become literally a matter of life and death, his statistics had a stinging accuracy. "Nieh Yuan-tzu's cannon fodder is limited in number; so is K'uai Ta-fu's. Sometimes three hundred; other times one hundred and fifty. How can this be compared with the number of troops under Lin Piao and Huang Yung-sheng? This time in one sally," the Chairman said, referring to the workers and soldiers he had sent into the universities, "we had thirty thousand."

But Mao's emotions in this intense family council seemed not unlike those of the more ordinary paterfamilias whose angry disappointment in his children has its origins in affection and extravagant hopes. Calling Wang Ta-pin over to him, Mao said, "Come over here, sit by my side," and mused, "In these matters, we should allow ourselves some leeway. All those involved are students. They did not engage in black gang [counterrevolutionary] activities. [. . .] The crucial point is that the two factions are engaged in armed struggle. They were bent on armed struggle. This kind of struggle-criticism-transformation does not work. Maybe struggle-criticism-quit will. The students are talking about struggle-criticism-runaway, or struggle-criticism-scatter."

Hours went by as the elders discussed the problem of fighting in the schools, and the younger members of the family sat silently and kept their thoughts to themselves. On more than one occasion, Chiang Ch'ing, placing the problem within the ancient and familiar structure of patriarchal authority which these young rebels had been called upon to overthrow, interjected: "Disgrace to the family!" But when her criticism of Han Ai-ching grew intense, Mao stepped in and stated, "Don't criticize him. You always blame others; you never blame yourself." And to Chiang Ch'ing's reply that Han Ai-ching lacked "a spirit of self-criticism," the Chairman commented thoughtfully:

> "Young people cannot stand criticism. His character [Han Ai-ching] is something like mine when I was young. Kids are very subjective, incredibly subjective. They only criticize others."

Perhaps speculating on what the young leaders must also have been thinking—that they had begun their rebel careers with encouragement from above and that their factionalism reflected the struggles of those with far greater political experience than themselves, Mao said:

> "Who could have foreseen this kind of fighting? Suspension of classes for half a year was originally planned. It was so announced in the newspaper. Later the suspension was extended to one year. As one year was not enough, it was extended to two years, and then to three years. I say, if three years are still not enough, give them as many years as necessary. After all, people are growing older every year. Suppose you were a freshman three years ago, you are now a junior. The schools may be suspended for another two, four, or eight years, you get promoted all the same, so what?"

The old revolutionary had moved into one of his favorite areas, the subject of education, and the fact that Engels, Stalin, and Maxim Gorki had had little education, which was also the case of most of the Chinese leaders, including himself. A great deal of what he said was reminiscent of, sometimes identical to, his remarks so widely circulated among the students in the early days of the Cultural Revolution: "Knowledge is not gained in schools. When I was in school, I did not obey the rules. My principle was just to avoid getting myself dismissed. As to examinations, my marks hovered between fifty or sixty per cent and eighty per cent, seventy per cent being my average." He spoke as he had done many times before of his lack of specialized training: "I have never attended any military school. Nor have I read a book on military strategy." And he reiterated once again his ideas on educational methods:

> ". . . Teaching is harmful. Organize a small group for self-study, a self-study university. The students may stay half a year, one year, two years, or three years. No examination is required. Examination is not a good method. Who examined Marx? Who examined Engels? Who examined Lenin? Who examined Comrade Lin Piao? [. . .] The needs of the masses and Chiang Kai-shek are our teachers. This was the case for all of us. Teachers are needed in middle schools, but everything should be made simple. [. . .] To study in a library is a good method. I studied at a library in Hunan for half a year and in the library of Peking University for half a year . . ."

However, now that the student "pathbreakers" were being informed that their role was over in a movement which had long ago left behind questions of educational reform for those of political power, the thrust of the Chairman's critique had a different direction.

> "Education revolution cannot make any headway. Even we cannot make any headway, not to mention you. You are hurt by the old system. Why can't we make any headway?"

Apparently Mao, like almost everyone else, was losing confidence in educational reform, or at least in the capacity of the current generation of students to effect it. Those whom he had expected to be the vehicles of change were themselves becoming an obstacle to progress. It was in reference to the fact that the Red Guards had become a problem rather than a means toward the solution of larger problems that Mao said:

> "Our Comrade Ch'en Po-ta was anxious at the Central Committee meeting. I said don't be so anxious. A few years later, they [the student Red Guards] will be gone, and that will be the end. As I see it, the education revolution consists of only a few things. Why should we engage in education reform. If we fail, that's the end of it. This is what the students say."

Mao's words were prophetic not only of the impending decision to send the students away from their role at the center of power to the practical schooling of the vast Chinese countryside, but to the indecisive state of educational reform long after the Cultural Revolution was officially over. Affirming the Chairman's theses, as all his colleagues did throughout the long session, Lin Piao remarked that he had studied for only four years in a middle school but had voluntarily withdrawn before graduation. And when Huang Yung-sheng replied to Mao's query about his education that he had had only one and a half years of schooling, Mao remarked: "All are country folks with so little knowledge. With that little knowledge, Huang Yung-sheng can be Chief of Staff. Can you believe it?" It was a return full circle to the earliest concerns of the Cultural Revolution.

The talk went on, weaving in and out of the same themes —the student violence, with all its specifics of torture, kidnapping, and forced confessions; the factional deadlock in Peking; the student reception of the workers, and the past, the memories of the old revolutionaries. The presence of the absent K'uai Ta-fu hung over the meeting as his name entered the discussion of one factional problem after another. To the old and the young, his absence from this most important of councils was the last symbol of the now discredited student rebellion. When his arrival, hours late, was at last announced, waves of relief and excitement must have swept over the intense assembly. Weeping, K'uai presented his report. He had been trapped in his fortress at Tsinghua University by his heavily armed opponents, the "April 14" Red Guards. Tsinghua University was in danger, he announced; the black hand was manipulating the workers to suppress the students. "I have become the black hand," the Chairman said. "Take me to the garrison headquarters."

With all its rambling and inconclusive quality, Mao's final meeting with the leaders of his revolutionary shock troops raised, in a far sharper way than later editorials, many of the central problems of the Cultural Revolution. He spoke of the failures of educational reform. He referred to the great difficulties the people had had in evolving political forms suitable to this superstructural battle of the Sixties out of their earlier experience with class struggle. In criticizing the student-invented "jet plane ride," in which those subjected to criticism were forced at meetings to stand with head down and hands back, Mao said with his usual irony, but with a clear understanding of the negative role of historical example:

> "I am the guilty one. In 'The Inspection Report on the Peasant Movement in Hunan,' I talked about 'parading people on the street in dunce hats,' but I did not mention 'jet plane ride.' "

However, it was from one of the now discredited "successors" that the central question came. The factional battles which had racked the Chairman's search for "those in the Party in authority taking the capitalist road" and finally, in essence, frustrated it, had been fought under a single flag— the banner of revolution and Mao Tse-tung Thought. As the Chairman himself had said earlier: "In the past, we fought North and South; it was easy to fight such wars. For the enemy was obvious. The present Great Proletarian Cultural Revolution is much more difficult than that kind of war." Every other class struggle in history had been fought out by forces which identified themselves by the politics of their class. However, under socialism, all defined themselves as revolutionaires, those who won established their position as "correct," and the only recognizable enemy was the one which had been defeated. It was the dilemma which the Cultural Revolution had challenged, but not resolved.

The student leaders initiated little during the many hours of talk; they spoke only when spoken to. But toward the end, Han Ai-ching, who had been the object of much criticism, suddenly said:

> "Chairman, I have a question. If, ten or one hundred years from now, civil war should break out in China, and if one faction claims that they represent Mao Tse-tung's Thought and another faction also claims that they represent Mao Tse-tung's Thought, resulting in a confused situation of splits and claims, what would we do?"

It was the central question to which thousands and perhaps millions of Chinese sought an answer. For the first time in the protracted meeting, there was a dialogue and, appropriately, it was between the Chairman and one of his twenty-three-year-old successors. It was a question that went to the heart of Mao's own assertion of a year earlier that "under the dictatorship of the proletariat there is no reason whatsoever for the working class to split into two irreconcilable factions." Nevertheless, this is precisely what had happened, and nothing in Marx, Lenin, or Mao Tse-tung himself had been able to explain it. The Chairman appeared interested in the question and answered it by reference to the struggles of the past:

> "There is nothing startling about it. The war against the Ch'ing dynasty lasted more than twenty years. We fought Chiang K'ai-shek for over ten years. Within the Chinese Communist Party, we had Ch'en Tu-hsiu, Li Li-san, Wang Ming, Po Ku, Chang Kuo-t'ao, Liu Shao-ch'i, and many more. These experiences are more valuable than our knowledge about Marxism."

His colleagues responded with the generalities with which the student leaders were quite familiar, and which, it seemed, had not aided in the resolution of the "unreasonable" factionalism. "We have Mao Tse-tung's Thought," Lin Piao said, to which Ch'en Po-ta added: "Han Ai-ching mentioned this problem before. With Comrade Lin Piao as Chairman Mao's successor and with Mao Tse-tung's Thought, I am not afraid of the emergence of revisionism." "The Chairman has already talked about this problem," Yao Wen-yuan chided, and Chou En-lai stated, "Comrade Lin Piao has studied the Chairman's writings well. Vice Chairman Lin has also mastered Soviet affairs and the works of Marx and Lenin."

Chiang Ch'ing, whose persistent criticism of the bold Han Ai-ching had already brought the Chairman's intervention several times during the afternoon, said with obvious annoyance:

> "Han Ai-ching wrote to me several times, discussing this problem. Why did Han Ai-ching keep bringing this problem up? In the first place, he is isolated from the workers and the peasants. In the second place, he is isolated from reality. As soon as I see him, he thinks about the future. He always talks about things that might happen decades from now. He even asked me when World War Three will break out."

Suddenly the Chairman appeared to realize that he might have more in common with this young rebel who had made fearful mistakes than with some of the country's senior leaders and he asserted with some heat: "It is good to think far ahead. He is good! He is good!" Perhaps the Chairman had found, as well as a "disgrace to the family," one of the successors he had been looking for.

## Chapter XI

# Consolidation At The Top:
# Again One Splits Into Two

IN THE LATE SUMMER of 1968, a pall hung over the capital city of the revolution. As we took long walks down the back lanes of Peking and rode the buses from here to there, silently observing the people who had learned about revolution by making it, there could be no question that the joy had gone out of the movement. The spirit of adventure had been replaced by a grimness reflected in the faces of a people who still marched behind crimson banners and portraits of the Chairman, but who did so out of habit. It was becoming clearer each day that Mao Tse-tung had wrung all that he could out of this cultural revolution. He had always believed in drawing the bowstring to the limit without letting it snap. Periods of tension, in the Chairman's view, must be alternated with periods of relaxation. It was a dialectical notion common to Chinese tradition.

By the time the five "small generals" returned to their respective campuses after their dialogue with the Chairman, the die had already been cast. It was too late for them to change their work-style; and even had they been willing, the opposition was too embittered to reach an accommodation. Consequently, the loudspeakers of Heaven and Earth filled the Peking air with one last impassioned round of exhortations. Heaven assailed Earth with the claim that Chairman Mao personally rejected the views of the Geology Institute militants, listing in detail the criticisms which Mao had directed against the leaders of the Earth faction. Earth reciprocated in kind. This was the last fusillade fired by the Red Guards of Peking. Thousands of workers and soldiers poured into the universities, overwhelming the students with their numbers and their coherence. "Struggle, criticism, and quit" had been rejected by the student leaders, so the Chairman had decided to "give them a little help" by sending in the workers and soldiers. Within six months to a year, the majority of the nation's students would be "sent down" to that great "school" in the countryside run by the peasants, having been declared incapable of completing the gigantic social movement which they had begun. The Cultural Revolution, after all, had been a drama staged by urban China for the benefit of the majority of Chinese living in the countryside. It was therefore fitting that the students, as part of society's superstructure, should go down, willingly or reluctantly, to the base upon which everything else rested. Only small teams of teachers, cadres, and a few students would remain on campus to discuss educational reform. In short, Chairman Mao's Headquarters had suspended the mass movement.

For more than two years, China had experienced that extraordinary level of popular participation in politics always associated with the great revolutions in world history. The Chinese people had experimented with new popular forms of government, while exposing a whole society and its institutions to merciless inspection and criticism. For an extended period of time, the Chinese mass social movement had lived a life of its own. The people had "stormed the heavens" and had set up representative organs of power in various localities. Like their predecessors, the peasants of the great Hunan uprisings in 1927, the cultural revolutionaries of the Sixties had "exceeded the limits" in order to right the wrongs of society. In 1927, Mao had written that, unless those limits were exceeded, "the wrong cannot be righted." But by 1968, many centers of power had proliferated throughout the land. Now editorials attacked what was called the "splittist theory of many centers," which, it was argued, amounted to a "theory of no center." Lenin was quoted to remind the people that "absolute centralization and rigorous discipline are an essential condition of victory over the bourgeoisie." The Cultural Revolution had challenged but not yet overcome the conflict between local and centralized power which has remained the key dilemma of all revolutions. However, the Chinese people had gone further than any other in the historic effort to confront that dilemma.

The threat of foreign military intervention that worked to undermine the spontaneous pattern of politics in the American, French, and Russian revolutions emerged once again to add to all the internal pressures forcing an end to the Chinese experiment with the mass politics of the Cultural Revolution. In one of the greatest mass airborne invasions in history, the Soviet Union occupied Czechoslovakia on August 20, 1968. More than a century after the publication of the *Communist Manifesto,* the specter haunting the socialist world turned out to be Soviet troops. Chinese leaders had little choice but grimly to face the new Brezhnev doctrine of limited sovereignty for socialist states. They knew that they might be next on the list. Mao was beginning to face outward for the first time in years and once again assess China's place in the world. In the new situation, the Army was given the job of reassembling the fragmented Chinese organizational structure, and it took full advantage of the opportunity.

Yao Wen-yuan, whose essay on Hai Jui had given the signal for the Great Proletarian Cultural Revolution, was assigned the task of providing the theoretical postulates for the final stages of the great rebellion. His essay "The Working Class Must Exercise Leadership in Everything" was published at the end of August 1968. His arguments were built on a new instruction from Chairman Mao publicized in every corner of the country:

> "Our country has seven hundred million people, and the working class is the leading class. It is essential to bring into full play the leading role of the working class in the great cultural revolution and in all fields of work. On its part, the working class should always raise its political consciousness in the course of struggle."[121]

In order for the revolutionary committees to carry out their work, it was necessary, asserted Yao, to "persist in leadership by the working class," to replace bourgeois dictatorship by proletarian dictatorship, and to ensure that every instruction emanating from the Proletarian Headquarters led by Chairman Mao "be carried out swiftly and smoothly." In addition, "The theory of 'many centers,' that is, the theory of no center,' mountain stronghold mentality, sectarianism, and other reactionary bourgeois trends undermining working class leadership must be opposed." The entry of the Workers' Propaganda Teams into the field of education was, according to Yao, "an earth-shaking event."

Certain people had sabotaged the Cultural Revolution, Yao said. They had incited the masses to struggle against each other, disrupted struggle-criticism-transformation, and undermined the great alliance and the "three-in-one" combination. This in turn had "aroused dissatisfaction among the masses." "Under such circumstances," the essay continued, "it is impossible for the students and intellectuals by themselves alone to fulfill the task of struggle-criticism-transformation and a whole number of other tasks on the educational front; workers and People's Liberation Army fighters must take part, and it is essential to have strong leadership by the working class." Yao stated unequivocally that "contradictions that the intellectuals have been quarreling over without end and are unable to resolve are quickly settled when the workers arrive." Moreover, Mao had now decided that the workers should remain permanently in the schools. In the future, "they will always lead the schools." In the countryside, according to the new formula, "the schools should be managed by the poor and lower-middle peasants—the most reliable ally of the working class." When the workers were combined with the People's Liberation Army, described as "the main pillar of the dictatorship of the proletariat," they would be able to stop "all erroneous tendencies contrary to Chairman Mao's revolutionary line and most effective in resolving all kinds of problems which have been described as long-standing, big, and difficult." The final stage of the movement called for the implementation of Mao's instructions on purifying the class ranks, rectifying the Party organization, simplifying organizational structures in the factories, changing irrational rules and regulations, and "sending people who work in offices to grass-root levels." The Party was to be rebuilt by expelling "bad" members and taking in new activists who had distinguished themselves in the movement.

The Mao Tse-tung Thought Propaganda Teams that descended on the schools and universities of the nation in the late summer of 1968 were massive. There was, for instance, something like one soldier or worker for every four or five students at the Peking First Foreign Languages Institute, a ratio which enabled the whole student body to be organized into small study groups with one worker or soldier assigned to each group. Since it was often impossible for either the workers or the soldiers to untangle the complex issues at stake in each organization, they often simply organized quasi-religious recitations by the students of Maoist ethical teachings. The "Three Old Articles" were once again called forth, and formal rituals devoted to "remembering the bitter past" became the order of the day. The hope was that the students would be shamed out of their factional loyalties through the realization of the high price paid by the Chinese people in their long revolutionary struggle for liberation. The practice of calling on old workers and peasants to recite the horrors of the past in contrast to the "happy present" for the benefit of the younger generation remains a key pedagogic practice up to the present day. In those waning days of the Cultural Revolution, middle school students partook of ceremonial meals of dried grass and roots such as starving peasants had eaten in pre-revolutionary times. These somber lessons perhaps served as a functional equivalent to the Christian practice of serving bread and wine in the ritual of the Communion, but, emotional as the experience might be, the length of the impact on the consciousness remains problematical. Mao, in his conversation with Edgar Snow in 1965, had himself cast doubt on the efficacy of attempting to experience revolution second hand. It was for this reason that he had tried to involve his successors in a real revolution.

During the fall and winter of 1968, the Army men and women were particularly guilty of pushing the Mao cult to impossible extremes. At one point, PLA teams fostered group therapy sessions all over Peking, at which members of opposing factions sat together and embroidered portraits of the Chairman. Proof of loyalty to Mao was determined by the size of the portrait. Statues of the Chairman proliferated to an unbelievable extent, the workers bowing to the benevolent plaster busts in the morning and reporting their successes to the same icon in the evening. However, there were many politically sophisticated participants in the movement who did not succumb to the cult, or who gave it ritual obeisance while following a larger politics. Among the leaders, Lin Piao was, without doubt, the chief offender in fostering the Mao cult. In the end, he was accused of having used it for ulterior purposes, but it was logical that the cult should have found its greatest support in the peasant army that constituted Lin's social and political base.

On a more sophisticated level, the Mao Tse-tung Thought Propaganda Teams did attempt to lead an intensive review of how well the various factions had carried out Mao's political instructions and formulations at each stage of the movement. In some cases, the factions admitted mistakes of orientation and line, thus achieving unity on the basis of a review of the whole movement. In other situations, discussions of the past only renewed old arguments.

Understandably, the most difficult task was convincing the masses that the revolution was over. On September 8, 1968, Chou En-lai, speaking for the Proletarian Headquarters, announced to the revolutionary multitude assembled in T'ien An Men Square, "Now the whole country is red." The evidence for this proclamation of revolutionary victory was the final establishment of revolutionary committees in all of China's twenty-nine provinces and major cities. The Premier himself had put in a twenty-hour day for over a year to accomplish this miracle of delicate accommodation which required soothing unruly factions who often refused to sit in the same room together. Signaling the end of mass revolutionary politics, the Premier told the million weary political actors who had gathered to hear him:

> "Now we can declare that through repeated struggles during the past twenty months we have finally smashed the plot of the handful of top Party persons in authority taking the capitalist road—counterrevolutionary revision-ists—renegades, enemy agents and traitors headed by China's Khrushchev to restore capitalism (applause), and fulfilled the great call issued by our great leader Chairman Mao, "Proletarian revolutionaries, unite and seize power from the handful of Party persons in authority taking the capitalist road.' (Applause. The masses shout; Long live the victory of Chairman Mao's revolutionary line!) This is a tremendous victory for the great proletarian cultural revolution, a great victory for the invincible thought of Mao Tse-tung."[122]

Chou reminded the masses that there was one province yet to be liberated—Taiwan. "Taiwan will be liberated without fail," he asserted. Warning that China's domestic and foreign enemies would not take defeat lying down, Chou called upon the people to "respond to the call of Chairman Mao and, under the unified leadership of the Proletarian Headquarters headed by Chairman Mao and with Vice-Chairman Lin Piao as its deputy leader, unify our understanding, coordinate our steps, and concert our actions." It was not the last time in the next few years that the foreign threat would be utilized to achieve unity at home, except that, in the future, that threat would be seen coming almost entirely from the north-ern border area shared with China's former fraternal neigh-bor, Soviet Russia.

The final stage of consolidation should be accomplished, Chou said, by establishing three-in-one committees in every unit, carrying out mass criticism and repudiation, purifying class ranks, consolidating the Party organization, and "sim-plifying the administrative structure, changing irrational rules and regulations, and sending office workers to the workshops." Young people, Chou added, "should go to the grass-roots levels, to the masses and to production, settle in the mountainous areas and the countryside, and take part in physical work in factories, mines, and villages." All these tasks were to be accomplished under the leadership of the working class, which was backed by the People's Liberation Army. The Red Guard movement was over. The mass organizations would be dissolved once the great alliance had been achieved.

Chou ended his peroration with the statement that the Great Proletarian Cultural Revolution "is a most extensive, thoroughgoing, and all-round political and military mobilization. Should enemies from abroad dare to invade China, we will wipe them out resolutely, thoroughly, wholly, and completely." In the beginning of the Cultural Revolution, Mao had subordinated the demands of foreign relations to the requirements of domestic politics; now domestic politics would be subordinated and increasingly influenced by the exigencies of China's world relationship.

Chiang Ch'ing addressed for the last time her political constituency, which would soon be dissolved. Stating as she had on previous occasions that she had been told "at short notice to say a few words here," she reminded all present: "We must not forget that the revolutionary youth and the young Red Guard fighters have made tremendous contributions at the initial and middle stages of the revolution," and while on the one hand the young Red Guard fighters should welcome the leadership of the working class, the working class "being the leading class [ . . . ] would do well to protect the young Red Guard fighters, help them, and educate them."[123] These improvised remarks were the last echo of an appointed committee which, at one time, hoped to have power second to none.

However, revolutions are as difficult to end as they are to start. One month after the Premier's announcement that the "whole country is red," Shanghai's *Wen-hui pao,* the reddest newspaper in the nation, once again raised the question of mass representation in the new organs of political power. On October 18, *Wen-hui pao* published an editorial called "Oppose Restoration of the Old." In its usual direct style, the paper called attention to the lack of representation on the newborn revolutionary committees of the masses who had made the revolution:

> "At the time when the Great Proletarian Cultural Revolution has won a decisive victory, the tendency to restore the old continues to be a trend deserving our serious attention.
>
> "The newborn revolutionary committee is the most representative form of revolutionary organ of power of proletarian dictatorship since liberation. Representing fully the revolutionary interests of the proletariat, it is full of the vigorous revolutionary spirit. However, Marx once said: 'Old things always seek to restore and consolidate themselves in newborn forms.' One way to restore the old is to attach a new label to the old and outmoded machinery and make it move in the newborn revolutionary committee.
>
> "Haven't such tendencies to restore the old appeared in certain units?
>
> "In these units, the leading groups are composed entirely of former personnel, have not drawn in proletarian new blood, and are not a revolutionary three-in-one combination. Even if in form they have absorbed revolutionary fresh blood they have done everything they could to get rid of fresh blood—like squeezing a tube of toothpaste."[124]

The editorial went on to explain that one of the leading cadres in a Shanghai factory was at a loss when it came to explaining the two-line struggle in his plant and had no idea when the rebel groups were formed there. The leading group in this factory was labeled by *Wen-hui pao* as a "stale group." In other cases, instead of "boldly arousing the masses and opening the doors wide in Party rectification and reconstruction," the leading personnel "rely on a few in finding fault with this or that behind closed doors." Even worse, according to the editorial, these same leading personnel exaggerated the faults of the revolutionary rebels as "a pretext for not admitting them into the Party." Once the Party was rebuilt as a vanguard party, the *Wen-hui pao* editorial writers implied, the revolutionary committees might become no more than a label for the old structural form of Party Committee.

As we watched the rebuilding of the Party apparatus in the late months of 1968, we could not help but wonder whether the Cultural Revolution had proved that the vanguard party was indispensable as a device for consolidating new revolutions. Whether the Cultural Revolution had come full circle in a return to Party rule or whether it had proceeded in a Hegelian spiral to reach a higher level, only the future could determine. Whatever the case, there were tens of thousands, perhaps millions in China, thanks to Mao and the Cultural Revolution, who would view the Party in the future as less than an infallible institution. The way in which it utilized its monopoly of power would be carefully scrutinized.

But in the late fall of 1968, Mao and his followers were absorbed with problems at the top—in particular, that of finally settling the question of the Chairman's fallen successor Liu Shao-ch'i. From October 13 to 31, 1968, Chairman Mao presided over the Enlarged 12th Plenary Session of the Eighth Central Committee of the Chinese Communist Party in Peking. The communiqué issued by the Plenum announced the decision to convene the Ninth National Congress of the Chinese Communist Party "at an appropriate time." It also formally decreed the expulsion of Liu Shao-ch'i. The former Chairman of the Republic was declared to be a "renegade, traitor, and scab hiding in the Party and [is] a lackey of imperialism, modern revisionism, and the Kuomintang reactionaries who has committed innumerable crimes."[125] A special panel set up by the Central Committee to investigate the background and history of Liu Shao-ch'i determined that he had "wormed his way into the Party in 1921" and for forty years had "consistently employed counterrevolutionary and double-dealing tactics to recruit renegades and defectors, to make contact with foreign countries, and to oppose wildly the proletarian revolutionary line represented by Chairman Mao. The report of the panel claimed that Liu had been arrested and had surrendered to the enemy in 1925, 1927, and 1929, but had kept this record secret from the Party. The charge was that he had been broken by the enemy during his arrests and agreed to work for the KMT, betraying the Party on numerous occasions. A further charge included the fact that "he married Wang Kuang-mei, a US secret agent sent to Yenan by the US Strategic Information Service of Peking. In May 1950, he sent his brother-in-law, Wang Kuang-ch'i, to Hong Kong to supply the US Central Intelligence Agency with much information 'of high value,' which was highly regarded by the Americans."[126]

The difficulty in believing the charge that one of the principal leaders of the Chinese Revolution helped found the Chinese Party only to destroy it, was one thing. The fact that Liu Shao-ch'i and Mao Tse-tung had long-standing theoretical and policy differences was another. Anna Louise Strong shared with us her notes of a private talk given in Peking at the beginning of 1968 by Premier Chou to a small group of foreigners on the differences between Mao and Liu. The Premier dated the dispute from the late 1940's. Chou described how Mao had foreseen that the main struggle when the communists took over the cities would be with the bourgeoisie, but that Liu had interpreted the alliance with the national capitalists in quite a different light. Liu emphasized a policy which called upon the capitalists to take a leading role in industry, while Mao hoped to win them over but to restrict them at the same time. According to the Premier, Liu admitted his errors after criticism and appeared to be won over to the Maoist line. A few years later, Liu, on his own initiative, stopped the peasants in Shensi from forming mutual aid teams, while Mao supported them. Again Liu made a self-criticism, but it was evident that he leaned toward a policy of increased agricultural production through mechanization and opposed Mao's plan for mobilizing the masses for collective effort.

Premier Chou provided some interesting insights into the conflict between the two leaders when he said that during the hard years (1959–62), Liu had encouraged the expansion of private plots and a return to a free market, while Mao believed that the answer to food shortages among the peasantry would be to allow the peasants to keep more of their own grain distributed to them by the commune. Each Chinese peasant household contains a huge earthen jar in which the family's private stock of rice or wheat is kept. Mao felt that if each peasant were allowed to increase his private store of grain from the commune reserves, he would then have no inclination to increase the size of his private plot. Mao has consistently believed in permitting the peasants to build up their own grain reserves to reassure them that the cities were not out to fleece the countryside. This was the exact opposite of the policy followed by Stalin in the 1930's. Stalin exacted the state quotas for grain delivery, much of which was used for export, whether the peasants starved or not.

During the early Sixties, the Premier said, Liu Shao-ch'i had panicked over the economy and wished to devalue the *renminbi*. But, according to the Premier, Mao maintained that, once production picked up, the currency problem would be solved. "And he was right," added Chou. "Now [1967–8] we are producing two hundred and forty million tons of grain a year" (a fact the West refused to admit until the 1970's, when Western experts confirmed 250-million-ton harvests).

The charge that Liu Shao-ch'i had been an enemy agent inside the Party ever since the early 1920's was more difficult to digest. When we were in Shanghai in the summer of 1969, we told a Party official there that it would be difficult to convince people in the West that the nation's president and a communist leader for over forty years had "sneaked into the Party" and, instead of being one of the principal figures of the Chinese Revolution, was in reality a spy. The cadre with whom we spoke said that such a reaction would be natural, since he himself and most Chinese had found it difficult to understand this question. He implied that somehow he had come to understand it, but that for Westerners it might be more difficult. Apparently, the accepted political pattern was that if a leader followed a "correct" policy in the present, his mistakes of the past were ignored; but if he were overthrown in a policy dispute, he would be found a "traitor" from the beginning. This was quite consistent with the practice followed by each Chinese dynasty of rewriting the official history of its predecessor. Of course, it also fit the Soviet record of rewriting history in light of present politics. Although history is often rewritten in the West, modern cultural and political traditions reinforce the conviction that there is more to history than the present. Whatever the truth in the case of Liu Shao-ch'i, it is probable that he will be judged by history as a representative of the Soviet model of communism who was for this reason rejected and overthrown by the Chinese people.

As 1968 drew to a close, a massive new campaign to send the students and youth to the countryside was begun. It would continue at an accelerating pace for the next few years, just as the rest of the population concentrated on the urgent tasks of production and the simplification of administration. It was a logical conclusion to the Cultural Revolution that the cities should turn to face the countryside, that one-third of the medical staffs in urban hospitals, and sometimes two-thirds, should be dispatched to set up clinics for the peasants, and that school graduates should take their place in the rural areas where they were needed. It was not surprising that many of the Red Guards perceived, in some cases perhaps correctly, that, rather than facing their revolutionary duty, they were confronting exile and punishment as scapegoats for the politics of the Cultural Revolution.

Mao's new instructions flowing out of the 12th Plenum were: "The Party organizations should be composed of the advanced elements of the proletariat and the revolutionary masses in the fight against the class enemy" and the slogan "The working class must exercise leadership in everything." However, it was the Army that was able to determine the composition of many key Party units and control the composition of the delegations elected to the forthcoming Ninth Party Congress. The bloody border clashes between major elements of the Chinese and Soviet armies on the frozen Ussuri River in March of 1969, just a few weeks before the opening of the Chinese Party Congress, served to strengthen this military bid for power. A grim and menacing atmosphere gripped Peking in the spring of 1969 as reports of the savage fighting with the Russians in the north filtered down to the average citizen. Peking was only some four hundred miles from the Mongolian border, where division upon division of Soviet troops were massed in offensive readiness. We met a close Chinese friend, who told us that spring that Chinese leaders were now debating whether, in case of an all-out Russian tank attack from Inner Mongolia, to make a fight for Peking or to abandon the city and retreat to the countryside. It was during this conversation that our friend flatly stated that the Russian leaders were madmen and that, in fact, the American leaders were much more reasonable than the Russians. In our previous four years in China we had never heard the case put that way. It was for us an augury of a new world outlook in the making.

Long overdue, the Ninth National Congress of the Chinese Communist Party opened in Peking on April 1, 1969. Time would quickly prove that its official title, "The Congress of Unity and Victory," was, in fact, a misnomer. The Ninth Party Congress, put together under the pressure of the imperatives of national consolidation and the Soviet military threat, failed to resolve many of the key problems in the economy, education, and the rebuilding of the State machinery. The main struggle at the Congress centered on the question of what groups would control a new vanguard party which had yet to be rebuilt. Even at the time, one had the impression that the Ninth Congress was somehow anticlimactic; no one seemed overly excited about this historic Congress marking the close of the Great Proletarian Cultural Revolution. Seen in retrospect, it was clearly a transitional event, a pause, before the final and fateful struggle at the very top which would be called by the Chinese "The Tenth Major Struggle Between the Two Lines in the History of the Chinese Communist Party." The internal dispute between the "victors" of the Cultural Revolution, a dispute which was masked, but which lay just under the surface of the documents and speeches issued by the Congress, concerned two basic issues:

How many of the old cadres should be restored to power and what was the relation of the Cultural Revolution to China's strategic world view? Foreign policy, long dormant, emerged as the most crucial determinant for Chinese politics of the post-Cultural Revolution era.

Lin Piao, reflecting his new position of power at the Ninth Congress, gave the main political report. Utilizing Mao's theoretical summary of the politics of the Cultural Revolution, he attempted to explain why the Cultural Revolution had been so complex: "The problem is that those who commit ideological errors are all mixed up with those whose contradictions with us is one between ourselves and the enemy, and for a time it is hard to sort them out." All previous movements in Chinese Communist history designed to wipe out revisionism had failed, Lin quoted Mao as saying, "because we did not find a form, a method to arouse the broad masses to expose our dark aspect openly, in an all-round way and from below. The answer was the Great Proletarian Cultural Revolution." Perhaps the most significant passages of Lin's long report concerned foreign policy. Lin Piao put forth a new strategic world orientation for the nation, the forerunner of more startling policies to come. There were, Lin stated, four major world contradictions:

> "The contradiction between the oppressed nations on the one hand and imperialism and social imperialism on the other; the contradiction between the proletariat and the bourgeoisie in the capitalist and revisionist countries; the contradiction between imperialist and social-imperialist countries and among the imperialist countries; and the contradiction between socialist countries on the one hand and imperialism and social imperialism on the other."[127]

For the first time in the history of the new China, it was officially proclaimed that imperialism and social-imperialism—that is, the United States and the Soviet Union—had become for China equal enemies. The Soviet Union had been elevated to the position of a principal or main enemy, a position previously occupied solely by the United States.

Within less than two years, the Soviet Union would stand alone as China's main enemy, and the United States, termed a "waning" imperialist power, would drop to the position of secondary enemy since, in Mao's view, there can be only one principal strategic enemy, and revolutionaries should never strike in two directions at the same time. The internal logic of Mao's Cultural Revolution was beginning to work itself out. It had been a revolution against the Soviet Union both as a system and as an external power seeking to control China's future. Therefore, the last stage of the Cultural Revolution was inevitably linked with the question of China's place in the world. Like all of the great world revolutions preceding it, the Chinese Cultural Revolution resulted in the consolidation of a modern independent nation state. Thus, the internal logic of a movement which, for a time, appeared to have no relationship to the outside world, evolved into a denouement that was a surprise to everyone except perhaps the Chairman himself.

Mao himself had signaled China's new strategic orientation as early as 1962, when he suggested that right opportunism in China be renamed revisionism, thus linking China's internal struggles with the Sino–Soviet conflict. It was just one more step to label the main internal target of the Cultural Revolution "China's Khrushchev." The Cultural Revolution, itself an internal revolt against the Soviet system, had finally produced out of that struggle a new Chinese world view. After half a century of struggle, the Chinese were ready to define Marxism–Leninism in their own way. Once the new Chinese synthesis of the materials they had appropriated from the 1917 Russian Revolution was near completion, Mao Tse-tung was even ready to jettison those Marxist–Leninist arguments which had constituted the Chinese polemic with the Russians over the general line of the international communist movement. Those arguments of the early Sixties had been based on the struggle against Russian–American collusion to control the world and were summarized by the Chinese statement that "Soviet–US collaboration is the heart and soul of the CPSU leaders' general line of peaceful coexistence." Although the Chinese would continue to "oppose the hegemony of the two superpowers," once America had been defined by Mao as a "waning" imperialism and Russia as a "rising" one, the entire Chinese polemic of the Sixties was no longer relevant. In the Fifties, Mao had "leaned to one side" toward the Russians; in the Seventies, he would advocate leaning the other way. The new Maoist global strategy inevitably impelled those revolutionary forces throughout the world threatened by US imperialism to develop their own strategies and to break with a Chinese line primarily designed to protect Chinese interests.

But in the spring of 1969, China's relationship to the rest of the world was far from clear. Lin Piao had been written into the Party Constitution as Mao's successor. The newly elected Central Committee of the Party, whose members averaged fifty-nine years of age, was heavily weighted with military leaders. Elected to the Standing Committee of the Political Bureau, the most powerful committee in the country were: Mao as Chairman, Lin as Vice Chairman, Premier Chou, Ch'en Po-ta, and K'ang Sheng. The fateful beginning of the "tenth major struggle between the two lines" must have begun either at the Congress or shortly after it had closed in the third week of April 1969. Mao, together with Chou, evidently wished to consolidate the gains of the Cultural Revolution, rehabilitate the old Party cadres as rapidly as possible, and move on to the final stage of defining China's relationship to the world system.

In retrospect, it appears that Ch'en Po-ta, the last of the ultra-left leaders on the Cultural Group, whose political base had been dissolved with the end of the mass movement, threw his support to Lin Piao and the Army, which seemed at the time to be an ascendant political force. Lin Piao and Ch'en Po-ta were probably in no hurry to rebuild the Party. They knew that a rehabilitated Party apparatus based on the old cadres would undoubtedly back the Premier and the State bureaucracy, since they had nowhere else to go. This potential political coalition was a threat to Army power. Chang Ch'un-ch'iao, Yao Wen-yuan, and the radical forces from

Shanghai possessed their own firm and formidable political base, enjoyed Mao's support, and had every reason to phase out military control in the rest of the country. Chiang Ch'ing, as Mao's wife, would be protected regardless of the errors she might have made. The tenth major line struggle, then, was a struggle between the Mao-Chou forces and the Lin-Ch'en coalition, which included a number, but perhaps not a majority, of the senior PLA officers.[128]

Significantly, at the end of a mass popular uprising, this final elemental struggle among the historic leaders of a great revolution took place behind the closed doors and high walls of the Ming Emperors' Winter Palace. The conflict between the two lines smoldered under the surface for more than a year and was finally decided in Mao's favor at the 2nd Plenary Session of the Ninth Central Committee held at Lushan in August 1970. There, the political forces led by Lin Piao and Ch'en Po-ta were defeated in a major fight over both foreign and domestic strategies. The Chinese masses were told the results once it was all over, the world a little later.

It would seem that the leaders of both high factions agreed at the Ninth Party Congress to set a new strategic line that would oppose both the superpowers. But when Mao forced Lin Piao, the Army Chief of Staff, and forty other top Chinese generals to choose between the two superpowers, and they chose the Soviet Union, these leaders, by definition, became counterrevolutionaries in an historic social revolution whose purpose was to smash Soviet influence on, and control over, China's destiny. Again and again, the major line struggles throughout the history of the Chinese Communist Party have been between Mao and those who have followed one or another policy line backed by Moscow. If the Chinese have for decades struggled to loose themselves from the Russian embrace, the Russians have been just as determined to exercise their authority.

As a result of the 1970 Lushan Plenum, Ch'en Po-ta, Mao's former secretary and confidant, who had no political base of his own, was cast out of the Party and renamed the "Chinese Trotsky." He had become a "left Russian," just as

Liu Shao-ch'i had become a "right Russian." Marshal Lin Piao, for forty years one of the military and political leaders of the Chinese Revolution, the Chairman's chosen successor, and "closest comrade in arms," presented a more difficult problem. Lin's life was too Chinese, too closely connected with the revolution and the Yenan tradition to end up as Russian. It was claimed that he tried to escape to Russia, a fact which labeled him as a "traitor," but in the end he would be linked with that most ancient of Chinese symbols—Confucius. In the end, only Lin's death could resolve the conflict, and it was many months after his violent death in September 1971 that the Chinese would announce it.

As a result of the victory of Chairman Mao over the Lin-Ch'en opposition, the top cadres in the Foreign Ministry, who had been carefully protected for four years against the formidable assaults of the radicals, returned to power in order to carry out "Chairman Mao's revolutionary foreign policy." Wu Leng-hsi and Chu Mu-chih, the pre-Cultural Revolution editors of the *People's Daily* and the New China News Service, labeled during the movement as top "capitalist-roaders" by all factions, reoccupied their desks so that they could exercise their skills in briefing the correspondents of the *New York Times* and the *Wall Street Journal*. After Lin Piao's death, Ch'en Tsai-tao, the "counterrevolutionary mutineer" at Wuhan, and his deputy in command, Chung Han-hua, were listed among the notables presiding over public and official occasions. Li Ching-ch'uan, the "monster" of Szechuan, Ulanfu, the "revisionist" Party leader of Inner Mongolia, and twenty-six provincial Party secretaries (of whom seventeen would rejoin the provincial secretariats) all returned to positions of power or respectability. T'an Chen-lin, the "counterrevolutionary" symbol of the 1967 Adverse February Current, and Yang Ch'eng-wu, the former Chief of Staff of the PLA associated with the Cultural Revolution counter-current of 1968, were also rehabilitated, while "leftists" were overthrown and disgraced for their identification with the radical policies of the Cultural Revolution.

Had all these targets of the Cultural Revolution remolded

their world outlooks? Perhaps. At least there was no question that they had accepted the Maoist strategic view of China standing as an independent nuclear-armed giant having broken decisively with the Soviet Union and the socialist bloc that the Russians had built. One of the tests for all cadres apparently became whether or not they supported the new strategic view. Teng Hsiao-p'ing, the organizational master in command of the old Liu Shao-ch'i Party machine, was, of course, the supreme symbol of what appeared to be a political trade-off, since it was he who would present China's new world view to the community of nations. Whether or not Mao had exchanged domestic concessions for his new foreign policy, a Faustian bargain which would have to be repaid, only time could reveal.

But neither we nor most of the Chinese people were aware of this new two-line struggle at the top that broke out between the Mao-Chou and Lin-Ch'en forces after the conclusion of the Ninth Party Congress in the spring of 1969. To us, China was still the pariah standing outside the world system of nation states, struggling alone, and aloof with the task of her own reconstruction and the historic effort to eliminate the gaps between mental labor and manual labor, town and country, leaders and led. The months passed slowly as we observed the end of an unprecedented and monumental social movement and disengaged ourselves from a social milieu of which we had become so much a part.

In the fall of 1968, we had once again visited Shanghai, this time to arrange the departure of our two younger sons, who were leaving for home. We did no formal visiting on that trip, but did watch from our hotel window the last upsurge of the factional opposition to the formidable Workers' Rebel Headquarters led by the able young revolutionary cadre Wang Hung-wen. Watching from an eighth-floor window, we had ringside seats to one final, futile effort by street mobs to overturn the revolutionary command in Shanghai. This motley army, directed by leaders from the old Diesel Engine Plant (a pre-revolutionary KMT stronghold), succeeded in rallying all the disparate and ragtail elements of Shanghai society, including children who were paid to hammer nails into the tires of trucks belonging to the fleet under the banner of the Workers' Headquarters. This guerrilla upsurge was finally quashed when the disciplined Shanghai revolutionary workers organized squadrons of trucks loaded with hardhat workers to invade the Diesel Engine Plant and put down the civil war, which had virtually wrecked the factory. The flames of this rather minor Vendée soon flickered out.

A year after waving our oldest son off on the weekly Shanghai to Paris Air France flight, we did the same with the younger two. And when we returned to Peking, aware that the Chinese were now fully engaged in putting their own house in order so that they could face the world on China's own terms, we began to plan our own departure. The Chinese, preoccupied as they were with their own affairs, had little time and less energy to consider how foreign teachers might be integrated into a qualitatively different post-Cultural Revolution future.

During the first six months of 1969, we spent a great deal of time with Anna Louise Strong, whose interest during this period of Chinese absorption in their own affairs had turned toward the struggles taking place in America. Her massive Chinese coffee table was covered with neatly organized piles of journals, underground newspapers, mimeographed newsletters, and personal letters from the myriad organizations in the United States spawned by the overextension of the American empire. Her increasing turn toward the problems of home was representative of the gradual shift in the political concerns of Peking's now small foreign community. Feeling, although not yet seeing, the outlines of China's new world stance, the community of foreign experts and teachers who had chosen to observe and even to act in China's historic drama of the Sixties, were now going home.

Packing cases lined the halls of the sprawling Friendship Hotel. The number of foreign experts from around the world had so shrunk that all could now be housed in only a few buildings of the formerly lively apartment complex. The vacated housing blocks were now hotel to a new kind of guest

—hundreds of high-ranking PLA officers from all over the country. They came to Peking to participate in month-long Mao Tse-tung Thought study sessions which would prepare them for their difficult leadership task in the political reconstruction of thousands of fractured civilian organizations. Their presence among the few remaining international inhabitants of the former home of thousands of Russian experts was a pointed symbolization of China's priorities. When the foreign guests and these groups of senior Army commanders passed each other on our ritual after-dinner walks around the now rather rundown garden, each group would nod in polite greeting to the other. The two worlds of the Friendship Hotel residents touched for a brief and poignant moment one evening as some of the old officers, the soldiers of the revolution, gathered silently around a group of small children from the five continents, and listened with solemn pleasure to the chorus of Chinese with which the children communicated with one another. To the Chinese, so long alone in the world, it was always a source of wonder and delight that anyone else could speak their language, whereas for Americans, it is equally surprising that there is anyone who cannot.

Although the parameters of China's new foreign policy were yet to be officially delineated, we began to sense a new mood in the Chinese people. Shortly after the bloody border clashes between Chinese and Russian troops on the northern border, a documentary film on that short war was shown in the Friendship Hotel, as everywhere else in China. We went one Saturday night to see it.

The audience was made up largely of the workers who performed the still extensive tasks of driving, cooking, carpentry, cleaning around the vast place, and of PLA men, not the old and distinguished officers whom we met on our walks, but the young peasant soldiers who had flooded into every troubled unit in the country. It was an emotionally charged film with its shots of huge Russian tanks and tracked vehicles plowing through groups of unarmed Chinese peasants, who beat on them with fists and sticks, and of Soviet naval gunboats turning their powerful fire hoses on a tiny dinghy with two Chinese fisherman, who fought back with their oars. We had, during our time in China, seen many Chinese war films—those of past Chinese struggles (the Boxer Rebellion, the war with Japan, the Korean War, the fight against Chiang Kai-shek) and those of the current struggles of China's allies, in particular, of course, the Vietnamese. But this was quite different. It was an ongoing Chinese war, an undeclared war in which their unarmed countrymen were being killed, and the customarily quiet Chinese audience responded with an anguish painful to share. Cries of "*Ai yah*," groans of anger and sympathy punctuated the entire film, and the crowd left the auditorium in a noisy storm, their faces dark and eyes narrowed. Ordinarily, no matter how serious the movie, the audience, leaving the theatre, would burst out upon the garden courtyard and clamber aboard their buses laughing and chattering. But on this evening, the grimness of the mood hung undissipated over the crowd.

There was nothing really surprising in the mass response to the Ussuri River documentary, but we soon were made aware that the realities shown there were part of a revised view of the Chinese situation which was clearly not short-term in nature. We had seen in China an infinite number of didactic skits, many of them centering around the Vietnam War. The enemy soldiers, including the representational American GI, were always caricatured in the same way, wearing a red wig, chewing gum, and swaggering nastily. Although we knew from our own experience that the Chinese did not classify foreigners by nationality so much as by "good" and "bad" categories within nationality, we always experienced a moment of discomfort at the justifiably harsh caricature. Our Chinese friends glanced at us uneasily at such moments and then would sometimes comfortingly pat one's hand or try to make an amusing comment on some other subject. The red hair remained a mystery to us until we learned that the red-haired character in Peking Opera who has long represented the evil personage had simply been transmuted into a contemporary "foreign devil." It was consequently with an abrupt shock of comprehension that we found ourselves

seeing for the first time in a similar skit the identical character with his signatory red wig now transformed into a Russian soldier. Such changes, in China, do not occur through
the creative caprice of local playwrights. And so, finally, at
the exhausted end of that enigmatically named "Cultural
Revolution," we were seeing, in the old form, the content of
the new culture.

Although we lived far from the intense realities of Chinese
life in this difficult period, we were aware of some of the
strains. Quite out of the blue, we were invited one evening to
tea and a briefing on the current situation by the newly
formed revolutionary committee of our Institute. There
were to be other successive committees in this school, as in
the many organizations where the attempts to form a new
coalition out of the still burning factionalism would again
and again flounder in the passion of unresolved questions.
But at this time, the public face of the committee was stud-
iedly confident. Their invitation to us, whom they had never
seen before, was clear indication that the PLA team that had
painstakingly put together the new committee was ready to
face the public. Like alien spirits returning home, we climbed
the stairs of the silent building on the east campus, where we
had once rushed through the crowded hallways and from
which we had been so long absent. When we entered the designated classroom, we found seated around the well-worn study
tables the familiar faces of a few English department teachers
and cadres and the new power in the school, the PLA Navy
men. Each place was arranged in the simple school style
which we had come to know so well, with a covered mug of
steaming tea, an apple, and a handful of wrapped candies. It
looked like any number of Institute functions of days past,
but the evening proceeded in an atmosphere different from
that in which we had felt so much at home. Our old colleagues greeted us with smiles, but there was to be no further
opportunity for conversation. The PLA man at the head of
the table, who prefaced his statements with the customary
modest remarks about his inadequate knowledge concerning
the situation in the school, was nonetheless the leading figure

of this compromise coalition. His remarks about the "excellent situation" in the school were general and doctrinaire, a verbal synthesis of many editorials we had read. Neither the pleasantness of his manner nor the general munching of apples seemed to warm the stiffness of the atmosphere. All of the questions politely invited from us were referred to him, and few of our colleagues spoke at all, those who did merely punctuating his statements.

As we were bade a cordial goodnight by our Hung-ch'i colleagues, who seemed truly glad to see us, and our Tsao-fan T'uan colleagues, who surely were not, we were far from convinced of the new unity that had been outlined to us that evening. The problem of imposing the PLA, by definition a command organization, upon the differences generated by several years of free-form politics were obvious even in this brief and superficial encounter. The Army had been the Chairman's ace. Without it, he could not have carried out his Cultural Revolution, but clearly the Army could not run the country, particularly a country so recently exhorted to resist commandism, no matter what benevolent guise it might wear.

The routine trips for foreign experts, along with many of the other amenities once taken for granted, had long been suspended. However, since we were preparing to leave for home, the Institute's new authorities decided that we should embark on a farewell tour which would include the sites of Mao's birth and youth, Shaoshan and Changsha, and his first historic Revolutionary Army base in the Chingkang Mountains. It was a fitting close to our years in China, spent among the violent social and political storms personally initiated and led by Chairman Mao, in a society in which not only the thought of the Chairman, but his presence, through statues, badges, and little red books, dominated every aspect of life. We had experienced the dramatic climax of a half-century revolution; the Chinese now wanted us to learn something about its beginning.

As we drove through the brilliantly green Hunan countryside, past the substantial yellow houses made of local clay, and crossed the broad rivers that crisscross the province under over-arching skies, we were aware for the first time of the roots of Mao Tse-tung the poet, the romantic revolutionary. We sat on a stone wall at the end of Orange Island among the tough and humorous fisherfolk who still live there as they did when young Mao was a Changsha student, and looked out at the vast Li River. We felt something not quite comprehensible in Peking of the visionary student who had swum in this fierce river and written:

> *Alone in the autumn cold*
> *I scan the river that flows northward*
> *Past the Orange Islet*
> *And the mountains crimson*
> *With the red leaves of the woods.*
> *On this broad stream of rich green water*
> *A hundred boats race with the currents*
> *Eagles dart across the wide sky,*
> *Fish swim in the shallows—*
> *All display their freedom in the frosty air.*
> *Bewildered by the immensity,*
> *I ask the vast grey earth: "Who decides men's destinies?"*
>
> *I brought hither hundreds of companions*
> *In those turbulent months and years.*
> *We were fellow students*
> *Then in our lissom youth.*
> *In the true manner of scholars*
> *We accused without fear or favor,*
> *Pointed at these rivers and ranges,*
> *And wrote vibrant words,*
> *Valuing marquisates as dust.*
> *Do you not remember*
> *How in mid-stream our boats struck currents*
> *And were slowed down by torrents?*[129]

Mao's poetic theme of 1926 was indeed strangely prophetic of the recent years in China when he, now himself the one who "decides men's destinies," would find once again that his boat had struck currents in mid-stream. It was in Changsha that the young Mao had become a thinker, had studied under the professors who would lead him to new ideas, to the history of the world outside China. However, the claim of the people of Changsha upon the philosopher-soldier-poet-leader of the Chinese Revolution rests easily on those who are accustomed to think of their city as an intellectual center which has produced remarkable men and women for centuries.

It is in Mao's birthplace, Shaoshan, a mountain village some miles distant from Changsha, that one finds the Lourdes of China. It is a shrine purified of all traces of ambiguous reality. There, Mao's rich peasant father has been transmuted into an "ordinary peasant," a category unknown to Mao's own explicit class analysis. The same authoritarian father against whom the great rebel exhibited some of his earliest rebelliousness is now sanctified as the most benevolent of parents. It was a distressing climax to the years of questioning, skepticism, and public examination of historical records and secret documents to encounter here hagiography more rigid than ever before.

In the Chingkang Mountains, one relived the earliest battles of Mao's first revolutionary peasant army on mountain precipices and now empty and peaceful meadows. The remembered history, told with great pride by local guides in these still isolated mountains, was deeply moving, but in the museum, which neatly summarized it all, one's sense of history was offended by the absence of any of the multitude of great figures of the time except for Mao and Lin Piao. Now, no doubt, Mao stands entirely alone to receive the accolades of a grateful people who, by the thousands, go to Chingkangshan as to Valley Forge. However, the real accomplishments of the Chinese Revolution and of Mao's singular contributions to it are evident not so much through the historical testimony of battlefields and buildings, but, as in all of China, through the lives of those now living. Perhaps Mao himself expressed most accurately the true significance of his birthplace, Shaoshan, when he returned there in 1959 and wrote:

*I curse the time that has flowed past*
*Since the dimly-remembered dream of my departure*
*From home, thirty-two years ago.*

*With red pennons, the peasants lifted their lances;*
*In their black hands, the rulers held up their whips.*
*Lofty emotions were expressed in self-sacrifice:*
*So the sun and moon were asked to give a new face to heaven.*
*In delight I watch a thousand waves of growing rice and beans,*
*And heroes everywhere going home in the smoky sunset.*[130]

We were also to find on this trip that that stormy and complex phenomenon, the Great Proletarian Cultural Revolution, was now in the process of canonization. Many of the remarkable achievements which, in 1964, had been credited to the Chinese Revolution were now attributed solely to the Cultural Revolution. We were startled to hear from various individuals that they had never been self-critical, had never done manual labor, had never been aware of the peasants, had never thought of serving the people before the awakening experience of the Cultural Revolution. Perhaps they were a breed of person whom we had never encountered before the Cultural Revolution, for we had previously met no one to whom these ideas would have come as revelations.

In our final visit to Shanghai, where we had seldom encountered dogmatism dominating realism, we once again felt that we were walking on comprehensible ground. We asked to spend our considerable time there talking with revolutionary committees, and our request could not have been more thoroughly fulfilled. We met morning, afternoon, and evening with committees representing small workshops and enormous factories, and although it was clearly impossible in these briefings for us to be told the different but equally complicated stories of the struggles in each unit, we received a very clear sense of the varying degrees of success that had been achieved. If one were to analyze the success of the Cultural Revolution, one would find in the entire country, we believe, what we found in Shanghai in the summer of 1969— that in some organizations, there had been considerable advances in new work relationships, new power relationships, and, most importantly perhaps, new ways of thinking about problems. In other organizations, matters were very confused and the final results as yet far from clear, with factional bit-

terness still so intense that a stranger could sense it upon
entering the room. In still other units, things were more or
less the same as they had always been, except for the replacement of certain leaders with others of a not very dissimilar
kind. Mao has taught the Chinese people that wherever human and social differences exist, there will always be struggle. No doubt the uneven results of the Cultural Revolution
that we saw in Shanghai were what he would have expected
any sensible person to have assumed from the beginning.

In Nanking, we were to encounter what we felt to be the
best and the worst of the great social experiment. In one elec-
tronics plant, we saw working relationships which seemed
superior to any we had encountered before. In every department into which we walked unannounced, workers and technicians were deeply involved in intense discussion, their
informality and enthusiasm giving the entire plant the air of
a giant research project staffed with volunteer workers. On
the other hand, we met in one of Nanking's huge chemical
plants the most arrogant cadre we had encountered in China
—a young man catapulted to the top by the political waves of
the Cultural Revolution. He was a living, breathing example
of Mao's warning that this was fundamentally a movement to
change men's thinking, that if that were not done, the present
Cultural Revolution might overthrow 2,000 or 3,000 revisionist leaders only to have 10,000 the next time around.

Our final departure, in the early days of November 1969,
was the occasion for a great show of unity, as teacher friends,
long absent students, and cadres from both sides of the factional divide joined PLA Navy men to bid us farewell on the
wintry field of Peking Airport. There was more unspoken
than spoken between ourselves and those we knew best. It
seemed a long time since we had seen each other almost
daily. Their concerns were still very difficult ones, and only a
few of them could have imagined when they urged us to
return to Peking that visits by Americans would soon be commonplace.

The great wrench that transfers one from China to the
West does not come at the end of the line on the weekly

Shanghai to Paris Air France flight, but in the Shanghai air-port. As one leaves the custody of the smiling and ingenuous Chinese stewardesses in their baggy cotton uniforms, little red books in pockets, braids down their backs, for their elegantly coiffed and tailored French counterparts, one has already changed worlds.

*Chapter XII*

# The New World View:
# Great Disorder Under Heaven

WE RESUMED LIFE in the United States in 1970. The historical waves which had washed over the country during our five-year absence had decisively altered the social contours of the land. During that crucial half decade, the American landscape reflected the fires of her central cities and echoed the sounds of a politics punctuated by political assassination. As early as 1966, Mao Tse-tung, following his strategic intuition, staked a great deal on his belief that the United States was a declining imperialism. In another decade, as America approached her revolutionary bicentennial, it was a view that would find greater acceptance.

During our readjustment to the rhythms of our own society, we, now the detached spectators, watched the two separate and polar worlds we had come to know gravitate toward each other, share for a time a mutual orbit, and connect. The *New York Times* reported the death of Anna Louise Strong, and we heard about the memorial meeting in Peking at which Premier Chou and other Chinese leaders paid their last respects to the "progressive American writer and friend of the Chinese people." She had written us one last letter asking for our assessment of the rigors of the plane flight home so that she might determine whether she might also make one last trip to the land where her ancestors had been pioneers. But it was too late. She was buried on the outskirts of Peking near the grave of her old friend Agnes Smedley, another extraordinary American woman who had supported the Chinese Revolution from the beginning.

Of the trio of American writers who over the decades had brought news of the Chinese Revolution to an uninformed world, only Edgar Snow remained. He would live just long enough to carry out one last mission which would contribute to the journey to Peking of Richard Nixon and Henry Kissinger. Praise for the New China would then flow from the pens of Joseph Alsop, James Reston, and finally William Randolph Hearst, Jr. Their writing would reflect the evolving perception in Washington that, in light of the Sino–Soviet conflict, China had ceased to be a threat and might well become an asset in the US effort to redress the global balance.

No longer guests in the Chinese house sharing the insights of the family members as they contested with one another, we now joined the myriad observers who watched that struggle from afar. Outsiders who share the visions but not the practical reality of a people involved in revolution tend to force their own visionary symmetry on a distant political process which, for the participants, constitutes a necessary disorder upon which social laws force their own end. Even so, the transformation of a politics of liberation, that heaven-storming art of the impossible, into the more familiar and mundane politics of interest comes as a shock. The demand for symmetry takes on a tenacious hold; the Nixon visit to Peking jarred aesthetically as well as politically, the product of some deformed logic of history. Mao Tse-tung, it may be argued, is not responsible for the world system of nation states, but at the same time it is equally true that the great revolution of the East has not yet begun to transcend that system. In the world, as within the nation, a politics of interest begets a politics of interest. It would seem that, a century after Marx defined the world as a system divided vertically by class, the horizontal division of the earth by unequally endowed states stands entrenched as a formidable factor determining historic outcomes. When the great states converse, the world listens, and as Kissinger and Nixon walked onto the Chinese stage, it was apparent to us that, in the future, insight into the nature of the new world configuration might require more dependence on the mind and less on the heart.

After the Ninth Party Congress, politics and power in

China once again flowed to the top, where the victors repeated the experience of previous revolutions by turning on one another. Chairman Mao defeated the Lin-Ch'en opposition at the August 1970 Central Committee Plenum held at Lushan. Ch'en Po-ta was purged, but it would take another year and a violent end to resolve conclusively the more crucial question of Lin Piao, who stood as Chairman Mao's legal successor. Mao later explained that Lin and Ch'en had tried to seize power at the Lushan Plenum by naming Lin as State Chairman and had organized "surprise attacks and underground activities" against the Chairman's strategic line.[131]

Mao Tse-tung's victory over his opponents at Lushan allowed him to move rapidly to implement his new look in foreign policy. Within a month after the closing of the Lushan Plenum, Edgar Snow conveniently arrived in Peking for another of his historic conversations with Mao, the last in a series which had spanned four decades.

Snow was called over during the October 1, 1970 National Day Parade to have his picture taken with Chairman Mao. The picture was held until the Chairman's birthday on December 26, when it was printed on the front page of the *People's Daily* as a signal to the Chinese people and the world of the emerging relationship between the United States and China. The message Mao gave to Snow to transmit to Washington was more explicit than the picture. In Snow's words, the Chairman told him:

> ". . . If the Soviet Union wouldn't do [point the way], then he would place his hopes on the American people. The United States had a population of more than two hundred million people. Industrial production was already higher than in any other country, and education was universal. He would be happy to see a party emerge there to lead a revolution, although he was not expecting that in the near future.
>
> In the meantime, he said, the foreign ministry was studying the matter of admitting Americans from the left, the middle, and the right to visit China. Should rightists like Nixon, who represented the monopoly capi-

talists, be permitted to come? He should be welcomed because, Mao explained, at present the problems between China and the USA would have to be solved with Nixon. Mao would be happy to talk with him, either as a tourist or as President."[132]

While the State Department had not been interested in what Snow had to say in 1965, President Nixon and his National Security Advisor Kissinger, after more than half a decade of disasters in Vietnam, must have been extremely interested in Snow's 1970 message. Within a year of its delivery, Edgar Snow succumbed to cancer. At his bedside to ease his last days was a team of Chinese physicians, including his old friend George Ma, whom Snow himself had introduced to the Chinese communists in the Yenan period.

However, it was not until the winter of 1971 that the new foreign policy put together by Chairman Mao and Premier Chou bore its first fruits. The Chinese waited until the North Vietnamese dealt their smashing defeat to the American-sponsored invasion of Laos before making a decisive move to test Sino–American relations. Mao then gave the signal for the now historic ping-pong diplomacy to begin. In July, after a long American press campaign heralding the new relations between the two great powers, Nixon announced his intention of visiting China. Nixon's July 6 speech in Kansas City must have pleased Chairman Mao and Premier Chou as much as it displeased Lin Piao and a faction of Chinese generals, since the speech appeared to confirm Mao's assessment of the United States as a waning imperialism. The American President announced that the world now consisted of five major powers, the United States, the Soviet Union, China, Europe, and Japan. The new Nixon formula suggested that the bipolar era was over and that China should be dealt into the game. Referring in gloomy tones to the challenges which faced the United States, Nixon said that when he viewed the classical architecture of Washington he was reminded of the decadence which had brought down Greece and Rome:

"Sometimes, when I see those columns, I think of seeing them in Greece and Rome and I think of what happened to Greece and Rome, and you see only what is left of great civilizations in the past—as they became wealthy, as they lost their will to live, to improve, they became subject to the decadence that destroys the civilization. The United States is reaching that period."[133]

At the very time when Chou and Kissinger were engaged in talks outlining the new relationship between the two countries, Lin Piao and Chief of Staff Huang Yung-sheng fought to prevent implementation of the Sino–US détente. Anti-American editorials appeared in the *People's Daily* to underline the fact that the Chinese leadership was far from united on Chairman Mao's new world strategy.

The showdown between the Mao-Chou forces and Lin Piao, backed by forty of China's senior generals, occurred within a few months after the Kissinger visit. Having lost in a major policy struggle, Lin, his wife Yeh Ch'un, and their son, were, according to the official Chinese account, killed as "they fled on September 12 toward the Soviet Union on a plane which crashed in the People's Republic of Mongolia." The Chinese statement on the Lin Piao affair was issued on July 28, 1972, after ten months of official silence. It declared that Lin Piao during "the Great Proletarian Cultural Revolution [ . . . ] appeared to support the thought of Mao Tse-tung and make propaganda in favor of this thought. He was thus able to hoodwink the masses to become in their eyes the successor of Chairman Mao Tse-tung. But," the statement asserted, "he was a double-faced man who was in reality opposed to the revolutionary line of Mao Tse-tung and to the revolutionary foreign policy worked out by him, especially after the Ninth Party Congress." Lin died, according to the Chinese account, after an "attempted coup d'état," in which he had "tried to assassinate Mao Tse-tung."[134]

In Mao's view, the United States, "sated with bread and sleep," as he had once put it, still possessed great technological and economic power and might well, in its own interest, share with China a desire to discourage the expansionism of the "New Tsars" threatening China from the north. It was a concept quite familiar to ancient China and to Emperor T'ai

Tsung of the T'ang dynasty, who believed it wise to "ally oneself with those who are far off against those who are near at hand." The Chinese would not again emphasize the question of foreign policy as a major basis for the differences between Mao and Lin. In the future, tens of thousands of words would be devoted to the subject of Lin Piao, but few would ever again be as precise or unambiguous as this first strained explanation to the world of the fate of Chairman Mao's "closest comrade in arms and successor." It was a startling end to what had been an unparalleled social movement. With the exit of Lin Piao and Ch'en Po-ta, the stage was set for Nixon and Kissinger.

We watched with strangely mixed emotions as television brought us the view of President Nixon and his entourage in Peking. Again and again in the months which followed, we would see some of our closest Chinese teaching colleagues and former students performing professionally as interpreters for the leading statesmen of the Western world. The American press campaign was skillfully orchestrated to overcome any major opposition to the opening to China. It was an opposition which soon proved not to exist. The press reflected the euphoria of an American establishment which had discovered a new option when all others had run out in Vietnam. If the empire was overextended and a retreat called for, then, by manipulation of the Sino–Soviet conflict, the United States could perhaps wield its power by other means. As the enthusiastic procession of American politicians, bankers, journalists, professors, doctors, and actors made the pilgrimage to Peking for a first view of the mysterious People's Republic, the feeling appeared to grow among at least some of the American elite that maybe China had not been lost after all. Samuel Casey, Jr., President of Pullman Incorporated, in an expression of unabashed optimism concerning the possibilities of trade with China, told a *New York Times* reporter: "We'll do fine with China. Their type of socialism is most exciting to us . . . We have a great conviction that the PRC has a greater profit potential than the Soviet."[135] Pictures on the financial pages of the American press revealed a smiling

David Rockefeller in a flowered sports shirt standing among a group of genial and equally informally attired Chinese bankers who had just negotiated ties between Chase Manhattan and the Bank of China. Yet the Peking the American elite encountered in the Seventies was no longer the semicolony which they had left in the late Forties. Henry Kissinger, after sitting in Mao's study, said later that Mao "conveyed this impressive atmosphere of tremendous power." After reviewing the transcript of the conversation between Nixon and Mao, Kissinger found the words of the Chairman to read "like the overture of a Wagnerian opera."[136]

Thus it was that China, by reshaping the Marxist–Leninist belief system appropriated from the West, reemerged as a great civilization state to take her place as one of the major world powers. The United States, the most powerful military state in the world, had been forced to deal with the People's Republic of China as an equal. There is little to indicate that the leaders of either powerful state were deceived by the trappings accompanying the exploitation of mutual interests. Kissinger hoped to use Peking as leverage against the Russians, and Mao was extrapolating to the world of nations from his protracted experience in manipulating the contradictions between Chinese warlords in order to establish stable base areas for his guerrilla armies. The same formula— "Make use of contradictions, win over the many, oppose the few, and defeat our enemies one by one"—guided the new Chinese international strategy as it had directed the internal communist strategy over the decades. Since contention rather than détente between the US and the USSR was, in the Chinese view, a social law of history, the Chinese probably felt they could hardly be faulted for exacerbating an elemental process. The Chinese Red Army had guaranteed communist independence in the national united front of the Thirties and Forties. In the Seventies, Chinese independence, in whatever coalition it might seek to form, would be guaranteed by nuclear weapons, guided missiles, and underground tunnels.

Who could have predicted that Teng Hsiao-p'ing would have been assigned the task of presenting China's new world view to the United Nations in the spring of 1974? Teng, excoriated during the Cultural Revolution for his pragmatic approach to the increase of private peasant plots during the "hard years" of the early Sixties, an approach symbolized by his famous statement "Black cats or white cats, as long as they catch mice, it's all right," was now needed for that very pragmatism in the world arena. And so it was Teng, the General Secretary of the Liu Shao-ch'i Party machine, who would proclaim from the UN rostrum in New York to an audience conditioned by a quarter-century of the cold war: "The socialist camp which existed for a time after World War II is no longer in existence." The world of social classes and the revolutionary coalition of communist parties and their allies against US imperialism, in the new Chinese view, had turned into a world of sovereign nations. That which divided the world, according to the Chinese analysis, was no longer capitalism and socialism but the conflict between national sovereignty and imperialism. The Chinese hoped to fashion a world-wide united front made up of those ready to oppose the superpowers of whatever social system.

China's new strategic view of the world as outlined by Teng was unique:

> ". . . The world today actually consists of three parts, or three worlds, that are interconnected and in contradiction with one another. The United States and the Soviet Union make up the First World. The developing countries in Asia, Africa, Latin America, and other regions make up the Third World. The developed countries between the two make up the Second World.
>
> The two superpowers, the United States and the Soviet Union, are vainly seeking world hegemony. Each in its own way attempts to bring the developing countries of Asia, Africa, and Latin America under its control and, at the same time, to bully the developed countries that are not their match in strength."[137]

Teng defined China as a "socialist country and a developing country as well" and stated that "China belongs to the Third World" and "is not a superpower, nor will she ever seek to be one." Whether most developing countries would consider China, a nuclear power ranking as the third most powerful military nation in the world and a permanent member of the UN Security Council, part of the third world was open to question. But that China offered to them a model of development more applicable than that of the industrial nations was unarguable.

Teng described contemporary international relations as reflecting a condition of drastic change. "The whole world is in turbulence and unrest. The situation is one of 'great disorder under heaven' as we Chinese put it." At the end of his speech, Teng Hsiao-p'ing told the assembled delegates that if one day China " . . . should change her color and turn into a superpower [ . . . ] the people of the world should identify her as social-imperialism, expose it, oppose it, and work together with the Chinese people to overthrow it." This was a revision of a similar statement heard in China in 1964, when the Chinese belonged to an international world of communist and revolutionary parties and proclaimed that if ever the Chinese Party turned into a revisionist party, the rest of the revolutionaries in the world must struggle against her.

The principle to which all other principles were subordinated in the new Chinese world view was national sovereignty, and it was under this standard that China would now march. It was this principle, not one of internationalism, that was dramatically symbolized in the gift that Ch'iao Kuan-hua presented to the UN from his country in October 1974. The gift, a giant tapestry of the Great Wall, now hangs in the delegates' lounge, exemplifying, as it has always exemplified, the inviolability of China's sovereignty, with particular reference to her neighbor in the North. China's message to the world was as simple as it was ancient—through self-reliance, replicate the Chinese experience. It was only natural that those who responded most fervently to China's new global stature and world view were millions of overseas Chinese, minorities facing discrimination in alien territories, who now embarked on pilgrimages to the homeland in order to associate themselves with a socialism they had not previously understood.

Henry Kissinger, in his address to the United Nations General Assembly in the fall of 1974, appeared to be in remarkable agreement with the Chinese evaluation of the state of the world. It was, he said, "a world ever more torn between rich and poor, East and West, producer and consumer; a world where local crises threaten global confrontation and where the spreading atom threatens global peril; a world of rising costs and dwindling supplies, of growing populations and declining production."[138] And Kissinger's analysis of this disordered world under heaven was further darkened by the prognosis of a general world depression which might sweep the capitalist world.

China's diplomats worked tirelessly to consolidate the newly-won legitimacy for the Chinese Revolution which had been wrested from a capitalist world system led by the United States. During this same period, when China was taking her place as a major power in the international system, the pattern of domestic politics forged in the fires of the Cultural Revolution continued to evolve within a context of heightened political sophistication. For more than three years after Lin Piao's death, a massive campaign was undertaken by the new leadership coalition to reconcile a positive evaluation of the Cultural Revolution with a condemnation of some of its main leaders. A return to the study of the Marxist–Leninist classics and the rejection of the little red book of Mao quotations marked aspects of the new campaign. Lin Piao, as the father of the red book and the Mao cult, was condemned for his "a priori idealism," a charge usually associated with an attack on leftists who try to skip historical stages, fail to cope with historical reality, and seek shortcuts to theoretical understanding. The new charges echoed some of the Russian criticisms of the Chinese communes and the Cultural Revolution for violating the objective laws of history through the substitution of consciousness for historically determined factors. Many of the excesses of the Cultural Revolution, including the worst aspects of the Mao cult, were corrected and put into perspective as the Chinese wrestled with the problem of summing up the experience of the greatest political movement in China's revolutionary history.

Difficulties in establishing a credible political line on the Lin Piao affair confronted leaders who wavered between condemning Lin as an ultra-leftist or as a rightist. There were, no doubt, many supporters of the overthrow of the Lin-Ch'en clique who interpreted that struggle as a repudiation of the Cultural Revolution itself, and again it was probably hard to sort them out. Perhaps it was for this reason that Lin was finally condemned as a rightist, labeled as a representative of the overthrown landlord and gentry class, and presented as the modern symbol of the feudal ideology of Confucius. The length and intensity of the P'i Lin, P'i K'ung campaign was apparently rooted in the reluctance of the masses to accept it all. Such a reluctance, if indeed it existed, might have stemmed not so much from the love of the masses for Vice Chairman Lin Piao, as from a determination not to be made the fools of history.

The return of the Chinese full circle to the great debates of the 1919 May 4 Movement and its historical criticism of Confucius was not fortuitous. It was one more sign that China had irrevocably severed her Russian connection and the ideology of the international movement which the Russians had founded. Reworking of the Chinese world view could once again proceed in the context of China's own history. The nation was ready to return to the study of Marxism as interpreted by the Chinese in an internal debate in which all the participants shared the same cultural referents.

That debate, however, was governed by the contention among political forces unleashed by the Great Proletarian Cultural Revolution of the 1960s. The very Chineseness of the new campaign against the political legacy of Confucius precluded its having much relevance to the outside world. Moreover, the Aesopian thrust to the new attacks on current leaders must have strained even the Chinese capacity for unraveling esoteric struggles among political contestants. The criticism of Confucius for his restoration of the feudal lords to power appeared to be a disguised attack on Premier Chou for returning national power to the old Party veterans. The Premier, an unsurpassed master in the political arena, deflected the attacks with his usual finesse. Once the campaign against Confucius was subordinated to the attack on Lin Piao, it proved difficult for the anti-Chou En-lai forces to forge a coherent ideological line in order to renew old struggles.

As the nation gradually recovered from the trauma of the Lin Piao crisis, a slow but steady effort was made to reconstruct governmental and administrative organs which could deal effectively with pressing social and economic problems. Gradually, the Party and government organization were rebuilt, often through compromises among contending ideological and political groupings. Loose ends were tied up, and many problems left in the wake of the social turmoil of the Sixties were at least temporarily resolved. One of these was the problem of the foreign community, which had been left in abeyance while the Chinese leaders occupied themselves with larger affairs.

On March 8, 1973, the remaining foreign experts who had participated in the Chinese Cultural Revolution were called to a meeting at the Great Hall of the People, where the Party's policy for the treatment of foreigners was explained by Premier Chou En-lai. Besides the Premier, the hosts included Chiang Ch'ing, Chang Ch'un-ch'iao, Yao Wen-yuan, Wang Hung-wen, Liao Ch'eng-chih, Ch'iao Kuan-hua, and others. Explaining why Chairman Mao's instruction of September 8, 1966 that "revolutionary foreign experts and their children should be treated exactly as the Chinese if they so wish" had not been carried out since 1968, the Premier stated that the mistreatment of foreign experts during the Cultural Revolution was due to excesses in the movement caused by the subversive actions of Lin Piao and his "anti-Party clique." Some of these wrongs were discovered earlier and some later, the Premier told his audience.

Chou listed a number of categories of people who had been mistreated. The first was those who had been cold-shouldered or made to feel unwelcome, and he listed some of their names. The second category included those who were treated discourteously before they left, and this included ourselves. "If they wish," the Premier said, "they are welcome to come back, so that we can make up for the mistake of not looking after them well." The next category of foreigners mentioned by the Premier were those who in the course of taking an active part in the Cultural Revolution had become entangled in the subversive activities of some "bad elements." Sidney Rittenberg was named by the Premier as one of these bad elements. Then the Premier went on to discuss the affair of Ch'en Li-ning and said that the plot involving Rittenberg, Wang Li, Kuan Feng, and Ch'i Pen-yü was unearthed through the play *Madman of the Modern Age*. Rittenberg's subsequent arrest, according to the Premier, involved some foreign friends—Israel Epstein, Michael Shapiro, and Elsie Cholmeley who had been taken in and deceived. He said that it had taken a long time to sort out their case, but now they were free and on behalf of the Chinese Government he expressed his apologies to the three who were present.

The case of David Crook, Chou stated, was a different matter. Some of the masses thought there were genuine grounds for being suspicious of him. But actually, the Premier said, the Foreign Languages Institute at the time Crook was captured was under the control of the Rebel Regiment, which had had May 16 elements as its backers. Liu Ling-k'ai and such people were to blame, and it was now clear that these heads of the Rebel Regiment were May 16 elements. Not only had Wang Li, Kuan Feng, and Ch'i Pen-yü had a hand in the Crook case, Chou said, but Lin Piao and Ch'en Po-ta had as well. Stating that the case was now cleared up and David Crook free, the Premier expressed the apologies of the Chinese Government to him.

Chou also referred to Bethune-Yenan as "a very good organization" which had split into two factions, with confusion occurring in its ranks and contradictions among the people changing into contradictions between the people and the enemy. Explaining that the Central Committee of the Party had made the decision to remove the foreigners from the Cultural Revolution in January 1968 because "some had supported this faction and some that, and then you have these bad people stirring up trouble," Chou went on to say that it had been five years or more since this decision was made, separating the political life of the foreign friends from that of the Chinese people. On behalf of the Government and the Central Committee of the Chinese Communist Party, he expressed his apologies to all the foreign experts.[139] Following the pattern of settlement in most Chinese organizations, the movement among the foreigners concluded with the enemy narrowed down to one symbolic figure—in this case Sidney Rittenberg. The Peking public struggle meeting attended by more than 10,000 people against Yao Teng-shan for his "counterrevolutionary" role in the Foreign Ministry plot confirmed the probability that there could be little hope for the rehabilitation of those involved in the May 16 conspiracy.

There was a historical consistency to the fact that the two men who had simultaneously participated in the founding of the Chinese Communist Party in Shanghai and Paris in 1921 presided, more than a half-century later, over the Tenth Party Congress in August 1973, which laid the basis for turning the revolution and the nation over to the next generation. Mao Tse-tung and Chou En-lai stand as living symbols of the dialectic of revolutionary social forces and administrative efficiency which produced the new China. Although there have undoubtedly been tensions between these two men, they have worked in tandem through every crisis in the long decades of the making of modern China, and history will associate their names above any others with the Chinese Revolution.

In political terms, the Tenth Congress represented a coalition of power which included representatives of the major social groupings in the world's most populous country. The old Party veterans, the Army, the workers, peasants, intellectuals, youth, and women were all represented, though not equally. Lin Piao and Ch'en Po-ta were officially cast into oblivion, the new foreign policy validated, and a new Party constitution adopted. History will record that it was the Tenth Party Congress and not the Ninth which marked the official close of the Great Proletarian Cultural Revolution. Perhaps the most significant action of the Tenth Party Congress was the reestablishment of the vanguard party, which, it was stated, "must exercise leadership in everything." Like Newton's formulations in physics, Lenin's vanguard party construct was founded on an indestructible logic. A party is either a vanguard or it is not; it is a concept that brooks no compromise. Revolutionary committees continued to exist as administrative bodies, but policy was made elsewhere. Eight million new members, presumably activists of the Cultural Revolution, were admitted into the Party, while the institution of the cultural revolution was written into the New Party constitution: "Revolutions like this will have to be carried out many times in the future."

The next few years saw a continuation of the national debate over the meaning of the Cultural Revolution and specific campaigns to condemn cadres who had connived to bring about the entrance of their children to universities through the back door. Chou En-lai, apparently again under attack, finally retired to the privacy of a hospital room and put together the Fourth National People's Congress, which met from January 13 to 17, 1975. Chairman Mao, having taken up residence in his native Hunan city of Changsha, was absent from the Congress. However, the Chairman demonstrated his continuing active role by meeting with the West German anti-Soviet politician Franz Joseph Strauss while the People's Congress was in session.

The coalition of Party, Army, and Shanghai Cultural Revolution leaders was reaffirmed at the Fourth People's Congress. The seventy-year-old Teng Hsaio-p'ing was named not only a Vice Chairman of the Party but was made Chief of Staff of the Army to make clear that the Party was once again controlling the gun. Chang Ch'un-ch'iao emerged as one of the most formidable political leaders in the nation, and Ch'en Yung-kuei, the much beloved peasant leader and salt of the Tachai earth, was named a Vice Minister of the Government and elevated to high posts in the Party. After the Congress, Ch'en traveled abroad as a roving ambassador of good will. The Congress solved the question of succession in a characteristically practical Chinese fashion by abolishing the office of the Chairman of the People's Republic.

Mao's personal demand, accepted by the Congress, that the right to strike be written into the constitution of the Republic stands as one of the final efforts of a revolutionary giant to institutionalize concepts of uninterrupted revolution and struggle from below. Reports of strikes by steel, mine, and transportation workers in the fall of 1974 indicate that the Chinese workers have not forgotten that they were promised a share of the nation's power. If that power should be denied them, they are prepared to fight for it.

Wang Hung-wen, the young Shanghai worker-cadre propelled into national leadership by the great rebellion of the Sixties, stated the unspoken feelings of the Chinese people in a speech to Party cadres when he said that the Cultural Revolution was a rather complex affair which he termed "a mixed kettle of fish." In the future, there was every indication that the struggle would be between those Party officials who had close ties with the masses and those more interested in consolidating their own power. The Chinese masses, educated in the great battles of the Sixties, are no longer as passive as some Peking editorial writers might wish, and there are few in China today who are unable to detect the manipulation of ideology for interest or lack the ability to decipher a politics cloaked in doctrinal verbiage. Continued struggle from below marks the transformation of the Chinese polity. This has been a legacy of Mao Tse-tung which will be difficult to revoke. The central authorities may prefer calm, but the wind will not subside.

For over 200 years, the ideals, concepts, and methods for a humane, rational, and effective social order have been generated by the great revolutions in history. It was during these brief but extraordinary periods that the people of various nations arose to debate and struggle over the most basic values of the society they wished to create. In terms of practical accomplishments, no revolution has ever measured up to the ideals it has proclaimed, a factor contributing to the disillusionment as well as the hope of its supporters. But somehow the great revolutions, despite their brevity, forge those ideas which nourish societies for centuries. Perhaps, besides their structural transformations, the concepts which revolutions pass on to future generations stand as their greatest accomplishment.

The Chinese Revolution, the first great political and social revolution of the East, after a half-century of revolutionary transformation, generated the concept of continuous revolution. For the first time in history, seventeen years after the seizure of power by representatives of the revolutionary class, those leaders called upon the masses to rebel against, to repudiate, and to criticize those in power who failed to serve the people. The Chinese Cultural Revolution of the Sixties extended the concept of equality, first spread by the American and French revolutions and noted by De Tocqueville as an irreversible idea, to the vision of wiping out the age-old differences between mental and manual labor, town and country, leaders and led. Karl Marx recognized long ago that the state is founded upon the contradiction between public and private life. Mao Tse-tung has shown that those appointed to serve the public interest may use their positions of trust for private gain and that even leaders brought to power by popular revolutions may become a class in their own right, utilizing political as well as economic power to exploit another class. Both Marx and Mao would agree that the key question facing society is who is to educate the educators, and the Chinese Cultural Revolution was the first social movement in history to attempt to put into practice the concept that leaders must become pupils of the masses and must be criticized and supervised by those who are led.

Every modern revolution, although national in form, has produced universal ideas, and the Chinese peasant revolution of this century, so different in content, structure, and style from Western revolutions, has generated ideas more relevant to the West than might have been expected. Because of centuries of Chinese experience with the bureaucratic state, their revolution has been logically an anti-bureaucratic revolution. The Cultural Revolution came at a time in history when the West was passing through the last stages of what had been a market economy into a world of bureaucratized administration, production, and control. This new system has been heralded by its advocates as the most rational means of exercising control over human beings, a system which, by its very nature, excludes the possibility of any other social organization. But more and more of those human beings controlled by the system, especially the young, are beginning to ask whether there may be other ways of running a modern technological society. As all modern nations move toward centralized and bureaucratized administration, it is not enough just to seize political control over the machinery. The problem cries for far-reaching structural reform of the apparatus itself, guaranteeing that policy inputs come from below as well as from above. Today the slogan "Democratize the bureaucracy" may seem a contradiction in terms; tomorrow it may become the battle cry of an advanced politics.

Though the great revolutions have produced universal concepts, they have all been a part of that historical process of creating strong, independent, and sovereign nation states. It is the contradiction between the universality of revolutionary ideas and the separateness of national revolution that constitutes a great dilemma of modern times. The units of the world system obey the nonrevolutionary law of national interest and power. China's Cultural Revolution was the final act in a long process which, though generating universal concepts, served as the political cauldron for forging an independent and modern Chinese nation beholden to none and ready to compete with the largest states in the game of nations.

It was a game to which China would bring her centuries-long diplomatic skills in political counterbalance, and which would find expression as much in the sayings of her traditional wisdom as in the Marxist terminology of recent years. Vice Premier Teng Hsiao-p'ing reminded the Philippines' President Ferdinand Marcos of the danger of "letting the tiger in through the back door while repelling the wolf from the front gate,"[140] while warning him, along with the leaders of other nations, of the dangers of a US military withdrawal from Asia. To the Vietnamese, whose recent victory might be interpreted, at least in part, as an astute handling of "letting the [Soviet] tiger in through the back door while repelling the [US] wolf from the front gate," it was a warning that must have seemed irrelevant. To the June 1975 Havana meeting of Latin American communist parties, for whom the US wolf at their front gate could be tolerated only at the greatest risk, China's maintenance of diplomatic links with the Chilean junta was interpreted as an alliance with the wolf.[141] In a world characterized by the Chinese as a "great disorder under heaven," each revolutionary people would follow its own line and go its own way.

The Chinese behind their Great Wall are well insulated from the storms threatening international upheaval. Their twenty-five years of hard work, sacrifice, and self-reliance seem to have borne fruit in the nick of historical time. Alone among the developing nations, they have achieved self-sufficiency in food, have one of the world's most stable currencies, owe no internal or long-term foreign debt, possess a health care system unsurpassed by any nonindustrial nation and few industrial ones, and have instituted a highly effective birth control program. Suddenly, the Chinese method of agricultural development, despised for so long by those technologists who put industrial growth before the organization of people, is the newly discovered model which starving nations will have to emulate in order to survive.

During that quarter-century of economic boycott and nuclear blackmail, there was no Chinese, working hard and possessing little, who did not from time to time renew his spirit with yet another reading or recitation of Mao Tse-tung's cherished version of the fable of "The Foolish Old Man Who Removed the Mountains." As they performed the herculean hand labor which produced the life-giving irrigation systems now crisscrossing the country, or as they simply worked patiently at whatever task the revolution assigned them, there were millions who drew strength from the words of the old man who directed his sons to dig up the two mountains obstructing the way in front of his house. "When I die, my sons will carry on; when they die, there will be my grandsons, and then their sons and grandsons, and so on into infinity. High as they are, the mountains cannot grow higher, and with every bit we dig, they will be that much lower." The fable ends: "God was moved by this, and he sent down two angels who carried the mountains away on their backs." Mao wrote, "We must persevere and work unceasingly and we, too, will touch God's heart. Our god is none other than the masses of the Chinese people." The masses of the Chinese people have indeed persevered and worked unceasingly, and it seems that they have at last touched God's heart. Estimates of China's newly discovered oil reserves indicate that they are among the largest in the world. By the end of the century, according to Premier Chou's report to the Fourth National People's Congress, China will rank among the greatest industrial nations on earth.

Protected by a growing nuclear missile deterrent, secure in their independence, and with their great cities honeycombed with underground bomb shelters, the Chinese are perhaps best able of all the world's people to survive the great disorder under heaven. And no doubt they now believe, as they have always believed throughout China's stormy millennial history, that if they can survive, they will win.

# Notes

1. For the full text of Mao Tse-tung's statements supporting the Panamanian, Japanese, and Dominican people's struggles against imperialism, see *Peking Review,* No. 5 (January 31, 1964); *Peking Review,* No. 20 (May 14, 1965).
2. For text of Chairman Liu Shao-ch'i's speech at the reception for the fifteenth anniversary of the founding of the People's Republic of China, September 30, 1964, see *Peking Review,* No. 40 (October 2, 1964).
3. For text of P'eng Chen's National Day speech, see *Peking Review,* No. 40 (October 2, 1964).
4. Chinese Government statement, "China Successfully Explodes Its First Atomic Bomb," October 16, 1964. Trans. New China News Agency release, October 16, 1964.
5. Related to the authors by Anna Louise Strong, who was present at the meeting with Mao and Du Bois.
6. Mao Tse-tung, "On the People's Democratic Dictatorship" (June 30, 1949), *Selected Works,* 4 vols. (Peking: Foreign Languages Press, 1964), Vol. 4, pp. 412–13.
7. Wang Fu-chih, quoted by Jerome Ch'en, ed., *Mao,* Great Lives Observed Series (Englewood Cliffs, N.J.: Prentice-Hall, 1969), pp. 2–3.
8. Mao Tse-tung, "On Practice" (1937), *Selected Works,* Vol. 1, p. 300.
9. For the full text of the Malraux interview with Mao of August 1965, see André Malraux, *Anti-Memoirs* (New York: Bantam Books, 1970), pp. 442–65. Quotation on pp. 444–45.
10. Owen Lattimore, *Inner Asian Frontiers of China* (Boston: Beacon Press, 1962), p. 531.
11. Mao Tse-tung, "Investigation of the Peasant Movement in Hunan" (1927), *Selected Works,* Vol. 1, pp. 23–4.
12. For a detailed description of the Yenan model, see Mark Selden, *The Yenan Way in Revolutionary China* (Cambridge, Mass.: Harvard University Press, 1971).
13. Quoted in "The Leadership of the CPSU and Ourselves," letter of the Central Committee of the Chinese Communist Party to CPSU, September 6, 1963, in *The Polemic on the General Line of the International Communist Movement* (Peking: Foreign Languages Press, 1965), p. 64.
14. Related to the authors by Anna Louise Strong, 1965.
15. "On the Ten Great Relationships" (April 25, 1956), in Stuart Schram, ed., *Chairman Mao Talks to the People* (New York: Pantheon Books, 1974), p. 68.
16. "Speech at the Lushan Conference" July 23, 1959), in *ibid.,* p. 142.
17. For details of the Sino–Soviet dispute, see William E. Griffith, *The Sino–Soviet Rift* (Cambridge, Mass.: MIT Press, 1964), and Walter C. Clemens, Jr., *The Arms Race and Sino–Soviet Relations* (Stanford, Calif.: Hoover Institute Publications, 1968).

18. Mao Tse-tung, quoted by Premier Chou En-lai in a talk with foreign residents in Peking, 1968.

19. For full texts of the Nine Comments, see *Polemic on the General Line*.

20. Quoted in Mao Tse-tung, Ninth Comment, Note on "The Seven Well-Written Documents of the Chekiang Province Cadres' Participation in Physical Labor" (May 9, 1963), in *Polemic on the General Line*, p. 447.

21. History of the struggle between the two lines in China's educational policy since 1949 based on conversations with teachers and students of the First Foreign Languages Institute, Peking. We also utilized the translation of "A Record of the Great Events in the Struggle Between Two Lines in the Field of Higher Education" in *Chinese Sociology and Anthropology* (International Arts and Sciences Press, White Plains, N.Y.), Vol. 2, Nos. 1–2 (Fall–Winter 1969–70).

22. Mao Tse-tung, "Sixty Articles on Working Methods" (January 1958). Partial text, *ibid.,* pp. 42–43.

23. Mao Tse-tung, "In Memory of Norman Bethune" (December 1939), *Selected Works,* Vol. 2, p. 338.

24. See "Decision of the Chinese Communist Party Central Committee on Certain Problems in the Present Rural Work" (draft), May 1963, known as the "First Ten Points." Text in *Documents of the Chinese Communist Party Central Committee, September 1956–April 1969* (Hong Kong: Union Research Institute, 1971), pp. 735–52.

25. "Provisions of Certain Concrete Policies of the CCP Central Committee Concerning the Socialist Education Movement in the Rural Areas" (draft), September 1963, known as the "Later Ten Points." Text in *ibid.,* pp. 753–86.

26. "Some Current Problems Raised in the Socialist Education Movement in the Rural Areas," January 14, 1965, known as the "Twenty-three Articles." Text in *ibid.,* pp. 823–35.

27. Edgar Snow, "Interview with Mao," *The New Republic,* January 20, 1965.

28. Chinese Foreign Ministry note to the Russians, *Peking Review,* No. 12 (March 19, 1965).

29. Lo Jui-ch'ing, "Commemorate the Victory over German Fascism! Carry the Struggle Against U.S. Imperialism Through to the End!" (Peking: Foreign Languages Press, 1965).

30. Announcement of change in Army ranking system, New China News Agency, May 25, 1965.

31. Full text of the Malraux interview with Mao in Malraux, *Anti-Memoirs,* pp. 442–69.

32. Lin Piao, "Long Live the Victory of People's War" (Peking: Foreign Languages Press, 1965).

33. See Edgar Snow, *The Long Revolution* (New York: Random House, 1971), p. 17.

34. Wu Han, *Hai Jui Dismissed from Office,* trans. by C. C. Hung with introductory essay by D. W. Y. Kwok, Asian Studies of Hawaii No. 7 (Honolulu: University of Hawaii Press, 1972).

35. Report on PLA Conference on Political Work, *Peking Review,* No. 3 (January 21, 1966).

36. Text of Lin Piao statement, March 11, 1966, quoted in *People's Daily,* June 19, 1966. Trans. New China News Service, same date.

37. Mao Tse-tung, "Strategy in China's Revolutionary War," *Selected Works,* Vol. 1, p. 233.

38. Abridged text in David Milton, Nancy Milton, and Franz Schurmann, eds., *People's China* (New York: Random House, 1974), pp. 93–100.

39. "Long Live Leninism" (1960), text in G. F. Hudson, Richard Lowenthal, and Roderick MacFarquhar, *The Sino–Soviet Dispute* (New York: Praeger Publishers, 1961), pp. 82–112.

40. "On Khrushchev's Phony Communism and Its Historical Lessons for the World," The Ninth Comment, text in *Polemic on the General Line,* pp. 417–80.

41. Text of Chou En-lai statement, April 10, 1966, *Peking Review,* No. 20 (May 13, 1966), p. 5.

42. Yao Wen-yuan, "On 'Three Family Village,' The Great Socialist Cultural Revolution in China No. 1" (Peking: Foreign Languages Press, 1966).

43. "Circular of the Central Committee of the Chinese Communist Party," May 16, 1966 (Peking: Foreign Languages Press, 1967).

44. Nieh Yuan-tzu, big-character poster, published in *People's Daily,* June 2, 1966. Trans. New China News Agency, June 2, 1966.

45. "Talk to Leaders of the Center" (July 21, 1966), in Schram, ed., *Chairman Mao Talks to the People,* p. 253.

46. Statement of Chairman Liu Shao-ch'i of the People's Republic of China, July 22, 1966, *Peking Review,* No. 31 (July 29, 1966), pp. 9–10.

47. Text of Mao Tse-tung big-character poster in Milton, Milton, and Schurmann, eds., *People's China,* p. 271.

48. Mao Tse-tung's talk with Albanian visitors, August 1967, in *People's China,* p. 262.

49. Text of "Sixteen-Point Decision" in *People's China,* pp. 272–83.

50. Mao Tse-tung, "Talk Before Central Committee Work Conference" (August 23, 1966), *Current Background,* No. 891 (Hong Kong: American Consulate General, October 8, 1969), p. 68.

51. Mao Tse-tung, "Strategy in China's Revolutionary War" (December 1936), *Selected Works,* Vol. 1, p. 191.

52. Mao Tse-tung's talk with Albanian visitors, August 1967, in *People's China,* p. 262.

53. *Ibid.,* p. 263.

54. Related to the authors by Anna Louise Strong, who heard the story from Australian Communist leaders on a visit to China during the Cultural Revolution.

55. Snow, *The Long Revolution,* p. 18.

56. Peking Red Guards, "Long Live the Revolutionary Rebel Spirit of the Proletariat" (June 24, 1966), in *People's China,* pp. 284–85.

57. Text of Mao's conversations with his niece in *People's China,* pp. 240–45.

58. Lin Piao, Address to Politburo, May 18, 1966. Trans. in *Chinese Law and Government* (International Arts and Sciences Press, White Plains, N.Y.), Vol. 2, No. 4 (winter 1969–70), pp. 42–62.

59. Talk at a meeting with Chinese students and trainees in Moscow (November 17, 1957), in *Quotations from Chairman Mao Tse-tung* (Peking: Foreign Languages Press, 1966), p. 288.

60. Lin Piao speech of December 11, 1968. Trans. in Hong Yung Lee, "The Political Mobilization of the Red Guards and Revolutionary

Rebels in the Cultural Revolution," unpublished Ph.D. dissertation, University of Chicago, 1973, p. 196.

61. "Victory for the Proletarian Revolutionary Line Represented by Chairman Mao," *Peking Review,* No. 45 (November 4, 1966), pp. 6–7.

62. *Red Flag* editorial, "Win New Victories." Trans. New China News Agency, December 13, 1966.

63. Mao Tse-tung, quoted by Lin Piao, "Report to the Ninth National Congress of the Communist Party of China" (Peking: Foreign Languages Press, 1969), p. 27.

64. Mao Tse-tung, quoted in a précis of an article by the Red Vanguards, a revolutionary mass organization of the Air Force Headquarters. Trans. New China News Agency, July 22, 1967.

65. Mao Tse-tung's talk with Albanian visitors, August 1967, in *People's China,* p. 262.

66. Letter from Mao Tse-tung to Chou En-lai, text in United States Joint Publications Research Service (hereafter JPRS) No. 49826 (February 12, 1970). Trans. of Communist China Digest No. 90, p. 22.

67. "Minutes of Talks with Leading Comrades of the Cultural Revolution Group at Interview Granted Representatives of the All-China Red-Workers Rebels' General Corps" (December 26, 1966), in Chung Hua-min and Arthur Miller, *Madame Mao: A Profile of Chiang Ch'ing* (Hong Kong: Union Research Institute, 1968), pp. 234–41.

68. *Ibid.,* p. 239.

69. The best analysis we have seen of economic interest groups in the Cultural Revolution is included in Hong Yung Lee, Ph.D. dissertation, Chap. 5, "Potential Grievances of the Chinese Workers and Their Mobilization into Rebels."

70. Text of Shanghai Message in *People's China,* pp. 293–98.

71. *Ibid.,* p. 299.

72. *Ibid.,* p. 303.

73. See *Daily Reports: People's Republic of China* (Washington, D.C.), Foreign Broadcast Report, April 1, 1967.

74. "Talks with Representatives of Revolutionary Masses of the Central Documentary Films Studio and the August 1 Movie Studio" (February 1, 1967), in Chung and Miller, *Madame Mao,* p. 254.

75. *Red Flag* editorial, "Long Live 'Peking People's Commune,'" February 10, 1967. Trans. New China News Agency, same date.

76. "Talks at Three Meetings with Comrades Chang Ch'un-ch'iao and Yao Wen-yuan" (February 1967), in Schram, ed., *Chairman Mao Talks to the People,* p. 277.

77. For the full text of Mao's "Directive on the Great Cutural Revolution in Shanghai," February 12, 1967, see JPRS No. 61269–2 (February 20, 1974), *Miscellany of Mao Tse-tung Thought (1949–1968),* Pt. 2, pp. 451–55.

78. *Ibid.,* p. 278.

79. Mao Tse-tung's talk with Albanian visitors, August 1967, in *People's China,* p. 265.

80. See Hong Yung Lee, Ph.D. dissertation, pp. 414–16.

81. Instruction to Lin Piao, February 1967, in *People's China,* p. 299.

82. *Red Flag* editorial No. 3, February 1, abridged text in *People's China,* pp. 307–15.

83. *Ibid.*, p. 311.

84. For T'an Chen-lin's reported statement, see Survey of the China Mainland Press (hereafter SCMP), Supplement No. 238 (November 8, 1968), p. 8, and SCMP No. 4169 (May 2, 1968), p. 7.

85. *Red Flag* editorial No. 4. Trans. in *Daily Reports: People's Republic of China* (Washington, D.C.), February 23, 1967.

86. Ch'i Pen-yü, "Patriotism or National Betrayal?—On the Reactionary Film 'Inside Story of the Ch'ing Court' " (Peking: Foreign Languages Press, 1967).

87. Ting Hsueh-li, "Class Struggle Is Essential to the Communist Party," *People's Daily*, May 10, 1967. Trans. New China News Agency, same date.

88. Mao Tse-tung, "Rectify the Party's Style of Work" (February 1, 1942), *Selected Works*, Vol. 3, pp. 49–50.

89. "Premier Chou Talks About Why Firepower Must Be Concentrated on Criticizing the Party's Top Person Taking the Capitalist Road," publication of the Revolutionary Rebel Alliance General Headquarters of the Kuan-tung Provincial Organs, text in JPRS No. 44574 (March 4, 1968). Trans. of Communist China No. 1, pp. 26–32.

90. Mao Tse-tung, "Directive on External Propaganda Work" (June 1967), in JPRS No. 61269-2 (February 20, 1974), *Miscellany of Mao Tse-tung Thought*, Pt. 2, p. 462.

91. Mao Tse-tung, quoted in *People's Daily* editorial, "Make a Class Analysis of Factionalism," April 27, 1967. Trans. New China News Agency, same date.

92. Mao Tse-tung, quoted in *Red Flag* editorial, "Hold Aloft the Banner of Unity of the Party's Ninth Congress and Win Still Greater Victories." Trans. New China News Agency, June 8, 1969.

93. Mao Tse-tung, "Khrushchev's Phony Communism," The Ninth Comment, text in *Polemic on the General Line*, p. 478.

94. Mao Tse-tung, "Report on the Investigation of the Peasant Movement in Hunan," *Selected Works*, Vol. 1, p. 28.

95. Edgar Snow, "The Army and the Party," *The New Republic*, May 22, 1971.

96. Article in *Wuhan Kang-erh-ssu*, August 22, 1967. Trans. in SCMP No. 4073 (December 5, 1967), pp. 1–18. Abridged version in *People's China*, pp. 335–41.

97. *Ibid.*; *People's China*, pp. 337–39.

98. For confirmation of this view see "A Mysterious American—How Rittenberg Usurped the Leadership of the Central Broadcasting Bureau," Cultural Revolution Bulletin No. 13, March 1968. Trans. in SCMP No. 4165 (April 26, 1968), pp. 1–3.

99. Peking Red Guards, "The 'Ultra-Left,' " in *People's China*, pp. 342–47.

100. Mao Tse-tung's talk with Albanian visitors, August 1967, in *People's China*, p. 263.

101. Lin Piao, speech of August 9, 1967, text in JPRS No. 43449, Communist China Digest No. 192 (November 24, 1967), pp. 57–64.

102. Chiang Ch'ing, statement at meeting of August 11, 1967, in *Current Background*, No. 844 (Hong Kong: American Consulate General, January 10, 1968), pp. 1–2.

103. Text of Chou En-lai order in SCMP No. 4088 (December 28, 1967), p. 13.

104. Chiang Ch'ing, "Speech to Rival Delegations from Anhwei" (September 5, 1967), *People's China,* pp. 348–53.
105. Text JPRS No. 43449, Communist China Digest, No. 192 (November 24, 1967), pp. 55–57.
106. See "Storming and Capturing the Sinister Stronghold of the 'May 16,' by the First Red Regiment of the Revolutionary Rebel Commune of the Peking Iron and Steel Institute," in SCMP No. 844 (January 10, 1968), pp. 18–19.
107. "Dialogues During Inspection of Central-South and East China" (September 1967), in JPRS No. 61269-2 (February 20, 1974), *Miscellany of Mao Tse-tung Thought,* Pt. 2, pp. 463–67.
108. *Ibid.*
109. See V. I. Lenin, *Left Wing Communism: An Infantile Disorder* (New York: International Publishers, 1934), p. 45.
110. Minutes of Premier Chou's interview with some representatives from both sides of Canton Local District, Great Hall of the People, November 8, 1967, text in JPRS No. 438 (February 19, 1968), pp. 13–22.
111. Premier Chou's Three-Point Instruction to the Foreign Ministry, March 5, 1967, and Ch'en Yi's Letter to the Premier, text in SCMP No. 4164 (April 25, 1968), pp. 4–6.
112. Text of Chiang Ch'ing's statement of March 15, 1968, in SCMP No. 4166 (April 29, 1968), pp. 1–3.
113. *Ibid.*
114. Letter of Mao Tse-tung to Lin Piao, Chou En-lai, and the Cultural Group, December 17, 1968, text in JPRS No. 61269-2 (February 20, 1974), *Miscellany of Mao Tse-tung Thought,* Pt. 2, p. 468.
115. For text of Chiang Ch'ing's statements, see SCMP No. 4181 (May 20, 1968), pp. 1–10; SCMP No. 4173 (May 8, 1968), pp. 1–5.
116. See SCMP No. 4166 (April 29, 1968), pp. 9–10.
117. *Ibid.*
118. *Ibid.*
119. Mao Tse-tung, quoted in "The Working Class Leading Struggle-Criticism-Transformation in All Spheres of the Superstructure Is Fine," *Liberation Army Daily.* Trans. New China News Agency, October 26, 1968.
120. The talk between Chairman Mao and the Peking Red Guard leaders was tape-recorded. The transcript, titled "Dialogue with the Capital Red Guards," was distributed widely throughout the country. Complete text of the dialogue in JPRS No. 61269-2 (February 20, 1974), *Miscellany of Mao Tse-tung Thought,* Pt. 2, pp. 469–97.
121. Yao Wen-yuan, "The Working Class Must Exercise Leadership in Everything," in *Peking Review,* No. 35 (August 30, 1968), pp. 3–6.
122. Text of Chou En-lai speech of September 8, 1967, in *Peking Review,* No. 37 (September 13, 1968), pp. 6–7.
123. Text of Chiang Ch'ing's speech of September 8, 1967, in *ibid.,* p. 8.
124. *Wen-hui pao* editorial, "Oppose Restoration of the Old," October 18, 1968, in SCMP No. 4300 (November 18, 1968), pp. 1–3.
125. Central Committee, "Communiqué Announcing the Expulsion of Liu Shao-ch'i from the Chinese Communist Party," in *People's China,* pp. 330–31.
126. Report of Central Committee panel, in SCMP No. 4334 (January 9, 1969), pp. 6–10.

127. Lin Piao statement at Ninth Party Congress. Trans. New China News Agency, April 27, 1969.

128. For a coherent analysis of the policy issues behind the Lin Piao–Mao Tse-tung split by an experienced Western correspondent with access to official Chinese sources before the struggle was reworked within an ideological framework, see *Le Monde* article by Robert Guillain, "The Fall of Lin Piao," trans. in *People's China*, pp. 381–85.

129. Mao Tse-tung poem, translated by Michael Bullock and Jerome Ch'en, in Jerome Ch'en, *Mao and the Chinese Revolution* (New York: Oxford University Press, 1965), p. 320.

130. *Ibid.*, p. 350.

131. See translation of the "Summary of Chairman Mao's Talks with Responsible Comrades at Various Places During His Provincial Tour" (from the middle of August to September 12, 1971), in Schram, ed., *Chairman Mao Talks to the People*, pp. 290–97.

132. Edgar Snow interview with Mao, December 10, 1970; text in Snow, *The Long Revolution*, p. 171.

133. Richard Nixon, quoted in *New York Times*, July 7, 1971, p. 16.

134. Text of statement on Lin Piao issued by the Chinese Embassy, Algiers, *New York Times*, July 29, 1972; *People's China*, p. 380.

135. "Pullman's Journey to the East," *New York Times*, Sunday, July 29, 1973, Financial Section.

136. Henry Kissinger, quoted by C. L. Sulzberger, *An Age of Mediocrity: Memoirs and Diaries 1963–1972* (New York: Macmillan Co., 1973), p. 7.

137. "Speech by the Chairman of the Delegation of the People's Republic of China, Teng Hsiao-p'ing, at the Special Session of the UN General Assembly," April 10, 1974 (Peking: Foreign Languages Press, 1974).

138. Henry Kissinger, quoted in *New York Times* editorial, September 29, 1974.

139. Notes on a talk by Premier Chou En-lai taken by a participant at the meeting and shared with the authors; therefore, not an official transcript.

140. Vice Premier Teng Hsiao-p'ing, quoted in an article by Geoffrey Godsell, *Christian Science Monitor*, June 17, 1975, p. 3.

141. See article "Peking Lambasted at Havana Parley," *Christian Science Monitor*, June 23, 1975, p. 10.

# Index

## About The Authors

David Milton was a merchant seaman during World War II and was active in the trade union movement during the late 1940's and 1950's. He is currently working on a doctoral dissertation in sociology at the University of California at Berkeley.

Nancy Milton is a graduate in creative writing from Stanford University with an M.A. from San Francisco State University. She is a teacher in the San Francisco Community College District and is co-editor of *Fragment from a Lost Diary* (Pantheon, 1973).

Both Nancy and David Milton taught at the First Foreign Languages Institute in Peking from 1964 to 1969 and co-edited *People's China* (Random House, 1974), with Franz Schurmann.